S0-EQS-534

International Advertising Handbook

International Advertising Handbook

A User's Guide to Rules and Regulations

Barbara Sundberg Baudot

Lexington Books
D.C. Heath and Company/Lexington, Massachusetts/Toronto

K
3844
.B38
1989

Library of Congress Cataloging-in-Publication Data

Baudot, Barbara Sundberg.
  International advertising handbook : a user's guide to rules and regulations / Barbara Sundberg Baudot.
    p. cm.
  Includes bibliographies and index.
  ISBN 0-669-17070-4 (alk. paper)
  1. Advertising laws. I. Title
K3844.B38   1989
343'.082—dc19
[342.382]   87-45968

Copyright © 1989 by Lexington Books

All rights reserved. No part of this publication may be reproduced or transmitted in any form or by any means, electronic or mechanical, including photocopy, recording, or any information storage or retrieval system, without permission in writing from the publisher.

Published simultaneously in Canada
Printed in the United States of America
International Standard Book Number: 0-669-17070-4
Library of Congress Catalog Card Number: 87-45968

The paper used in this publication meets the minimum requirements of American National Standard for Information Sciences—Permanence of Paper for Printed Library Materials, ANSI Z39.48-1984. ∞™

Year and number of this printing:

89 90 91 92 10 9 8 7 6 5 4 3 2 1

This book is dedicated to Alan Whipple, William Sprague Barnes, Audrey Beardsley, and Ruth Sundberg.

> *They which builded on the wall, and they that bare burdens, with those that laded, everyone with one of his hands wrought in the work. . . . So the wall was finished. . . " Neh. 4: 17, 6: 15.*

Contents

Figures xi

Tables xv

Maps xvii

Foreword xix

Preface xxiii

Acknowledgments xxix

Part I Background 1

1. Setting the Stage 3
   Theory and Definitions 5
   Early History 6
   The International Development of Commercial Advertising 7
   The Spread of Multinational Advertising 10
   The Development of Regulation 11
   Notes 14

2. The Actors 17
   The Industry: Regulatory Target 18
   The Critics 27
   The Regulators 31
   Final Remarks 37
   Notes 37

3. Advertising Issues 39
   Perceptions of Advertising 40
   Product-Specific Issues 41
   Societal Issues 42
   Relevance of Solutions 46
   Notes 48

4. **Advertising Regulation** 51
    National Regulation 51
    International Regulation 59
    Self-Regulation 61
    Notes 63

Part II Industrialized Market-Economy Countries 65

5. **Advertising in Industrialized Market-Economy Countries** 67
    Notes 74

6. **The United States** 75
    Administrative Law and Regulation 81
    Free Speech 86
    Self-Regulation 88
    Advertising and Private Claims for Injury 89
    International Reach of U.S. Advertising Law 96
    Overview 100
    Notes 100

7. **Europe: By Parts and Community** 105
    The European Communities 105
    The United Kingdom 116
    Other Developed Commonwealth Countries and South Africa 126
    France 132
    Scandinavia 139
    Notes 142

8. **Japan** 149
    The Advertising Industry 153
    Environmental Influences on Advertising 156
    Regulation of Advertising 158
    Notes 160

Part III Socialist Countries 163

9. **Advertising in Socialist Countries** 165
    Notes 168

10. **Eastern Europe** 169
    The Soviet Union 170
    Future Outlook 178
    Other Eastern European Countries 180
    Notes 182

11. China and Socialist Asia 185
    China 185
    Other Low-Income, Centrally Planned Asian Countries 198
    Notes 199

Part IV Third World Countries 201

12. The Third World: Special Considerations 203
    Notes 209

13. The Arab Middle East 211
    Characteristics of Advertising 216
    Regulation of Advertising 219
    Notes 222

14. Latin America and the Caribbean 225
    High-Income Latin America 231
    Middle-Income Latin America and the Caribbean 242
    Notes 244

15. Third World Asia 249
    Low-Income Asia 250
    Middle-Income Asia 260
    High–Middle-Income Asia 272
    Notes 277

16. Africa South of the Sahara 281
    Low-Income and Middle-Income Anglophone Countries 289
    Middle-Income Francophone Countries 295
    Low-Income Countries 297
    Notes 299

Part V International Controls 301

17. Global Advertising and International Control 303
    Notes 305

18. International Guidelines and Standards 307
    General Code on Advertising 307
    Guidelines on Consumer Protection 308
    Code of Conduct for Transnational Corporations 311
    The Work of the Codex Alimentarius Commission 313
    Pharmaceuticals 317
    Tobacco 319

Alcohol   320
Appendix: Ethical and Scientific Criteria for Pharmaceutical Advertising   320
Notes   321

19. The International Code of Marketing of Breast-Milk Substitutes   327
The Crusade against the "Baby-Killer"   327
Characteristics of the WHO Code   331
The Legal Nature of the Code   333
The Impact of the Code   334
The Future of Similar Codes   336
Notes   337

20. Concluding Observations   341
National Systems   341
Self-Regulation   343
International Rules and Regulations   343
A Word on the Future   344

Index   347

About the Author   359

Figures

2–1. Advertising Expenditure of Principle Advertisers, 1987   28
2–2. Per Capita Advertising Expenditures in Selected Countries and Regions, 1986/87   34
5–1. Total Advertising Expenditures in the Industrialized Nations, 1987   68
6–1. Gross Multinational Agency Billings and Total Advertising Expenditure in the United States, 1987   76
6–2. Per Capita Advertising Expenditure and Per Capita GNP in the United States, 1986/87   77
6–3. Advertising Expenditure by Media and Non-measured Media in the United States   78
7–1. Gross Multinational Agency Billings and Total Advertising Expenditure in Europe, 1987   106
7–2. Per Capita Advertising Expenditure and Per Capita GNP in Europe, 1986/87   107
7–3. Advertising Expenditure by Media and Non-measured Media in the United Kingdom, France, Germany (F.R.), and Scandinavia   108
7–4. Gross Multinational Agency Billings and Total Advertising Expenditure in Australia, Canada, New Zealand, and South Africa, 1987   128
7–5. Per Capita Advertising Expenditure and Per Capita GNP in Australia, Canada, New Zealand, and South Africa, 1986/87   129
7–6. Advertising Expenditure by Media and Non-measured Media in Australia, Canada, New Zealand, and South Africa   130

8–1. Gross Multinational Agency Billings and Total Advertising Expenditure in Japan, 1987   150

8–2. Per Capital Advertising Expenditure and Per Capita GNP in Japan, 1986/87   151

8–3. Advertising Expenditure by Media and Non-measured Media in Japan   154

10–1. Distribution of Media Used by Foreign Advertisers in the Soviet Union, 1988   173

11–1. Gross Multinational Agency Billings and Total Advertising Expenditure in China, 1987   189

11–2. Per Capita Advertising Expenditure and Per Capita GNP in China, 1986/87   190

11–3. Advertising Expenditure by Media and Non-measured Media in China   191

12–1. Total Advertising Expenditure in the Third World, 1987   205

13–1. Gross Multinational Agency Billings and Total Advertising Expenditure in the Middle East, 1987   217

13–2. Per Capita Advertising Expenditure and Per Capita GNP in the Middle East, 1986/87   218

14–1. Comparison of Advertising Expenditure in High- and Middle-Income Latin American Countries, 1987   231

14–2. Gross Multinational Agency Billings and Total Advertising Expenditure in High- and Middle-Income Latin America, 1987   233

14–3. Per Capita Advertising Expenditure and Per Capita GNP in High- and Middle-Income Latin America, 1986/87   234

14–4. Advertising Expenditure by Media and Non-measured Media in High- and Middle-Income Latin America   235

15–1. Gross Multinational Agency Billings and Total Advertising Expenditure in Low-Income Asia, 1987   253

15–2. Per Capita Advertising Expenditure and Per Capita GNP in Low-Income Asia, 1986/87   254

15–3. Advertising Expenditure by Media and Non-measured Media in Low-Income Asia   255

15–4. Gross Multinational Agency Billings and Total Advertising Expenditure in Middle-Income Asia, 1987   263

15–5. Per Capita Advertising Expenditure and Per Capita GNP in Middle-Income Asia, 1986/87   264

15–6. Advertising Expenditure by Media and Non-measured Media in Middle-Income Asia   265

15–7. Gross Multinational Agency Billings and Total Advertising Expenditure in High-Income Asia, 1987   274

15–8. Per Capita Advertising Expenditure and Per Capita GNP in High-Income Asia, 1986/87   275

15–9. Advertising Expenditure by Media and Non-measured Media in High-Income Asia   276

16–1. Gross Multinational Agency Billings and Total Advertising Expenditure in Africa, 1987   282

16–2. Per Capita Advertising Expenditure and Per Capita GNP in Africa, 1986/87   283

16–3. Advertising Expenditure by Media and Non-measured Media in Zimbabwe   291

Tables

2-1. Comparison of Gross Billings of Top Multinational Agencies with Total World Advertising Expenditure, 1987   19

2-2. World's Top Fifty Agencies, 1987   20

2-3. World Wide Operations of Selected Multinational Advertising Agencies, 1987   22

2-4. International Advertising Conglomerates as of February 1989   23

2-5. Geographic Distribution of International Advertising Activities by Type of Investment, 1987   25

2-6. World Advertising Expenditure by Region, 1987   32

6-1. Regulatory Profile: United States   79

6-2. Summary of Theories of Liability   95

7-1. Regulatory Profile: European Communities   110

7-2. Regulatory Profile: United Kingdom   117

7-3. Regulatory Profile: Other Developed Countries   127

7-4. Regulatory Profile: France   133

7-5. Regulatory Profile: Scandinavia   140

8-1. Regulatory Profile: Japan   152

10-1. Regulatory Profile: Soviet Union   171

11-1. Regulatory Profile: China   186

13–1. Regulatory Profile: Near East   213
13–2. Regulatory Profile: North Africa   214
14–1. Regulatory Profile: High-Income Latin America   232
14–2. Regulatory Profile: Middle-Income Latin America   243
15–1. Regulatory Profile: Low-Income Asia   252
15–2. Regulatory Profile: Middle-Income Asia   261
15–3. Regulatory Profile: Upper-Income Asia   273
16–1. Regulatory Profile: Low-Income and Middle-Income Anglophone Africa   290
16–2. Regulatory Profile: Low-Income and Middle-Income Francophone Africa   296
16–3. Regulatory Profile: Other Low-Income Africa   298

Maps

1–1. World 2
5–1. First World 68
7–1. Western Europe 109
9–1. Second World 166
10–1. Eastern Europe 170
12–1. Third World 204
13–1. Arab Middle East 212
14–1. Latin America 226
15–1. Asia 251
16–1. Africa 284

Foreword

Since the early 1970s the "business" of advertising has been affected by two major and parallel developments: an immense increase in regulation and an impressive augmentation in the level and sophistication of self-regulation. Equally, these developments have taken place, not only at the national level, but also at international levels. Starting in the most developed industrialized countries, these parallel developments have spread to the smaller developed nations and into the less-developed Third World.

As Barbara Baudot says, the debate goes on and the pendulum swings back and forth. Her chronicle of how this tug-of-war started and of how it is developing is a most valuable addition to the literature about the state of the business as distinct from the state of the art of advertising. Especially for the layman, she has performed a most valuable service, providing an understanding of the legalities involved and also giving a rich documentation to the reader. Her book could be subtitled "From Galbraith to Greyser" in that she provides an incisive assessment of the problems of marketing communications in both planned economies and those commonly called market economies. One thing is certain. There is no such thing as totally free enterprise or laissez-faire in the world of advertising. Whatever is done must be circumscribed by both national, and even international, regulation and self-regulation.

Advertising confronts a "jungle of codes, regulations, laws, unwritten customs, and practices" says Dr. Baudot quite correctly and further, advertising is affected by all nuances of culture, religion, and tradition. Even after the internalization of the European Common Market in 1992, advertising will be bound by language and culture, by the tools of the trade, and by changing transmission devices. And, despite the trend toward larger regional and multinational market entities, anti-foreign sentiments may actually increase in these areas. Such international bodies as the World Intellectual Property Organization (WIPO) and the United Nations Conference on Trade and Development (UNCTAD) and the General Agreement on Tariffs and Trade (GATT) are dealing with these matters. With all of this turmoil, one thing does stand out. There is an almost universal acceptance by all governments and international bodies that misleading advertising must be guarded against, if not punished. And the advertising industry is in total agreement. The only question is whether government or industry is the better watchdog—or perhaps there should be a combination of efforts by both.

On the international scene there have been major milestones that have heightened the debate and set the stage for international regulation. These have been: the adoption by the World Health Organization of the International Code of Marketing of Breast-milk Substitutes (1981), the United Nations Guidelines for Consumer Protection (1985), the establishment of the UN Centre on Transnational Corporations (1974), and UNESCO's so-called MacBride Report (1980) preceded by its adoption of the so-called Declaration on the Mass Media in 1978. Dr. Baudot traces these developments and their impact with care and attention.

On the one hand, there now exists a far more robust international consumer movement, dominated by the International Organization of Consumer Unions (IOCU), pushing for more and more national and international regulation. On the other side, not only defending their territories from attack but also pushing hard for freedom of commercial expression and more open markets are the numerous industry associations and organizations such as the International Chamber of Commerce (ICC) and the International Advertising Association (IAA), both of which pre-date World War II. This book delineates the roles of each of these players. The IOCU is the great proponent of the protection of vulnerable groups such as children and the illiterate and it strongly favors the demarketing of pharmaceuticals, infant formula products, and many food and health care products, not to mention alcohol and tobacco. IOCU wants strict international bans or regulatory codes. Its targets are the products themselves, but the starting point is the most visible part of the marketing process, the products' advertising.

So complicated are the problems that many world bodies such as the Food and Agriculture Organization (FAO) and the World Health Organization (WHO) have so far resisted legally binding codes, leaving the regulation and regulatory administration to individual governments, but at the same time encouraging the "rational use" of products and defining their essentiality through recommended guidelines.

There is growing conscious awareness but also enhanced expectations for better products and the right to make choices. The regulators run the risk of throwing out the baby with the bath water. As Dr. Baudot rightly claims "organized consumerism is the handmaiden of industrialization and open markets." Some of Dr. Baudot's important chapters deal with how new problems of commercial communication and more open markets are evolving, how the debate rages in the Third World, and how the desire for more commercial expression and more open markets is now affecting the huge markets of the Soviet Union and China as well as the vibrant but smaller ones of

Eastern Europe, all areas in which advertising is now an accepted fact of modern day mass communications. In these countries, new regulatory and self-regulatory codes are being enacted, following the examples and experiences in most cases of the industrialized Western nations that have lived with them for decades. But, all of these are adopted and adapted with a view to national legal systems, culture, tradition, and usage.

This book provides a clear understanding of the forces at play and emphasizes the inevitable march of new market development. The pendulum may be swinging finally toward greater freedom, less statism and government restriction, and indeed toward more and more necessary self-regulation in the best interest of the consumer who must be the ultimate victor, regardless of the type of government or economic system. In such a world advertising will continue to thrive and perform a service everywhere.

—Sylvan M. Barnet, Jr.
Former Chairman
Advisory Council of the
International Advertising Association
Riverside, Connecticut

Preface

Before there was law there was human behavior. That precept forms the basis for much of the work contained in this book. Regulations governing international advertising reflect the environments from which they originate and the interplay of a variety of actors including consumers, bystanders, governmental authorities, and the advertisers themselves. Through consideration of the social, political, and economic characteristics of the world's advertising countries, and through an analysis of the objectives and attitudes of the actors, it should be possible to reach a deeper understanding of a sometimes bewildering maze of laws, regulations, and rules on international advertising.

Thus, this handbook considers such laws and regulations in light of their origins and purposes, and provides clues to assessing the overall advertising regulatory regimes in representative countries and regions around the world. It examines selections from the relevant regulations that exist in any one country, and these selections figure forth the character of the overall regime. It is conceived as a complement rather than a substitute for massive legal compilations. By raising questions, providing environmental clues, and outlining relevant aspects of socio-economic and political culture, it should guide the law seeker to perceive the "laws behind the laws." It also considers the responses of the intergovernmental community to controversies arising from problems not covered by national regulatory systems. Those practitioners looking for a detailed or comprehensive summary of regulations affecting advertising in any one country should be redirected to multivolumed compilations of advertising law.

Part I establishes the basis for presenting the vast array of regulations confronting advertisers in various national and regional markets. It sketches the development of advertising regulation in the major regions of the world. Thereafter, the principal players are introduced with an indication of their respective roles in the regulatory process. An overview of the main issues confronted in regulatory forums is further provided to aid in understanding the variety of underlying rationales for regulation. Part I concludes with an introduction to the principal regulatory environments found around the world.

Parts II, III, and IV consider the issues, laws and regulations, and the positions of various players in the western industrialized countries, the socialist countries, and the Third World developing countries, respectively. The substance ranges over national and regional initiatives, extraterritoriality, the role of private suits and the judiciary, and self-regulation, as appropriate. Part II focuses on the advertising environment in the industrialized market economy countries giving particular attention to the United States, the European Communities, and Japan. Part III covers the socialist countries including the Soviet Union, Eastern Europe, China, and low income socialist Asia. Part IV centers on the Third World divided into groups of countries in the Middle East/North Africa, Latin America, Asia, and Africa.

Part V describes the role played by international organizations as they attempt to bolster measures protecting third world countries and as they attempt to fill international regulatory voids.

Regulations are not conceived in a void, and there is a variety of approaches to analyzing relevant factors and resultant regulations. One approach would be to see the decision-making process as a rational phenomenon through which policymakers would gather statistical data on the impact of advertising and then design scientific policies to remedy negative excesses, as if the regulatory game was one of facts and figures, empirically determined policy objectives and prescribed remedies.

Such an approach might prevail in some circumstances, but in this book, regulations are the outcomes of bargaining games in which social and economic benefits are implicitly weighed against perceived abuses and social costs. The chess-pawns, in the case of advertising, are positive and negative perceptions of the impact advertising has in particular scenarios. The players are the various competing interest groups: business, consumers, legislators, etc. The outcomes depend on how the players use their pawns to influence others and thereby amass the greatest amount of power in terms of popular support. Data can be manipulated to support any contention. The winners have their views reflected in the design or absence of a particular policy or piece of legislation affecting advertising.

In short, regulation is a fact of life and may be best understood in terms of the motives, biases, and relative power of influential players. These factors provide clues to the impact of regulations in a particular environment. Beyond the game, the legislative process also reflects opposing philosophical schools on the role of business and its relations with individuals, society, and government. One school places supreme value on the autonomy of the individual: the world is better left to millions of random decisions of sovereign individuals; survival is the reward of intelligence, wisdom, and discernment; and ultimately reasoned self-interest will control the excesses of individual behavior. The other school places "society" at the pinnacle. Society is an organic whole directed by the "state," which is the main agent of change, defining and enforcing the common good. The individual, inherently selfish, needs to be checked by the "rational state" for the good of society. An underlying question concerns the extent to which current national and international doctrine and practice regarding codes and regulations reinforce one or the other school. The answer offers further clues to the nature of a particular advertising environment.

In the global context, the concept of "international morality" confronts the political reality of "national sovereignty." Questions of values, culture-bound or universal, must be faced when uniform international regulations are considered. Such questions have been posed. Is national sovereignty being undermined by international prescrptions for advertising behavior and international selection of products permitted for trade? Or, is sovereignty already undermined by the power and persuasiveness of multinational advertisers? The answers are left to the reader.

In international business relations, commercial advertising is controversial. Proponents may identify advertisers of brand-name comestibles, beverages, tobacco, pharmaceuticals, and other consumer products as the true heroes of the twentieth century responsible, for improved health and higher standards of living. Adversaries may compare these advertisers to the hucksters of snake oil, relics from the turn of the century.

The benefits of advertising are obvious to many. Through the demonstration effect, it stimulates socio-economic development; brand-name competition leads to improved products, lower prices, and an expanded range of product choice. Advertising is also essential to the existence of a free competitive economy, and it provides information for the consumer that could not otherwise be so easily obtained.

Controversy stems from advertising's perceived pervasiveness in daily life and hypotheses about its negative impact on personal values, health, and economic decisions. Commonly identified abuses range from the mere existence of glossy advertising to misconduct arising out of particular practices or concerning specific products, targets, and effects. Within the range are several product—and audience-related issues. They include promotion of "unhealthy," "unsafe," or "useless" products, and advertising messages that exploit the credulity of the ignorant, the illiterate, or the young.

Some of today's concerns are peculiar to modern commercial life. Rapid expansion of world trade and investment and technological advancement in communications have offered business a vast range of market opportunities in an expanding global community. Advertising's international dimension enlarges problems and widens perspective, reflecting notable differences in market structure and situations. Advertising across national frontiers raises issues with cultural and environmental implications. Between rich and poor countries, and between countries with open and closed economies, broadcast commercials and glamorous ads have brought controversial issues into sharp relief. Particularly problematic has been the injection of sophisticated commercial messages into less materially sophisticated, developing societies.

National regulatory regimes exercise the strongest legal control over international advertising within national boundaries. By the end of the nineteenth century, concerned individuals and organizations in the United States and Western Europe began seeking and obtaining increasing protection from excesses of advertising through laws, regulations, and standards imposed on advertisers and their agencies. In general, the stronger the consumer organization in a free market country, the more effective has been the protective legislation.

Since the 1920s, the socialist countries have exercised near monopoly control over advertising allowed within their borders. There has been a slow evolution toward permitting commercial advertising under strict conditions. This varies from country to country. Today dramatic shifts in attitudes toward commercial advertising are occurring in the Soviet Union and China.

Many developing countries have adopted legislation to curb certain advertising practices. In the past, their rules were often modeled on the laws of the ex-colonial powers. Recently, however, the unique problems of developing countries have been reflected in revisions or new laws and regulations.

National legislation has proven most potent in western industrialized market economy countries and socialist countries where there are respected means for enforcement. In developing countries where legislation exists, difficulties with enforcement pose serious obstacles to effective implementation.

Self-regulation by the advertising industry began even before 1900. Members of the industry took steps to discourage dishonest and unfair practices threatening the integrity of their profession. They formed organizations and proposed codes and guidelines for advertising even prior to the adoption of government regulations. Since then, national and international self-regulatory organizations have grown in size and number. The effectiveness of their voluntary codes is not to be underestimated in governing advertising.

Consumers injured by products misrepresented by advertisers may seek judicial recourse to control advertising practice. Under various theories of tort and contract law, individuals have successfully sought compensation for their losses in civil liability suits. The threat of such a suit, under U.S. law, is one of the most potent controls on advertisers.

International measures include "soft-law" codes and guidelines. These are intended to serve a number of purposes, including guidance for national legislators, support for domestic legislation, or calling public attention to international activities of enterprises beyond the reach of effective national controls.

Since the 1960s, many U.N. specialized agencies, the U.N. itself, and regional intergovernmental groups have probed "advertising" from a variety of perspectives. Thus far, WHO, FAO, and the U.N. have adopted recommendatory measures. These reflect the weight attached to views of negative health and social consequences of advertising. Although these measures are universal in scope, they are more specifically aimed at protecting the peoples of the Third World.

Taken together, national laws and administrative fiats, international codes and guidelines, self-regulatory codes and standards, and private claims for injury form a complex regulatory web in the global market place.

Summation

This book, global in scope, covers the richest and poorest countries in the world, and compares advertising regulation in a vast range of countries with different cultures, religions and ideologies, different levels of economic development, and, different economic and political systems. It provides an overview of regulation, examining the various types and their sources—whether they be national governments, international organizations, or self-imposed intra-industrial organizations. In the process of studying these regulations, it also takes into account the perspectives of all the interested principals: business, consumers, and governments.

It is hoped that the comparative analyses of the various measures affecting advertising and marketing throughout the world and the attention given to idiosyncrasies of the legal systems that produce and apply them will be helpful. It is also hoped that this book will be of use to those who seek to understand not only the what but mainly the *why* of international regulatory efforts. Advertising regulation also has its own metaphysics. Knowledge of this underlying framework should help readers to anticipate regulation and regulatory change, not simply to react to such changes.

Finally, a word of advice to the reader. The laws and other regulatory prescriptions, as well as institutional organizations in any one country or international system, are in a continual state of flux. It is very likely that many changes will have already taken place in rules and institutions mentioned in this book. Again, the purpose of this work is to guide inquiry and to create awareness of different advertising and advertising regulatory environments. The reader is therefore advised to appreciate this material with a degree of historical perspective, to use this book as a base, and to build on it with the very latest information needed for practical purposes.

—Barbara Baudot

Acknowledgments

Professionals, academics, international civil servants, my special assistants, family, and many friends deserve infinite votes of thanks for their part in bringing this book to reality.

Professor William Sprague Barnes of the Fletcher School of Law and Diplomacy, as my Ph.D. adviser and mentor, has been a vital part of this project from the initial stage of research on my dissertation on international advertising until present. His advice and judgments were valuable contributions to this book.

To my dear friends, philosopher-writer-scholar Alan Whipple, who has since passed on, and to his wife Monika, I am particularly indebted for their time, vision, and encouragement in conceiving this project.

Vital to the task's successful completion were the members of the industry who have contributed information, comments, and their valuable time. I am grateful to Sylvan M. Barnet, Jr., former chairman, Advisory Council of the International Advertising Association and to Ed Lucaire, also of the IAA. Great appreciation is also due to Neils Menko of Young & Rubicam; Graham De Villiers and Roger Murray of McCann Erickson; Alexander Mudrov of Veneshtorgreklama, Kaede Seville of Kaede Media and consultant to Dentsu; Lobna Reda, Egyptian marketing consultant; and John McCaffrey of Pan Am. I am also indebted to Ilsa Cermak of *Advertising Age* for her advice on statistics.

Among those in the legal profession who contributed to this work should be mentioned Dominique Borde of Simon, Borde, Moquet; Jean Claude Fourgoux, avocat au Barreau de Paris; Robert Angarola of Hyman, Phelps & McNamara; and Louis Frumer, of the New York bar.

Many in the academic world also contributed to this work. Among them I am particularly indebted to Professors Ingo Walter, New York University; Paul Savage, St. Anselm College; Jim Post, Boston University; John Spencer, Fletcher School of Law and Diplomacy; R.G. Lawson, Faculty of Law, University of Southampton; N.T. Wang, Columbia University; Stephen Greyser and Frank Aguilar, Harvard Business School; and Thomas Schuller, Lawrence Academy.

Several officials in the secretariats and delegations to United Nations and the World Health Organizations made vital contributions to the substance of this work. Those to whom I am particularly indebted include Peter Hansen and Karl Sauvant of the UN Centre for Transnational Corporations; Luis Maria Gomez, Karina Gerlach, and Gus Feissel in the UN Secretariat; and Sev Fluss, Sami Shubber, Jim Acre, F.K. Kaferstein, Marcus Grant, John Dunne in the World Health Organization. Jeremy Sheehan and Patrick Latham of the Commission of the European Community were also very helpful.

No less important were those involved in the logistics of preparing the book. To Terry Murbach of Lawrence Academy I offer my most humble gratitude for this editorial work and for his persistence as an enthusiastic and critical test audience. I am also deeply appreciative of my ever patient and most efficient secretary, Margie Provost. Never to be forgotten is my totally reliable and effective research assistant, Christopher Flanagan, St. Anselm College. I am also indebted to Jerome Coffey for his work on statistics and to Ann Richardson for her creativity and skill in preparing all the final tables and graphs.

A special note of appreciation is addressed to my mother, Ruth Sundberg, who has served as my "jack of all trades"; proofreader, baby sitter, audience, prodder, chauffer, photocopier, printer . . . you name it, she did it all. Also vitally important to this project was my husband Jacques and my daughters Elise, Laura, and Amélie who willingly pitched in to help whenever they could.

Part I
Background

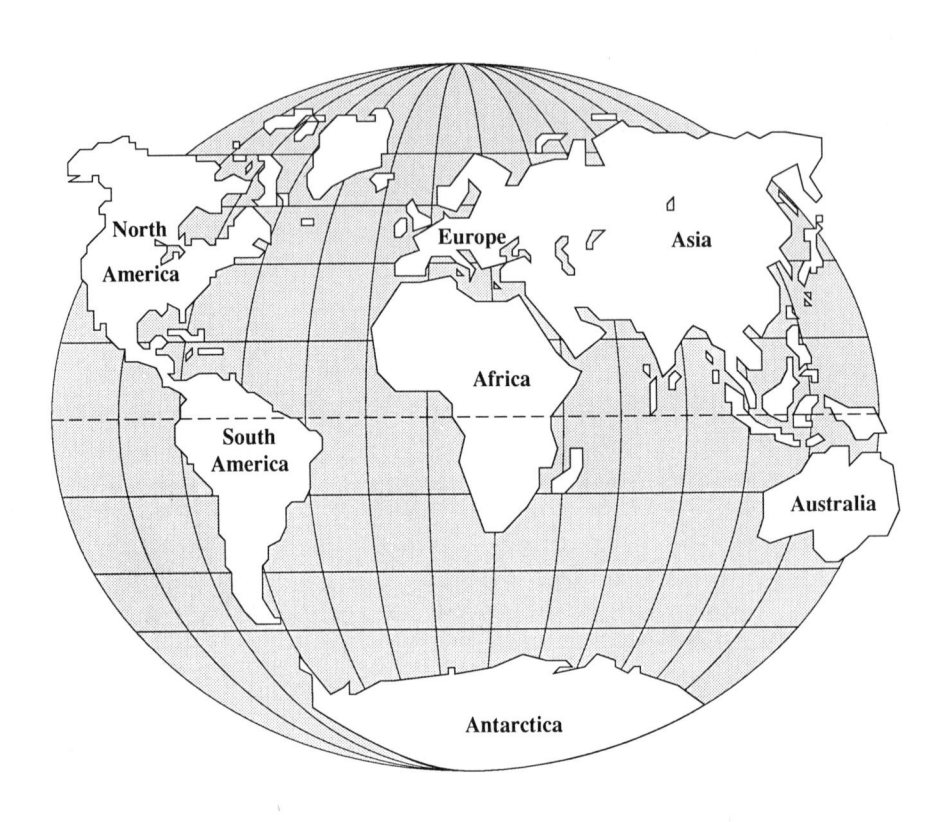

1
Setting the Stage

Founded on the basic principle of truth in advertising and pursued in response to the various needs and values of societies around the globe, the regulation of advertising is integrated into highly complex systems, the criteria and variables of which are drawn from multiple phenomena embedded in the cultures, philosophies, and ideologies of national and international societies. Thus, advertisers and the agencies seeking to promote commerce beyond their national frontiers are embarking on a journey through a veritable jungle of codes, regulations, laws, unwritten customs, and practices of all forms and natures. In view of this, what advertisers need is a "road map" to international advertising regulation. A useful map would set in relief the characteristics defining regulatory environments and the public priorities, values, and perspectives that give spirit to a particular advertising control system.

The intent of this book is to provide such a map. It investigates the economic, political, and cultural influences that underlie advertising regulations in different parts of the world. It begins to explain how and why regulations are put in place and what is their likely impact. It does not pretend to be a comprehensive catalogue of laws and administrative rules on a country-by-country basis. Such a survey would fill volumes and be rapidly outdated.

An understanding of the essential elements of legal systems is necessary in order to comprehend the nature and spirit of rules of law and to evaluate their impact on the social fabric. Thus, according to legal scholar John Merryman, legal systems should be characterized in terms of their elements, including extension and penetration, cultures, structures, actors, and processes. These elements define the functioning, the internal logic, and the boundaries of each legal system.[1]

Merryman observes that legal *extension* and *penetration* vary from one country to the next and together reveal the significance of legal legislation in terms of human behavior and conditions in a particular society. Extension relates to the substantive scope of the law. Societal behavior gives rise to conflicts open for legal or nonlegal solutions. Examples of the latter are custom and tradition, religion, informal negotiation procedures, social conventions, and peer pressure. The boundary between the legal and nonlegal domains defines the extension of the law. Differences in legal extension are illustrated, for example, by the major and minor roles played by law and lawyers in Western and Asian societies, respectively.

Penetration as distinct from extension refers to the actual role of law in the lives of the various segments in society. Differences in penetration are notably related to levels of socioeconomic development; in many poor societies, social interrelations in rural areas are beyond the reach of the law. Given differences in important aspects of social life and degrees to which law can reach and affect it, the divergencies can be substantial between two or more regulatory systems, including those with the same paper laws.

No less important are the related concepts of legal *culture, actors, structures,* and *processes*. The legal culture determines the internal logic of the system, its structure and operation. It reflects the historical and social environmental conditioning of a society toward law. The actors, structures, and processes are the more tangible or visible components of the legal system. Courts, parliaments, and public administrations are examples of structures. The various roles played by legal professionals and other participants animate the processes. Regulation is the result of the processes or, in other words, the interactions of the actors within the legal structures to bring about legislation or administrative actions, judicial proceedings, or the ordering of legal relations. In respect to all these elements, there are greater or lesser divergencies and similarities among countries. The legal structures, actors, and processes are products of the ethos of each state whose divergencies stem from historical, cultural, and developmental roots.

These concepts and components are particularly relevant to understanding the variegated landscape of international advertising regulation, featuring national rules and regulations of over one hundred different types, a number of international codes and guidelines, and a multitude of self-regulation guides and guidelines, not to mention the more extensive extralegal controls. Although the laws and systems of many countries seemingly resemble models established in advanced legal and commercial societies, such as the United States, the United Kingdom, France, Germany, or the Soviet Union, the resemblance is often superficial or illusory. Deeper investigation reveals dramatic divergencies in the aspects of social and commercial life that the laws seek to affect and in the extent to which they actually do.

Before examining in subsequent chapters the map through the maze of international advertising regulation, it is worthwhile to take a brief detour to recall the theoretical basis of advertising, the early history of its practice and its expansion as a multinational activity to the major regions of the world, and the origins of the international regulatory system.

Theory and Definitions

Advertising is bound by language and culture. Commercial advertising is the skillful use of all the capacities of language organized into a system of tools, techniques, and transmission devices. The system is used to relate ideas and impressions about characteristics and goods and to align them to human needs in order to promote sales. An advertising artist designs with words all kinds of realities, at times more believable than the actual physical world. The rationale for advertising is the satisfaction of human needs according to manners dictated by culture and expressed in language.

The theoretical basis for advertising is found in the concepts of *utility, economic goods,* and *value* developed by W.S. Jevons and Carl Menger in the 1870s. Jevons defined utility as "the abstract quality whereby an object serves our own purpose and becomes entitled to rank as an 'economic good.'"[2] Menger defined economic goods as possessing four qualities: relevance to human need, capacity to satisfy the need, knowledge of the object's capacity for satisfaction, and the technical ability to direct the object of the satisfaction of the need. "The value of goods arises from their relationship to our needs, and is not inherent in the goods themselves."[3] According to Menger, men's needs arose from drives deeply embedded in human nature.

In business practice, *advertising* connotes a concrete commercial transaction. According to the Definitions Committee of the American Marketing Association, advertising is "any paid form of non personal presentation and promotion of ideas, goods or services by an identified sponsor."[4] Advertising is one among other sales promotion activities. These also include product development, packaging, personal selling, availability (including display), price appeals, premiums, and contests.

There are multiple forms of advertising. The term embraces both *commercial* and *noncommercial* expressions. The former denotes advertising of goods and services by commercial enterprises, whereas the latter denotes promotion of ideas by nonprofit organizations, such as governments and charitable, religious, and political organizations. Commercial advertising is directed to individual consumers or to businesses (industrial advertising). A distinction is also drawn between institutional advertising and product advertising. *Institutional advertising* is used to sell the idea of patronizing a particular producer or retailer. It is designed to improve a firm's image for public relations purposes or to promote a particular cause. Commercial advertising may be targeted to primary and/or selective markets. *Primary demand* refers to the promotion of generic products, while *selective demand* means brand-name advertising. This book focuses principally on selective demand advertising, or the commercial advertising of mass-produced consumer products in international trade.

Early History

Advertising, performed in some way in all cultures, has probably been practiced as long as mankind has been exchanging goods and services. Its precise origins are unknown. Some believe the oldest example to be a Mesopotamian tablet announcing a reward for a runaway slave.[5]

In the works of Han Fei (280–233 B.C.) is a story about a man in the Song Kingdom of China who opened a wine shop and hung a flag prominently to attract customers. The earliest print ad found in China was produced from a bronze-etched block that dates back to the early 1100s A.D. Today, the block is on display in the China Historical Museum in Beijing. It was used to print handbills or packaging paper, advertising a needle shop in Jinan, "Jinan Liu's Fine Needle Shop." It signals a white rabbit as a trademark, and its message is "purchase fine steel bars and make excellent needles."[6]

Ironically, the term *advertising* or *publicité* appeared for the first time in a French dictionary in 1694 denoting "a crime committed with many witnesses." Then, until the end of the nineteenth century, the term was synonymous with information. The French attribute the birth of the modern advertising agency to their seventeenth century philosopher and essayist Michel de Montaigne. In his writings he suggested that each town open an office for *petites* annonces. He also conceptualized the practices of cultural sponsorship by demonstrating that rich people would fulfill a social function by supporting artists and writers. He further conceived the idea for a newspaper, called *La Gazette,* which actually appeared in the early 1600s. Founded by a medical doctor, Theophraste Renaudot, it carried, among other things, ads for health spas. This commercial purpose of newspapers was affirmed in the nineteenth century by the father of modern French journalism, Emile de Girardin. In his view a newspaper consisted of two parts: *polemiques* and *publicité*. According to this concept, advertising consisted of the continual repetition of information, longer and louder than the competitor.[7]

From early on, advertising appealed to basic human needs, particularly health concerns. In Paris during the early decades of the 1600s, charlatans, such as the famous doctor Montdor, staged skits simultaneously promoting and ridiculing their medicinal drugs and other miracle concoctions.

The first recorded published food advertisement in England, appearing May 26, 1657, in the *Publick Advertiser,* promoted coffee as a medicinal panacea.

> In Bartholomew Lane, on the backside of the old Exchange, the drink called coffee, which is very wholesome and physical drink, has many excellent virtues, closes the orifices of the stomach, fortifies the heat within, helpeth digestion, quickeneth the spirits, maketh the heart lightsum, is good against eye-sores, coughs, or colds, thumes, consumptions, head-ache, dropsy, gout,

scurvy, King's evil, and many others; is to be sold both in the morning and at three of the clock in the afternoon.[8]

Formal criticism of advertising also dates years back in history. In the Western world, the earliest comments and criticisms of advertising are attributed to Joseph Addison, publisher of *The Tatler* in the early eighteenth century. His writings indicate that, even before the Industrial Revolution, advertisers used special methods to catch the reader's eye to develop product awareness. They did this by glamorizing products, by comparisons and denigration of competing products, and by promises of consumers' satisfaction.

> The great Art in writing Advertisements, is the finding out a proper Method to catch the Reader's Eye; without which, a good Thing may pafs of unobferved, or be loft among Commiffions of Bankrupt. . . .
> But the great Skill in an Advertiser is chiefly feen in the Style which he make Ufe of. He is to mention the univerfal Efteem, or general Reputation, of Things that were never heard of. . . .
> A Second Ufe which this Sort of Writings have been turned to of late Years has been the Management of Controverfy, infomuch that above half the Advertisements one meets with now-a-Days are purely Polemical. The Inventors of *Strops for Razors* have written against one another this Way for feveral Years, and that with great Bitternefs. . . .
> The Third and laft Ufe of thefe Writings [advertisements] is to inform the World where they may be furnifhed with almoft every Thing that is neceffary for life. If a Man has Pains in his Head, Cholicks in his Bowels, or Spots in his Clothes, he may here meet with proper Cures and Remedies . . . ; if he wants new Sermons, Electuaries, Affes Milk, or any Thing elfe, either for his Body or his Mind, this is the Place to look for them in.[9]

The International Development of Commercial Advertising

The growth of commercial advertising has accompanied economic development, industrialization, international trade, and foreign direct investment. It has been most rapid in the *First World,* the industrialized, market-economy countries, where the functioning of the competitive market had depended on the widespread distribution of product information. There, advertising grew from simple media brokerage firms to full-service national agencies between 1850 and 1900. Modern commercial advertising grew most dramatically in the United States, where it was well established by 1900. In that year national advertising expenditure totaled $500 million, the equivalent of 3.2 percent of the gross national product (GNP).

During the decades between World War I and World War II, advertising took on a new look in the United States and Europe. Radio became a popular advertising media; photography replaced artistic drawings in the printed media. In the 1920s low-priced consumer goods, soda pops, soaps, deodorants, and toothpaste were mass marketed. Large-scale production of cigarettes began, and smoking by men and women was in vogue, encouraged by advertising campaigns employing slogans such as Reach for a Lucky Instead of a Sweet and Les Hommes Preferrent les Brunes (Gitanes). For the next twenty years, there would be no significant increase, the result of economic conditions during the depression and World War II.

During the 1950s television became a major communications medium, the middle-class consumer was the majority, and brand names proliferated. The largest advertisers were in the high volume/turnover product fields, including processed foods, beverages, pharmaceuticals, and tobacco products.

Since the 1950s advertising has made considerable strides in technique and technology in the United States as well as in Europe. Expenditures have increased by multiples. Moreover, the opening of a single common market in Europe in 1992 is expected to stimulate accelerated expansion. At the same time, the advertising boom has been tempered by the growth of consumerism and public regulation. To a large extent, advertising in the industrialized free-enterprise countries is more responsive to the needs of the general public than in any other part of the world. Advertising and its regulation in the First World form the subject of part II of this book.

The development of advertising was at first stymied, then redirected in more or less controlled channels in the Soviet Union, Eastern Europe, and China—the *Second World*. In these societies, there has been heavy reliance on advertising to sell to the citizenry the merits and goals of the socialist state. It was, and to some extent remains, an instrument for propaganda and social integration.

Although apparently never making explicit reference to advertising, Karl Marx held that the only activities benefiting society were those that embodied labor value. "Costs of circulation which originate in a mere change of form of value, ideally considered, do not enter into the value of commodities."[10] According to Marx's disciples such costs include market research, sales promotion, and advertising.[11]

Despite Marx and despite Lenin's disdain for advertising, the necessity for advertising of a limited nature has always been apparent to public administrators. Lenin permitted the practice in the mid-1920s along with some free enterprise under his New Economic Policy. During this period, according to Marshall Goldman, "Newspapers carried ads, poets wrote copy, and advertising was not too different from that in the rest of Western Europe."[12] When Joseph Stalin came into power and introduced his Five-Year Plan, commercial advertising and free enterprise were virtually swept out.

After Stalin's death, advertising began to enjoy a limited renaissance. The change came about slowly. Even in Stalin's time, officials recognized the need for product labeling to facilitate administrative controls on output. And, as production increased, planners introduced trademarks to encourage repeat sales and to save on inspection costs. In the post-Stalin period, self-service shops were introduced, and display advertising began to fulfill the information function of the salesperson. With increased production, advertising was also needed to encourage sales of newly introduced products and to clear overstocked inventories. Thus, advertising was progressively acknowledged as a necessary commercial tool.

Advertising policy was outlined at the first Conference of Advertising Workers in Socialist Countries held in December 1957 in Prague, and the first All Soviet Conference held in August 1958. The recommendations adopted in Prague are enshrined in the current policies of Eastern European countries. Accordingly, socialist advertising's aims are to influence demand for goods by educating consumers' tastes, to help consumers by giving them information about the most rational forms of consumption, and to improve service to the consumer in the retail trade.[13]

In China, after the revolution of 1949 and during the Mao culture, advertising barely survived as an arm of public policy. Commercial advertising was denounced, and commercial services were either neglected or suppressed.

Maoist policy stemmed partly from Marxist tradition and partly from Chinese historical experience that associated services with servitude—in semifeudal and semicolonial contexts familiar to the Chinese proletariat. Economic hardship was also an important factor. According to Chinese economic expert N.T. Wang, "Under conditions of centralized purchase and allocation as well as general scarcity, advertising was hardly required to push sales. Moreover, in a time of general scarcity, the provision of services such as marketing was tantamount to granting a favor."[14] During the Cultural Revolution, advertising was linked to capitalistic practices and was banned.

Local advertising agencies that existed prior to the turbulent years of the 1960s and 1970s survived for a period by producing political posters but finally ceased all activities. During the 1950s foreign advertising, so prevalent in domestic Chinese media, continued only a short while and in limited fashion. Foreign advertising through foreign Chinese-language publications continued into the early 1960s, ceased, and slowly began to reappear in the early 1970s.[15]

Today, advertising throughout most of the Second World is enjoying a dramatic renaissance. Current developments and controls are described in part II of this book.

Trade and colonial expansion brought foreign commercial advertising to *Third World* countries in Latin America, Asia, and Africa during the early decades of the twentieth century. In these countries advertising was not used extensively for sales promotion except by foreign importers, most frequently by those promoting patent medicines and cigarettes. Prerevolutionary China was one of the earliest and most important centers for foreign advertising activity. The largest advertisers in China in the early 1900s included the British American Tobacco Company and the American Singer Sewing Machine Company. In the 1920s foreign firms of many industrialized countries operated freely in China. Important advertisers included enterprises from the United States (Procter & Gamble, Kodak, and Ford Motor Co.), from Britain (Dunlop, Imperial Chemical Corp., and Dr. Williams' Medicines), from Germany (Agfa Films and Bayer Aspirin), and from Switzerland (Nestlé and Hoffman-La Roche).

In its earliest years, international advertising in Third World countries was carried out by specialized departments of the large advertisers. In China foreign advertisers established the media that carried their ads. In the fifty years that followed the Opium War, foreigners established some three hundred newspapers. Later in the 1920s, radio stations were founded by the foreign enterprises. The first neon signs in China were brought in for the American Royal Typewriter Co. Commercial advertising in India had appeared since the turn of the century, when Dunlop, among other British firms, began promoting its products in Bombay and Delhi. The advertising departments of Unilever were among the forerunners of commercial advertising in the Third World and the precursors of Lintas Worldwide. In 1928 Unilever/Lintas established the first commercial advertising firm in West Africa. Commercial advertising was also introduced in Indonesia in 1938 by Unilever/Lintas.

Foreigners were also instrumental in establishing the advertising industry in most Third World countries. The first advertising agency was established in Brazil in 1914, when an American businessman and a journalist joined forces to introduce American techniques of mass advertising. Foreign firms established local agencies in Brazil in the 1930s. In the 1920s British, French, and American firms established a number of medium-sized firms that were concentrated in Shanghai. In the late 1920s and early 1930s, the establishment of foreign advertising agencies in India heralded the beginning of the Indian advertising industry. The first advertising agencies in Africa were established by the British in Nigeria in the 1930s.

By the 1960s significant advertising industries had been established in many Third World countries in Latin America, Asia, and parts of Africa and the Middle East. The nature of this industry in the Third World, including policies and regulations, is the subject of part IV of this book.

The Spread of Multinational Advertising

Although foreign advertising was well established in the fifty or so independent countries that existed at the end of World War II, most advertising activity was domestic, and 75 percent of recorded world expenditure was concentrated in the United States. In 1962 total world advertising expenditure was estimated to be about $20 billion, of which 90 percent occurred in the United States and Europe (65 percent and 25 percent, respectively).[16]

A study conducted by *Advertising Age* in 1963 of foreign advertising businesses "showed billings of $2 billion by 375 agencies located in 48 countries outside the United States and indicated that foreign business was growing at a rate considerably higher than in the United States." This trend continues.[17]

The growth in international advertising was particularly rapid after the 1960s, when hundreds of foreign-based companies established offices abroad. Another study conducted for the period July, 1960, through June, 1961, revealed that 690 U.S. firms participated in over one thousand new activities overseas. Of them, 54.6 percent were new establishments, 18.3 percent were expansions, and 27 percent were license agreements.[18]

This unprecedented growth in international advertising occurred for several reasons. First, world markets for consumer goods expanded rapidly. Second, multinational advertisers competed with each other in promoting needs for greater services from technologically advanced agencies with overseas production facilities. Third, local agencies desiring access to modern marketing techniques invited foreign participation in the founding and building of local enterprises. Finally, attractive incentives to the establishment of foreign affiliates included advantages in reduced tax costs on foreign advertising.

Expansion has taken several forms, but the style, concepts, techniques, and technology used have been heavily influenced by the American advertising industry.[19] In other industrialized countries and many parts of the Third World, there has been heavy emphasis on brand names and image. Moreover, studies of the products advertised by the international enterprises in the late 1970s showed remarkably similar products in most countries. Of international advertising, 80 percent to 90 percent was concentrated on five or six product categories. These categories included internationally recognized brands of processed foods, soft drinks, beer and wine, cigarettes, drugs, and toiletries, which account for about 40 percent of current national advertising in the United Kingdom and the United States.[20]

The Development of Regulation

Precedents for modern commercial regulation of advertising occur in legal doctrines found in Roman and medieval cultures. One is the ancient principle of a manufacturer's responsibility for his products. Under the Roman *jus civile*, the buyer had protection against hidden defects if the seller committed fraud or had given an express warranty. Fraud, according to the law, included nondisclosure of known defects as well as misrepresentation and concealment. Administrative or aedilian law offered additional remedies against bona fide sellers who gave no express warranty. The *corpus juris* merged the civil and aedilian law, preserving the two systems and warranty liability.[21] These early maxims gave rise to proscriptions against selling short-weight or adulterated goods, to concepts of decency, to just prices, and to laws against usury and the manipulation of markets.

The responsibility of suppliers of foods and drinks for human consumption has also long been recognized in English common law. According to William L. Prosser, the leading expert on producers liability:

> Even in the ancient days . . . there were innumerable local regulations governing weight and measure and quality. The baker of bad bread went to the pillory, and the ale-wife who sold sorry beer "journeyed to the tumbrel with distaff and spindle." The year 1266 saw the first of a series of English criminal statutes imposing penalties upon victualers, vintners, brewers, cooks and others who marketed "corrupt" food and drink for immediate consumption.
>
> Beginning about 1431, there were dicta in a line of decisions, and occasional statements of text writers, to the effect that the seller of food incurred a strict liability, in the nature of an implied warranty.[22]

Of the safeguards derived from common law, the most important—embodied in England's Sale of Goods Act of 1893—states that whenever a buyer, expressly or by implication, makes known to the seller the particular purposes for which the goods are required, showing that he relies on the seller's skill or judgment, there is an implied condition that the goods sold shall be reasonably fit for such a purpose. Today the English common law precludes misrepresentation of facts, defamation, passing off, and breach of confidence in advertising. Similarly, under Confucian teachings personal trust is the fundamental tenet of social order, and deception is not to be countenanced.

In contradistinction to the principle of manufacturers' responsibility is the age-old common-law precept of caveat emptor, which, as a corollary of the emerging laissez-faire economic ideology, enjoyed a renaissance in the seventeenth century. The principle of caveat emptor is the source of fundamental tension between buyers and sellers and holds that the buyer is served best by free competition between sellers. Since the beginning of the twentieth century, this concept has slowly withered away with each passage of consumer legislation. The regulators have observed that the changes in the nature of business and technology have rendered fundamental assumptions of caveat emptor largely invalid.

According to the proponents of regulation, modern economic realities have destroyed the possibilities for rational consumer choice for a number of reasons. First is the alleged absence of free choice due to prevalent monopolistic and oligopolistic forces. Also, product complexity resulting from modern technology is seen as exceeding the capacity of the ordinary consumer to absorb information. Moreover, say these proponents, the heavy reliance of producers on persuasive and emotional techniques, instead of informational advertising, have subjected consumers to choice by influence and persuasion rather than by reason.

Modern regulation dates to the turn of the century in the First World. Initial emphasis was placed on acts of unfair competition. Gradually, consumer protection became the stronger motive. Over the course of the twentieth century, the regulation of the advertising industry became increasingly rigorous. The rigor subsided, and a revival in the direction of deregulation slowly began in the 1980s.

In the United States, federal regulation of corporate behavior began with the adoption of the Sherman Anti-Trust Act of 1890. It declared acts of restraint on competition with an adverse effect on interstate and international commerce illegal. Congress passed the Food and Drug Act in 1906 and in 1914 the Federal Trade Commission Act.[23,24] The intention of the Food and Drug Act was to enable the government to act against blatant, reckless deception. It prohibited misbranding or making false claims concerning drugs. The Federal Trade Commission (FTC), created by the 1914 act, had the authority to prohibit unfair competition and strengthened the Sherman Anti-Trust Act. The phrase *unfair practices* referred especially to advertising deemed to be injurious to competitors. At this stage consumer protection was only a by-product of restraints on anticompetitive practices. Consumer protection, however, was the main objective in 1938, when Congress passed the Wheeler-Lea amendment to the Federal Trade Commission Act, providing restrictions on the advertising of foods, drugs, and cosmetics. This act extended the powers of the Federal Trade Commission to include advertising adversely affecting consumers.[25]

Over this same period, self-regulation initially developed in the United States. Industry responded to repeated charges of false advertising with the initiation of organized self-regulation. The first attempt to coordinate self-regulation nationally and internationally was the truth in advertising resolution, proposed in 1911 at a convention assembled by the Associated Advertising Clubs of America and the World. The convention adopted the slogan Truth in Advertising, referring to the one kind of advertising that would be "permanently profitable."[26] In 1919 the International Chamber of Commerce (ICC) was established to promote fair business practices on an international scale. In 1938 it established its Code of Standards of Advertising Practice, providing the framework for coordinated self-regulation in the global community.

The enhanced technical possibilities for advertising following World War II raised renewed ethical and social concerns. Consumer protests emphasized the negative aspects of the overall social orientation of advertising, particularly its pervasiveness in daily life, its promotion of materialism, and its lack of "good taste." Protests had national and international reach. Measures for reform were prompted by fear and indignation over the manipulative techniques and emotional appeals of the advertisers and by the dramatic rise in the volume of advertising that permeated everyday life. The regulatory response in the United States extended the machinery that was in place by 1938, including the extension and development of the food and drug laws, the adoption of the Consumer Product Safety Act, and the establishment of the Consumer Product Safety Commission.[27]

In Western Europe, the most significant legislative initiatives in the interest of consumer protection were taken in the late 1960s and early 1970s, updating and extending earlier laws on anticompetitive behavior and on social responsibility and liability for deception. These initiatives brought European regulation up to par with that of the United States.

Government control of foreign investment and advertising began to appear in Latin America in the late 1940s and the 1950s. More extensive legislation was enacted in the 1970s and 1980s. Advertising excesses in other Third World countries, notably in Africa and Asia, were initially controlled under rules and regulations established by colonial rulers. Indigenous controls began to appear in the 1970s.

Until the 1960s, international regulation was concentrated on the ICC's Code of Marketing Practices and primarily concerned with anticompetitive practices. In the 1960s, however, the representatives of academic and government sectors formally acknowledged the existence of multinationalism and multinational corporations as an international phenomena of foreign trade and investment. From this time onward, advertising, as the promotional tool of the multinational corporations, has attracted increasing attention from the international community.

Notes

1. John Henry Merryman, "The Convergence (and Divergence) of the Civil Law and the Common Law," in *New Perspectives for a Common Law of Europe,* ed. Mauro Cappelletti (Boston: Sythoff Publishing, 1978), 222–27.

2. W.S. Jevons, *The Theory of Political Economy,* 4th ed. (London: MacMillan, 1911), 38.

3. Carl Menger, *Principles of Economics,* trans. James Dingwall and Bert F. Hoselitz (Glencoe, Ill.: Free Press, 1950), 120.

4. "Report of Definitions Committee," *Journal of Marketing* 12 (October 1948): 202.

5. For information on the history of advertising in the Western world refer to Raymond A. Bauer and Stephen A. Greyser, *Advertising in America: The Consumer*

View (Boston: Division of Research, Graduate School of Business Administration, Harvard University, 1968); Henry Sampson, *History of Advertising* (London: Chatto and Windus, 1875); Ralph M. Hower, *The History of an Advertising Agency,* rev. ed. (Cambridge, Mass.: Harvard University Press, 1949); James Playstead Wood, *The Story of Advertising* (New York: Ronald Press, 1958); Frank Presbrey, *The History and Development of Advertising* (New York: Doubleday, Doran and Co., 1929; New York: Greenwood Press, 1968); S. Watson Dunn, *Advertising* (New York: Holt, Rinehart and Winston, 1961); Steven R. Fox, *The Mirror Makers: A History of American Advertising and Its Creators* (New York: William Morrow and Co., 1984).

6. Xu Bai-yi, *A Brief History of Advertising in China* (Shanghai: Gestetner Technique and Service Center, 1986).

7. Gérard Lagnaud, "Une histoire de comédiens et de médecins," *Autrement,* October 1983, 10–15.

8. Presbrey, *Development of Advertising,* 48.

9. Ibid., 64–67, quoting *The Tatler,* 14 September 1710.

10. Karl Marx, *Capital* (Moscow: Foreign Languages Publishing House, 1957), 136, as cited in Marshall I. Goldman, "The Soviet Union," *International Handbook of Advertising* (New York: McGraw-Hill Book Co., 1964), 494.

11. See Marshall I. Goldman, "Product Differentiation and Advertising: Some Lessons From Soviet Experience," *The Journal of Political Economy* 68 (August 1960), 346.

12. Marshall I. Goldman, "The Soviet Union," 494.

13. Everett M. Jacobs, "New Developments in Soviet Advertising and Marketing Theory," *International Journal of Advertising* 5, no. 3 (1986): 244; see also V.E. Demidov and I.P. Kardashidi, *Reklama v Torgovli: Teoria i Praktika* (Moscow: Ekonomika, 1983), and P. Hansen, *Advertising and Socialism* (London: Macmillan, 1974).

14. N.T. Wang, *China's Modernization and Transnational Corporations* (Lexington, Mass.: Lexington Books, 1984), 6.

15. Scott D. Seligman, "China's Fledgling Advertising Industry," *The China Business Review* (January/February, 1984), 12.

16. Research Committee of the International Advertising Association, *International Advertising Expenditure* (New York: International Advertising Association, 1963).

17. "Foreign Agency Report," *Advertising Age,* 4 March 1963, as cited in S. Watson, Dunn, *International Handbook of Advertising,* p. 666.

18. Study carried out by the management firm of Booz, Allen and Hamilton reported in *Media/scope* as cited in S. Watson Dunn, *International Handbook of Advertising* (New York: McGraw-Hill Book Co., 1964), p. 666.

19. Karl P. Sauvant, "The Potential of Multinational Enterprises as Vehicles for the Transmission of Business Culture," in *Controlling Multinational Enterprises, Problems, Strategies, Counterstrategies,* ed. Karl P. Sauvant and Farid G. Lavipour (Boulder, Colo.: Westview Press, 1976), 57–63.

20. Global studies on advertising have been carried out in the last ten years by the UNCTC and UNESCO. See UN, *Transnational Corporations in Advertising,* ST/CTC/8 (1979), 32. Information in the UN study was obtained from American Association of Advertising Agencies (AAAA), *The Advertising Agency Business*

around the World: Reports from Advertising Agency Associations and Agency Readers in 51 Countries (New York: AAAA, 1975). UN, UNESCO, *Mass Communications and the Advertising Industry* (Reports and papers on mass communication) no. 97 (1985): 15; and "100 Leading National Advertisers," *Advertising Age,* 26 September 1985.

21. Freidrich Kessler, "The Protection of the Consumer under Modern Sales Law: A Comparative Study (Part 1)," *Yale Law Journal* 74 (1964): 263–64.

22. William L. Prosser, "Assault upon the Citadel: Strict Liability to the Consumer," *Yale Law Review* 69 (June 1960): 1103–4.

23. United States, *Food and Drug Act,* 34 Stat. 768 (30 June 1906).

24. United States, *Federal Trade Commission Act,* 38 Stat. 719 (1914).

25. United States, *Wheeler-Lea Act,* ch. 49, 52 Stat. 111 (1938), in 15 U.S.C., sec. 41 et seq.

26. Fox, *The Mirror Makers,* p. 68; see also Bauer, Greyser, *Advertising in America,* 7–10.

27. United States, *Consumer Safety Act,* Pub. L. 92573, 86 Stat. 1207 (1972).

2
The Actors

Advertising and its regulation are, after all, human activities; as with all other such activities, a knowledge of the people involved sheds light on the activities themselves. In the national and international regulatory processes, thousands of people actively help to shape both the advertising and the regulations. Conditioned by culture, history, and development, they interact according to the directions of their different ideologies, attitudes, and perceptions of advertising's impact on socioeconomic well-being. These thousands of people may be placed into three categories: the *targets,* the *critics,* and the *regulators.*

The targets of regulation are the various sources and disseminators of advertising, as legislation and administrative regulations set limits on how, what, when, and where advertising may be carried on. The targets include *advertisers*—the producers, suppliers, retailers, and other direct dealers of economic goods and services; *advertising agencies*—the producers of the promotional images and messages; and the *media*—the disseminators of messages through newspapers and magazines, television and radio, billboards, loudspeakers, and cinemas. A staunch supporter of free, competitive marketplaces and the regulatory-burden bearer, the advertising industry resists regulations that limit commercial speech or are otherwise deemed unreasonable in the prevention of unfair competition or in the protection of consumers.

Critics fall into two subcategories: the *interest groups* and activists and the *general public*. Among the former the most visible groups have asserted their influence on advertising regulation through what has come to be called *consumerism*. Aimed at protecting the general public from the effects of imperfect market conditions, including misinformation and product defects, consumerism is a complement to a vigorous private-enterprise system. Thus, consumer-interest groups and activists play their most effective roles in First World countries. They also lend support to consumers of Third World countries through debates in international forums, where they have provided the impetus for the United Nations' guidelines on consumer protection and the World Health Organization international code on breast-milk substitutes, to cite two examples.

Elsewhere, consumer groups are of only secondary importance or are virtually nonexistent, as in Second World countries where prevailing socialist systems have obviated their emergence. In most Third World countries, consumer-interest groups are hard to find. Instead, officials of ministries of commerce, economic planning, and health have performed the functions of the critics for the protection of local consumers and industries.

Be it in the First World, Second World, or Third World, the general public is for the most part apolitical, even in the most democratic societies. When blatant controversy arises, responsive chords may be struck and interest aroused such that enthusiastic public support for regulatory proposals may ensue. Because such enthusiasm is difficult to sustain, activists gain popular acclaim only periodically. Once the wave of popularity has ended, years of relative inactivity follow. Presently, consumerism in the First World is at a relatively low ebb. Many of the goals of the activists and interest groups have been attained. Political conservatism appears to be the dominant ideology, and deregulation in general is in vogue. Only some product-specific issues remain alive. This quiet spirit also is prevalent in intergovernmental organizations.

The primary regulators are the decision makers in national governments. They determine policy, legislate and administer the law, and adjudicate resultant conflicts. Secondary roles are played by diplomats, experts, and international executives in various forums when controversies over advertising are put on the agendas for international discussion. The industrial regulators impose voluntary restraints on their industry members. Some perform a watchdog function by building up respected systems of self-regulation in order to protect industry from itself and from outside regulation.

The Industry: Regulatory Target

Multinational advertisers and advertising agencies are primary actors on the international commercial stage. In practically all countries where advertising is commercially significant, the multinational agencies play an important role. Figures shown in table 2–1 indicate that the billings of the top fifty agencies worldwide were equivalent to between 30–40 percent of total world commercial advertising expenditure in 1987. Concentration in the industry also is very high. Figures in table 2–1 also show that in 1987 the top twenty agencies accounted for 80 percent of the billings of the top fifty agencies. Table 2–2 identifies the world's top fifty advertising agencies, as reported by *Advertising Age* in 1988.

Many of the top world advertising agencies are both multinational in terms of transfrontier operations and transnational in terms of international ownership.[1] While the U.S. agencies have long dominated the world adver-

Table 2–1
Comparison of Gross Billings of Top Multinational Agencies with Total World Advertising Expenditure, 1987

Agencies	Gross Billings (Billions $)	As Percentage of Total Advertising Expenditure
"Top Ten" Multinational Agencies	41.8	20
"Top Twenty" Multinational Agencies	59.0	29
"Top Fifty" Multinational Agencies	73.8	36
"Sweet 16" United States Firms[a]	46.6	23

Source: derived from *World Advertising Expenditure,* 1987, 22nd ed., Starch INRA Hooper, Inc. in cooperation with IAA; "Foreign Agency Report," *Advertising Age,* 9 May 1988; "US Agency Income Report," *Advertising Age,* 30 March 1988.

[a]The sixteen largest agencies in the United States, all are billion dollar agencies.

tising market, Western European and recently Japanese, Australian, and Brazilian agencies have expanded or merged operations with agencies in other countries and are playing increasingly important roles in international advertising. Today, of the world's top twenty agencies, eleven are home based in the United States, four in the United Kingdom, three in France, and two in Japan. Australia and Switzerland are the newest additions to this group of home countries. Each of these countries has one major multinational incorporated in their territory. However, Australia's multinational advertising agency, Mojo, merged in January 1989 with Chiat/Day, the U.S. advertising firm based in Los Angeles. Brazil's largest advertising agencies in recent years have been classified among the world's top fifty foreign firms. State advertising enterprises of several Second World countries are involved in joint operations with multinational agencies in the United States and Western Europe, thus far primarily to promote their own exports. Table 2–3 provides financial and geographic indicators of the extent of operations of twenty-five multinational advertising agencies (all among the world's top fifty agencies).

Increasing concentration and pluralism have been the advertising trends in the 1980s. During this period, the advertising industry has undergone substantial change through takeovers and internal expansion. Following a number of mergers and takeovers beginning in the mid-1980s, the profile of the industry has been significantly altered.

Today many of the largest multinational agencies have regrouped into multimillion- and billion-dollar multiservice transnational holding companies, home-based either in the United Kingdom, the United States, France, or Belgium. The composition, home-base, and operations of the ten largest holding companies are shown in table 2–4.

Most multinational advertising agencies are privately owned, profit-seeking entities. They conduct foreign activities through a number of alternative arrangements with host countries. These fall into one of two broad categories: equity (ownership) agreements or nonequity (contractual) agreements. The legal implications vary with the vehicles chosen for foreign operations. Multinational advertising firms may be single enterprises or holding companies. In either case they are conglomerates of various corporate and affiliated entities bound together by a center of operations—the parent corporation seated in the home country.

Table 2–2
World's Top Fifty Agencies, 1987

Rank 1987	Rank 1986	Agency	Gross Income	Billings
1.	(1)	Dentsu Inc.	$884.5	$6.78 billion
2.	(2)	Young & Rubicam[1]	735.5	4.91 billion
3.	(3)	Saatchi & Saatchi Advertising Worldwide[2]	693.6	4.61 billion
4.	(4)	Backer Spielvogel Bates Worldwide[3]	600.7	4.07 billion
5.	(7)	BBDO Worldwide[4]	537.0	3.66 billion
6.	(6)	Ogilvy & Mather Worldwide[5]	528.6	3.66 billion
7.	(8)	McCann-Erickson Worldwide[6]	512.5	3.42 billion
8.	(5)	J. Walter Thompson Co.[7]	483.0	3.22 billion
9.	(15)	Lintas: Worldwide[8]	417.9	2.79 billion
10.	(12)	Hakuhodo International	383.4	2.90 billion
11.	(10)	D'Arcy Masius Benton & Bowles[9]	371.3	2.49 billion
12.	(14)	Leo Burnett Co.	369.2	2.46 billion
13.	(13)	Grey Advertising	369.2	2.46 billion
14.	(9)	DDB Needham Worldwide[10]	358.5	2.60 billion
15.	(11)	Foote, Cone & Belding Communications[11]	344.6	2.30 billion
16.	(—)	WCRS/Belier[12]	230.2	1.63 billion
17.	(—)	HDM[13]	204.0	1.38 billion
18.	(16)	Bozell, Jacobs, Kenyon & Eckhardt	185.2	1.33 billion
19.	(18)	N W Ayer	166.1	1.22 billion
20.	(19)	Publicis International	164.3	1.09 billion
21.	(—)	Lowe Group[14]	137.3	968.3
22.	(26)	Roux, Seguela, Cayzac & Goudard[15]	115.7	830.1
23.	(21)	Wells, Rich, Green	114.0	765.0
24.	(24)	Tokyu Advertising Agency	107.1	879.9
25.	(22)	Dai-Ichi Kikaku	109.4	836.7
26.	(25)	Daiko Advertising	107.1	879.9
27.	(27)	Scali, McCabe, Sloves[16]	93.1	653.2
28.	(28)	Ketchum Communications	88.1	660.0
29.	(31)	Ogilvy & Mather Direct Response	84.0	560.0
30.	(33)	TBWA	79.0	545.0
31.	(38)	Asatsu Advertising	73.4	489.3
32.	(34)	Ross Roy Inc.	71.3	475.3
33.	(37)	I&S Corp.[17]	65.8	540.4
34.	(41)	Yomiko Advertising	64.7	477.3
35.	(36)	Campbell-Mithun	63.9	425.8

Table 2–2 (continued)

Rank 1987	1986	Agency	Gross Income	Billings
36.	(40)	Wunderman Worldwide	62.1	414.8
37.	(42)	GGK[18]	59.3	415.0
38.	(45)	Asahi Advertising	54.4	340.6
39.	(43)	Chiat/Day	52.5	350.0
40.	(—)	Mojo MDA[19]	52.5	348.0
41.	(—)	Dorland Worldwide	49.6	331.0
42.	(44)	Tracy-Locke	47.3	326.0
43.	(35)	Lowe Marschalk[20]	45.6	304.2
44.	(—)	Doremus & Co.	45.4	304.1
45.	(—)	BDDP Group[21]	44.6	297.6
46.	(—)	George Patterson Pty.[22]	44.3	295.3
47.	(48)	Hill, Holiday, Connors, Cosmopulos	43.4	289.6
48.	(—)	McCaffrey & McCall	42.1	308.9
49.	(47)	Laurence, Charles, Free & Lawson	41.5	302.0
50.	(46)	HBM/Creamer	40.9	272.0

Notes: Dollars are in millions unless otherwise noted.
Included in agency figures are income and revenues from the following subsidiaries and affiliates: [1]Young & Rubicam: HDM (33 percent); Wunderman Worldwide; Sudler & Hennessey; Stone & Adler; Creswell, Munsell, Pultz & Zirbel. [2]Saatchi & Saatchi Advertising Worldwide: McCaffrey & McCall; Rumrill-Hoyt; Klemtner Advertising, Cochrane Chase, Livingston & Co. The holding company, Saatchi & Saatchi PLC, London, reported world gross income of $1.68 billion on billings of $11.36 billion. [3]Backer Splevogel Bates Worldwide: Campbell-Mithun; AC&R/DHB&Bess; Kobs & Draft. [4]BBDO Worldwide: Tracy-Locke; Doremus & Co.; Ingalls, Quinn & Johnson, MARCOA DR Group; Lavey/Wolff/Swift; Frank J. Corbett Inc.; Blair Advertising; Franklin Spier Inc.; Caravetta Allen Kimbrough/BBDO. [5]Ogilvy & Mather Worldwide: Ogilvy & Mather Direct Response; Rolf Werner Rosenthal. [6]McCann-Erickson Worldwide: Part of the Interpublic Group of Cos., New York, which reported world gross income of $992.9 million on billings of $6.62 billion. [7]J. Walter Thompson Co.: Brouillard Communications. JWT Group was acquired in June 1987 by WPP Group PLC, London. [8]Lintas: Worldwide: Part of the Interpublic Group of Cos. In October 1987 SSC&B: Lintas and Campbell-Ewald were joined to form Lintas: Worldwide. [9]DMB&B: Medicus Intercon International: Ted Colangelo Associates. [10] DDB Needham Worldwide: Kallir, Philips, Ross; Bernard Hodes Advertising Group; Rapp & Collins USA; Kresser, Craig/D.I.K. [11]Foote, Cone & Belding Communications: Lewis, Gilman & Kynett; Albert Frank-Guenther Law; Vicom/FCB. [12]WCRS/Beller: Delta Femina, Travisano & Partners; HBM/Creamer; Creamer Dickson Basford: Heller Breene; Robert A. Becker; Cohn & Wells. In September 1987 London-based WCRS acquired 49 percent of Paris-based Groupe Belier, owned by Eurocom. Earlier in 1987 WCRS aquired the Ball Partnership from the Ogilvy Group. [13]HDM: HDM (Havas, Dentsu, Marsteller) is an equal partnership (33 1/3 percent) between Young & Rubicam, Tokyo-based Dentsu and Havas Conseil. [14]Lowe Group: Lowe International; Allen Brady & Marsh; Laurence, Charles, Free & Lawson. [15] Roux, Seguela, Cayzac & Goudard: includes offices in Austria, Belgium, France (Paris and regional), Germany, Netherlands, Italy, Spain, Sweden, Switzerland, U.K. and O'Rielly O'Brien Clow/RSCG in the U.S. Also, RSCG Export which does business in Africa, the Middle East and French Caribbean and Creative Business International. [16]Scali, McCabe, Sloves: Martin Agency, Fallon McElligott. [17]I&S Corp.: Formerly Dai-Ichi Advertising, Tokyo, which merged in 1986 with SPN Co., a communications and sales promotion company of the Seibu Saison Group. [18]GGK Holding: A Basel, Switzerland-based agency group with offices in Austria, Germany, France, Netherlands, Spain, U.K., Italy and Brazil. Lois Pitts Gershon/GGK, New York, is also part of the group. [19]Mojo MDA: 14 offices in Australia, New Zealand, Hong Kong, Singapore, U.K. and the U.S. [20]Lowe Marschalk: Interpublic Group of Cos. holds 70 percent of LM; Lowe Howard-Spink & Bell PLC, London, the other 30 percent. [21]BDDP Group: Boulet, Dru, Dupuy, Petit, Paris, lists nine regional agencies and 10 affiliated companies. [22]George Paterson Pty: Part of Backer Spielvogel Bates. Compiled by Ilse Cermak Reprinted with permission from 9 May 1988 issue of *Advertising Age*. Copyright 1988 by Crain Communications, Inc.

Table 2-3
World Wide Operations of Selected Multinational Advertising Agencies, 1987

Agency and Group	Home Country	U.S. Income (% of total)	U.S. Billing (% of total)	Concentration of Operations[a]	Classification of Foreign Operations[b] MJ / MN / NE
Dentsu Inc.	Japan	—	>6	US, E, A	7 / / 9
Young & Rubicam	USA	52	53	US, LA, E, A	125 / 10 /
Saatchi & Saatchi (Saatchi WW)	UK	48	48	US, E, A	85 / / 35
Backer Spielvogel Bates WW (Saatchi/Saatchi)	US/UK	44	44	US, LA, E, A	(102)
BBDO Worldwide (Omnicom)	USA	58	62	US, LA, E, A	(112) / 8
Ogilvy & Mather (Ogilvy Group)	USA	49	49	US, LA, E, AF, A	185 / 49 / 12
McCann-Erickson WW (Interpublic)	USA	32	32	US, LA, E, AF, A	115 / 5 / 25
J. Walter Thompson Co. (WPP Group)	US/UK	50	50	US, LA, E, AF, A	29 / 9 / 8
Lintas: Worldwide (Interpublic)	USA	40	39	US, LA, E, AF, A	55 / 4 / 26
Hakuhodo	Japan	1	3	US, A	4 / 2 / 2
D'Arcy, Masius, Benton & Bowles	USA	53	52	US, LA, E, A	45 / 4 / 22
Leo Burnett Co.	USA	63	64	US, LA, E, A, ME	42 / 5 / 3
Grey Advertising	USA	59	60	US, LA, E, AF, A	(34)
DDB Needham WW (Omnicom)	USA	61	63	US, LA, E, A	32 / 11 / 4
Foote, Cone & Belding	USA	71	71	US, LA, E, AF, A	83 / 19 / 9
WCRS/Belier	UK	40	41	US, E, A	17
HDM	USA	13	14	US, E, A	43
Bozell, Jacobs, Kenyon & Eckhardt	USA	86	87	US, LA, E, A	5 / 21 / 33
NW Ayer	USA	70	71.1	US, E, A	10 / 3 / 23
Publicis	France	2	2	US, E	24 / 14 /
Lowe International (Lowe, Howard, Spink & Bell, PLC)	UK	52	53	E	10
Roux, Seguela, Cayzac & Goudard	France	1	1	E	10
TBWA Advertising	USA	25	23	E, A	15 / / 10
GGK	Switzerland	18	21	US, LA, E, A	13 / 2 /
Chiat/Mojo	USA	50	52	US, UK, A	7 / / 6
UNIVAS (Eurocom)	France	0	0	E	6

Source: derived from "International Agencies Report," *Advertising Age,* 11 July 1988; Dentsu Data Book, Dentsu Inc., 1 April 1988.

[a] A—Asia, AF—Africa, E—Europe, LA—Latin America, ME—Middle East, UK—United Kingdom, US—United States.
[b] MJ—Subsidiary, MN—Minority Associate, NE—Non-equity and branch offices.

Table 2-4
International Advertising Conglomerates as of February 1989

Agency	Home Country	Advertising Companies (within)	WW Gross Income[a]	Non-US Gross Inc. (% of total)	WW Billings[a]	Non-US Billings (% of total)	Adv. as % of total Activity	Other Activities
Saatchi & Saatchi PLC	U.K.	Saatchi & Saatchi Adv. WW, Backer Spielvogel Bates WW, McCaffrey & McCall, AC & R/DHB & Bess, Campbell-Mithun, Wm. Esty, Co., Rumrill-Hoyt, Klemtner, Conill, Cochrane Chase, Livingston & Co., KHBB, and Hall/Harrison Cowley	$1.68b	51	$11.36b	50	79	P.R., Design, Sales Promotion, Direct Marketing, Consulting, Crisis Management, Financial Services
Interpublic Group of Companies	U.S.	Lintas: WW, [Lowe Marschalk 30%], McCann-Erickson WW	992.9	61	6.62b	61	[100][b]	—
Omnicom Group	U.S.	BBDO Worldwide, DDB Needham WW, Blair Advertising, Bernard Hodes Advertising	895.5	39	6.27b	38	99	Diversified Agency Services, Direct Marketing, Communications
WPP Group, PLC	U.K.	J. Walter Thompson, Lord Geller Federico & Einstein	892.5	45	5.95b	45	58	P.R., Market Research, Sales Promotion, Design & Graphics, Communications
Ogilvy Group	U.S.	Ogilvy & Mather Adv.; Scali, McCabe, Sloves Group, Euramerica Int'l Adv., Cole & Weiler	723.9	49	5.04b	51	93	P.R., Diversified Agency Services, Sales Promotion, Direct Marketing, Research
Eurocom	France	[WCRS/Belier 51%], [Polaris 50%], Univas, Havas	420.1	—	2.76b	—	[93][b]	Direct Marketing, Sales Promotion
WCRS/Belier Group	U.K.	WCRS Adv., Belier Adv. Interests, Ball Partnership, Helle Breene, R.A., R.A. Becker	230.2	60	1.63b	59	94	Direct Marketing
Lowe, Howard, Spink & Bell PLC	U.K.	Lowe Int'l, [Lowe Marschalk 70%]	183.8	48	1.27b	47	[100][b]	—
Alliance International	Belgium	Warwick Adv., Assorted Alliance Agencies	83.6	na	557.1	na	[100][b]	—
Chiat/Day:Mojo	U.S.	Mojo Agencies, Mojo/MDA, Allen & Dorward	52.5	50	348.0	52	[100][b]	—

Source: derived from information provided by the staff of *Advertising Age* and the UN Centre for Transnational Corporation.
[a]In millions of dollars unless noted.
[b]Estimated.
WW = Worldwide, P.R. = Public Relations.

Wholly owned subsidiaries, minority-share associations, joint ventures, and nonequity contractual arrangements are all employed in the organization of multinational advertising activities. The choice depends on a number of factors, such as the importance and conditions of the market, the geographic horizon of the agency, the amount of resources the firm decides to commit to the host country, and the entry and operating rules set down by the host country. The preferred strategy for many enterprises is the wholly owned subsidiary. Although equity commitment in establishing an advertising subsidiary is minimal and the use of local personnel is extensive, parent corporations prefer to maintain control over management and profit where feasible. The variety of investment arrangements, the concentration of certain forms of arrangements in certain regions, and the overall geographic distribution of multinational advertising activities are illustrated in table 2–5.

As shown in table 2–5, majority-owned subsidiaries loom largest in the advertising industries of Western Europe, the United States, and high-income countries in Latin America, except Argentina. In Third World countries, majority-owned subsidiaries compete with minority ownership and nonequity arrangements. For political and economic reasons in middle-income Latin American countries, minority affiliations and nonequity contractual relations appear to be more frequent than majority-owned subsidiaries. This is also true for high-income Argentina. Minority-share affiliations are frequently found in Asian countries whose investment laws tend to limit foreign participation in service sectors of their economies. As of 1987 no majority-owned foreign advertising subsidiaries were established in India, where investment laws favor minority association or nonequity contracts. Investment laws of many countries in the Middle East and of South Korea and Indonesia permit, in principle only, nonequity contractual arrangements with foreign firms.

With China's *modernization* and the Soviet Union's *perestroika,* foreign advertising is becoming important in China and is opening up in the Soviet Union. Joint ventures with majority or even 99 percent share ownership by western firms are now permitted in China and in the Soviet Union.

Billings by local agencies in some way tied to multinational advertising agencies account for a significant percentage of the total national expenditure on advertising in many countries throughout the world. High percentage estimates in Europe are shown for France, West Germany, and Portugal. High percentage estimates are also shown for some Caribbean and Central American countries, and the Philippines, Hong Kong, Singapore, and Malaysia. The average range for most other countries appearing on table 2–5 is from 20 percent to 50 percent. Below average range percentages show for Pakistan, countries in the Middle East, and the socialist countries.

Table 2–5 shows that multinational agencies dominate the advertising industry in the United States, West Germany, the Netherlands, Spain, Hong Kong, France, Switzerland, and the United Kingdom, where at least eight

Table 2–5
Geographic Distribution of International Advertising Activities by Type of Investment, 1987[a]

Country/Region	Foreign Billings/Total Adv. Exp. (%)	Saatchi & Saatchi WW	McCann-Erickson WW	Lintas WW	BBDO WW	DDB Needham WW	J. Walter Thompson Co.	Young & Rubicam	Ogilvy & Mather WW	DMBB	Foote, Cone & Belding	Grey Advertising	Leo Burnett Co.	Bozell, Jacobs, Kenyon & Eckhardt	Publicis International	Eurocom/WCRS-Ball/Belier	Roux, Seguela, Cayzac & Goudard	Backer, Spielvogel, Bates WW	NW Ayer	Other MNE's[b]	Local Agencies
Industrialized Market Economy Countries																					
Australia	53	16	8	13	(2)	4	11	5	6	9	15		12			17		1		3	7, 10, 14
Austria	52	7		3	8		17	9	5	16		15					14	12		1/6/13	2, 6, 10
Canada	20	11			9		2	3	1	14	12	7	10					13			4, 5, 6, 8
Cyprus	—				(1)																
Denmark	50	14		5	(3)		16	4	6	15		(10)	13					1			2,7,8,9,11,12
Finland	15		2	10					13			1						3			4-9,12,14,15
France	72	11	14	7		10	17	8	13		15	16		(6)	1	2/9	3			4/12	1, 3, 5
Germany, FR	79	9	3	2	1	11	8	6	4	14		5	12					7	(13)	(10)	
Greece	38	3	8	4	6/13	9	(1)		15	(7)		5						12			2,10,11,14
Ireland	50	3/4						8	1	12											2, 5-7, 9-11
Italy	52	8	1	9	(7)		5	4	(10)	13	11	12	17	20		6		14	15		
Japan	41		9		(6)		14													1/2/3	1-5,7,8,10,11-13
Netherlands	39	7	8	4	1/9	11		2	3			14								6/10/12	5, 13
New Zealand	54	3	9	10	1,6/14	4		12	8	5	(15)		11	2				(7)	13		
Norway	41		11	4				3	5	8								1			2,6,7,9,10,12+
Portugal	89	(5)	1	2	12	11	4		8		3/6				9			(10)			7, 13
South Africa	40		4	5	7		6	2	(3)				(1)								11, 14
Spain	28	10	2	4	5	(7)	3	15	13	9								1	6	8	11, 12, 14
Sweden	35		10		14	13		7				5			11			3			1,2,4,6,8,9,12
Switzerland	24	(13)	5	9	(1)	11	14	6	12				10		8			4		2/3/7	
Turkey	47	1	3	(7)			(2)		(6)		(12)	5	(13)								4, 8-11
United Kingdom	48	1/7/14	6	16		18	3	8	2	12		4	17			9		15		11	1,3,5,7,9-11,13,14
United States	24	3	14	13	2	6	8	1	5	11	7	10	9	12				4	15	16	all but 3, 4, 8
Socialist Countries[c]																					
China, Peop. Rep.	5		★	★		★		★											★		
Hungary	—			★					★												
U.S.S.R.	2	★					★	★													
Latin America																					
Argentina	15	7		(12)	(6)		1	11	(4)		(8)		10						(13)		2, 3, 5, 9
Bolivia	—																				
Brazil	35	10	6	9			4	7	5				11	8					2		1, 3, 14
Chile	48			4	2/9		1/8	7			(6)		8								
Colombia	20	1	4		5		3			8		2						6			7
Costa Rica	49		2		1					3											
Dominican Rep.	90		2				1			3	4										
El Salvador	19				(2)					4		3							1		
Guatemala	82		2	5	(1)					4		3									
Jamaica	52	1	2							(4)											3
Mexico	41	14	2	(12)	15	5	8	7	3/13	11		6	(10)								1, 4
Peru	13		2	3		1				4								(5)			
Trinidad & Tobago	84	3	1							(4)		(5)									2
Venezuela	27	9	4				2	5/11	(1)		6	10	3	8				(7)			
Middle East																					
Bahrain	23										2										1, 3
Israel	22																				1-8
Jordan	—																				
Kuwait	—																				
Lebanon	—										1/2										3
Morocco	—																				
Saudi Arabia	7							3				1									2

Table 2–5 (continued)

Country/Region	Foreign Billings/Total Adv. Exp. (%)	Saatchi & Saatchi WW	McCann-Erickson WW	Lintas WW	BBDO WW	DDB Needham WW	J. Walter Thompson Co.	Young & Rubicam	Ogilvy & Mather WW	DMBB	Foote, Cone & Belding	Grey Advertising	Leo Burnett Co.	Bozell, Jacobs, Kenyon & Eckhardt	Publicis International	Eurocom/WCRS-Ball/Belier	Roux, Seguela, Cayzac & Goudard	Backer, Spielvogel, Bates WW	NW Ayer	Other MNE's[b]	Local Agencies
Asia																					
Hong Kong	88	7	6	8	13	9	3		2/16		11	12	1	15	10/14			4		17	5
India	27	(5)	(1)	7			2/9	(3)	4		8										6, 10-15
Indonesia	41	3		1	6		4		(5)				2								
Korea, South	36	4		5				3				7	8								1, 2, 9-11
Malaysia	75	(2)(5)	6	11	(7)(3)		(1)		(9)(14)	4	(17)		12				(8)(13)(16)	10, 15
Pakistan	8		1																		2, 3
Philippines	98	4	2	(8)	6		3		(1)(12)	7	10							5			9, 11
Singapore	77	8	3	7	14		6	2		(10)	4	9		12			11				1, 5, 15
Sri Lanka	30							(2)					(1/3)								
Taiwan	16	7	3	12	(15)(14)			2				11									1, 8-10
Thailand	63	15	6	1	(17)(3/5)	8		2/14 (13)(7)(9)	4	16		12							10, 11
Africa[d]																					
Kenya	37		1																		
Zambia	27							1													
Zimbabwe	40	1		3				(2)													

Source: derived from "Foreign Agency Report," *Advertising Age*, 11 May 1987 and 9 May 1988.
Note: Numbers indicate approximate rank of agency in advertising industry.

[1] Subsidiary   (1) Minority share   [1] Non-equity arrangement   [★] Rank not available.
Joint ventures are absorbed in minority or majority arrangements.
[a]Based only on agencies reporting to *Advertising Age*. *Advertising Age* seeks as complete coverage of principle agencies as possible, including major locally owned agencies.
[b]Including Dentsu, Hakuhodo, Mojo, Alliance, HDM, etc.
[c]All multinationals operate with large Socialist country agencies or directly with state controlled media. The relative ranking of the socialist advertising organizations is not available.
[d]Lintas reports operations in Ivory Coast and Namibia.

of the top ten agencies reporting billings in 1987 were subsidiaries or parent corporations of the world's largest agencies. In Brazil, Mexico, and Venezuela, at least five subsidiaries of the international agencies are reported among their ten top agencies. Local agencies having minority and/or majority affiliations with the multinationals play significant roles (i.e., five or more agencies among the top ten national agencies) in the advertising industries in Malaysia, Thailand, India, Argentina, Chile, South Africa, and New Zealand.

The spread of foreign advertising has followed the expansion of the activities of the multinational advertisers. The largest clients of the multinational advertising firms are the multinational advertisers that the firms have followed around the world. Besides the large Japanese, American, and Western Europe automobile companies, those clients include the advertisers of low-cost, mass-produced consumer goods, processed foods, soft drinks, gums and candies (notably Nestlé SA, Mars Inc., RJR Nabisco, Coca-Cola Co., PepsiCo Inc., Cadbury Schweppes PLC, Philip Morris Cos., Kellogg Co., and McDonalds Corp.), pharmaceutical products and cosmetics (Johnson & Johnson, Ciba-Geigy AG, Pfizer, Inc., Warner-Lambert Co., Bristol-Myers Co., Bayer AG, American Home Products Corp. and Gillette Co.), soaps and cleaners (Unilever NV/PLC, Procter & Gamble Co., Colgate-Palmolive Co., and Henkel KGaA), tobacco companies (Philip Morris Cos., B.A.T. Industries PLC, American Brands, Rothmans International, Dunhill, Peter Stuyvesant, and Grand Metropolitan P/C), alcoholic beverages (Joseph E. Seagrams & Sons, Bacardi Corp.), and airlines and hotels.

Advertising expenditures as a percentage of sales for the low-cost consumer products is high relative to sales. Figure 2–1 shows the percentage of advertising expenditure to sales, ranging from 15 to 19 percent for candies and cosmetics; 10 to 12 percent for pharmaceuticals and soaps and cleansers; and 6 to 10 percent for alcoholic beverages, tobacco products, foods, and soft drinks. All other products were below 2 percent.

The Critics

The most visible and vociferous critics in First World countries are the consumer interest groups who provide the driving force behind consumerism. Their proliferating demands make real the otherwise theoretical consumer issues. The term *consumerism,* like *advertising,* has many connotations in the industrialized market-economy countries. A popular connotation is "an organized movement to increase rights and powers of buyers in relation to sellers in an imperfect market."[2] Like many movements, it consists of a relatively small number of interest groups led by political figures and by consumer activists. These interest groups, although often small, become occasionally very powerful. Operating most effectively in First World countries and international forums, consumer groups differ markedly in strength, approach, outlook, tactics, and financial support.

Consumerists come in two general varieties: consumer organizations and loose confederations of sympathetic individual activists. The organizations are relatively stable. They maintain offices with hired staffs and formal publications. The activists are issue oriented, and their presence often is more unpredictable, as is their behavior.

Consumerism accompanies increased public awareness of problems that impact consumer well-being. The higher the organizational form and the greater the political effectiveness of consumer groups, the more likely is the

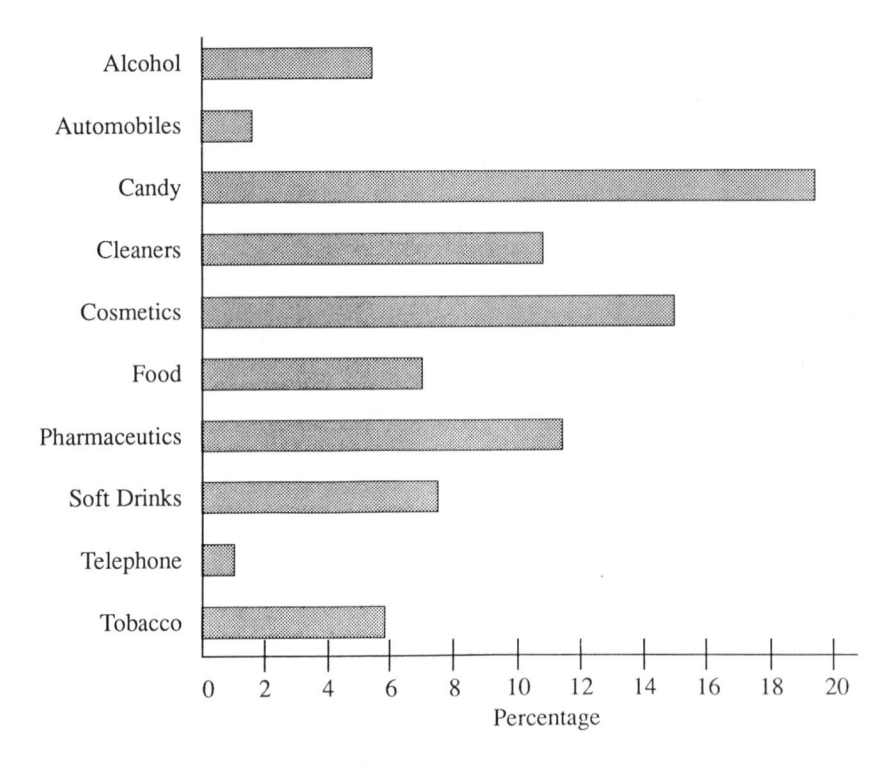

Figure 2-1. Advertising Expenditure of Principle Advertisers, 1987

Source: derived from "100 Top Advertisers," *Advertising Age*, 28 September 1988.

field of operation to be a free-market country with high standards of living. In general, the most restrictive free-market countries have the largest and most active consumer organizations. The strong influence of consumerism on advertising regulation was ascertained in a study commissioned by the International Advertising Association.[3] This finding also is sustained by general observation.[4]

Although some form of consumer movement has existed since the mid–nineteenth century in Europe and the United States, the muckrakers of the turn-of-the-century time are the precursors of today's consumer advocates. Periodic waves of consumerism in the 1930s and 1950s brought increasing legislation in the interest of consumers.

President John F. Kennedy's milestone message to Congress on March 15, 1962, stimulated by rapid growth in international advertising, was a clarion call to consumers worldwide and a significant stimulus to the pursuit of consumerist objectives on an international scale.

In his speech, President Kennedy outlined four fundamental consumer rights:

1. The right of safety—to be protected against the marketing of goods hazardous to health or life.
2. The right to be informed—to be protected against fraudulent, deceitful, or grossly misleading information and to be given adequate information.
3. The right to choose—to be assured access to a variety of products and services at fair and/or competitive prices.
4. The right to be heard—to be assured that consumer interest will receive full and sympathetic consideration in the formulation of government policy.[5]

Western Europe and the United States were loci for the most concerted efforts to balance consumer interests against the multinationals operating in these industrialized countries and in the Third World. Protests were also brought on behalf of Third World consumers to the United Nations (UN) and its specialized agencies.

As a result of this heightened and expanded political activity, the decade and a half following Kennedy's speech witnessed a continuum in consumer legislation and regulation on national and international planes. Many governments in Europe and North America established administrative machinery to deal with consumer issues, and multivarious laws and regulations addressing a variety of consumer concerns were adopted. In international organizations several codes and guidelines were drafted to curb business practices accused of having negative implications for national economies and consumers.

Disparities today among consumer organizations reflect gaps in socioeconomic development, but the common perception that consumerism is unique to the prosperous countries of North America, Scandinavia, and Europe is no longer valid. Consumer movements have been developing in the larger countries of Latin America since the late 1960s. Consumer organizations exist in Nigeria, Egypt, India, Malaysia, Thailand, and Singapore and in other developing countries. In general, although the formulation of consumer demands and the organization of groups to politicize consumer interests has been slow, it does not mean that consumerism will not come to fruition. It is safe to generalize that organized consumerism will come to all countries as the handmaiden of industrialization and open markets.

Still, on the whole there is a lack of consumer representation in governments of most Third World countries, and what exists may be relatively weak when weighed against political support for the growth sectors of the economy, such as manufacturers, wholesalers, and retailers—foreign and domestic. This does not mean that most Third World consumers are totally unprotected. Health ministries often have worked for consumers, even though general political concern for individuals and their well-being is outweighed by the pressing problems of underdevelopment, such as overpopulation, malnutrition, disease, and persistence of poverty.

Generally, the critics' roles in the Third World are actively played by government officials and local industry interest groups whose concerns are predominately economic—protection of local commerce and industry and achievement of development objectives. To the extent that foreign advertising promotes displacement of local goods by higher-cost imported processed goods, discouragement of foreign advertising is pursued by these groups.

Moreover, to protect Third World countries as well as consumers in general, the international consumer movement was organized after 1960, when the International Organization of Consumers Unions (IOCU), an independent, nongovernmental foundation, was founded to promote worldwide cooperation for the protection of consumers. IOCU, headquartered in the Hague, the Netherlands, has an office in Washington, D.C., and has regional offices in Penang, Malaysia, and Montevideo, Uruguay. Since its inception IOCU's activities have included information provision, product testing, lobbying, legislation drafting, and representation in international forums, including the European Communities (EC), the UN, and the UN-specialized agencies. In the United Nations, IOCU has called attention to the need for more emphasis on improvement in quality of life as a balance to traditional emphasis on GNP growth.[6]

Suspicions concerning the political orientation of consumer organizations lies behind the apparent tendency of the industry to distrust the initiatives of consumerism. In fact, consumer organizations run the gamut from radical to moderate to conservative and include groups who are generally apolitical. In some cases, however, the consumerist sympathy with leftist ideology is apparent. Stephen Greyser, a professor at Harvard Business School, has identified these organizations as anti-industrialists, "the most radical members of the consumerism industry."[7] These organizations promote the demarketing of pharmaceuticals and infant formula in Third World countries, strict control over use of technology, and strong environmental protection. Similar demands, however, have also been pursued by more moderate groups indentified by Greyser as the *nationals* or the *feds*. The feds include large, broad-based groups, such as the Consumer Federation of America, and national special interest groups, such as Action for Children's Television, the American Association of Retired Persons (AARP), and the Group Against Smoking and Pollution (GASP). Unlike the radical groups that pursue their aims with provocative literature, demonstrations, and boycotts, the more moderate groups tend to work discreetly through congressional lobbies, focusing on legislation, constitutional reform, enforcement of consumer protection laws, and education. Other moderates include the federal agencies in the United States and the consumer ombudsman in the Scandinavian countries. Typical examples of conservative groups are organizations, founded by industry, that seek deregulation and self-regulation as they aim to resolve consumer complaints and improve products and performance.[8]

Consumerists are particularly concerned with protecting the social order. Executives are its principle targets, particularly advertisers. According to economist E. Scott Maynes, the failure of contemporary economies to satisfy consumers has manifested itself in a set of consumer problems that gave rise to the need for consumer protection. The problems directly linked to advertising include: (1) the classical exercise of monopoly powers expressed in high prices and low-quality output; (2) imperfect markets characterized by seller control of information, persuasion, and resources; (3) manipulation of consumer preferences through want-creation (John Kenneth Galbraith's theory); and (4) consumer dissatisfaction with purchases that did not conform to expectations.[9]

The Regulators

To simplify this chapter's introduction, the individual actors in advertising are assimilated into the institutions through which they play out their regulatory politics. Thus, the regulators are referred to as *host countries* and *home countries,* the *international organizations,* and the *self-regulatory bodies.*

Host and Home Governments

Host countries are the receivers of international advertising activity and foreign direct investment. They include all countries where foreign multinational agencies have established branch offices or affiliates or have contracted for another arrangement. Today, virtually every country in the world is a host country for one or several foreign advertising agencies.

The host countries are the principle regulators of international advertising. Their role is established under international law that accords the national state sovereignty over all peoples, resources, and activities within their territorial limits. The capacity, willingness, and effectiveness of the host countries to perform such roles vary considerably according to level of development and prevailing ideology. This capacity is also challenged by technological advances in electronic information transmissions and a cross-frontier media. Increasingly, host countries are seeking support for their regulatory objectives through international cooperation. The work of the European countries in this regard is illustrative.

Foreign investments in host countries are strongly influenced by commercial and historic ties. Most foreign advertising activity is between industrialized market-economy countries. The largest hosts, as measured by total advertising expenditure, are the industrialized market-economy countries. Table 2–6 shows that 95 percent ($195 billion) of total world advertising expenditure in 1987 ($207 billion) was concentrated in these countries. Latin America is host to about two-thirds of investments of U.S.-based multinational enterprise (MNE) advertisers in the Third World. Asia and Africa are host for investments in British, French, and more recently U.S. firms.

Table 2–6
World Advertising Expenditure by Region, 1987

Country/Region	Total Advertising Expenditures (in millions of US$)	Average Per Capita Expenditures (in US$)	Share of World's Expenditures in each Region
First World	195,319	241	95
US	109,650	451	53
Western Europe	48,896	119	24
Japan	27,273	223	13
Other [a]	9,968	148	5
Second World	1,110 [b]	0.4	—
China	310	0.3	—
USSR/Eastern Europe	800 [b]	2	—
Third World	10,077	6	5
Middle East/N. Africa	850 [bc]	5 [e]	—
Latin America	5,115	14 [f]	3
Asia	4,031	3 [g]	2
Africa	81	0.6	—
Total	207,417 [d]	52	100

Source: derived from *World Advertising Expenditure*, 1987, 22nd ed., Starch INRA Hooper, Inc. in cooperation with IAA.

[a] Includes Commonwealth countries of Australia, Canada, New Zealand, and the Republic of South Africa.
[b] Estimated.
[c] Of which Middle East 300; N. Africa 100; Israel 450.
[d] Total for 75 countries.
[e] North African and conservative Middle East > $2; Kuwait $22; Israel $102.
[f] Argentina, Venezuela $26; Mexico $6.
[g] Hong Kong, Singapore $60; India, Indonesia < $1.

As host countries, the industrialized market-economy countries have the toughest regulatory regimes. Moreover, foreign and domestic firms are obliged to comply or face prosecution. The stringency of these rules and regulations is a continual source of irritation between business and government. At the same time, markets are becoming saturated with a vast range of consumer products, and possibilities for expansion are relatively limited. Combined, these factors have provided the impetus for expansion into Third World markets.

Today the advertising industries of most Third World countries are small and underdeveloped when compared with the First World. The gaps in national advertising industry size is clearly shown in table 2–6 and in figure 2–2, which compare the total advertising expenditures and the per capita advertising expenditures of various countries and regions. With little competition to offer, Third World host countries offer attractive frontiers for the global marketers of processed foods and drugs and other low-cost consumer goods. As a result many Third World countries have significant foreign elements in their consumer goods industries. The degree of indigenous control over these foreign operations varies depending on the development of the government infrastructure, the policies of public authorities, and the degree of independence from foreign pressure of each government. It is in regard to Third World countries that the regulation issue is most controversial.

Only a handful of countries are home countries for multinational agencies. Home countries provide the bases for international advertising activity. Here the parent corporations of advertisers and agencies are incorporated. For years the United States has been the principal home country for international advertising. The United Kingdom and France also have been significant players in advertising in industrialized and Third World countries. Today, the relative role of the United States is diminishing as the United Kingdom, France, and Japan extend their foreign operations in ever-widening international circles and purchase controlling interests in multinational agencies.

As international regulators, home-country advertising policies are important when they exert influence on central decision-making organs of parent companies and, in turn, on operations of affiliates in third countries. The extraterritorial application of antitrust, taxation, and securities laws are obvious examples of the application of home-country law to international business operations. Rarely, however, have any of the home countries invoked national legislation to protect foreign consumers. To ensure consumer protection, international advertising firms are expected to abide by consumer laws established by host countries.

Self-Regulators

Since the turn of the century, self-regulatory bodies have been organized across horizontal industry lines or by individual industry groups. Their intent

34 • *International Advertising Handbook*

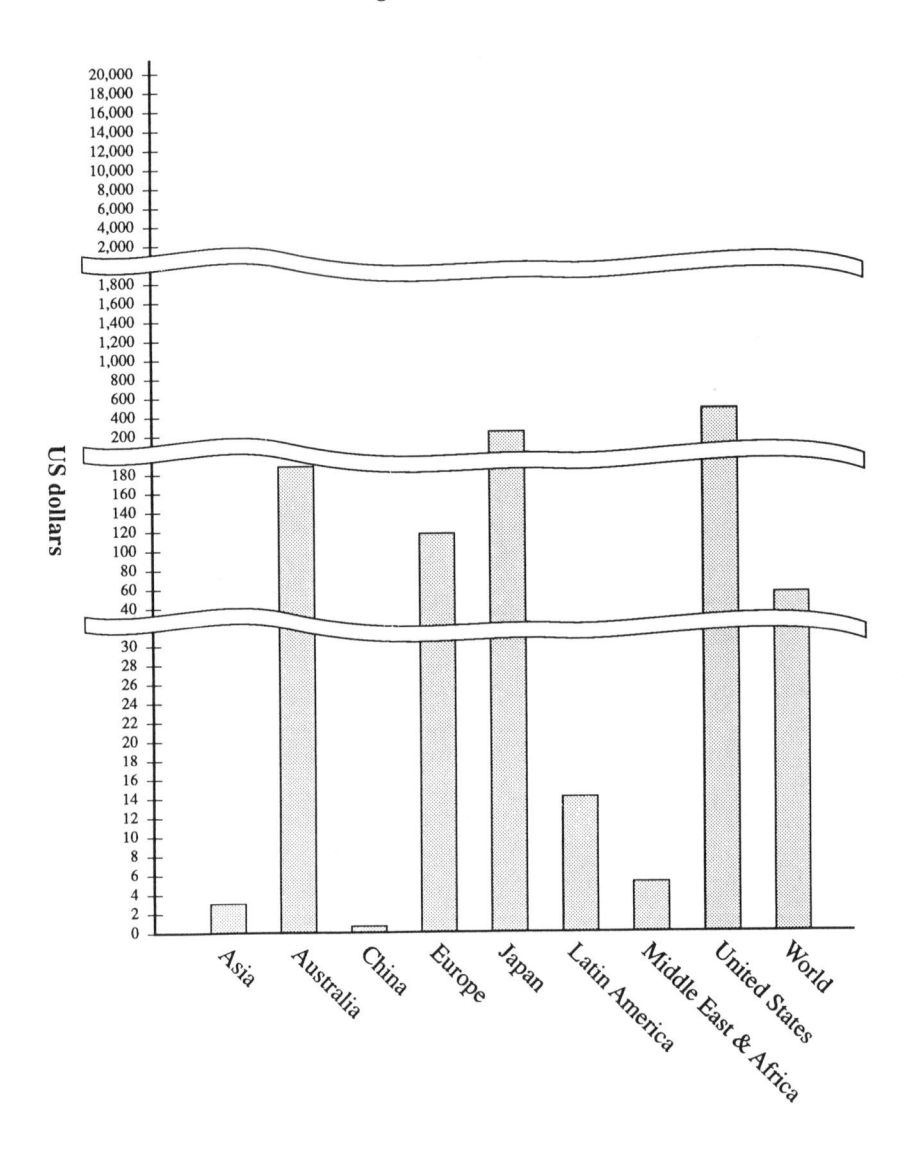

Source: derived from *World Advertising Expenditure,* 1987, 22nd ed., Starch INRA Hooper, Inc. in cooperation with IAA.

Figure 2–2. Per Capita Advertising Expenditures in Selected Countries and Regions, 1986/87

was to establish orderly marketplaces for competitors and to provide protection for consumers. Self-regulation is national and international in scope. Generally, the greater the threat of government regulation, the more willing is industry to impose self-regulatory systems. Today, self-regulatory systems are in effect in the United States and Western Europe and in increasing numbers of developing countries.

Self-regulation began at the turn of the century with the foundation of local clubs of agents, advertisers, and media representatives in the United States. In 1904 these clubs united in a loose federation called the Associated Advertising Clubs of America (AACA). This organization later became the American Advertising Federation (AAF). Other splinters of the AACA included the American Association of Advertising Agencies (AAAA) and the Association of National Advertisers (ANA). These were all rejoined in a central organization, the National Advertising Review Board (NARB), established in 1971.

Another root of self-regulation can be traced to the convention assembled by the AACA in 1911, which proposed establishment of a vigilance committee to discover and correct advertising abuses. The National Vigilance Committee was formally established in 1912. After 1915 the committee became the Better Business Bureau.

In the interest of fair competition, the advertising community provided impetus for the establishment of the U.S. Federal Trade Commission in 1914. Since then national and international self-regulatory organizations have grown in size and number. The national crusade for fair business practices spilled over onto the international scene in 1919. That year the International Chamber of Commerce (ICC) was established to promote business interests at international levels, to foster the greater freedom of international trade, and to harmonize and facilitate business and trade practices.

In the late 1930s, the ICC, together with its principal national branches, established the International Code of Advertising Practice with the full support of the organizations representing the three interests involved: advertisers, agencies, and the media.[10] The code reflected a change in emphasis in national advertising regulations from unfair anti-competitive practices to consumer protection, thereby recognizing the social responsibilities of business. Over the years since World War II, the ICC has established national committees in about fifty countries and representation in some thirty others. Its code serves as the model for national codes.

In 1938 the Export Advertising Association of New York was founded, and in 1954 became the International Advertising Association (IAA). The IAA has worked to elevate the standards, practices, and ethical concepts of advertisers, advertising agencies, and allied services. It has sought improvements in marketing proficiency and the professional status of people in the international advertising business. To these ends it has worked to create an environment wherein international advertising may thrive while exerting a positive influence on the general public. Moreover, coordination of national advertising industry codes has been provided by the IAA. Established with a membership of sixty-seven, the IAA has now grown to a membership of over two thousand. Since the 1940s, the IAA has held biennial world congresses.

In addition to general organizations, several specific industry associations have established international bodies to monitor the marketing behavior of its members. Examples are the Nestlé Audit Commission, the International Association of Infant Food Manufactures (IFM), the International Federation of Pharmaceutical Manufacturers Association (IFPMA), and the Federation Internationale des Vins et Spiritueux (FIVES). These organizations are active in addressing public complaints and pressing for remedial measures when, after their investigation, complaints prove justified.

Intergovernmental Regulators

The largest intergovernmental organizations dealing with advertising are the United Nations and its specialized agencies. The UN unites 160 countries in an organization whose purposes, powers, and limitations are set out in a charter adopted in 1947. The UN reaches the world through five regional economic and social commissions, a number of information offices, and the principal offices and branches of its multiple components.

The UN system includes the United Nations and more than a dozen specialized agencies, each of which is entirely independent of the UN in terms of constituencies, direction, and financing. Universal in character, they attempt to coordinate their programs and to cooperate on certain projects through the Economic and Social Council and the General Assembly of the United Nations.

These organizations lack the attribute of sovereignty, or the legislative authority of a world government to legislate enforceable regulations. Thus, their roles are restricted to the development of voluntary codes and guidelines whose effectiveness depends on moral suasion and public acceptance. These codes may be translated through national legislation into laws. By consensus, members also may decide to adopt regulations by treaty, which becomes enforceable law in ratifying countries. Alternately, countries may decide to adopt conventions or resolutions binding members in accordance with voting rules in organizational charters. No binding rules in respect to international advertising have yet been adopted by intergovernmental organizations.

A number of organizations in the UN system have been active in areas of international advertising. The scope and nature of their activities conform with the terms of reference of each body. The UN, acting through its Economic and Social Council and the Centre for Transnational Corporations, has focused on aspects of consumer protection and general corporate behavior. The World Health Organization (WHO) and the Food and Agricultural Organization (FAO) are concerned with the health effects of multinational commercial activities. Shared concerns of these organizations are met by cooperating through the joint WHO/FAO Codex Alimentarius Commission. The United Nations Educational Scientific and Cultural Organization

(UNESCO) focuses on the cultural effects of global advertising. The United Nations Conference on Trade and Development (UNCTAD) has carried out studies on subjects related to the international advertising of specific manufactured products. In addition, the General Agreement on Tariffs and Trade (GATT) has been involved in the reduction of trade barriers in respect to advertising materials. Moreover, advertising is one of the areas covered in a potential GATT agreement on trade in services currently being discussed in the eighth round of GATT world trade negotiations. The present round of negotiations is referred to as the "Uruguay Round" because the decision to undertake the eighth round was signed in Montevideo.

Regional intergovernmental organizations also deal with important aspects of international advertising. For example, the Organization for Economic Cooperation and Development (OECD), whose membership consists of all the industrialized market-economy countries (the First World), has dealt with problems raised by advertising practices such as endorsements and advertising directed at children. The European Common Market has adopted a directive on misleading advertising and a related directive on product liability. International advertising also has been affected by the investment laws of the Andean Common Market (ANCOM).

Final Remarks

The efficiency of national and international regulatory initiatives, whatever their nature, is reflected in the increased attention of the business community to self-regulation and to activities of national governments and international organizations. Main concerns are to prevent further interference, by way of regulations, with the flow of international commerce and advertising and to gain recognition of the efficiency and effectiveness of self-regulation in international advertising activities.

This chapter has introduced in aggregate groups the major participants in the advertising regulatory process. Within these groups one finds thousands of politicians, executives, lawyers, judges, notaries, and other active citizens involved in the regulatory process. The regulatory outcomes of their interactions are the result of the interplay as they vie for power in support of their particular interests. These interests are cloaked in issues on which actual debate leading to regulatory solution takes place. The participants' viewpoints on the issues are examined in chapter 3.

Notes

1. Examples of transnational organizations include Lintas Worldwide (United States and the United Kingdom); HDM (Japan, France, and the United States); Euro-

com (France and the United Kingdom); and Backer Spielvogel Bates Worldwide (United States and the United Kingdom).

2. Stephen A. Greyser and Steven L. Diamond, "Business in Adapting to Consumerism", *Harvard Business Review,* (September-October, 1974) 38.

3. John R. Ryans, Jr., and James R. Wills, Jr., *Final Report on Consumerism's Impact on Advertising: A Worldwide Study* (New York: International Advertising Association, 1979).

4. See also Greyser and Diamond, "Business Is Adapting to Consumerism," 38–44; and Greenwald, ed., *Encyclopedia of Economics* (New York: McGraw-Hill Book Co., 1982) 195.

5. U.S. Congressional Quarterly Service, "Kennedy Recommends Consumer Protection," Presidential Messages, *Almanac XVIII,* 87th Congress, 2nd Session, 1962. (Washington, DC: Congressional Quarterly Inc.), 890.

6. UN, Economic and Social Council, *Transnational Corporations: Proposal for Consumer Protection under United Nations Auspices; Statement Submitted by the International Organization of Consumers Unions, A Nongovernmental Organization in Consultative Status, Category 2,* E/NGO/52 (19 July 1976), 1; Peter Goldman, *Multinationals and the Consumer Interest* (The Hague: International Organization of Consumer Unions, 1974), 7. Today the membership of IOCU comprises at least one hundred private consumer's associations and government-financed consumer agencies of more than forty-four countries—on every continent and at all stages of development.

7. Paul N. Bloom and Stephen A. Greyser, "The Maturing of Consumerism," *Harvard Business Review* (November–December 1981): 135.

8. Ibid., 134–136.

9. E. Scott Maynes, "Consumer Protection: The Issues," United Nations Center on Transnational Corporations, subject file 72 (11 February 1978), 1–13. Typescript.

10. The code is discussed on page 62.

3
Advertising Issues

A host of complex issues underlies the laws and regulations governing advertising. Identifiable actors compete in the presentation and resolution of these issues. In all policy debates, the adversaries weigh the perceived advantages and disadvantages of advertising. In the free industrialized market economies, there are three principal viewpoints expressed by the *industry,* the *critics,* and the *regulators,* respectively. In this setting, consumer advocates vie with business executives and advertising professionals for the attention of the policymakers.

Similar scenarios exist in virtually all regulator settings, be they national governments or international assemblies. In centrally planned economies, the state enterprises and the concerned ministries are typical adversaries. In Third World countries, little overt conflict of this type arises because of the dominant concerns for economic growth and development. Instead, Third World concerns are aired in international assemblies, where consumer advocates strongly defend their perceptions of the problems posed by advertising for Third World consumers. Regardless of the setting, however, to appreciate the regulatory game fully it is essential to understand the nature of the issues as seen from different perspectives.

In international business relations, commercial advertising is itself an issue. Proponents extol advertisers of brand-name foods and drugs and other consumer products as missionaries of the technological age, responsible for improved health and higher standards of living. Critics tend to label these advertisers as high-tech snake-oil salesmen, descendants of the hucksters of the turn of the century. Advertising's high visibility only intensifies the controversy.

The benefits of advertising, however, are appreciated by most interest groups. By encouraging competition, economies of scale, and product development, advertising stimulates economic growth; brand-name competition leads to improved products, lower prices, and greater variety. In most countries, developed or developing, market oriented or centrally planned, all contenders seem to agree that advertising serves many purposes. Advertising by public or private enterprise communicates the benefits, the availability, and the effective use of products and services to the consuming public. It also is used to disseminate public information, to promote politicians, and to publicize numerous social causes. It is particularly crucial to the existence of a competitive market economy, which depends on the flow of commercial information.

The disadvantages of commercial advertising—according to its critics—include its pervasiveness in daily life and its potential for negative effects on health, personal values, and economic decisions. The most radical critics decry the mere existence of commercial advertising; the majority are concerned with deceptive practices, misleading messages, and an alleged exploitation of vulnerable consumers. Many critics point to promotion of so-called unhealthy, unsafe, or useless products and to advertising messages that take advantage of the ignorant, the illiterate, or the young. Such problems have long been established, but technological advancements in communications have increased the number and complexity of these issues and have heightened the tensions between the conflicting interest groups.

In international debates differing perceptions of a particular issue are compounded by differences in cultures, backgrounds, ideologies, and a myriad of other phenomena that influence biases and objectives. Thus, the spread of advertising across national frontiers and the development of the concept of global advertising have had a number of controversial effects that are perceived either to accentuate notable differences in market structures and situations or to open up more opportunities for cooperation and to narrow cultural and economic gaps. No one will deny that between rich and poor countries, advertising has introduced new products and stimulated development. Nor can one ignore that international advertising has raised new concerns, with significant health, economic, cultural, and environmental implications. Between traditionally open and closed economies, advertising is breaking down barriers and building avenues for future cooperation.

Perceptions of Advertising

The differing perceptions, when related to attitudes toward advertising itself, resolve themselves into three distinct types. In a national study of advertising's social effects, Stephen Greyser has identified three divergent views of advertising operations: the *manipulative model,* the *service model,* and the *transactional model.*[1]

The manipulative model sees the advertiser's role as one of persuading or even seducing reluctant consumers to buy. Advertising is the all-important and powerful weapon; the market is the consumer's overpowering adversary. In this view advertising tends to obscure social values and promote materialism as essential to a good life; therefore, it must be carefully monitored. This model implies the need for a strong governmental role to protect consumers from the deleterious effects of advertising—a government tending toward what John Kenneth Galbraith has called the rational state or, at the extreme, such as prevails in centrally planned economies. The rational state is one wherein corporations pursue rational and purely economic goals in obedience to the regulatory hand of the law and actions of the political system and as custodians of public well-being direct corporate goals to the common good.[2]

The second model, the service model, portrays the successful marketer as the one serving the consumer best. It predicts failure for those who do not serve. Consumers are portrayed as more rational, independent, and intelligent than those depicted in the manipulative model. Advertising supports consumers' choices, and the consumers know what they want. This view evokes the "invisible hand" philosophy of Adam Smith and suggests that the most effective regulator of advertising is the marketplace. Smith's theory states that every individual, in selfishly pursuing only personal good, is led as if by an *Invisible Hand* to achieve the highest good for society and any interference by government is bound to be deleterious.[3] There is a minimal need for rules and regulations.

The third model, the transactional model, denotes a middle-of-the-road perception of advertising in the marketplace. Consumers trade time and attention to advertising for information and entertainment; they trade money for products offering functional or psychological satisfaction. This model presupposes a degree of consumer sophistication and claims that for the majority of people, advertising causes no significant problems. It is a part of the daily social landscape, sometimes irritating, sometimes entertaining. This model depicts advertising as an indispensable, or unavoidable, dimension of a modern economy—part of the price consumers pay for the goods they want. According to this model, the public realizes, however vaguely, that advertising permits mass production, hence long-term price decline and greater access to goods and services. From this perspective advertising should provide the largest and best choice in both a quantitative and qualitative sense. Here, the role of government is to ascertain the value of the information provided and to regulate it only as much as is necessary to keep advertising on the track of its stated objectives.

Whether the contending parties subscribe to the manipulative, the service, or the transactional view of advertising's operations, they focus their attention on certain issues that are significant to the development of regulations. These issues may be categorized as either *product specific* or *societal*.

Product-Specific Issues

The first group of issues concerns products that directly influence a consumer's health and physical well-being. Such issues often arise when consumers have been adversely affected by products. In some societies these issues also stem from fears or dangers evoked by religious beliefs or cultural traditions. Though the physical harm may have been caused by product chemistry, product misuse, or consumer overindulgence, blame is frequently extended to include advertising appeals and suggestions. If a particular product has few socially redeeming attributes and is inherently toxic, the mere advertising of the product is a potential health menace. When a society determines that a product's health costs outweigh its benefits, the assumption is made that the product's appeal must have resulted from advertising's persuasive powers to create demand and not to serve human needs. Particularly vulnerable to this kind of criticism is the advertising of processed foods, pharmaceuticals, alcohol, and tobacco.

Societal Issues

Into the second category fall a significant number of societal issues deriving from factors not directly product oriented and whose influence is diffuse and more resistant to definition. These factors are economic, social, ethical, and environmental. They include the impact of advertising on market structure, allocation of resources, prices, and development; on cultural diversity, values, and public welfare; on ethics and freedom of speech; and generally on individuals' well-being in society. Satisfactory answers to these issues, as well as to those that are more product specific, depend to a large extent on the solutions given to three fundamental and vexing questions. They concern (1) the measurement of advertising's impact on demand, (2) the determination of its impact on society, and (3) the concept of truthfulness in advertising.

Impact of Advertising on Demand

First is the question of whether advertising increases demand. From the producer's perspective, the purpose of advertising any product is to preserve and increase market shares. Advertising serves this end by erecting an expenditure barrier to new entrants, confirming and strengthening people in their established behavior, and creating brand loyalties.

Common sense and general economic theory suggest that demand for most products should be greater in market economies where advertising is more extensive than in environments without advertising. This follows from advertising's role of providing information about products and sellers. Further, it is argued, if advertising were not beneficial to an industry, it would not exist. At the same time, the question arises whether advertising creates the demand by stimulating awareness of a need or whether it is consumption that directs advertising. Observations of increased consumption of alcohol and tobacco products in centrally planned economies where these products are not generally advertised lend validity to the latter possibility.

The theory that advertising "is the creator of want" has been formulated by John Kenneth Galbraith. According to Galbraith, advertising's venerable place in economics results from its function in demand management designed to sustain the industrial economy. Advertising has upset the delicate automatic mechanism of supply and demand by artificially inducing demand for the sake of ever-increased production.[4]

A review of empirical literature on the effect of advertising on general demand and on the demand for alcohol and tobacco was carried out by the U.S. Federal Trade Commission. Although this report pointed out that economic theory predicted a positive correlation between advertising and demand, it concluded that nothing had been determined empirically about the magnitude of the effect.[5]

The FTC study demonstrates the difficulties in measuring advertising's effect on demand. Bearing in mind the theory of diminishing returns, one should distinguish between the effect of total advertising on total demand and the marginal effect of an incremental dollar on advertising expenditure. Typically, economists are able to measure only marginal effects. The major studies reviewed in the FTC report used statistical techniques that treated as constant the effects of such variables as industry prices and consumer incomes. Most of the studies addressed the effect of marginal changes in advertising expenditure on total demand or consumption over a period of a decade or more. Several studies concluded that little or no effect of advertising could be discerned on broadly based industries, such as tobacco or alcoholic beverages. However, it is recognized in such studies that reliability is hampered by problems of data and methodology and that more positive correlation could not be excluded.[6] Equally thorough investigations produce contrary evidence, suggesting that advertising alters market share and/or total demand under certain circumstances. Such circumstances depend on the nature of the advertising and the structure of the industry.[7]

A review of major findings of some European studies on advertising's impact on demand was carried out by Theo Van Iwaarden.[8] According to his review, theories as well as empirical findings on the influence of advertising on purchasing behavior were conflicting. Moreover, Galbraith's hypothesis "that because advertising influences the formulation of consumers' tastes, it can also influence spending decisions" was not confirmed.[9] At the same time, Iwaarden found that the "null-hypothesis that advertising had no impact" also had little support.[10]

Impact of Advertising on Society

A second overall and vexing theoretical question concerns advertising's impact on society, particularly through what is termed the *demonstration effect.* The demonstration effect, as defined by R. Nurkse, is the bundle of psychological changes that occur when people come to know superior goods or patterns of consumption, for example, new articles or new ways of meeting old wants. These changes include the tendency to feel restlessness and dissatisfaction, the stimulation of imagination, the arousal of new desires, and the upward shift in the propensity to consume.[11]

The frustrations created by persuading people to want something that their neighbors have or that may not be obtained are shared by people of all ages. One hypothesis, outlined by Charles Kindleberger, is that advertising demonstrates new goods and alternative tastes and lifestyles. Also through demonstration, consumption patterns of developed countries are transferred to developing countries, and shifts are made from local staples or traditional remedies to luxury or prestige items imported or locally produced by multinational affiliates. Furthermore, according to this school of thought, the idyllic picture of people and the world painted in advertisements presents a distorted view of health and happiness as dependent on the consumption of certain foods and drugs. In his analysis Kindleberger also notes that the implications of the demonstration effect are not all negative, and he stresses that the appeal of new goods to the consumer has always been a powerful factor in economic development.[12]

The power of the demonstration effect is based on a presumption that people are easy targets for persuasion. In advanced industrialized countries, the groups commonly considered to be the most vulnerable to the seductive entreaties of advertising are the children, the poor, and the elderly. On the international scale, the illiterate masses of the Third World are generally considered the most gullible and most vulnerable. Because of their age or their poverty, these groups also suffer the greatest harm from advertising's alleged exploitation.

Many studies and experiences, however, have indicated that all people, including the so-called vulnerable groups, may not be as open to persuasion as is commonly purported. A study prepared at the Harvard Business School has questioned the persuasive aspect of advertising in at least four circumstances: (1) when advertising is directed to consumers who are without means to purchase the products offered, (2) when products are not wanted or needed, (3) when the means of persuasion is unknown or only subtly conscious to the recipient, and (4) when product differentiations are barely perceptible.[13]

Other studies also indicate that there is no empirical way to determine whether and to what extent advertising influences people positively or negatively. Age and education, while generally linked to persuasibility and miscomprehension, are only two among many factors that may or may not determine a particular individual's response to advertising.[14]

Personality and wealth are also determinants of the extent to which advertising's enticements are entertained. According to Galbraith, vulnerability to the persuasive power of advertising in creating wants (demand stimulation) is in direct relation to affluence. His hypothesis is that only in a comparatively affluent country are people open to persuasion on how to spend their money.[15] He argues that the fact that wants can be synthesized by advertising, catalyzed by salesmanship, and shaped by persuaders shows that these wants are not very urgent. The poor man is inspired by his appetite: only those who are so far removed from physical want that they do not already know what they want are open to persuasion.[16]

Galbraith's hypothesis is consistent with Maslow's hierarchy of needs, which states that man's first priority is survival and the satisfaction of basic psychological needs. Abraham H. Maslow's central assumption is that higher needs will not be activated until relatively more basic needs have been reasonably satisfied. In developing societies, once the most basic needs have been satisfied, other priorities must be fulfilled before the average individual could even imagine the satisfaction to be gained by having what the affluent possess in their own society or in a distant world.[17]

According to a French study on the impact of the media and advertising, the persuasiveness of advertising is extremely limited when the target audience has strong feelings or strong views on the item being advertised. To take an extreme example, an advertising campaign by a government against the use of tobacco will have very little effect if the smokers are convinced by their environment and by their peers that smoking is a pleasant and harmless entertainment. Conversely, according to this thesis, advertising is very persuasive when the target audience has little involvement with the issue. If a product is advertised on television and if the audience does not have strong feelings about this product, be it a shampoo or a mode of behavior, the audience will tend to buy.[18]

Consistent with this view is the frustration of some nutritionists working in the Third World and trying to influence food consumption patterns. A number of experts have confronted significant cultural barriers to information campaigns built on modern advertising principles and employing sophisticated promotional techniques.

Truthfulness in Advertising

The third question concerning societal issues in advertising is that of the truthfulness of advertising. Underlying the advertising controversy is the elusive nature of human truth; variations in human personalities reflected in different thresholds of credulity, persuasibility, and comprehension; and the large part played by emotions in purchasing decisions. Thus, while deliberate dishonesty with the intention to defraud generally is considered a crime, the acceptability of many other practices may depend on prevailing social philosophies and values and on the elusiveness of human truth. The following are examples of contentious questions: What are the criteria for determining false advertising? What is deception? To what extent is exaggeration permissible? What is the link between disclosure and truth? *Truth* is relative to the perception of the audience. Literal truth can be misapprehended or misleading to some audiences. Many governments and private organizations have outlined broad criteria for measuring fallacy, misleading statements, and deception. Nevertheless, a charge of breach of honesty often must be determined in the particular context of its occurrence.

A concrete example of legally permissible mendacity is so-called puffing. However, the courts have yet to establish definitive criteria for distinguishing puffing from false or misleading advertising. This decision, more often than not, depends on the material situation in a particular case. *Puffing* is commonly defined as the use of exaggeration of an unmeasurable nature, such as Esso's slogan Put a Tiger in Your Tank. Periodically, puffing is widely countenanced, particularly in societies with high general levels of practical education, but the margin for permissibility is often changing.[19] In international advertising transference of culture-bound exaggerations to foreign societies where education differs, particularly to countries where beliefs in enchantment or sorcery are widespread, raises questions on the extent of the consumers' possible susceptibility to amplifications in commercial truth.

A measure of integrity in advertising is positive consumer satisfaction, which, too, is an illusive concept, resulting from a subjective comparison of expected and received product attribute levels. There are many explanations for failure to meet expectations. Obvious ones are defective products and deluded expectations. But these basic elements interact with other variables, including consumer personalities and situations and variations in environments.[20]

Relevance of Solutions

The elusiveness of agreement on these fundamental questions reflects inherent difficulties confronting advertising research.[21] In general, consumption decisions are based on many determining factors, of which advertising is only one. Deciphering the factors poses significant theoretical statistical difficulties. Further difficulties arise because advertising achieves a range of effects with varying degrees of emphasis and because the marketing context of advertising is in constant flux. Because demands on research vary with the interests of the parties concerned, the relevance of the survey data is inherently subjective. In the absence of agreement on the fundamental issues, Neil Borden was inspired in the early 1940s to write the following:

> Advertising is under fire. Its adverse critics come from many camps and their complaints tend to become increasingly vehement. . . . The discussion on both sides have [sic] often been characterized by sweeping generalizations, by paucity of fact, and by lack of closely-knit logical reasoning. There has been much wishful thinking and rationalization. . . . What is needed is evidence bearing upon the issue.[22]

Today, as yesterday, as long as empirical evidence bearing on the fundamental issues is lacking, then subjective judgment, fiction, and unsubstantiated fact will hold sway. The regulations that are adopted or not adopted reveal the viewpoint that has garnered the greatest amount of political support.

In the generation of rules and regulations, product-specific and societal issues vary according to the environmental context. The issues most commonly bartered in the industrialized market countries are product specific, social, and political. They relate to problems and merits of advertising tobacco, alcoholic beverages, and prescription drugs and to the nutritional contents of food. The overexposure of children as a target and audience of advertising is another concern. Business groups have been concerned with overregulation and its challenge to the freedom of commercial speech. In the EEC debate is focused on the standardization of advertising rules and regulations in order to remove barriers to the development of a European cross-frontier broadcasting system and to facilitate commercial relations among member countries. Agreement on a directive on unfair practice continues to elude EEC governments. In France use of the French language in advertising is a central concern.

In the centrally planned countries, ideological and socioeconomic issues underlie advertising policy. Discussions about foreign advertising are focused on the amount and type of foreign advertising that is to be permitted and its consistency with socialist objectives for development. In countries where foreign advertising of consumer products is permitted, corruption of socialist values is an issue. For example, the information content and accuracy in advertising about foods, medicines, and durable goods is a serious issue in China, where there is a rapidly expanding decentralized advertising industry with elements of private enterprise.

Issues arise concerning advertising in Third World countries in different milieus. Third World countries themselves are seriously concerned with the economic consequences of foreign advertising, including the displacement of local advertisers and the increased importation of consumer goods. In many countries international advertising's threat to social and/or religious values and cultural traditions is another important issue. Numerous issues concerning advertising in Third World countries are raised by advocates in industrialized countries. Many of these issues reflect concern for consumers and are ethical and product specific in nature. Promotion of unnecessary, inappropriate, or dangerous products; exploitation of the credulity of the uneducated; destruction of cultural diversity; and the spreading of Western materialistic values are some examples of such issues.

Finally, international organizations are also centers for expressed concerns about advertising. The nature of the issues corresponds in general to the terms of reference of the particular forum in which the issues are raised.

And so the debate moves on, and the success of one legislative measure changes the tally. Another player has scored. Advertising goes on, other problems are perceived, and the debate resumes.

Notes

1. Stephen A. Greyser, "Understanding the Social Impact of Advertising" (Paper delivered at the Crichton Symposium, Advertising Educational Foundation, Chicago, November 1983), 20–22.

2. John K. Galbraith, *The New Industrial Estate* (Boston: Houghton Mifflin Co., 1967), 178.

3. Adam Smith, *Wealth of Nations,* Edwin Cannon (ed.), (New York: Modern Library, Inc., 1937, originally published in 1776), 423.

4. John Kenneth Galbraith, *The Affluent Society,* rev. 2d ed. (Boston: Houghton Mifflin, 1969), 149–50.

5. U.S. Federal Trade Commission, Bureau of Economics, *Alcohol Advertising, Consumption, and Abuse,* prepared by Mark Frankena et al., included as appendix A in United States, Congress, 99th Senate Hearings before the Subcommittee on Children, Family, Drugs and Alcoholism, of Committee on Labor and Human Resources, 7 February 1985 (Washington, D.C.: U.S. Government Printing Office, March 1985).

6. R.C. Ashley, W.J. Granger, and R. Schmalensee, "Advertising and Aggregate Consumption; An Analysis of Causality," *Econometrica* 48 (July 1980): 1149–67; Chiplin, B.T. Sturges, and Dunning, *Economics of Advertising* (New York: Holt, Rinehart and Winston, 1981); H.G. Grabowski, "The Effects of Advertising on the Inter-Industry Distribution of Demand," *Explorations in Economic Research* 3 (1976): 21; B.T. Sturges, "Dispelling the Myth: The Effects of Total Advertising Expenditures on Aggregate Consumption," *Journal of Advertising* 11 (Fall 1982): 201; P.S. Kyle, "The Impact of Advertising on Markets," *Journal of Advertising* 11 (Fall 1982): 345.

7. W.S. Comanor and T. Wilson, *Advertising and Market Power* (Cambridge, Mass.: Harvard University Press, 1974); B. Rush and A. Osborne, eds., "Is Advertising Effective for Public Health Policy," *Evaluations Research in the Canadian Addictions Field* 146 (1983).

8. M.J. Van Iwaarden, "Advertising, Alcohol Consumption, and Policy Alternatives," *Economics and Alcohol,* ed. Marcus Grant, Marcus Plant, and Alan Williams (New York: Gardiner Press, 1983) 223–37.

9. Ibid., 225.

10. Ibid., 227.

11. R. Nurkse, *Problems of Capital Formation of Underdeveloped Countries* (Oxford: Basil Blackwell and Matt, 1953).

12. Charles P. Kindleberger, *Economic Development,* 3d ed. (New York: McGraw-Hill, 1977), 82–83.

13. Market Science Institute, *Appraising the Economic and Social Effects of Advertising: A Review of the Issues and Evidence,* staff report (Cambridge: Harvard Business School, 1971).

14. James William Carey, "Personality Correlates of Persuasibility," *Measuring Advertising Effectiveness: Selected Readings,* John J. Wheatley, ed. (Homewood, Ill.: Richard D. Irwin Inc., 1969), Article reviews mainly the work of Carl Havland and Irving L. Janis at Yale University in the late 1950s and early 1960s; Jacob Jacoby and Wayne D. Hoyer, "Viewer Miscomprehension of Televised Communication: Selected Findings," *Journal of Marketing* 466 (Fall 1982): 12–26. See also David M. Gardiner and Ivan Ross, "Potential Contributions of Consumer Psychology to Deceptive Advertising Determinants and Corrective Measures," paper presented at the 44th Annual Meeting of the Eastern Psychological Association, Washington, D.C. (1973), and David M. Gardiner, "Deception in Advertising: A Conceptual Approach," *Journal of Marketing* 39 (Winter 1975): 40–46.

15. John Kenneth Galbraith, *The New Industrial State* (Boston: Houghton Mifflin, 1967), 325.

16. Galbraith, *Affluent Society,* 151–52.

17. Abraham H. Maslow, *Motivation and Personality,* 2d ed. (New York: Harper & Row, Inc. 1970), 35ff.

18. Jean-Noël Kapferer, *Les chemins de la persuasion: Le mode d'influence des média et de la publicité sur les comportements* (Paris: Dunod Entreprise, 1986).

19. Ivan L. Preston, *The Great American Blow-Up: Puffery in Advertising and Selling* (Madison, Wis.: University of Wisconsin Press, 1975).

20. Jacob Jacoby and James Jaccard, "The Sources, Meaning, and Validity of Consumer Complaint Behavior: A Psychological Analysis," *Journal of Retailing,* New York University Institute of Retail Management 57 (Fall 1981): 4–24.

21. These are summarized in Mark Lovell, "Advertising Research," *Consumer Market Research Handbook,* ed. Robert M. Worcester and John Downham (Amsterdam: North Holland/Esomar, 1986), 471–508.

22. N.H. Borden, *The Economic Effects of Advertising* (Chicago: R.D. Irwin, 1942), 1.

4
Advertising Regulation

No one questions the power of advertising to inform people, but countries question the uses to which that power might be put. This concern takes its most directed expression in the regulations a country adopts toward advertising. The stringency of regulation reflects the reigning power's perception of advertising as predominantly positive or negative. The promotion of certain products may be more limited or less so; the use of the media for commercial advertising may be more restricted or less so; the content of advertising may be more censored or less so. Society's understanding of advertising's net impact comes from a weighing of the negative effects against the socially redeeming features of the products, the messages, and their alternatives.

The principal sources of advertising regulation are national governments, international governmental organizations (global and regional), and nongovernmental institutions, including associations of individual advertisers, the media, and advertising agencies. They adopt many different types of regulatory controls to govern advertising, such as national legislation, administrative rules and orders, intergovernmental recommendatory codes and guidelines, and national and international self-regulation guidelines and codes. Together, these controls form the complex regulatory web spanning the global marketplace.

National Regulation

In classic international relations, the power of law to control the operations of multinational enterprises rests with national governments. Accordingly, it is up to each government to choose which products to allow in its markets and the manner in which these products are to be promoted. This responsibility follows from the principle of territorial sovereignty, a basic rule of international law.[1] This principle is reaffirmed in the OECD Declaration on International Investments and Multinational Enterprises:

Every State has the right to prescribe the conditions under which multinational enterprises operate within its national jurisdiction, subject to international law and to the international agreements to which it has subscribed. The entities of a multinational enterprise located in various countries are subject to the laws of these countries.[2]

International recognition of the rights of host states to regulate advertising within their borders, including messages originating outside their borders, has been reaffirmed in the Guidelines on Consumer Protection, adopted by consensus by the United Nations General Assembly in April 1985.[3] This resolution calls upon all enterprises to obey the relevant rules and regulations of the countries in which they do business.

National administrative and private laws, rules, and regulations set out on paper the parameters for legal operations of the international advertiser and advertising agencies. They are public expressions of the values of a particular society and the extent to which that society is prepared to protect these values. These primary rules of obligation are important because they are directed toward controlling undesirable behavior and encouraging beneficial activity.

Behind the paper laws, which in phrase and content may or may not differ from one country to the next, are all-important questions relating to the spirit and actual application of the law. These questions concern the penetration of the legal system into the daily lives of ordinary citizens; the culture of a society; and the characteristics, uses, and development of a country's legal machinery (including its participants, structures, and processes). Each of these key elements in a national legal system provides critical dimension for divergence and convergence.[4]

A comparative study of all these elements in national legal systems would fill volumes and is beyond the scope of this book. Suffice it then to note their existence and the necessity to consider them in the process of evaluating the regulatory system of any country on any aspect of commercial activity.

Points of divergence and convergence can, however, be gained by identifying some of the important characteristics of six major groups or families of legal systems existent today. Significant similarities or differences exist among national systems incorporating elements of one or more of these primary systems of law: *Romano-Germanic civil law, common law, socialist law, Islamic law, Confucian law,* and *traditional (customary) law.* Civil law traces its roots to Roman law and, largely through its interpretation in the Napoleonic code, defines the modern legal systems of the majority of countries in continental Europe and Latin America and many countries in Africa and Asia. English common law is traced to Germanic tribal custom and is a direct legacy of the Middle Ages in England. It has been adapted to local conditions by countries formerly colonized by the British.[5] Socialist law is a pragmatic expression of the antilegal ideology of Marx and Lenin and, at this point in history, gives unique character to the legal systems in Eastern Europe and China. Islamic law, grounded in the theology of Islam, permeates social and economic life in the Arab Middle East and in predominantly Islamic countries in Africa and Asia. Confucian philosophy and its inherent aversion to legalism have fundamentally influenced and slowed the development of legal systems in China, Korea, and Japan. Finally, the law of traditional societies is an important body of unwritten law rooted in customs and, to some extent, religion and morality and is applied in the courts of many African societies.

In civil-code countries, law rests its authority on statutes and administrative regulations that derive from some authoritative body. The code is the embodiment of legislation, executive regulations, and the deductions of legal scholars. Primary responsibility for application and interpretation of the written law rests on public administrators and is accomplished through detailed administrative rulings and ordinances. Custom and concepts of equity are subsidiary sources of law to be used by judges when the application of legislation is not clear or when there are gaps in written law. Civil-code countries tend to rely heavily on government officials in legal matters, they attach considerable prestige to the civil service in public-law matters, and they rely on the notary public in the application of private law. Jury trials are reserved for criminal cases; judges and lawyers decide civil suits.

Common law is an accumulation of principles, customs, and rules that may or may not base their authority on the explicit expression of some legislative body. Thus, common law, as distinct from civil law, lacks definitive written form and is better described as a dynamic process powered by the machinery of a court system through which the principles of law are discovered and applied to specific problems. Disputes, framed in legal terms, examined according to legal procedures, and resolved in terms of legal practice and precedent, provide the input for judicial decisions, which in turn supply legal precedents and evidence of law. Each legal case thus adds dimension to the common law. Lawyers and judges play key roles in the discovery and application of law in the common-law tradition. Trial by jury is the defendant's right in criminal and many civil cases. Social issues are often important in case decisions in countries where precedent, custom, and equity are primary sources of law.

According to classic Marxism, the principle source of socialist law is the economic infrastructure that conditions and determines the legal system. In the communist utopia, law would not exist. Until the communist system achieves that utopia, socialist law serves three functions: national security and peaceful coexistence between countries, the development of economic production on the basis of socialist principles, and elimination of antisocial behavior. The system establishes the centrally planned state with the dual functions of sovereign and subject. Significant aspects of the present system are (1) the interrelation of the state plan and the law, (2) the law of property and contract, and (3) the law for remedy of economic crimes. Legislation is the main source of socialist law. In the Soviet Union, legislative power is exercised by the Supreme Soviet and through its presidium. (All policy to be translated into law in fact originates from the Politburo of the Central Committee of the Communist Party of the Soviet Union whose membership overlaps with the presidium of the Supreme Soviet.) The execution of the law is the responsibility of the ministries and the collective enterprises or government "corporations," which are individual legal entities with capacity to sue, to be sued, and with rights of property and contract.[6]

In the Marxist planned economy, the concept of large-scale private ownership is abolished in favor of state ownership. The contract constitutes a general volitional act by the parties, wherein the planning and regulating members of the state establish obligations of civil law between the contracting parties, according to overall objectives of the society.[7] In short, contract arrangements are arrangements of convenience aimed at economic objectives subordinated to overall goals of society. A special system of economic courts, State Arbitrazh, protects the government by providing for the adjudication of property and contract disputes between state enterprises belonging to different economic councils or ministries. Socialist criminal law addresses, among other crimes, economic crimes against the property of the state, such as sabotage and negligence and willful misconduct of state economic management.

Islamic law, one of the facets of the Islamic religion, incorporates religion, society, and politics in a unified system, the foundation of an ideal theocratic state. The *Shari'a* embodies the law, in which the Western concept of law as legislated commands that are enforced by the state is but one integral element. *Shari'a,* literally "the way to follow," is the Islamic term denoting the whole duty of man. The system embodies moral and pastoral theology and is centered on man's obligations and duties to God and to his fellow man. The principal origins of the Shari'a are found in the *Qu'ran* (the word of God) and the *Sunna* (the practices of the Prophet). Other important sources are the *ijmā,* or consensus of legal scholars on apparent discrepancies in the teachings and gaps in the law, and the *kiyās,* juristic analogical reasoning relevant in interpreting and applying the law. The various chapters of the Qu'ran set out the teachings and philosophy of the Prophet Muhammad based on messages from God as revealed by the angel Gabriel. On the basis of the Qu'ran, numerous principals of law have been derived. The Sunna is composed of the collected traditions, or *hadith,* of the acts and sayings of Muhammad and his companions, handed down by intermediaries. Two great scholars of Islam Al-Bukari and Muslim worked to establish the authentic hadith in the nineth century A.D. Islamic law is specifically relevant to interpersonal relations among Muslims. Its principles, however, may permeate many of the secular laws establishing the framework for commercial relations.[8]

Many Asians, in keeping with Confucian tradition, have associated law with impersonal and arbitrary power and have traditionally been adverse to legalism as the means to assure peace and social order. Confucianism conceives the universe in purely moral terms and puts a premium on virtuous conduct at all levels of society. Followers are admonished to uphold the sanctity of the five human relationships (father-son, husband-wife, ruler-subject, older brother-younger brother, and friend-friend). Today, stable interpersonal relationships remain highly valued in Far Eastern countries. Law in the Western sense plays a subsidiary function only when less confrontational means of dispute settlement have been exhausted. Trust and trustworthiness, predisposition for conciliation, and willingness to compromise are fundamental to commercial as well as social relations. Therefore, many Far Eastern countries are at comparatively early stages in the development of legal machinery to accommodate transnational business.

Traditional law generally refers to the law of preindustrial societies in Africa. Its distinction from other families of legal systems lies in the proportionate weighting of different sources of law. A body of unwritten doctrine, it derives its existence from certain customs, to some extent from morality and religion, and from values and cultural postulates. Variations in the machinery, substance, and procedure of traditional legal systems exist among societies with different political and economic structures. Each variety is indigenous and localized. Procedures may involve resorting to the supernatural, such as so-called ordeals. In general, traditional law is less concerned with individual rights and justice than with those of the community. Superseded for years by Western laws in colonized Africa, traditional law is making a comeback in African societies seeking their own legal identity.[9]

In theory and history, distinctions between these fundamental legal systems seem clear. In reality, national systems are hybrids of multiple varieties containing in varying proportions different elements of the fundamental systems. A body of written legislative law builds from parliamentary decisions in common-law countries; case law provides precedents for legal interpretations in civil-code countries. Many Islamic countries have developed secular legal codes modeled on the French civil code.

The socialist countries are fundamentally civil-code countries. The Japanese legal system combines German civil-law concepts with Anglo-American law and unique Asiatic attitudes toward law. Chinese law is an amalgam of traditional philosophy, socialist law, and American and European commercial codes. African societies apply European laws and traditional customary principles in their courts.[10]

Legal systems are also dynamic in their continuous evolution in response to changes in public policy and the sociopolitical environment. The Soviet Union currently is establishing a modern commercial code comparable with Western Europe and the United States. Currently, the United Nations and other institutions are offering technical assistance in the development of the commercial laws of China and the Soviet Union. The Chinese patent and copyright laws will be modeled on U.S. law. Former colonial countries are reevaluating their systems with intention to discard laws reflecting the colonial legacy and are restoring, where practical, precolonial traditions, rights, and obligations in their laws.

Such dynamism also exists in the development of public policy regarding advertising. Public policy reflects a nation's ethos (its socioeconomic, political, and ideological tenets) in constant flux and varies from country to country and region to region. Truth in advertising is the only universally accepted principle, since it appears in some form in the regulations of every country. It is frequently accompanied by other ethical values, including fairness and decency. In some countries, economic ideology—capitalism or Marxism—has been the most powerful policy determinant. Social welfare objectives are strongly emphasized in countries where consumers have established power bases. Religion and cultural traditions have strongly influenced social perceptions of advertising in still other countries. Historical, commercial, and colonial ties have determined the character of regulation in a vast number of countries. The influence of nationalism as a control on foreign advertising cannot be ignored.

Reflecting in varying degrees the influence of the aforementioned variables, the regulation of advertising serves different objectives in different countries. In industrialized market-economy countries, regulation has two main aims: (1) fair competition and (2) consumer protection. Three different assumptions provide the rationale for devising measures to achieve these goals. The first emphasizes advertising's power to inform and strives for integrity in content. The second suggests advertising is the creator of demand for products deemed dangerous, inappropriate, or useless and proposes restrictions, such as outright bans on advertising, as a means for demarketing potentially dangerous products. The third recognizes the potential for consumer misuse of products or misunderstanding of product information, thus necessitating the restriction of product knowledge and promotion to certain audiences.

For the Third World, national development objectives are paramount. Consumer welfare and fair competition are incorporated in the overall aim to the extent that they are consistent with development objectives. Economic policy may require keeping the temptation of Western consumer goods to a minimum, particularly in societies where private consumption has low priority in development plans. In encouraging the development of local industries to meet consumer needs, countries may also restrict foreign advertising to a prescribed minimum. Local ownership of or controlling interest in affiliates of foreign advertising agencies is a policy of many developing countries. Preservation of cultural values and local languages complements overall development objectives and serves as another rationale for restrictions on foreign advertising. Finally, religious principles justify regulations that prohibit the contents of certain advertising or the advertising of certain products.

In centrally planned countries, advertising is a tool of socialist policy objectives; it promotes growth in the socialist commodity economy. As such, advertising is carried out by public agencies, ministries, and state-owned enterprises. Public policy stresses the informational and educational functions of advertising.

Regardless of their differences, nearly all countries regulate some aspects of advertising within their borders. Rarely do governments extend the application of their laws extraterritorially. When this does occur, the objective is to curtail anticompetitive practices having a negative impact on domestic commerce, and only incidentally to protect consumers.

Advertising regulations take many forms. They can be classified into three categories: (1) general laws on misleading and/or unfair advertising; (2) specific product, media, and audience regulation; and (3) indirect laws and regulations.

General Laws on Misleading and Unfair Advertising

General regulations include comprehensive consumer protection laws and/or advertising laws setting out broad parameters for advertising practice. Such laws focus on advertising content and claims that are false, misleading, or unfair with respect to material facts about a good or service promoted for commercial gain. They also may set out rights and obligations of advertisers and consumers. Violations of these laws encounter criminal or civil actions and sanctions. Most advanced industrialized free-market countries have adopted some form of general legislation. The European Economic Community has adopted recently a directive making such legislation mandatory among member states. A few developing countries also have adopted general legislation of this nature. Notable examples are Mexico and China. Another form of general restriction is governmental monopoly over the advertising industry in a country. This is found in centrally planned countries in Eastern Europe.

Specific Laws and Regulations

In the group of specific laws and regulations falls a spectrum of legislation, regulations, and administrative orders concerning advertising content and practices. These may be directed against the promotion of specific consumer products most closely associated with bodily health and safety. Pharmaceuticals, alcoholic beverages, tobacco, and infant formula are the most frequent objects of advertising regulation. Other foods, cosmetics, and children's products are also important targets. Frequently, these regulations are translated into media restrictions. For example, the advertising of tobacco and alcohol products often is prohibited on television and radio broadcasts and is restricted in print advertisements. In most Western European countries and in a growing number of Third World countries, advertising prescription drugs and infant formula to the public through mass media is forbidden. In the case of pharmaceuticals, licenses permitting their advertisement in the media are frequently required. Terminology is important in the advertising of all these products. Prior substantiation of claims often is required for food and medicine advertisements. Television and radio advertisements frequently must receive approval before being broadcast.

Media restrictions per se are another example of specific regulations. For example, all commercial advertising is forbidden on radio and television in Scandinavia (except Finland) and in some Middle Eastern countries. Time restrictions are placed on television and radio advertising in the Federal Republic of Germany, in Austria, in the Middle East, and in some Eastern European countries.

Advertising to certain target audiences is another area for specific regulation. Advertising directed to children or employing children is meeting increasing restrictions. These restrictions are encountered most frequently in Europe. The ICC International Code of Advertising Practice also advises sensitivity in advertising aimed at children.

"Foreign" advertising has given cause for special legislation in a number of countries. Some of these countries have adopted specific laws restricting the use of foreign languages and materials. Further, they may require that all ads originate in the receiving country and employ local people, customs, and expressions. For example, unauthorized use of a foreign language in advertising in France is punishable as fraud under the penal code. English is allowed only in fully sung commercials in Thailand. The Philippine government encourages the use of the Tagalog language for preserving the national heritage and independence from foreigners. Nationalism, the desire to keep or forge a regional identity, the protection of consumers, and the preservation of cultural traditions and national nomenclature appear to be compelling motives in France, Malaysia, Peru, and Mexico.[11]

Indirect Controls

In many countries advertising by foreign firms is indirectly controlled through restrictions on foreign investment and trade. Stringent ownership requirements exist in Ghana, Nigeria, a number of Asian countries, the Middle East, and Eastern Europe. These requirements have been effective in discouraging the establishment of foreign agencies and advertisers and in causing others to move out of the country. Such restrictions aim to protect local business and encourage the development of local skills. They also limit foreign influence on the society. They do not necessarily preclude joint ventures or contractual arrangements with foreign agencies.

Taxation policies also can be an impediment to advertising. Almost all countries in Europe impose heavy taxes on advertising. These vary with the media, the highest being imposed on television advertising.

Private law is another source of control in advertising. In some developed-market countries, notably the United States and increasingly the EEC, the courts applying liability law permit consumers injured by products misrepresented by advertisers to sue for compensation. Under various theories of tort and contract law, individuals have successfully recovered their losses in civil liability suits. The threat of such a suit is one of the most potent controls on advertisers under U.S. law.[12]

The impact of regulation on the industry depends on the particular operational environment. Regulation is largely nominal in environments poorly equipped to enforce its prescriptions. In many developing countries, for example, the greatest obstacle to eliminating alleged advertising excesses is the lack of the administrative and legal infrastructure necessary to breathe life into the letter of the laws. In Western industrialized market-economy countries and socialist countries, however, the administrative and judicial capacity exists to enforce existing laws.

International Regulation

Since the 1960s the UN, many of its specialized agencies, and regional intergovernmental groups have probed advertising from a variety of perspectives. The work has been both general and product specific and has taken several forms, including studies on marketing problems and public policies, debates in various forums, resolutions calling for further investigations, and the adoption of codes and guidelines.

The voluntary codes and guidelines are the international counterpart of national regulation. Because international organizations lack the power to enforce their rules, these so-called soft laws gain strength from the moral and political commitment of the countries that adopt them. Their legal effect comes through translation into national law. International soft laws serve a number of purposes, including providing guidance for national legislative validity for domestic legislation in weak countries, acting as an instrument for harmonizing national laws and regulations, and offering some control over excesses falling outside municipal law.

General advertising practices have been the concern of the UN and UNESCO. The UN has focused on overall principles of consumer protection, and UNESCO has considered the need for a code of advertising practice to protect cultural integrity and social values. The UN General Assembly adopted its Guidelines on Consumer Protection by consensus on April 9, 1985.[13] The guidelines are of a general nature and relate to overall trade in consumer products and to the provision of product information. Advertising also falls under the rubric "consumer protection" in the UN's Draft Code of Conduct on Transnational Corporations. Provisionally agreed-upon paragraphs express the need for respect of host-government laws and regulations, regard for standards, provision of adequate information (particularly on products with health implications), and accurate advertising.[14]

WHO is the main forum sought by countries to air problems on the advertising of health-related products, specifically foods, drugs, tobacco, and alcoholic beverages. International recommendations affecting the advertising of foods in general and infant formula in particular have been adopted with the primary objective of protecting consumers' health and safety. This work was accomplished by the WHO/FAO Codex Alimentarius Commission and by WHO. The recommendations are embodied in codes and guidelines on the promotion of food products. These include the FAO/WHO Joint Food Standards Program Guidelines on Claims and Code of Ethics for International Trade in Food, and the WHO Code of Marketing of Breast-Milk Substitutes. Of these, the WHO code is most directly aimed at advertising practices.

The Guidelines on Claims emphasizes the principle that "No food should be described or presented in a manner that is false, misleading or deceptive or is likely to create an erroneous impression regarding its character and respect."[15] The Code of Ethics for International Trade in Food also stresses that food in international trade must be properly labeled and honestly presented in order not to mislead consumers. Particular emphasis is given to claims of nutritional value. The code aims to protect consumers in importing countries where these principles of ethics are not embodied in national laws and regulations.[16]

The WHO Code of Marketing of Breast-Milk Substitutes recommends, among other things, a ban on direct advertising to the public of all products covered in the code as a measure to promote better infant nutrition.[17] National restrictions and even bans on the advertising of infant formula have spread since the late 1970s in response to the infant formula controversy over allegations that infant formulas promoted by multinational food and pharmaceutical companies, notably Nestlé, were responsible for illness and even death of millions of infants in the Third World.

Many international organizations have received proposals to initiate work on a code of conduct for the pharmaceutical industry. Few phases of the activities of this industry, be they production, sales, research and development, advertising and direct sales, or exports or imports, have escaped public scrutiny and designs for control. Studies have been carried out by the UN, UNCTAD, United Nations Industrial Development Organization (UNIDO), OECD and WHO. The OECD, the UN Centre for Transnational Corporations (CTC), UNCTAD, and UNIDO have studied measures for promoting drug self-sufficiency through national policy-making and increased production capacity. Advertising and direct sales promotion by the multinational enterprises may be considered detrimental to these ends.[18]

Specifically, advertising of drugs has long been a preoccupation of WHO. In 1968 member countries adopted a strong resolution on pharmaceutical advertising recommending adherence to certain fundamental principles and urging Member States to enforce the application of ethical and scientific criteria for advertising.[19] More recently issues of pharmaceutical advertising have been discussed in WHO Expert Meetings held in Nairobi and Belgrade in 1985 and 1987 respectively. Given the peculiarities of the product and the differences in country health profiles, further regulation of pharmaceutical advertising is appropriate at the national level. This position has been maintained despite calls for an international code on pharmaceutical advertising.[20]

Special reports and meetings have been held by WHO on tobacco- and alcohol-related health problems and their possible link to advertising. In laying the basis for the development of anti-smoking policies, the WHO has convened expert committees to examine the issues.[21] In 1985 a study was published on the implications of production and trade of alcoholic beverages.[22]

The UN, the CTC, WHO, and the United Nations Environment Program (UNEP)—through the International Register of Potentially Toxic Chemicals (IRPTC)—have been concerned with the trade of potentially harmful products. Important in this context is the Consolidated List of Products Whose Consumption and/or Sale Have Been Banned, Withdrawn, Severely Restricted or Not Approved by Governments, the compilation of which was approved in UN General Assembly Resolution, 37/137 adopted 17 December 1982. Although product specific, this work has implications for international advertising since it aims to alert governments to regulatory action that might be needed concerning the marketing of products on the list. As many as 6000 manufactured brand name products are concerned. The list is updated periodically.

Self-Regulation

Self-regulation is an outgrowth of industries' awareness that promotion of goods and services is a controversial activity arousing public suspicion and antipathy and even organized opposition. It denotes the morally suasive, self-restraining measures taken within an industry to monitor the actions of its members, particularly in light of the impact of these actions on competition and on consumers' welfare. Self-regulation consists in the establishment of standards of conduct consonant with recognized principles of ethics, the development of complaint review processes, and the elaboration of sanctions.[23] By establishing its own codes of fair practice, the industry has to some extent obviated the necessity for governments to adopt unnecessary rules and regulations.

In 1937 the ICC established its Code of Standards of Advertising Practice with the support of advertisers, agencies, and the media. While primarily an instrument for self discipline, the code has come to be used by the courts as a reference document. Over the years this code has served as a model for self-regulation in over thirty countries and by more than 200 organizations.

Since 1937 the code has been revised periodically to reflect changes in the industry, and in public sentiment and policy toward advertising.[24] The most recent revision was adopted by the Executive Board in 1986. It reflects increased recognition of social responsibilities and the need to establish a fair balance between the interests of business and consumers.[25] On the international plane the principles, general rules, and special provisions of the code are administered by the International Council on Marketing Practice which, on request, investigates and tries to resolve allegations of unfair practices. All involved business interests are represented on the Council. The question of consumer representation has been studied.

The 1986 revised code provides an umbrella for growing numbers of industry/product specific and media-specific codes based on ICC principles but tailored in detail to the particular products or media activities. The Code of the International Federation of Pharmaceutical Manufacturers (IFPMA) is an example. According to the IFPMA code preamble, the role of advertising is to inform consumers of the existence of products by providing with objectivity and good taste useful scientific information and to provide clear statements with respect to indications, contraindications, tolerance, and toxicity. The code establishes ethical criteria for advertising drugs, and it is adhered to by member associations in fifty countries accounting for 80 percent of total production of pharmaceuticals. Violations of the code are reported to national associations, are investigated, and are brought to the attention of the offending company for correction. In the first six months of 1987, more than one hundred complaints were handled.[26]

In summary, it has been said that regulations are scores in the bargaining matches played out in various national and international political forums. In these events various issues have been the pawns positioned according to the motives and objectives of the principal players. The results often reflect dominant views of advertising's net social benefits. They are expressed in general rules and regulations, specific rules, and indirect regulations. The regulatory process in individual countries and in international governmental and nongovernmental forums constitutes the remainder of this book.

Notes

1. *S.S. Lotus (France v. Turkey)*, 2 Hudson, P.C.I.J. Rep. 20, at 18–19, (1927); Hans Baade, "The Legal Effects of Code of Conduct for Multinational Enterprises," *Legal Problems of Codes of Conduct for Multinational Enterprises,* Norbert Horn, ed. (Deventer, The Netherlands: Kluwer, 1980), 16.

2. UN, OECD, *Guidelines for Multinational Enterprises,* annex to the declaration of 21 June 1976 by governments of OECD member countries on international investment and multinational enterprises, rev. ed. (1979), par. 7.

3. UN, General Assembly, *Resolution on Consumer Protection,* res. 39/2488, A/C. 2/39/L. 2 (9 April 1985).

4. John H. Barton et al., *Law in Radically Different Cultures* (St. Paul, Minn.: West Publishing, 1983), 1–4.

5. Civil code law and legal science is rooted in Roman law, first codified in the 6th century under the aegis of Emperor Justinian I, and elaborated on through the ages in universities and monasteries in accordance with the changing needs of society. Under Emperor Napoleon in 1804, a modern version of the fundamental code was established. It serves as the blueprint for many national codes. The formal beginnings of common law mark back to medieval England on the arrival of William the Conqueror to take the throne of his uncle as the legal heir.

6. Rene David and John E.C. Brierley, *Major Legal Systems in the World Today* (London: Stevens and Sons, 1978), 147–208; Harold J. Berman, *Justice in the USSR; An Interpretation of Soviet Law* (Cambridge, Mass.: Harvard University Press, 1963), 152–67.

7. E. Allen Farnsworth and Victor P. Mozolin, *Contract Law in the USSR and the USSR and the United States,* vol. 1 (Washington, D.C.: International Law Institute, 1987). Citing F.T. Gavze, *Sotsialislicheskii grazhdansko-pravonoidogover* [*The Socialist Contract in Civil Law*] (Moscow: Iruridicheskaia Literatura, 1972), 6–7.

8. Majid Khadduri and Herbert J. Liebesny, eds., *Law in the Middle East,* vol. 1 (Washington, D.C.: Middle East Institute, 1955).

9. Barton et al., *Different Cultures,* 43–44; Hilda Kuper and Leo Kuper, eds., *African Law Adaptation and Development* (Berkeley, Calif.: University of California Press, 1965), 216–40; David and Brierley, *Major Legal Systems,* 505–33.

10. David and Brierley, *Major Legal Systems,* 143, 431 ff.

11. UN, CTC, *Transnational Corporations in Advertising: Technical Paper,* (ST/CTC/8), 1979, 38; J.J. Boddewyn, *Foreign Language, Materials, Trade, and Investment in Advertising: Regulation and Self-Regulation in 46 Countries* (New York: International Advertising Association, 1985).

12. Barbara Baudot, "Advertising: A Case for International Regulation?" (Ph.D. diss., Fletcher School of Law and Diplomacy, 1986). 4:1–4:180.

13. UN, General Assembly, *Resolution 39/248 on Consumer Protection,* A/INF/39/7 (9 April 1985), 67–73.

14. UN, ECOSOC, *Report of the Intergovernmental Working Group on a Code of Conduct on its Fourteenth Session,* E/C.10/79, annex 1 (26 June 1981).

Labeling, *Report of the Thirteenth Session,* Ottawa, 16–20 July 1979, ALINORM 179/22, par. 4–7 and appendix 2.

16. UN, Joint FAO/WHO Food Standards Program, Codex Alimentarius Commission, *Code of Ethics for International Trade in Food,* CAC/RCP 20 (1979), art. 4.2, 5.10, and 6.2.

17. UN, WHO, *International Code of Marketing of Breast-Milk Substitutes,* adopted by the 34th sess. of the World Health Assembly, 4–22 May 1981.

18. See e.g., UN, CTC, *Transnational Corporations in the Pharmaceutical Industry of Developing Countries,* ST/CTC/49 (1984); UN Conference on Trade and Development, *Technology Policies and Planning for the Pharmaceutical Sector in the Developing Countries,* TD/B/C.6/56 (1980), together with a series of individual national profiles; UN, UNIDO, *Global Study of the Pharmaceutical Industry,* ID/WG.331/6 and add. 1 (22 October 1980); OECD, *Multinational Enterprises, Governments, and Technology: Pharmaceutical Industry,* report by M.L. Burstall, J.H. Dunning, and A. Lake (1981).

19. UN, WHO, Assembly, *Resolution WHA 21.41,* 21st sess. (1968), in *Who Handbook of Resolutions and Decisions of the World Health Assembly and the Executive Board 1948–1972,* vol. 1 (1973), 144.

20. See UN, WHO, "Introduction by the Director General," in *The Work of the WHO 1982–1983: Biennial Report of the Director General, 1984,* xiii; UN, WHO, *The Rational Use of Drugs* (Report of the Conference of Experts, Nairobi, 25–29 November 1985).

21. UN, WHO, Assembly, *Resolution 33.35,* 33d sess. (1980), in *WHO Handbook of Resolutions and Decisions of the World Health Assembly and the Executive Board, 1973–1984,* vol. 2 (1985), 175; UN, WHO, Assembly, *Resolution WHA39.14,* 39th sess. (1986), in *WHO Handbook of Resolutions and Decisions of the World Health Assembly and the Executive Board, 1985–1986,* vol. 3 (1987), 15–16.

22. UN, WHO, *Public Health Implications of Alcohol Production and Trade,* prepared by Brendan Walsh and Marcus Grant, WHO offset pub. 880 (1985).

23. James P. Neelankavil, "Advertising Self-Regulation: Concepts, Prospects and Problems; A World Wide Study" (Sponsored by the International Advertising Association, Typescript).

24. Updated versions were issued in 1955, 1966, 1973, and 1987.

25. ICC, Executive Board, 47th session, *International Code of Advertising Practice,* Paris, 2 December 1986.

26. International Federation of Pharmaceutical Manufacturers Association, *IFPMA Code of Pharmaceutical Marketing Practices: Sixth Status Report,* Geneva, July 1987.

Part II
Industrialized Market-Economy Countries

5
Advertising in Industrialized Market-Economy Countries

As principle host and home countries of the multinational advertising firms, the industrialized market-economy countries of North America, Western Europe, and Japan, Australia, and New Zealand are the central focus of international advertising activity (see map 5-1). These countries account for 95 percent of global advertising activity (see figure 5-1 and table 2-6). Per capita expenditures on advertising in all these countries, averaging $241 and ranging from $53 to $458, exceed comparable figures for all other countries in the world, except Singapore and Israel ($60 and $103, respectively). Well over 50 percent of all advertising expenditure in the First World is concentrated in the United States; Western Europe accounts for about 25 percent of the total; Japan for 13 percent; and the other industrialized countries, including the developed Commonwealth countries and the Republic of South Africa, for 5 percent (see figure 5-1).

Mature markets, affluent populations, priority placed on the production of consumer products, advanced communications technology, and adherence to liberal economic ideologies advocating free competition and promoting consumer choice, all conducive to the flourishing of advertising, are trademarks of these national advertising environments.

Not only do these countries boast the world's highest advertising activity, they also have the most highly developed legal systems for regulatory regimes. Their regimes provide models for regulatory systems worldwide and are instructive about the way regulation works throughout the world. However, they also are interesting in and of themselves.

The industrialized market-economy countries, with the exception of Japan, are the principal bastions of legalism, having adopted law as the main organizational framework for government in society. The United States is the paradigmatic example; Japan leans the farthest toward nonlegal tradition. Japan shares with other Asian societies an underlying aversion both to legalism and to the resort to litigation as the principal means of dispute settlement. Secularism is another characteristic of law practiced in the industrialized societies. This contrasts with other legal cultures in which religion and law are closely associated (such as Islamic law, Hindu law, and the laws of

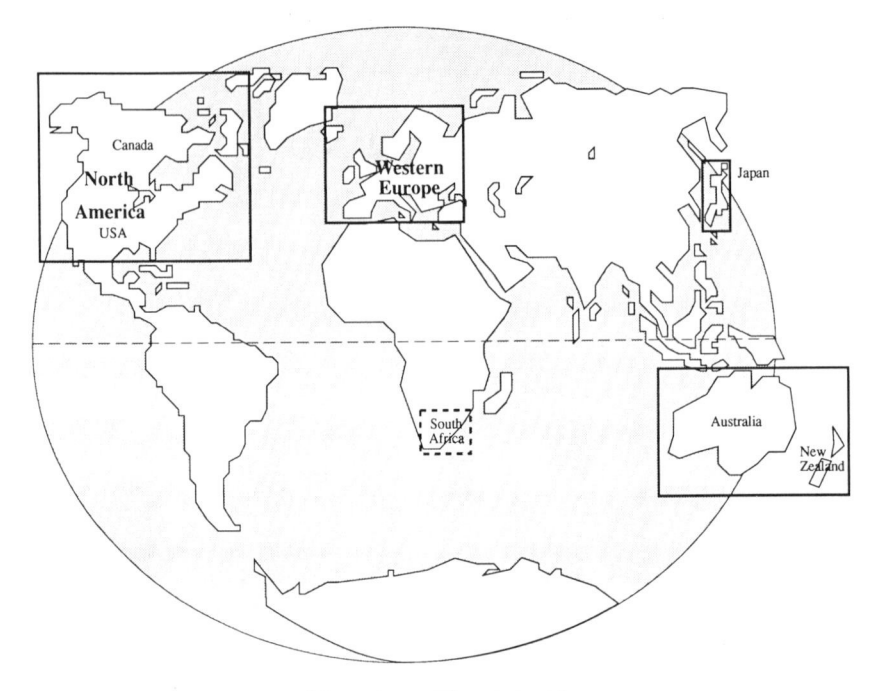

68 • *International Advertising Handbook*

Map 5-1. First World

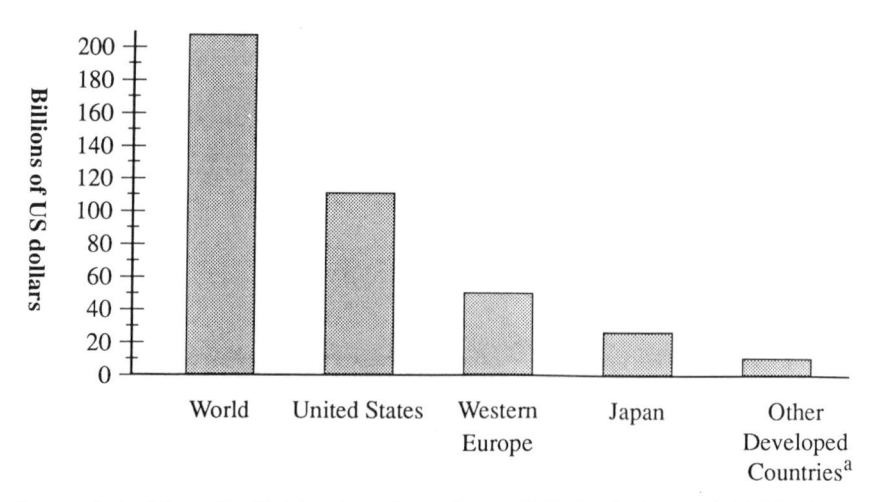

Figure 5-1. Total Advertising Expenditures in the Industrialized Nations, 1987

Source: derived from *World Advertising Expenditure,* 1987, 22nd ed., Starch INRA Hooper, Inc. in cooperation with IAA.

[a]Including Australia, Canada, New Zealand and the Republic of South Africa.

many traditional cultures). Western law is peculiarly imbued with the concern for rights of individuals, with constitutionally protected rights (speech, due process, etc.) and ordinary subjective rights (property, tort, and contract). This concern for rights contrasts with Asian systems, notably Japan, with their emphasis on duty and the social hierarchy of interpersonal relations.

Most industrialized market-economy countries initially approached advertising regulation with the goal of maintaining fair competition. Over the years these regimes developed a second focus, the protection of consumers. Presently, unfair advertising embraces both anticompetitive acts (including disparagement, passing off, tendentious arguments, and false statements that might injure the commercial reputation of another person) and anticonsumer acts involving moral judgments (such as appeals to fear; promotion of discrimination; exploitation of the credulity, trust, or lack of experience of the consumer; or other improper influence). The concept of misleading advertising has taken precedence over unfair advertising as the main rationale for regulation.

In order to assure advertising's benefits for consumers, business, and the marketplace, general rules are predicted on the principle of truth in advertising and reasonable guarantee of the freedoms of speech and the press. In the United States and West Germany, it has been determined that reasonable restrictions on advertising are necessary and do not violate guarantees of freedom of speech. Throughout the United States and Europe, advertisers generally accept a responsibility to provide a minimum of truthful information to enable consumers to make reasonably informed purchasing decisions. Specific regulations focus on consumers' health and safety (which are priority concerns of public policy). To these ends all governments have adopted specific regulations directed at the advertising of at least some of the following products: foods, drugs, tobacco, alcohol, and other health-related merchandise. Furthermore, liability laws (when relevant to advertising) allow private individuals to sue advertisers and agencies for injuries sustained while relying on advertising; suits may be brought either as breeches of contract or under various theories of tort.

In many senses a laudable determination to operate by professional and ethical standards, and in other senses a survival mechanism, self-regulation plays a varying role in the overall regulation of advertising in all these countries. By their own rules, advertisers observe local standards of fairness, taste, and decency. These principles are embodied in the voluntary Code of Advertising Practice as set down by the International Chamber of Commerce, headquartered in Paris. Self-regulation, when it works, obviates the necessity in many instances for resorting to law. In most countries self-regulation is an intraindustry operation, albeit with some outside participation. National codes tend to follow the guidelines established in the ICC Code of Advertising Practice.

Although they impose restrictions of various kinds, particularly on foreign labor, foreign investment laws in the industrialized market-economy countries are mutually advantageous and generally favorable to foreign investment. Not surprising, then, is that all these countries (with some exceptions for Japan and Scandinavia) share the same top advertising firms in their countries (as illustrated in table 2–5).

Differences in national regulatory regimes reflect, to varying extents, basic distinctions in political, cultural, and legal environments. The prevailing political ideology, whether it be economic liberalism or social conservatism, influences the extent to which advertising is permitted to permeate the communications media. The broadcast advertising regimes of Sweden and Italy demonstrate the extremes. The social mores of each society are reflected in the substance of restrictions in respect to truth, decency, and language usage. Explicit nudity has been commonplace in advertising in France and West Germany; it is unusual in the United States and Japan. Differing attitudes toward legalism are reflected in the amount of restrictions imposed on advertising and the processes for dealing with abuse. Private suits and public prosecution concerning advertising are unusual in Japan; they are most frequent in the United States.

The actual operations of these regimes demonstrate other significant differences stemming from the legal "systems" to which each country belongs. These idiosyncracies are worth noting if only for the light they may shed on the regulatory practices within these countries. Equally important, these fundamental differences significantly affect advertising and its regulation throughout the world.

Two basic families of law operate prominently here: civil code and common law. A third, the Confucian antilegalist tradition, is highly relevant for Japan. Based on different premises and different imperatives, these types of law operate through different agents and different structures. Civil-code countries, all countries in Western Europe except the United Kingdom, operate through compilations of legal precedent and legislation, statutory law, and a complex governmental infrastructure. Civil-code countries share the same general branches of law and the same fundamental formulations (constitutional law, administrative law, criminal law, and commercial and civil law—sometimes called private law). Common-law countries, the United Kingdom, the United States, Canada, Australia, and New Zealand lean heavily on both statutory law and case law and rely on the courts for administration of the law. Japan tends to avoid strict reliance on codes, statutory stipulations, and courts and emphasizes instead deeply ingrained notions of personal honor and communal obligation in private and commercial relations.

In civil code countries, notably France, the best means for achieving justice is to rely on enacted legislation. Legislation, the primary source of law, is authoritative in nature and has general applicability. Administrative rules and decrees are fundamental to applying and interpreting law. The solution to legal cases is sought in judicial interpretation of code and statutory laws. The underlying assumption is that the state and the public administration are best equipped to coordinate the different sectors of social activity and to determine where the common interest lies. This coordination is effected through the administrators' enunciations of rules covering complex social relations that demand precision and clarity.

Basic to advertising law in the code countries is the civil-law concept of obligation, the duty of one person to do or not do something for the benefit of another person. Advertising rules expound general principles of unfair and misleading practices. The emphasis on the state and the public administration results in lesser roles for the courts or for self-regulation. Clearly, major players in the code countries' regulatory schemes are administrators.

The Scandinavian countries present variations based on code-system regulation. Although grounded in Roman and canon law, the Scandinavian countries did not adopt the model of the Napoleonic code in 1805, when much of the continent did so. Instead, they continued to build upon their own versions of the Roman code and to develop unique structures and processes. Of most significance is the office of ombudsman. Legally empowered to mediate between the government and private parties, the ombudsman performs functions much the same as the FTC in the United States. Not only do ombudsmen monitor advertising practices, they also may evaluate cases, issue guidelines, or refer cases to the courts for judicial disposition. Established as an independent entity, the ombudsman is equally accessible to consumers, marketers, manufacturers, or the government.[1]

By contrast, in England and most of the Commonwealth countries, statutory law, case law, and self-regulation form partners in the monitoring and correction of advertising. In England the formulation of statutory laws is in style and structure consistent with case law. Laws adopted are detailed and open ended, leaving the judges to discover further rules under the law as cases arise. Thus, the judges play a key role in the interpretation and application of law.

No general principles of advertising have been formulated in British legislation. The majority of advertising rules fall into the category of public criminal law. In the United Kingdom, the procedural requirements under criminal statutes make prosecution through the courts a lengthy and unpopular solution. Hence, self-regulation that introduces more flexibility and efficiency into the system plays an important role.

The U.S. regulatory regime, in many ways the most comprehensive, reflects the dual influence of common law and code law. Common law comes into play most when private law is concerned. Code law is most clearly reflected in the U.S. development and application of administrative advertising law. The United States has an extensive body of administrative law and utilizes an administrator (the FTC). Violations are generally treated as civil offenses. Self-regulation plays a more modest role than in the United Kingdom and is more comparable to self-regulation in France.

In striking contrast to the philosophies and regimes of Europe, Scandinavia, and the United States, Japan demonstrates a basic aversion to legalism, reflecting its Confucian tradition. Thus, while Japan has nominally adopted the European code system as well as advertising rules and regulations, actual impact of law on commercial activity is quite different in Japan as compared with the United States. However, Japan's increasing involvement in international marketplaces is creating pressure toward greater conformity with European and U.S. regulatory practices.

The different treatment of advertising violations in each industrialized market-economy country illustrates basic differences in advertising regulation, differences that stem from the different legal origins. Truth in advertising has been established variously under criminal law, private law, or administrative law—private law in relation to anticompetitive practices, criminal law on the premise that false and fraudulent statements made irresponsibly or negligently are contrary to public morals and the public interest, and administrative law in that the action is investigated according to the regulations of an agency established (in part) to protect the principle. Such distinctions are necessary because under criminal law culpability must be established, which private suits do not require. As mentioned earlier the starting point for advertising legislation in the United Kingdom, Ireland, and other common-law countries is in the public (criminal) law. In code countries (West Germany, Austria, the Benelux countries, and Italy), the general legal basis for advertising regulation is private law. This does not exclude criminal prosecution for fraud in cases of false advertising. Both civil and criminal law underlie French advertising law.[2] Administrative law governs advertising for the most part in the United States and Scandinavian countries. Violators subsequently may be prosecuted for violations or for misdemeanors. Penal law may be imposed for violations affecting the health and safety of consumers.

Contrary to general practice on the European continent, where the principle of unfairness is deeply ingrained, the United States and the United Kingdom permit and protect comparative advertising as a source of important information for consumers and as a stimulant to the production of better products. Under common law in the United Kingdom, there is no concept of unfairness, and comparative advertising is permitted as long as it does not involve disparagement. United States policy encourages the naming of or reference to competitors and requires clarity and disclosure to avoid deception of consumers. Brand comparisons are supported when bases of comparison are clearly identified. According to the FTC, the use of truthful comparative advertising should not be restrained by business or self-regulatory entities. Moreover, industry codes prohibiting practices of denigration are subject to FTC challenge.[3] Disparaging advertising (denigration) is permissible as long as it is truthful and not deceptive. A shift toward permitting comparative advertising is occurring on the continent, notably in France, where consumer power has increased greatly in recent years.

Generally, national regulations have only territorial effect. France is an exception in that certain laws may be applied extraterritorially. The United States also will apply unfair competition rules outside its boundaries. However, among all these countries, there have been efforts to develop common standards of misleading and unfair advertising. These efforts have recognized that satellite and cable communications have allowed advertising to overflow national boundaries in a manner that is no longer controllable by national authorities. This has not been an easy operation. The EEC took almost ten years to obtain an agreement on its first directive on advertising. In September 1985 the Council of Ministers of the European Communities adopted a directive on misleading advertising, which will require the harmonization of laws and regulations of the 12 member states by October 1989.[4] Further directives on advertising through electronic media and on unfair advertising are under consideration. Meanwhile, member countries of the EC are making adjustments in their regulatory regimes to bring their controls on misleading advertising into conformity with the directive.

Understanding legal systems in general and advertising regulatory regimes of the industrialized market-economy countries in particular is key to understanding the approaches to regulation in many other countries throughout the world. Because the industrialized market-economy countries wield strong economic power, their methods of advertising and of regulating that advertising echo throughout the world. For that reason the evolution of advertising regulation in these countries is of even greater interest, and trends in this area are mirrored in the growth and development of other countries' regulatory schemata. English law, legal institutions, and self-regulation provide a model that may not be adhered to in all respects but that is more or less generally respected and taken into consideration in several countries, including most Commonwealth countries (of which there are thirty-one) and, to some extent, the United States. The civil-code system and approach to regulation have been adapted by countries of Latin America, by French-speaking and Spanish-speaking Africa, and in Indonesia. In these countries the commercial and legal heritage of French, Spanish, and Dutch colonialism is strongest. The U.S. legislation also provides models for consumer protection sought today in many Third World countries, particularly in Latin America. Principles of consumer protection and unfair competition developed in the home countries of the transnational advertising agencies also have inspired intergovernmental and nongovernmental organizations to establish voluntary codes and guidelines for international advertisers and agencies.

Notes

1. The incorporation of the office of ombudsman in the European Communities' recent Directive on Misleading Advertising (see chapter 7) points to the importance of this feature of the Scandinavian regime.

2. See, for example, Norbert Reich and Hans W. Micklitz, *Consumer Legislation in the EC Countries; A Comparative Analysis,* prepared for the EC Commission (London: Van Nostrand Reinhold, 1980), 48.

3. 16 U.S.C. sec. 14, 15 (January 1985).

4. European Community, Council, *Directive Relating to the Approximation of the Laws, Regulations, and Administrative Provisions of the Member States Concerning Misleading Advertising, Official Journal of the European Communities-Legislation* 210 (7 August 1985): 29 et seq.

6
The United States

The United States is the advertising capital of the world. It is a market of 240 million people, or about 4 percent of the world's population. Advertising expenditures exceed $110 billion—over 53 percent of the world's total advertising expenditure. In the United States, modern commercial advertising has grown to its fullest potential, and from the United States, the latest techniques of the trade have been exported to the rest of the world.

The terms *bigness,* and *leadership* characterize the U.S. advertising industry. The gross worldwide billings of the sixteen largest U.S. agencies amounted to $47 billion in 1987 equivalent to 23 percent of the world's total advertising expenditure (see table 2–1). The "sweet sixteen" billion dollar advertising agencies, the sixteen largest agencies operating in the United States, are all included among the world's twenty largest agencies as reported in *Advertising Age* in 1988. Of these sixteen multinational agencies all but three, Saatchi & Saatchi WW, Walter Thompson Co., and Backer, Spielvogel, Bates WW are home-based in the United States. The latter two are American firms that are held by British based holding companies (see tables 2–2, 2–3, and 2–5).

The role played by multinational advertising agencies in the U.S. advertising industry is also significant although percentage-wise it might appear to be lower than in many other developed or developing countries. On the basis of figure 6–1 one can calculate that the combined U.S. billings of the sixteen top multinational agencies were equivalent to 24 percent of total U.S. advertising expenditure in 1987. The figure becomes more significant when one considers that it represents $23 billion or close to one-half of total advertising expenditure in all of Western Europe.

The size of the U.S. advertising industry is also indicated by per capita expenditure that amounted to $451 in 1987, a figure surpassed only by Switzerland and a figure more than twice that of Japan, the country with the second largest advertising industry in the world. Total advertising expendi-

76 • *International Advertising Handbook*

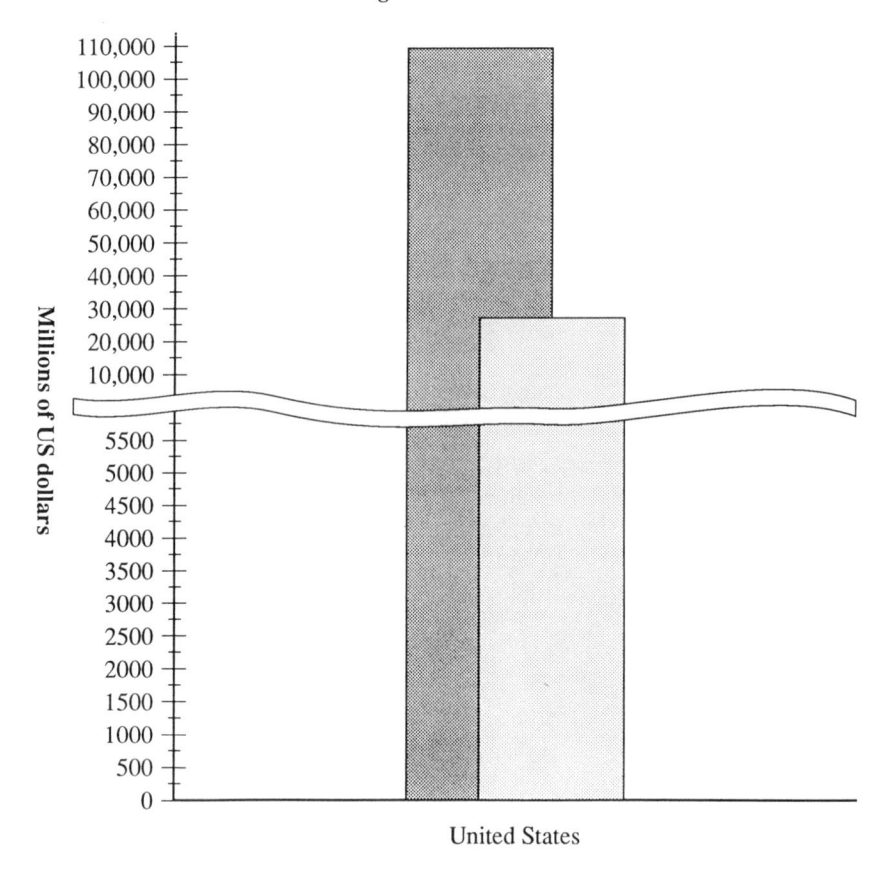

[Bar chart showing two bars for United States: Total Advertising Expenditure (~110,000) and Multinational Agency Billings (~28,000), in Millions of US dollars. Y-axis has a break between 10,000 and 5500.]

▨ -Total Advertising Expenditure   ▢ -Multinational Agency Billings[a]

Source: derived from *World Advertising Expenditure,* 1987, 22nd ed., Starch INRA Hooper, Inc. in cooperation with IAA; "US Advertising Agency Profiles," *Advertising Age,* 30 March 1988; "Foreign Agency Report," *Advertising Age,* 9 May 1988.

[a]The term "Multinational Agency" in the present context is equivalent to the expression "Foreign Agency" used in *Advertising Age* where the parent foreign agency operates in more than one country.

Figure 6–1. Gross Multinational Agency Billings and Total Advertising Expenditure in the United States[a], 1987

ture in the United States was equivalent to 2.4 percent of GNP in 1987, the highest percentage GNP ratio in the world (see figure 6–2).

Although it does not hold monopolies in any one field, the U.S. advertising industry provides world leadership in creativity, technique, organization, and management, as well as marketing research. Table 2–3 shows that U.S.-

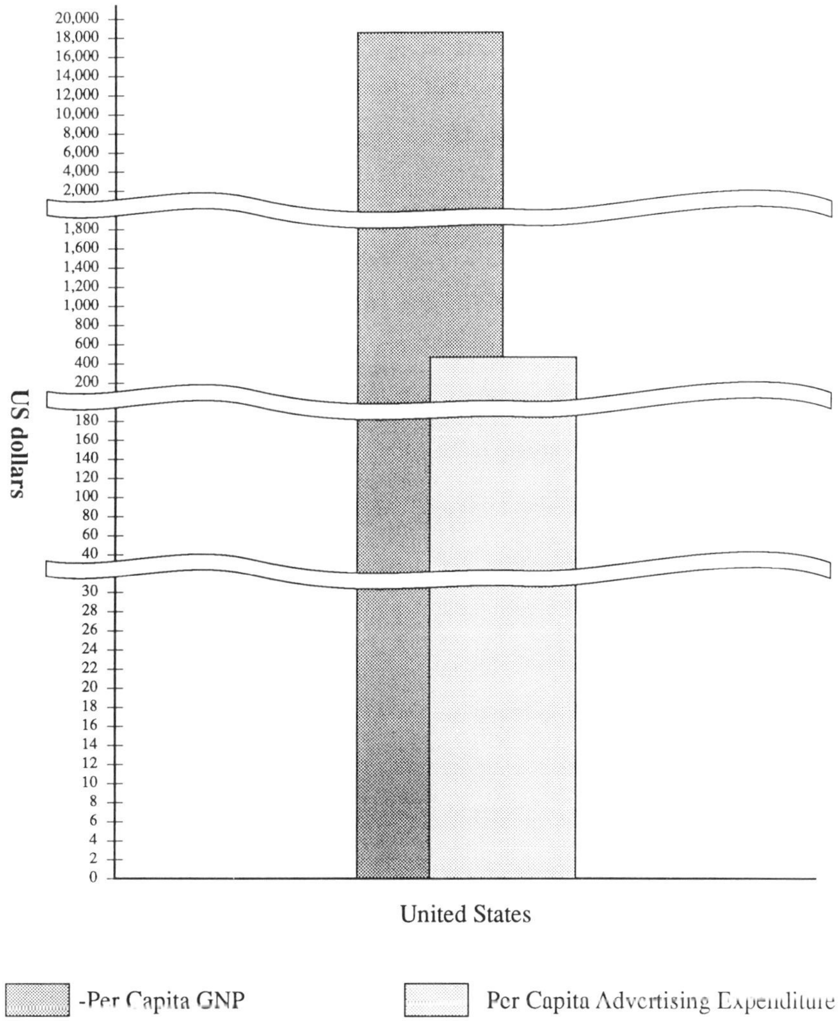

Source: derived from *World Advertising Expenditure,* 1987, 22nd ed., Starch INRA Hooper, Inc. in cooperation with IAA; *World Development Report, 1988,* World Bank.

Figure 6–2. Per Capital Advertising Expenditure and Per Capital GNP in the United States, 1986/87

based multinationals have a much broader sweep of operations around the world than the multinational agencies home-based in other countries including Japan, France, Switzerland, and Belgium. Only the British-based Saatchi & Saatchi offers competition in worldwide reach.

78 • *International Advertising Handbook*

Unlike many western European countries, where media reliance is heavily weighed toward print, the United States, as well as Canada and to some extent Japan, distributes its media advertising more evenly between print and radio and television. Unlike other countries, except Canada and perhaps West Germany, a large percentage of advertising expenditure is non-measured (see figure 6–3).

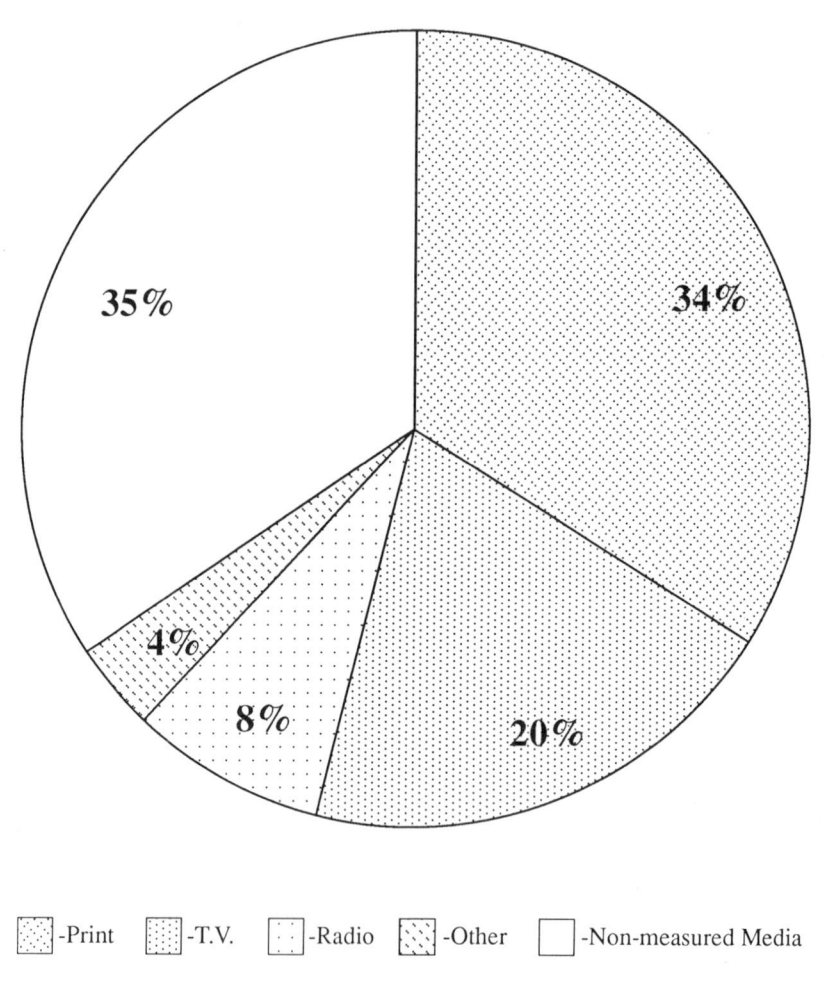

[Pie chart: Print 35%, T.V. 34%, Radio 4%, Other 8%, Non-measured Media 20%]

▨ -Print ▦ -T.V. ▢ -Radio ▨ -Other ☐ -Non-measured Media

Source: derived from *World Advertising Expenditure*, 1986, 21st ed., Starch INRA Hooper, Inc. in cooperation with IAA.

Figure 6–3. Advertising Expenditure by Media and Non-measured Media in the United States (percentage shares)

Despite the colossal strength of its advertising industry, this country has one of the most restrictive regulatory systems among free-market countries, a system that provides a model of standards of integrity for many other countries and international organizations (see table 6–1). Though rooted in England's common-law tradition, the legal system is unique in many profound respects. The distinctive features express to some extent a former colony's rejection of its colonial ruler, but more significantly, these features highlight its unique socioeconomic history and environment, as well as its federalist government. Retained from England, however, is a common-law frame of mind and common-law values.[1]

Rather than resort to a body of unwritten law as the highest legal authority, the framers of the U.S. government established a written constitution as the supreme and fundamental law of the land. Thus, U.S. federal administrative law (public law), which includes advertising laws and regulations, has always been in theory and form distinct from the British advertising regulatory regime rooted in English common law. In addition, over the years the U.S. government has amassed a huge body of statutory law, including federal statutes, uniform state laws, and administrative laws stemming from such sources as Congress, government agencies, and state legislatures.

Because the Constitution is largely silent about such matters as interper-

Table 6–1
Regulatory Profile: United States

Government:	Republic; presidential system; pluralist/elitist democracy; two dominant political parties
Politico-economic ideology:	Constitutionalism/legalism; capitalism with conservative and liberal approaches
Economic system:	Free enterprise with moderate public regulation
Legal system:	Anglo-American common law; elements of Romano-Germanic code system buttressed by statutory and administrative law; federal and state systems
Investment policy:	Liberal; adherence to OECD principles
Ad regulation:	Rigorous control by federal regulatory commissions; effective self-regulation
Ad expenditure:	$110 billion; per capita: $451; %GNP: 2.4
Consumer market:	Mature; reaching saturation for many products
Social indicators:	
Population:	240 million
Urbanization:	74%
Per capita income:	$17,500
Language:	English
Class structure:	Predominant middle class
Life expectancy:	72–80 years
Literacy:	90+%

sonal (private) legal relations, contracts, and torts, the question of the nature of law administered by the federal courts in private cases has been left open. However, since the Constitution empowered the states to develop their own legal systems, an alternative source of law for private suits is available. In 1938 in *Erie v. Tompkins,* the Supreme Court declared that, in absence of explicit constitutional or federal legislative authority, federal courts are bound to follow state laws in private suits where Federal jurisdiction is based on diversity of citizenship.[2] Law applied in private suits is derived largely from U.S. case law, although in the 1800s, recourse to English customary law was not uncommon.

A decisive difference between the English common-law approach and the U.S. approach is the American resort to more than precedents in deciding a case. In adjudication U.S. judges take into account not only law and precedent, but also the real interests at stake, or the social consequences of their decisions and the balancing of party interests in lawsuits. Thus, considerable extralegal data are admitted when relevant to a case. In doing so, the judge not only seeks to decide the issues, but also to predict the most desirable consequences of various alternative solutions. This broader approach to law is a distinctive feature of liability law and advertising regulation and contributes to the U.S. position as a leading country in advertising and liability law.

Advertising is subject to many types of federal, state, and local regulations.[3] The main components of the federal regulatory framework are the following: (1) general administrative laws governing unfair and deceptive advertising, (2) specific rules and regulations governing products and media, (3) the body of case law developed in the application of administrative law, and (4) self-regulation.

The elaboration of the regulatory regime has accompanied consecutive waves of consumer activism. The first significant wave occurred at the turn of the century and was led by the muckrakers and certain government officials. Dr. Harvey Wiley's campaign to expose common and dangerous practices in adulterating food and to demonstrate that the composition of various home remedies, promoted as miracle cures, was manifestly useless or even dangerous stirred public attention to needs for consumer protection. But it was the publication in 1905 of Upton Sinclair's novel *The Jungle,* which revealed unsanitary conditions in the meat-packing industry, that aroused such popular indignation that President Theodore Roosevelt was motivated to demand food and drug reform.[4]

A second wave of consumer activism came in the 1930s. By the depression years, a new round of sensational literature aroused the public and precipitated further reforms. A 1932 best-seller, *100,000,000 Guinea Pigs,* charged that fallacious consumer advertising deluded the public and lead consumers to buy over-priced products competing with one another in a display of economic waste.[5] The regulatory response came in 1938.

The last major wave came in the late 1950s and early 1960s, when enhanced technical possibilities for advertising media raised many renewed ethical and social concerns. The leading publication of this period was Vance Packard's *The Hidden Persuaders*. Measures for reform were prompted by fear and indignation over the manipulative techniques and emotional appeals of advertising and the dramatic rise in the volume of advertising that permeated society.[6] Thus, over the years statutory additions and amendments, administrative regulations, and an accumulation of case law have continued to shape an elaborate scheme of proscriptions and guidelines.

Since the turn of the century, self-regulation also has grown. This growth has occurred primarily as the industry's response to criticism threatening the credibility of the profession.

In response to increasing restrictions on its advertising activities, the business community has sought constitutional relief from regulation by seeking protection under the First Amendment to the Constitution. As a result, the courts have developed criteria for protection of commercial speech under the First Amendment, thus checking the regulatory authority of the federal commissions.

In addition to the public law and self-regulatory frameworks, the judicial system offers recourse under private law for persons suffering physical injury or economic losses from misrepresentation in advertising. This opportunity is due to product liability theories developed by courts and legislatures of several states. Control over advertising through liability suits may be particularly effective in bringing about responsible advertising, as it obliges advertisers and/or their agencies to take into account potential social costs.

Because the United States is the advertising capital of the world, the question often is raised of whether this country has a moral responsibility to apply its laws to home-based agencies in their foreign operations. Thus far, the United States has limited such action to unfair competition under the Sherman Anti-Trust Act and the Clayton Act, leaving the responsibility of consumer protection to host countries.

The remainder of this chapter examines in detail the following: (1) the development of general and product-specific regulations, including the authorizing of a federal commission to regulate advertising (according to certain objectives and guidelines), (2) self-regulation, (3) advertising regulation and the guarantee of free speech, (4) regulation through private claims for injury, and (5) the international reach of U.S. legislation.

Administrative Law and Regulation

Although more than twenty federal administrative bodies exercise control over advertising in one way or another, in interstate commerce the Federal

Trade Commission and the Food and Drug Administration (FDA) exercise the main jurisdiction. The U.S. Postal Service (USPS), the Federal Communication Commission (FCC), and the Securities and Exchange Commission (SEC) are also involved, but within more limited terms of reference. The Senate Committee on Commerce, Science, and Transportation and the House Committee on Energy and Commerce review the work of the FTC, carrying out inquiries and promulgating new legislation. These agencies and legislative bodies are concerned with advertising deemed (1) fraudulent, deceptive or misleading; (2) unfair in its methods of competition; and (3) injurious to public safety and health. The general, societal, and product-specific regulations are outlined in the following sections.

General Laws

The Federal Trade Commission Act is the principal federal law authorizing power to regulate advertising and promotional practices in interstate commerce.[7] The law was enacted on September 26, 1914. It established the Federal Trade Commission as an independent administrative agency to prevent "unfair methods of competition in commerce."[8] In 1938 the scope of the act was widened with the adoption of the Wheeler-Lea Act amendment on March 21, 1938. The commission was thereby empowered to prevent "unfair and deceptive acts or practices in commerce."[9] The Wheeler-Lea Act extended the basis of jurisdiction of the commission to all cases in which an injury to the public existed, regardless of the presence of injury to a competitor, thereby shifting emphasis of advertising regulation from "unfair competition" to "consumers' welfare."[10]

Powers of the Commission. Although the act gives the commission only broad directions for the necessary regulation of advertising (within the meaning of this provision), it authorizes the commission to prescribe interpretive rules and general statements of policy concerning unfair or deceptive acts and practices, as well as rules that specifically define acts or practices that are unfair or deceptive.

The commission's rule-making authority is subject to congressional review before final rules may be promulgated. Upon specific request from any interested person stating reasonable grounds, a rule also may be subject to judicial review. The rule making authority of the commission extends to all products except those that are excluded or limited in respect to banks, meat packers, alcohol and prescription drugs, subject to regulation under other legislation and by other agencies of the administration.[11]

Once rules are promulgated, violators are served with complaints and orders to cease and desist from violations charged in the orders. The commission also may initiate civil actions against violators.

Under its initiative the commission issues industry guides that are administrative interpretations of law. Guides may relate to practices common to many industries or to specific practices of a particular industry. They are only advisory, but failure to comply with them can result in corrective action by the commission under applicable statutory provisions.

Although the power of the FTC to take action against false and misleading advertising exists under the commission's general authority over unfair or deceptive acts or practices, the act also gives the commission specifically defined powers in respect to the false advertising of particular products, notably food, drugs, devices, and cosmetics.[12] The following sections summarize the evolution of the concepts of *false advertising, deception,* and *unfairness* and illustrate the application of the general laws on advertising.

False Advertising. False advertising is defined as an unfair and deceptive act or practice in commerce and is therefore unlawful. The act provides that:

> The term "false advertisement" means an advertisement, other than labeling, which is misleading in a material respect; and in determining whether any advertisement is misleading, there shall be taken into account (among other things) not only representations made or suggested by statement, word, design, device, sound, or any combination thereof, but also the extent to which the advertisement fails to reveal facts material in the light of such representations or material with respect to consequences which may result from the use of the commodity to which the advertisement relates under the conditions prescribed in said advertisement, or under such conditions as are customary or usual. No advertisement of a drug shall be deemed to be false if it is disseminated only to members of the medical profession, contains no false representation of a material fact, and includes, or is accompanied in each instance by truthful disclosure of, the formula showing quantitatively each ingredient of such drug.[13]

In general, false advertising must be misleading in a material respect, and the commission, in determining its existence, takes into account both acts and omissions concerning the nature of the product and the consequences of its use as portrayed in the advertisement. Further, the judiciary has affirmed that the meaning of *advertisement* and its tendency or capacity to mislead or deceive are questions of fact to be determined by the commission. Such findings are to be upheld by the reviewing court unless arbitrary or clearly wrong. In addition, the commission may evaluate the capacity to deceive on the basis of advertising content alone without the testimony of actual purchasers.[14]

Deception. The development of the concept of deception (as well as unfairness) in advertising has been an evolutionary process of rule making, review, and adjudication, occurring often when commission decisions have been challenged. According to the commission, deceptive acts and practices in advertising cases usually have taken three forms: (1) advertising containing direct representations, (2) advertising containing representations that, with reason, may be implied by the advertising (television image messages), or (3) advertising failing to disclose material facts.[15]

The ascertainment of deception is a subjective operation. A number of standards, however, have been applied by the commission with enough consistency to approach some semblance of rules for determining deception. The capacity to deceive is based on net impressions conveyed at first glance to the average public.[16, 17] Subsequent court rulings have upheld commission interpretations on the following: (1) truthfulness does not preclude deception;[18] (2) ads capable of several interpretations, one of which is false, are deceptive;[19] and (3) incomplete disclosures and material falsehoods are forms of deception.[20]

Whether the standard for deception is the average intelligent consumer or whether protection extends to the more vulnerable, less educated, or aged groups is not altogether clear. The record appears to indicate that essentially all persons are to be protected, in particular those who are naive, trusting, and of low intelligence.[21, 22, 23]

Unfairness. When the original 1914 act gave the FTC power to prevent unfair methods of competition, the basis for jurisdiction was injury to a competitor. Injuries to the public as a result of deceptive advertising were not under the commission's jurisdiction. Only cases involving competitors or injury to them were covered.[24]

In 1934 the Supreme Court broadened the interpretation of unfairness to include consumer protection.[25] Later, in preparing in 1964 to regulate the advertising of cigarettes, the commission undertook a review of its precedents in respect to unfairness.[26] The commission concluded that an exact and comprehensive definition of unfair acts and practices was not possible, but that an idea of the broad scope of the concept might be gathered. The commission considered the marketing methods that it had in the past forbidden as unfair, but that involved neither deceptive (false advertising) nor restraint of trade (anticompetition) principles. On the basis of some forty cases, the commission found three general grounds for determining unfair practice: (1) when the practice offends public policy or rules that have been established by statutes, the common law, or otherwise; (2) when the practice is immoral, unethical, oppressive, or unscrupulous; or (3) when the practice causes substantial injury to consumers (or competitors or other business executives). Subsequently, the commission added a fourth ground: when the practice makes advertising claims lacking adequate and well-controlled studies and tests.[27]

Specific Legislation

As described above, the Federal Trade Commission has specifically defined powers in respect to false advertising of food, drugs, devices and cosmetics.[28] Moreover, it has authority to develop rules and general statements of policy on unfair or deceptive acts or practices. Under this authority, the commission also has developed industry guides defining deceptive and unfair acts or practices. The numerous rulings, guides, administrative interpretations, and general policy statements constitute an intricate industry and/or product-specific regulatory regime governing product advertising.

Other agencies as well as the Congress also have power over product advertising. In general, regulation of food and drug labeling and advertising of prescription drugs fall under the purview of the Federal Food, Drug, and Cosmetic Act adopted June 25, 1938.[29] This act applies only to foods, drugs, devices, and cosmetics in interstate commerce. Further, Congress has adopted special legislation on the advertising of tobacco products.

Pharmaceuticals. Each year drug manufacturers spend over 5 percent of gross sales on the promotion of prescription drugs to physicians and pharmacists (about half of these manufacturers' total advertising expenditures). The media utilized include medical and pharmaceutical journals, direct mailings, brochures, and radio commercials.[30] Prior to 1962 there was no effective mechanism for controlling and regulating prescription drug advertising.

As discussed earlier, the Wheeler-Lea Act amending the FTC act specifically exempted prescription drug advertising from the authority of the FTC.[31] Although divested of responsibilities for prescription drugs, the commission retained primary responsibility for regulating advertisements for over-the-counter drugs and other commodities in media intended for the general public. The Federal Food, Drug, and Cosmetic Act omitted reference to prescription-drug advertising regulation on the presumption that physicians, given their expertise, were capable of discerning false and misleading advertising claims and did not, therefore, require protection.[32]

This situation changed in 1962 after numerous complaints were brought to congressional attention. In that year Congress passed the drug amendments of 1962, which gave authority to the Food and Drug Administration to promulgate detailed regulations for implementing the Food and Drug Act in respect to prescription drug advertising.[33] The law provided that all prescription drugs would be deemed misbranded unless all advertisements and other descriptive printed matter provided (1) a true statement of the established name of the drug, (2) the drug formula, and (3) information relating to side effects, contraindications, and effectiveness.

The FDA initially was satisfied with urging voluntary compliance, but faced with continuing problems, it invoked a regulatory procedure enforcement, including civil and criminal prosecution.[34]

A notable distinction in U.S. prescription drug advertising is the fact that the FDA cannot require advance clearance for a new drug's advertising and promotional campaign. Prior approval under normal circumstances has been considered an abridgement of the First Amendment. Copies of advertising and other promotional material must be sent to the FDA on publication.[35]

A current issue confronting the FDA is the permission to advertise prescription drugs to the general public. It should be noted that there never has been a legal or regulatory ban against consumer-directed prescription drug promotion. Tradition has, until today, kept such promotions out of the mass media.

Despite its rules and regulations, the FDA continues to be troubled by numerous problems in drug advertising. Some typical advertising defects include poor quality research; misuse of data; failure to include necessary material facts; non sequiturs; whole or partial omissions; and vague, distorted, and open-ended claims.[36]

Tobacco Products. In the United States, special legislation also has been adopted to restrict advertising of tobacco products. The first Federal Cigarette Labeling and Advertising Act was adopted July 27, 1965.[37] The act embodied the findings of the U.S. surgeon general's report issued a year earlier and forbade the production and trade in the United States of any cigarettes whose package lacked the statement, "Warning: The surgeon general has determined that cigarette smoking is dangerous to your health." The act also rendered unlawful as of 1971 the advertisement of cigarettes and small cigars on any medium of electronic communication subject to the jurisdiction of the Federal Communications Commission. The authority of the FTC to deal with cigarette advertising in print media remained untouched. However, the FTC was ordered to transmit to Congress annual reports on the current practices and methods of cigarette advertising and promotion.

Congress reinforced and strengthened the law in 1984 when, under growing pressure, it adopted further legislation requiring four new labels for packages and advertisements.[38] The labels would be rotated periodically, and they warned of cancer, heart disease, and other health problems and advised smokers that cigarette smoke contained carbon monoxide. This time, contrary to the case with earlier legislation, the tobacco industry participated in developing the legislation.[39]

Free Speech

Federal Trade Commission restrictions on advertising have been challenged as violating the First Amendment, which guarantees freedom of speech. This charge has been addressed by the courts. The present position of the judiciary is that commercial speech is entitled to qualified protection under the First Amendment.

Commercial speech originally was accorded no protection under the First Amendment. The Supreme Court had held in *Valentine v. Chrestensen* that "the Constitution imposes no . . . restraint on government as respects purely commercial advertising."[40] Consequently, a municipal ordinance forbidding the distribution of advertising matter on public streets was upheld.

In 1976, however, the Supreme Court, in the landmark case *Virginia State Board of Pharmacy v. Virginia Citizens Consumer Council* explicitly overruled the Valentine decision. The issue was the validity, under the Constitution's first and fourteenth amendments, of a Virginia statute declaring it unprofessional conduct for a licensed pharmacist to advertise the prices of prescription drugs. In its decision the Court stated that commercial speech is not wholly outside the protection of the First Amendment and the Fourteenth Amendment.[41] The Court drew a line between protecting the public from unethical advertising and protecting it from straight information. In its opinion, regulation of the latter is not justified: "Where straight information is at issue, the better alternative is to assume that information is not harmful, and that people will perceive their own best interests if only they are well informed. Thus, it is preferable to open the channels of communication rather than to close them."[42] In sum, the Court ruled that protection should be accorded to commercial speech because society has a strong interest in the free flow of commercial information, because advertising is indispensable to the proper allocation of resources in a free-enterprise economy, and because advertising is indispensable to the formulation of educated opinions on how the system should function.

Protection of commercial speech under the First Amendment is not unconditional. Because First Amendment protection of commercial speech is based on the informational function of advertising and the right of consumers to be informed, the Court continues to maintain that untruthful commercial speech was never intended for protection and upholds regulations supressing information found to be deceptive or misleading. Moreover, when there is an overriding public interest, commercial speech also is subject to regulation.

In 1980 in *Central Hudson Gas v. Public Service Commission,* the Court establishes a four-part test for determining the constitutionality of regulations on commercial speech. For commercial speech to come under the protection of the First Amendment, (1) it must concern a lawful activity and not be misleading, (2) the government interest must be substantial, (3) the regulation must advance the substantial government interest, and (4) the government regulation must not be more extensive than necessary to achieve its objective.[43]

The issue of freedom of speech is not limited to the United States. It is also stated as a fundamental right of man in the United Nation's Universal Declaration of Human Rights. In the international advertising setting, the issue came to force upon the adoption of the WHO Code of Marketing of Breast-Milk Substitutes. The U.S. delegate explained his country's opposition to the code on the grounds that it was in violation of the First Amendment. In the view of business, the code would restrict the freedom of commercial speech that is necessary for informed consumer choices. In fact, the dispute was over the target audience's capacity to make choices, given the degree of sophistication of the advertising information and taking into account the underdeveloped environments in which it was being received. Given these considerations, the proponents of restrictions on infant-formula advertising contended that the target audience lacked the capacity to understand the information contained in the advertising or to follow the instructions on the packaging. Thus, they were unable to make an informed decision. This audience, argued the proponents, required special protection through restrictions on advertising.

Self-Regulation

Self-regulation in the United States is a form of industrial self-defense. According to a report on self-regulation sponsored by the International Advertising Association,

> In the face of the increased government controls and increasing consumer criticism, the advertising industry has formed a centralized body for self-regulation. Its purpose is to define a position for the advertising industry and to defend it against the onslaught of consumerism and of legislative efforts that would severely limit its ability to function as part of a system in a competitive business environment.[44]

Although various self-regulatory bodies have been operating for several years, including the American Association of Advertising Agencies, the American Advertising Federation, the Association of National Advertisers, and the Council of Better Business Bureaus (CBBB), a central body was established only in 1971. This body absorbed and expanded the National Advertising Division (NAD) of the CBBB. The central body is now called the National Advertising Review Board and is sponsored by a Delaware corporation, the National Advertising Review Council, Inc. (NARC). This corporation is formed of the four self-regulating advertising bodies (the AAAA, AAF, ANA, and CBBB).

Today the regulatory work is done by the NAD (the first tier of regulation) and the NARB (the appeal level) on the basis of voluntary industry cooperation. The review procedure can be initiated by an individual, group, or company. It focuses on questions or complaints concerning the truth or accuracy of an advertisement or its capacity to mislead. Other subjects, such as those involving considerations of taste, ethics, and social responsibility, are considered only if they concern broadly applicable questions or techniques in frequent use.

Although cooperation and compliance with decisions of the NAD is voluntary, in situations where a company refuses to cooperate with the NAD, that case can be referred to the FTC. From 1971 to 1989, the NAD handled 2,371 complaints confined largely to consumer advertising of which 1,344 have resulted in modifications to or discontinuance of the advertising concerned. Only forty-four cases have been appealed to the NARB. Very few companies have refused to cooperate with the NAD and thus it is estimated that less than 1 percent of all cases have gone to the FTC.

Advertising and Private Claims for Injury

In the United States, few view the FTC, the FDA, and the FCC as offering sufficient guarantees that advertising will perform with full integrity its essential function for the benefit of the public. The insufficiency of the purely regulatory approach is demonstrated by the large number of liability suits brought for injuries related to product misrepresentation in advertising. Indeed the threat of liability suit deriving from advertising is sufficiently serious that lawyers have counseled advertisers to consider precautionary measures, including limiting advertisements to supportable claims or to broad general statements to ensure that no segment of the population will be misled.[45]

In the United States, liability actions are in the domain of the individual states. Thus, there are fifty sets of liability law and no federal law to date. Nevertheless, successful efforts have been made to compile preferred state-control and tort laws into uniform codes. The first attempt was the Uniform Sales Act of 1906, adopted by thirty-six states. This act was superseded by the Uniform Commercial Code (UCC) adopted in 1965 by virtually all states. It embodies statements on express and implied warranty under contract law. Preferred laws of tort are embodied in the Restatement (Second) of Torts, compiled in 1965. (American Law Institute publishes the Restatement as an unofficial consensus of the rules generally applied in the courts of the United States. Since no federal common law exists, the Restatement provides an authoritative compilation of private law in the field of Torts.) More recently, on October 31, 1979, the Department of Commerce published a model, entitled the Model Uniform Product Liability Act, for voluntary use by states.[46] The intent of the model act is to set forth uniform standards for state product-liability law, because the system at the time did not address interstate commercial reality or the needs of users, sellers, and bystanders.

Its success depends on its adoption by the states. It preempts the UCC and is in accord with the Restatement (Second) of Torts. Efforts to adopt a national product-liability law have been unsuccessful thus far.

Advertising and product liability are related in a number of ways. For example, U.S. courts have maintained that reliance on advertising leads to contractual relationships between buyers and sellers and raises consumers' expectations concerning the design, function, and performance of products.[47] Advertised claims that items are safe, wholesome, and free from dangerous elements, or statements concerning product use have led to liability suits when those claims were unfulfilled and consumers suffered injury or loss.

Many theories of civil liability law are relevant. They fall under either contract law or tort law. Under contract or commercial law, a party is liable for breach of express or implied promise or set of promises in an exchange of economic goods and services. Thus, the relevant theories concern liability for breaches of expressed or implied warranties made by the seller to the consumer. Under tort law a party is liable for civil or private wrongs or injuries resulting from breach of duty implicit on society's expectations in interpersonal conduct. Thus, the relevant theories of liability falling under tort are negligence, strict liability, and misrepresentation (also referred to as strict liability).

The roles of advertising change under the various liability theories. In some express-warranty and negligence suits, the content or nature of the advertising has helped to form the basis for findings of liability. In implied warranty suits, advertising may clarify the circumstances. In other cases advertising may identify the party liable for the injury or dramatize the intent of the defendant. In all cases advertising must be related to the injury or loss, and the plaintiff must prove reliance on the advertised statement.

The following paragraphs review advertising control through private suits for injury under several theories. These include *negligence, warranty and advertising,* and *strict liability.*

Negligence

Under the theory of negligence, advertising has been identified as the direct cause of injury even if the product per se was not defective. Cases have established that advertising renders a product dangerous by creating unjustified confidence in the safety of the product, that advertising in the form of overpromotion could distract users and cause them to overlook warnings, and that, advertisers should take extra precautions with respect to advertising products with potential health implications. In general, false and misleading advertising resulting in harm to a consumer provides just cause for suit for negligence if it is established that the defendant, in making the statements, neglected a duty to the consuming public.[48] The charge is sustained if the courts can be convinced that the plaintiff relied on the advertisement and that the negligence in the advertisement led to the injury or harm. The literature contains multiple examples of this.[49]

A classic negligence case linking advertising to product-related injury is *Crist v. Art Metal Works,* in which the court decided it was not necessary to prove an article defective per se to establish liability.[50] The plaintiff, a minor, was injured as a result of flames emitted by a toy revolver. Advertising was seen as the cause of the injury because the advertising incited the consumers to use the product without taking necessary precautions. The defendant, a manufacturer of toy revolvers, had "advertised the same for use, especially by children and infants of tender years, as a means and source of fun, play, joy, and amusement."[51] The advertising matter described in bold print the revolver as "absolutely harmless" and used other statements indicating that no harm could come to an infant user.

Case law also shows that advertisements that cause the client to overlook warnings also may be held negligent. Promotional activities extolling the attractive and beneficial aspects of a product that also contains potentially dangerous ingredients have been held to distract the customer from appreciating the potential dangers of the product even though adequate warnings are provided on labels and in the cartons. Sales efforts with the effect have also been identified as "advertisements causing traverse warnings," "overpromotion," or "watered down warnings."[52] The classic case is *Love v. Wolfe.*[53] The case involved a dangerous antibiotic, allegedly oversold by advertisements and representatives of Parke-Davis and Co. The court held that if overpromotion could have induced the doctor to disregard warnings, the warning was thereby cancelled. Further, if the doctor prescribed the overpromoted product to cure the condition for which the sellers had recommended use, the seller's negligence was an inducing factor causing the injurious result.

Warranty and Advertising

The relationship between warranty and advertising rests on the premise that promises, *express* or *implied,* are characteristics of virtually all advertising and that consequently an advertisement can amount to a contractual promise (a warranty) thus, an injury is an actionable breach of that promise. However, there is no rule of thumb stating that all advertised statements amount to warranties. The facts, circumstances, and language of the advertisement in each case must come into play.[54]

The generally accepted judicial definitions of warranties are embodied in the UCC.[55] Accordingly, a statement in an advertisement may create an express warranty if it is construed as a promise, affirmation of fact, description of the goods, sample, or model that becomes a part of a bargain. An implied warranty is applicable to a sale without regard to express statements by the sellers. In other words, in each sale there is an implied undertaking by the seller that a product will be of a certain minimum quality and that a product is fit for the purpose for which it is sold. In many cases of express warranty, the courts have found a direct link between advertising and a breach of express warranty. In cases of implied warranty, the relationship is best described as indirect. Advertising is seen as supporting evidence of the seller's commitment to the consumer in marketing the product.

Express Warranty. The key to determining whether an advertisement constitutes an express warranty depends on whether it is a factual representation. The general rule is that advertisements constituting express warranties must be factual. Mere affirmations of the value of goods or statements purporting to be the sellers' opinion or commendation of the goods (puffing) do not constitute express warranties.[56] (As mentioned earlier, puffing refers to loose general praise of goods or statements considered scientifically unconfirmable.) Often these statements are so obviously exaggerated that the average consumer would not take them seriously (for example, the slogan Put a Tiger in Your Tank). It has been suggested that representations of safety, strength, durability, or performance abilities would probably be deemed factual in nature.[57]

Nevertheless, the distinction is not always evident, and the choice is often controversial. Determination of the nature of the advertisement is left to the jury, which decides this point on the criterion of whether the statement constitutes a question of material fact. If so, it is actionable.

The advent of mass advertising has resulted in frequent liability suits under commercial law. In the landmark case *Rogers v. Toni Home Permanent,* the Ohio Supreme Court recognized that the consumer might take legal action against a manufacturer for breach of express warranty derived from advertising misstatement.[58] In general, a manufacturer's product liability is affirmed in cases of express warranty upon proof that (1) a statement of fact relating to the character or quality of the product has proven to be false, (2) the user has relied on the statement, and (3) the breach of warranty has caused harm to the user.

Advertisements also can cause customers to overlook fine-print warranties and thus give rise to breach of express warranty. Such was the case of *Ducote v. Chevron Chemical.* Special advertisements stressed that an herbicide quickly readied cotton for harvest, controlled weeds to make harvesting clean and more efficient, and took the guesswork out of defoliation. These claims were held to outweigh the fine-print warranty on the product label that the product's use could inhibit development and cause immature cotton balls. The advertisements had led farmers to believe that the product would produce desired results with little or no risk.[59]

Implied Warranty. In matters of implied warranties, the courts have differed over whether advertised statements give rise to a manufacturer's liability. The relationship depends on the degree of involvement of advertising and is strongly product related. In the view of some courts, the very act of putting a product on the market constitutes an implied warranty. In such cases advertising used to induce the purchase of the products also presumes a warranty on the article sold. Certainly this has been the decision in suits concerning the sale of food or beauty products. By contrast, in some cases (for example, sales of an automobile, a crop fertilizer, and a glass-container machine) the courts held that the advertising did not give rise to implied warranties.[60]

Strict Liability

The general application of strict liability as a legal theory is a relatively recent extension of the common-law rule holding those engaged in selling foods for human consumption responsible for their products. It provided the exception of privity in legal cases at the turn of the century, when sellers of foods were held liable to the ultimate consumer without proof of negligence.[61] Strict liability, like warranty, is an umbrella term for two independent theories of liability: *strict liability* per se and *misrepresentation*.

The overall strict liability doctrine is embodied in the Restatement (Second) of Torts and in the Model Uniform Product Liability Act.[62] Accordingly, strict liability per se provides that the seller of a product in a defective state, unreasonably dangerous to the user, is liable for physical harm thereby caused the user. According to the model act, the courts require the plaintiff to prove that the product was defective by a preponderance of evidence and that the same product caused the plaintiff's injury. The defect may be inherent to the product or in information about the product. The theory of misrepresentation concerns defects in the representation of the product (the advertising of a product) and is distinct in that recovery is allowable even in the absence of a product defect.

The doctrine of strict liability is distinct from absolute liability. Liability is said to be *strict* in contrast to the theory of negligence because it is imposed without subjective fault. To this extent, strict and absolute liability are the same. The difference lies in the concept of defect. Under absolute or no-fault liability, the plaintiff must prove only that a particular product was the cause of the damage, whereas under strict liability, the plaintiff must prove that the damage was caused by a defect.

Strict Liability Per Se. The general application of strict liability overcomes inadequacies of traditional negligence principles that place the burden of proof on the plaintiff, requiring the plaintiff to establish that the manufacturer knew in advance of the defect, the magnitude and likelihood of the danger that the product could cause, and the existence of safer alternatives. Strict liability facilitates redress for victims by providing that they may recover for harm upon proof that a product was defective when placed on the market and that the defect caused the harm.

Advertising is implicated in strict liability cases even though the main issue is an unreasonably dangerous defect that directly caused harm.[63] Thus, the court has reiterated among reasons for applying strict liability in tort that "the manufacturer by marketing and advertising the product impliedly represents that it is safe for its intended use."[64] See table 6–2.

The information defect as described in the Restatement (Second) of Torts, is distinct from the material properties of the product. It is inherent in the consumer's concept of the qualities or utilities of the product, determined by the nature of information provided, not provided, or overlooked for some particular reason. Information is distinguished from advertising as misrepresentation in that it generally is interpreted to be limited to warnings and instructions. The advertising defect is defined explicitly as misrepresentation; however, advertising often is inseparably linked to informational defects under strict liability per se.

Advertising has given cause for strict liability, as under theories of negligence and warranty, when the promotional aspects of manufacturers' communications have caused warnings or instructions to be overlooked or watered-down. This creates an information defect as described in 402 A. of the Restatement (second) of Torts.

Two cases are illustrative. In *Carmichael v. Reitz,* the plaintiff brought action against a doctor and a pharmaceutical company for illness attributed to the doctor's having prescribed the drug Enovid.[65] In considering the case against the manufacturer (Searle) of the drug, the court affirmed the opinion in *Love v. Wolfe* that when "promotional features of communications to the doctors by the manufacturer unfairly and unreasonably predominate, a warning otherwise adequate may become inadequate and the adequacy of the warning may present a jury question."[66] In *Berkbile v. Brantly Helicopter,* the court considered that the jury should have been permitted to consider the impact of advertising on directions and warnings provided to pilots as to what to do and how fast they had to act in the event of an emergency.[67]

Misrepresentation. Misrepresentation provides judicial reflection on society's reaction to the influence of mass advertising. According to the courts, the merchandising world is no longer the realm of direct contact. Instead, it is the world of advertising—where marketing communications are expressed and disseminated through mass communications. When these communications prove false and the consumer is harmed by reason of his or her reliance on the representation in the advertisement, it is difficult to justify the manufacturer's denial of liability.[68]

Table 6–2
Summary of Theories of Liability

Theory	Legal Sources	Brief Description	Prerequisites for Sustaining A Change	Relevance to Advertising	Liability
Negligence	Case Law see Macpherson VS Buick Motor Co. (1916) W.H. Elliot VS King (1961) Bryer VS Rath (1959)	Failure of supplier to exercise reasonable care	Defective product Physical harm related to product	High	Tort
Warranty					
a) Express	Uniform Sales Act 1906– (superseded by Uniform Commercial Code) Case law see	Statement of fact about a product proves false	Defective product Statement influenced purchase Physical harm or economic loss related to product	High	Contract
b) Implied	Uniform Commercial Code Section 2–314, case law	Breach of terms of sale; by virtue of sale supplier has undertaken to guarantee certain minimal quality	Defective product Physical harm or economic loss related to product		
Strict Liability	Restatement of Torts 2d (1965) para 402a, case law	Supplier responsibility for sale of a defective product	Defective product Unreasonably dangerous Physical harm caused by product	*	Tort
Misrepresentation	Restatement of Torts 2d (1965) para 402b case law	Misrepresentation of a material fact about a product	Physical harm and economic loss** sustained by user due to reliance on statement	High	Tort

*Warnings and labeling on pharmaceutical products common cause for action.
**Courts disagree on whether or not plaintiff can recover for economic loss.

Liability for misrepresentaion is embodied in the section 402 B of the Restatement (Second) of Torts. This section provides that misrepresentation of a material fact in an advertisement subjects the seller to liability for physical harm to the consumer who has relied on the advertisement. Section 402 B reads:

> One engaged in the business of selling chattels who, by advertising, labels or otherwise, makes to the public a misrepresentation of material fact concerning the character or quality of a chattel sold by him is subject to liability for physical harm to a consumer of the chattel caused by justifiable reliance upon the misrepresentation, even though
>
> - [a] It is not made fraudulently or negligently, and
> - [b] The consumer has not bought the chattel from or entered into any contractual relation with the seller.[69]

Misrepresentation, like the information defect, is not dependent on defects in the material properties of the product. However, proof of reliance on the representation must be established. The misrepresentation theory is the exception to other theories of product liability in that recovery is allowable in the absence of a product/information defect. It provides a judicial means to react against fraudulent or innocently inaccurate advertising. Successful pursuit of claims under this theory is contingent, however, on the sustainment of physical and/or mental harm, commercial loss, consumer reliance on the warranty represented, and a causal relationship between the harm and reliance on the misrepresentation of fact.

Courts seeking earlier precedents have identified *Baxter v. Ford* as the leading case in the application of the theory of misrepresentation.[70] For example, *Baxter* was identified as the landmark case in the decision in *Klages v. General Ordinance Equipment*.[71] Prior to *Baxter,* a consumer did not have direct cause of action in tort against a manufacturer for the failure of the product to conform to the manufacturer's representations. The only recognized claim in such a case was breach of express warranty. When privity of contract prevented direct suits against a manufacturer for breach of warranty, the plaintiff had to prove some degree of fault in order to recover against the manufacturer. In fact, since *Baxter v. Ford* courts have been virtually unanimous in imposing strict liability on product sellers when statements about their products prove to be untrue.[72]

International Reach of U.S. Advertising Law

Since the United States is the principal home country for international advertising, the extraterritorial application of relevant laws is a significant issue.

Thus far, the application of advertising regulations for purposes of consumer protection is confined to U.S. territory. The long arm of the FTC and the FDA governing extraterritorial advertising by U.S. agencies and advertisers has been explicitly cut off in both the Federal Trade Commission Act and the Food and Drug Act. According to the former, the powers of the commission are limited only to unfair methods of competition involving commerce with foreign nations.[73]

The act does not protect foreign consumers who are victims of deceptive or unfair practices when no harm to the U.S. public interest has been shown. In general, the powers of the commission to deal with unfair and deceptive practices committed overseas by U.S.-based multinationals rest in three conflicts-of-law principles contained in the *Restatement (second) of Foreign Relations Law*. [The *Restatement* is an attempt by the American Law Institute to codify international law as it is interpreted by the United States. The *Restatement* (second) was approved in 1978.] First, if a significant or essential part of conduct occurs within the United States, the issue falls under the principle of subjective territoriality. Second, if a substantial effect occurs in the United States as a result of conduct outside the United States, the activity falls in the category of objective territorial principle of jurisdiction and justifies the extension of U.S. law to subjects beyond the territorial reach of U.S. law.[74] And third, if the activity is carried out by U.S. nationals, the basis for jurisdiction is the nationality principle justifying territorial or extraterritorial application of U.S. law, depending on the location of the defendant.[75]

Like the FTC, the FDA has limited authority over products sold overseas, including their advertising. With respect to foods, drugs, health devices, or cosmetics to be exported, the Federal Food, Drug, and Cosmetic Act provides that a food, drug, health device, or cosmetic intended for export may not be deemed adulterated or misbranded if it, among other things, accords to the specifications of the foreign purchaser or is not in conflict with the laws of the country to which it is intended for export.[76]

At the same time, foreign prescription-drug products may not be directly marketed in the United States. According to the FDA Division of Drug Advertising and Labeling, all foreign prescription drugs must have a local U.S. firm to act as distributor. A foreign drug, once cleared by FDA new drug approval process, is no longer considered foreign and is treated as any other drug in normal U.S. channels of commerce. Unapproved foreign drugs in U.S. channels of commerce are subject to seizure.[77]

In general, protection of foreign consumers from misrepresentation by U.S. advertisers or agencies has been left to the legislative and judicial processes of local (host) governments. A leading case on this question is *Branch v. Federal Trade Commission*.[78] The case is explicit on the point that injury to foreign consumers alone would not empower the commission to act against U.S. citizens for acts committed abroad when no injury to the public interest (in other words, U.S. competitors) could be shown.

Under U.S. security laws, however, foreign consumers are not systematically outside the protection of U.S. courts in cases concerning fraud.[79] Although protection under the antifraud provisions of the federal security laws appears to be more favorable to U.S. citizens abroad than to foreigners (as demonstrated in *Bersch v. Drexel Firestone*) these provisions do, nevertheless, apply to foreign plaintiffs when acts (or failures to act) committed on U.S. territory directly cause losses.[80]

Likewise, foreign consumers suffering injuries or harm from deceptive or fraudulent advertising are not bereft of recourse to U.S. legal protection. In accordance with state liability laws and practices, foreign victims of advertising malpractice can bring civil suits in U.S. courts, under theories of tort or contract law, against perpetrators or advertising misrepresentation.

The United States has the most advanced legal infrastructure for seeking redress for harm caused by products defective in their inherent physical properties or defective by virtue of their representation. This conclusion is based on assumptions that (1) the U.S. legal system is amenable to such actions, (2) its laws recognize the advertising/product liability link under many theories of liability law, and (3) its courts are free to apply procedural law favorable to plaintiffs in international or liability suits.[81]

The feasibility of bringing foreign product liability claims to U.S. federal courts is attractive to foreign plaintiffs in instances when the "better rule" may be applied in absence of comparable liability law in plaintiffs' countries. ("Better Rule of Law" is a validation principle generally applied where most favorable results are produced for the plaintiff.) In such cases the courts of the states of the principle place of business of the supplier would be chosen. Under the system of contingency payments, the cost of such a suit to a foreign plaintiff would not be insurmountable. A few cases won or lost on legitimate grounds by foreign plaintiffs in U.S. courts would give muscle to international regulation, with a limited objective of maintaining an orderly system of international commerce prescribed by principles of social responsibility outlined, for example, in the UN's Universal Declaration of Human Rights.

Given the advantages offered by American courts, several liability cases have been brought to the United States and have involved injuries suffered by foreign plaintiffs in foreign locations. The assumption has been that more favorable awards would be achieved than if the cases were tried under domestic laws. Thus, "forum shopping" in the United States is a strong temptation in international liability cases. Overburdened with cases brought by its own citizens and aware that U.S. competitiveness might be jeopardized, the courts have taken a tougher stand in recent years against international suits brought by foreign plaintiffs.

Since 1980 there has been an acceleration in the increase of international liability suits brought against U.S. parent corporations for injuries occurring abroad and attributed to products manufactured or services provided by independent subsidiaries. The most publicized case is the catastrophic industrial accident in Bhopal, India, that gave rise to a claim on behalf of thousands of Indian victims. The case was heard in the federal district court in New York City.[82] In addition, there have been at least five international suits brought against U.S. pharmaceutical manufacturers, including Wyeth Laboratories, Inc.; Searle Laboratories, Inc.; Merrell Dow Pharmaceuticals Inc.; Syntex Laboratories, Inc. (California); and American Home Products (New York). All cases except the one against Syntex have been dismissed *forum non conveniens*. (*Forum non conveniens* is a declaration by the court that it is not the most appropriate place for the action to be brought. Such rulings usually result in judgment for the defendant. Due to overcrowding of dockets more and more international suits are being thrown out on this finding.) The case against Merrell is under appeal.[83]

Today a leading case on forum non conveniens is *Piper Aircraft v. Reyno*.[84] The case concerned the instigation of wrongful-death litigation in a California state court by the representatives of estates of citizens and residents of Scotland killed in a plane crash in Scotland during a charter flight and was filed against manufacturing companies in Pennsylvania and Ohio. The plane was registered in the United Kingdom and owned and operated by a company organized in the United Kingdom. Respondents sought to recover from petitioners on the basis of negligence or strict liability and *admitted* that the action was filed in the United States because its laws regarding liability capacity to sue and regarding damages were more favorable to the respondents' position than those of Scotland. A ruling of forum non conveniens was given by the federal district court of appeals, holding that "dismissal is automatically barred where the law of the alternative forum is less favorable to the plaintiff than the law of the forum chosen by the plaintiff."[85]

Subsequently the case was heard by the Supreme Court. The court's restrictive interpretation of forum non conveniens reflected increasing concern over the attractiveness of U.S. courts to foreign plaintiffs and the fear that a favorable decision would make the courts even more attractive, intensifying an already congested and overcrowded situation. In its interpretation, the Court dissolved the presumption of a link between choice of forum and application of the law most favorable to the plaintiff; restated public and private criteria for determining forum non conveniens based on an earlier decision (*Gulf Oil v. Gilbert*);[86] drew a distinction between foreign and U.S. plaintiffs, giving the former's choice of forum less weight than the latter's; and rejected the social responsibility argument as a reason for hearing foreign cases in U.S. courts.

On the issue of social responsibility, the court held that;

> As to the respondents' argument that American citizens have an interest in ensuring that American manufacturers are deterred from producing defec-

tive products and that additional deterrence might be obtained by trial in the United States where they could be sued on the basis of both negligence and strict liability, any incremental deterrence from trial in an American court is likely to be insignificant and is not sufficient to justify the enormous commitment of judicial time and resources that would be required.[87]

It might appear from *Piper Aircraft v. Reyno* that foreign plaintiffs are going to have more difficulty in bringing suits to U.S. courts in most states. Moreover, the attractiveness of U.S. courts for international liability suits will diminish with the court's rejection of the argument of social responsibility and the link between choice of forum and application of the law most favorable to the plaintiff, as well as the court's acceptance of the principle of deference in favor of hearing U.S. plaintiff cases over foreign plaintiff suits. This court ruling will contribute to lessening the threat to U.S. competitiveness from foreign liability suits in U.S. courts.

Overview

The United States has one of the most complex and controversial advertising regulatory systems in the world. Besides being subject to a host of federal, state, and local regulations, advertising also is exposed to control by individual citizens through private suits for injury. The regulation of commercial speech has raised important constitutional issues as well. The attractiveness of the U.S. legal system in terms of consumer protection has resulted in numerous suits against U.S. advertisers by foreign plaintiffs in U.S. courts. The protections offered in this country have provided incentives for international regulation. The complexity of the system emanates from the prevailing ideology of legalism, reflected in the growth of a massive judicial system and the enormous prestige attached to the legal profession.

Notes

1. Calvin Woodward, "Common Law and Common Law Legal Systems," *Encyclopedia of the American Judicial System,* ed. Robert Janosik (New York: Charles Scribner's Sons, 1987), 500–17.

2. *Erie Railroad v. Tompkins,* 304 U.S. 64 (1938).

3. Because this book's focus is on international advertising and because federal advertising law supersedes state law in interstate and international advertising situations, this work does not cover state and local regulations.

4. Upton Sinclair, *The Jungle,* (1905; reprint, New York: New American Library, 1973).

5. Arthur Kallet and F.J. Schlink, *100,000,000 Guinea Pigs* (New York: Vanguard Press, 1933).
6. Vance Packard, *The Hidden Persuaders* (New York: David McKay, 1957).
7. *Federal Trade Commission Act*, ch. 311, sec. 1, 38 Stat. 719 (1914), 15 U.S.C. sec. 41 et seq. (1982).
8. Ibid., sec. 41.
9. *Wheeler-Lea Act*, ch. 49, 52 Stat. 111 (1938).
10. *Ray S. Kalwajtys et al. v. Federal Trade Commission*, 237 F.2d 654, Annot. 65 A.L.R. 2d 220 (30 October 1956), Annot. Federal Trade Commission Powers, at 233.
11. Banks and meatpackers: ibid., sec. 45 (a) (2); alcohol: 27 U.S.C. sec. 205 (f); prescription drugs: 15 U.S.C. sec. 55 and 21 U.S.C. sec. 352 (n).
12. 15 U.S.C. sec. 52-55.
13. 15 U.S.C. sec. 55 (a) (1). The definition of false advertisement in section 55 generally has guided the commission in dealing with false and misleading advertising of many commodities other than those falling under section 52 of this act.
14. Annot. 65 A.L.R. 2d 220 (30 October 1956), at 222; *Rhodes Pharmacal v. Federal Trade Commission*, 208 F.2d 382 (1953), at 383.
15. *Pfizer Co., Inc.* 81 FTC. 23 (1972).
16. *Charles of the Ritz Dist. v. Federal Trade Commission*, 143 F.2d 676 (1944), at 677.
17. *Colgate Palmolive v. Federal Trade Commission*, 58 FTC 422 (1961).
18. *Ray S. Kalwajtys v. Federal Trade Commission*, 237 F.2d 654, Annot. A.L.R. 65 2d 200.
19. *Rhodes Pharmacal v. Federal Trade Commission*, 208 F.2d 382 (1953).
20. *Lorillard Co. v. Federal Trade Commission*, 186 F.2d 53 (1950).
21. *Ray S. Kalwajtys v. Federal Trade Commission*, 237 F.2d 654, Annot. 65 A.L.R. 2d 220.
22. Annot. 65 A.L.R. 2d 220, at 223, *Parker Pen v. Federal Trade Commission*, 159 F.2d 509, 511 (1946).
23. *Feil v. Federal Trade Commission*, 285 F.2d 879 (9th Cir. 1960).
24. Annot 65 A.L.R. 2d 220, at 234; *Federal Trade Commission v. Raladam Co.*, 283 U.S. 643, 75 L.Ed. 1324, 51 S.Ct. 587, Annot. A.L.R. 1191, *motion denied* (U.S.) 76 L.Ed. 1300, 52 S. Ct. 14 (1931).
25. *Federal Trade Commission v. Keppel and Bro.*, 291 U.S. 304 (1934).
26. Federal Trade Commission, *Trade Regulation Rule for the Prevention of Unfair or Deceptive Advertising and Labeling of Cigarettes, and Statement of Basis and Purpose of Trade Regulation Rule 408, Unfair or Deceptive Advertising and Labeling of Cigarettes in Relation to the Health Hazards of Smoking*, 29 Federal Register 8234 (2 July 1964).
27. *Pfizer Co., Inc.*, 81 FTC 23 (1972).
28. 15 U.S.C. sec. 52-55.
29. *Federal Food, Drug and Cosmetic Act*, ch. 675, 53 Stat. 1040 (1938), 21 U.S.C. ch. 9 sec. 301 et seq. (1982).
30. "Keeping Prescription Drug Advertising Honest," *American Pharmacy* no. 20 (May 1980): 280-84.
31. See the definition of false advertising cited from 15 U.S.C. sec. 55.

32. H.W. Chadduck, "In Brief Summary: Prescription Drug Advertising, 1962–71," *FDA Papers,* U.S. Department of Health, Education, and Welfare, FDA 72-3026, February 1972 Reprint. Chadduck was director of the Division of Drug Advertising, Office of Compliance, Bureau of Drugs, FDA.

33. 21 U.S.C. sec. 352.

34. "Keeping Prescription Drug Advertising Honest," 280.

35. G. Millstein, "The Regulation of Prescription Drug Advertising," *American Pharmacy* no. 23 (September 1983): 490–93. Millstein is the most recent director of the Division of Pharmaceutical Advertising at the FDA.

36. Peter Rheinstein and Paul S. Hagstad, "The Regulation of Prescription Drug Advertising," *Legal Medicine Annual 1978,* (Wichita, Kans.: International Reference Organization in Forensic Medicine, 1978) 405–19. Rheinstein was also director of the Division of Pharmaceutical Advertising at the FDA. Millstein, "Prescription Drug Advertising," 491.

37. *Federal Cigarette Labeling and Advertising Act,* Pub.L. No. 89–92, 79 Stat. 282 (1965), 15 U.S.C. ch. 36, sec. 1331–37 (1982).

38. H.R. 3979, Pub.L. 98–474, 96th Cong., 2d sess. (26 September 1984).

39. U.S. Congressional Quarterly Service, "New Cigarette Labels," *Almanac* 40, 96th Cong., 2d sess. (1984): 478.

40. *Valentine v. Chrestensen,* 34 F. Supp. 596, 314 U.S. 604, 316 U.S. 52 (1941), at 54.

41. *Virginia State Board of Pharmacy v. Virginia Citizens Consumer Council,* 425 U.S. 748 (1976).

42. Ibid., at 770.

43. *Central Hudson Gas v. Public Service Commission,* 447 U.S. 557, 100 S.Ct. 2343, 65 L.Ed. 2d 341 (1980).

44. International Advertising Association, *Advertising Self-Regulation; A Global Perspective,* prepared by James P. Neelankavil and Albert B. Stridsberg (New York: International Advertising Association 1980) 130.

45. Fred W. Morgan, "The Products Liability Consequences of Advertising," *Journal of Advertising* 8 (Fall, 1979): 30–37; Michael Hoenig, "Influence of Advertising in Product Liability Suits," *Journal of Product Liability* 6 (May 1982): 321–29.

46. U.S. Department of Commerce, *Model Uniform Product Liability Act,* 44 *Federal Register* 212 (31 October 1979) (hereinafter cited as Model Act).

47. *Rogers v. Toni Home Permanent,* 167 Ohio St. 244, 4 Ohio Ops.2d 291, 147 N.E.2d 612, Annot. 75 A.L.R. 2d 103 (1958).

48. *Rogers v. Toni Home Permanent,* 75 A.L.R. 2d 103, (1958) at 123.

49. 63 Am. Jur. 2d *Product Liability* (1984), 643–47.

50. *Crist v. Art Metal Works,* 230 App. Div. 114, 243 N.Y.S. 496, *aff'd without op.,* 255 N.Y. 624, 175 N.E. 341 (1930).

51. Ibid. at 496.

52. William P. Richmond, "Present Trends in Drug Product Liability Law in the United States," *Report of the International Conference on Pharmaceutical Product Liability Law* (London: Powder Advisory Center, 1979), 55. See also Morgan, "Products Liability Consequences."

53. *Love v. Wolfe,* 226 2d Cir. 378, 38 Cal. Rptr. 183 (1964), and 249 Cal. App. 2d, 58 Cal. Rptr. 42 (1967).

54. 63 Am. Jur. 2d *Products Liability; Advertising As Affecting Products Liability* sec. 638-5 (1984) 900-18.
55. U.C.C. sec. 2-313-18 (1978).
56. *Model Act,* sec. 105.
57. Hoenig, "Influence of Advertising," 321.
58. *Rogers v. Toni Home Permanent,* 167 Ohio St. 244, 147 N.E. 2d 612, 75 A.L.R. 2d. 103 (1958).
59. *Ducote v. Chevron Chemical,* (La. App.) 227 So. 2d 601 (1969).
60. 63 Am. Jur. 2d *Product Liability* sec. 642 (1984) 906-7.
61. *Restatement (Second) of Torts* sec. 402A, comment b (1965).
62. *Restatement (Second) of Torts* sec. 402 A, 402 B (1965); *Model Act,* sec. 104 (A), (B), and (C).
63. See *Mc Cann v. Atlas Supply,* 325 F. Supp. 701 (D.C. Pa. 1971).
64. *Kassab v. Central Soya,* 432 Pa. 217, 246 A.2d 848 (1968).
65. *Carmichael v. Reitz,* 17 Cal. App. 3d 958, 95 Cal.-Rptr. 381 (1971).
66. Ibid., at 401.
67. *Berkbile v. Brantly Helicopter,* 225 Pa. Super. 349, 311 A.2d 140 (1975).
68. See *Randy Knitwear v. American Cyanamid,* 11 N.Y.2d 5, 226 N.Y.S.2d 363, 181 N.E.2d 399 (1962), at 367, at 402.
69. *Restatement (Second) of Torts.* 402 B.
70. *Baxter v. Ford,* 168 Wash. 456, 12 P.(2d) 409, 88 A.L.R. 525 (1932).
71. *Klages v. General Ordinance Equipment,* Pa. Super., 367 A.2d 304 (1976).
72. Refer to *Model Act,* sec. 104, analysis (D).
73. 15 U.S.C. sec. 45 (a) (3).
74. The reach of U.S. law beyond territorial limits is referred to as the extraterritorial application of U.S. laws.
75. *Restatement (Second) of Foreign Relations Law* secs. 17, 18, 30 (1965).
76. 21 U.S.C. sec. 381.
77. William V. Purvis, assistant to director, Division of Drug Advertising and Labeling Office of Drug Standards, FDA, letter to author, 24 May 1984.
78. *Branch v. Federal Trade Commission,* 141 F.2d 31, (7th Cir. 1944).
79. These consist of six interrelated statutes administered by the Securities Exchange Commission, including the Securities Act of 1933, which is the disclosure and antifraud statute; 15 U.S.C. sec. 77(a) et seq.
80. *Bersch v. Drexel Firestone,* 519 F.2d 974 (2d Cir. 1975), *cert. den., 423* U.S. 1018 (1975).
81. These points repeatedly have been emphasized by W.L. Reese, renowned expert on U.S. and international liability law, in his articles on product liability law. See for example "Further Comments on the Hague Convention on the Law Applicable to Products Liability," *Georgian Journal of International and Comparable Law* 8 (1978): 311.
82. In re *Union Carbide Corp. Gas plant disaster* 809 F.2d 195 (2nd Cir. 1987).
83. *Harrison v. Wyeth Lab.,* 510 F.-Supp. 1, E.-Distr.-Pa. (1980); *Jones v. Searle Lab.,* 93 Ill. 2d 366, 444 N.E. 157 (1982); *Chambers v. Merrell Dow Pharmaceutical,* Ohio Ct. App., 1st App. Div., Hamilton County, *on appeal* Ohio Sup. Ct. (December 1986).
84. *Piper Aircraft v. Reyno,* 454 U.S. 235 (December 1981).

85. Ibid., at 236.
86. *Gulf Oil v. Gilbert,* 330 U.S. 501 (1947), at 508–9.
87. *Piper Aircraft v. Reyno,* at 237.

7
Europe: By Parts and Community

European advertising, like politics, is dominated by the five largest countries: the United Kingdom, the Federal Republic of Germany (West Germany), France, Italy, and Spain. These countries account for more than two-thirds of total advertising expenditure. This fact does not discount the importance of the industry in smaller countries whose per capita expenditures in many cases exceed those of the bigger players.

Europe's advertising industry blends sophisticated European and U.S. technology and is nearly as important in the daily life of the average citizen as it is in the United States. The percentage of foreign advertising expenditure is high throughout most of Europe. Media trends vary sharply among countries, as do the regulatory measures that influence commercial communication means. All variations in advertising in Europe reflect the mosaic of independent cultures that continue to define this continent (see figures 7–1, 7–2, and 7–3).

The European Communities

Europe today is on the brink of enormous change. Vital to consider are the efforts being made throughout Europe to overcome differences and to establish a free market for the circulation of goods and services. The most significant of these initiatives has occurred in the European Communities (EC, or the Common Market, formerly referred to as the European Economic Community (EEC)). The 1957 Treaty of Rome foresaw the removal of obstructions to the freedom to provide services within the EC and the institution of a system to ensure that competition in the EC is not distorted.[1] EC members include Belgium, Denmark, France, West Germany, Greece, Ireland, Italy, Luxembourg, the Netherlands, Portugal, Spain, and the United Kingdom (see map 7–1). Table 7–1 presents a regulatory profile of these countries.

By 1992 harmonization is intended to be in place, according to an overall plan expedited by the adoption in February 1986 of the Single European Act,

■ -Total Advertising Expenditure   □ -Multinational Agency Billings

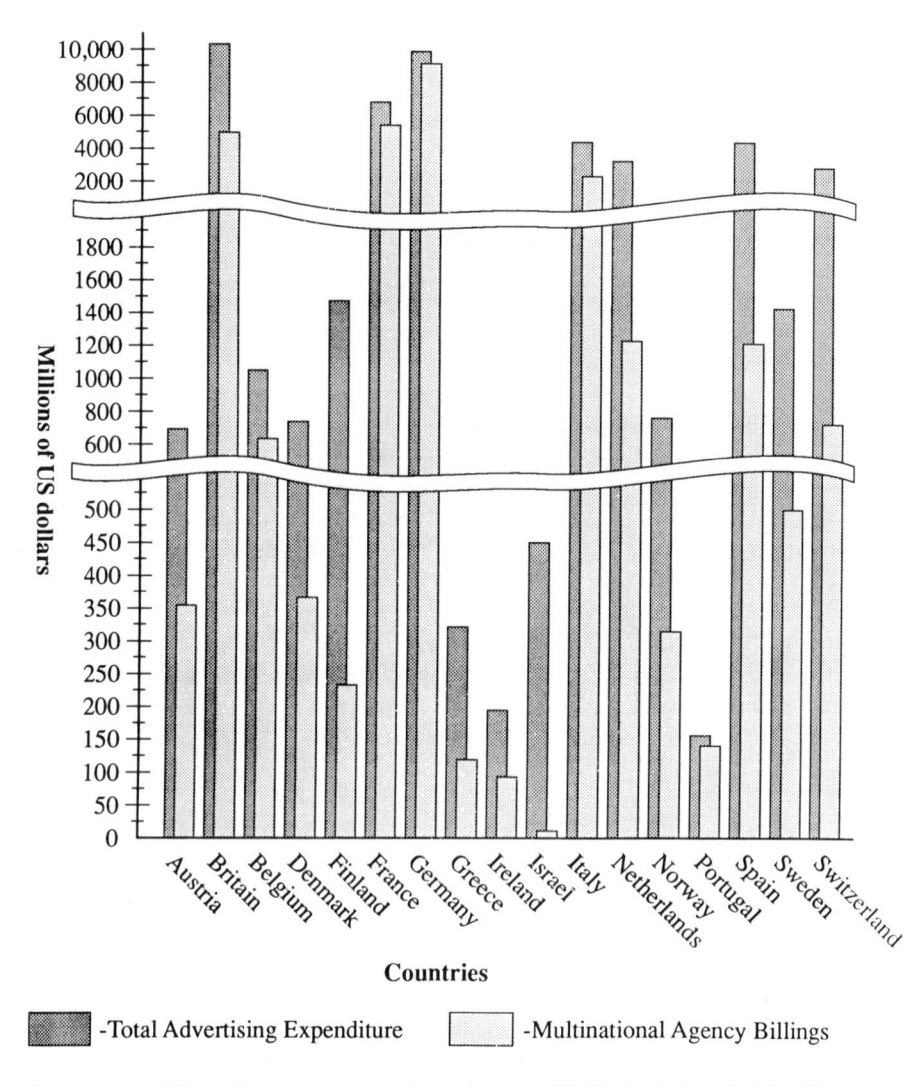

Source: derived from *World Advertising Expenditure,* 1987, 22nd ed., Starch INRA Hooper, Inc. in cooperation with IAA; "Foreign Agency Report," *Advertising Age,* 9 May 1988.

Figure 7–1. Gross Multinational Agency Billings and Total Advertising Expenditure in Europe, 1987

which amends the 1957 Treaty of Rome.[2] The plan is an array of some 280 directives designed to remove physical, fiscal, and technical barriers to trade among the twelve European Community members. The act defines the internal market as "an area without frontiers in which the free movement of

[Figure: bar chart with y-axis labeled "US dollars" showing Per Capita GNP and Per Capita Advertising Expenditure for countries: Austria, Britain, Belgium, Denmark, Finland, France, Germany, Greece, Ireland, Israel, Italy, Netherlands, Norway, Portugal, Spain, Sweden, Switzerland]

▨ -Per Capita GNP   ☐ -Per Capita Advertising Expenditure

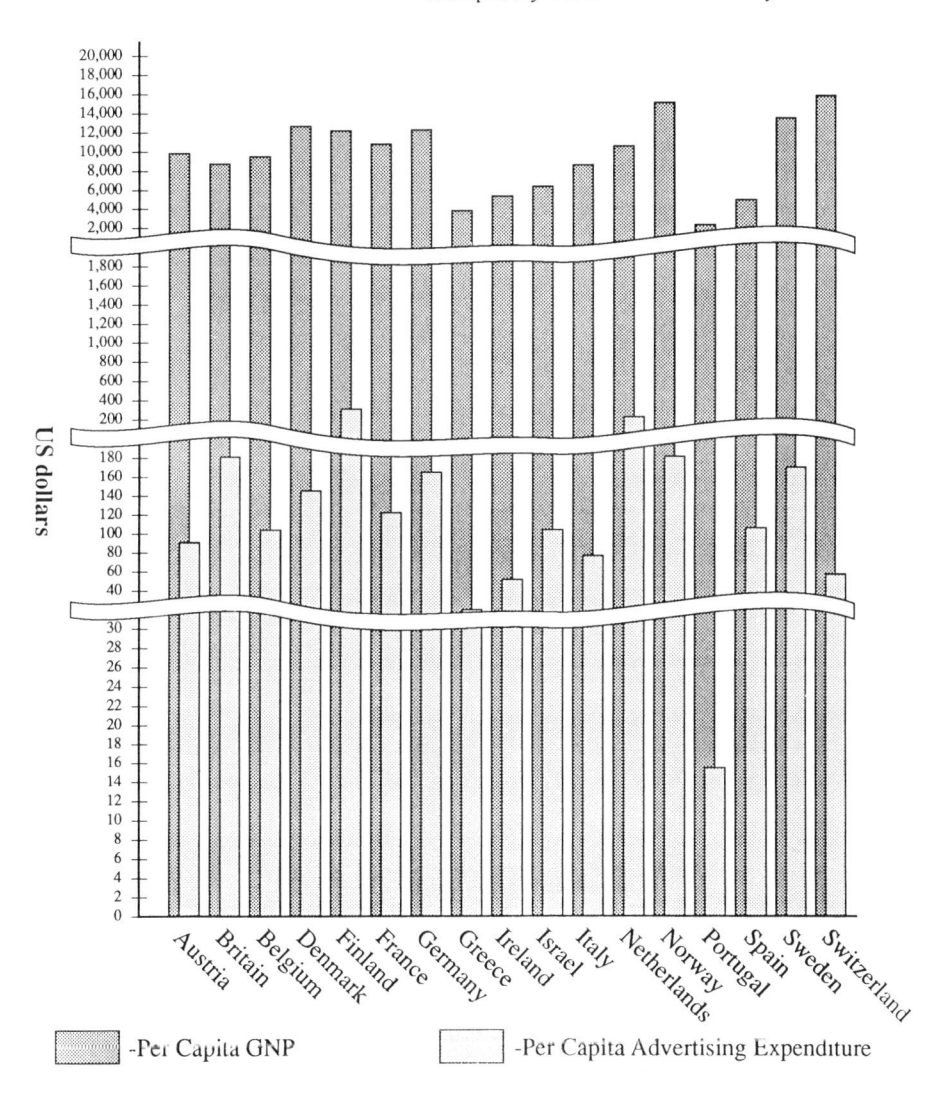

Source: derived from *World Advertising Expenditure*, 1987, 22nd ed., Starch INRA Hooper, Inc. in cooperation with IAA; *World Development Report, 1988*, World Bank.

Figure 7–2. Per Capita Advertising Expenditure and Per Capita GNP in Europe, 1986/87

goods, persons, services, and capital is ensured in accordance with the provisions of this Treaty."[3] Besides projecting the completion of the internal market by 1992, the act calls for requisite progress in a number of specific

108 • *International Advertising Handbook*

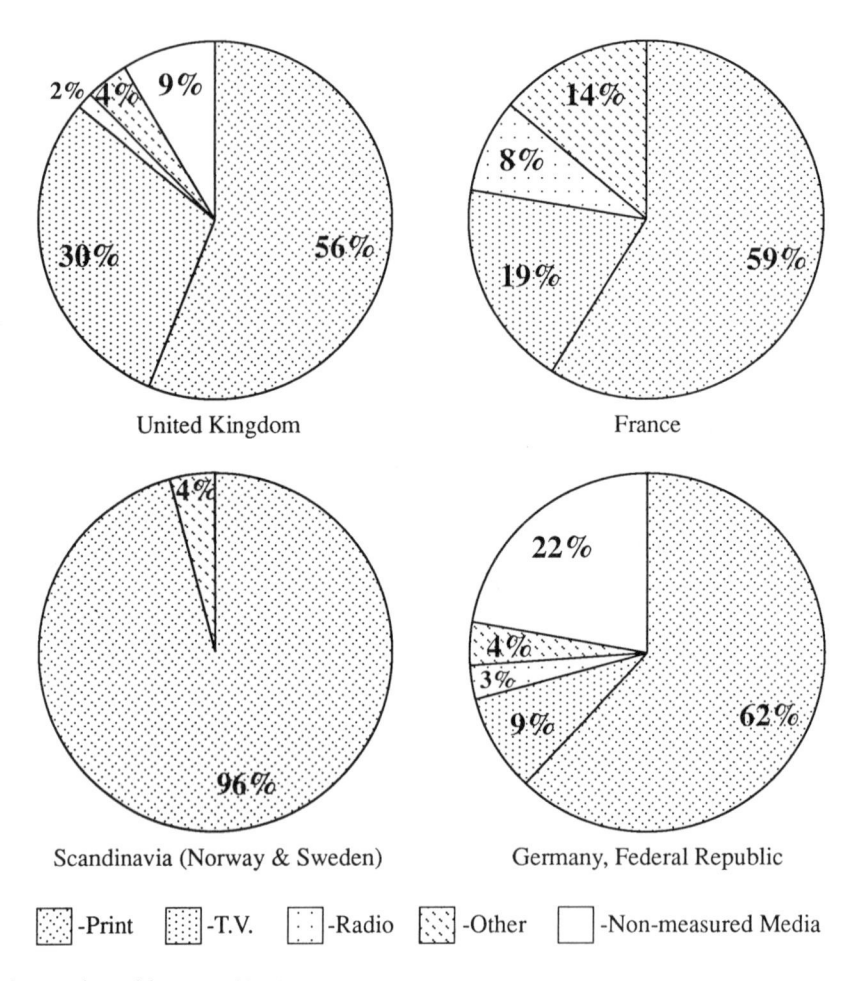

United Kingdom: Print 56%, T.V. 30%, Radio 2%, Other 4%, Non-measured Media 9% (plus 4% segment shown)

France: Print 59%, T.V. 19%, Radio 8%, Non-measured Media 14%

Scandinavia (Norway & Sweden): Print 96%, Other 4%

Germany, Federal Republic: Print 62%, T.V. 9%, Radio 3%, Other 4%, Non-measured Media 22%

Legend: -Print, -T.V., -Radio, -Other, -Non-measured Media

Source: derived from *World Advertising Expenditure*, 1986, 21st ed., Starch INRA Hooper, Inc. in cooperation with IAA.

Figure 7–3. Advertising Expenditure by Media and Non-measured Media in the United Kingdom, France, Germany (F.R.), and Scandinavia (percentage shares)

areas, including research and development, economic and monetary harmonization, and the environment and working conditions. To accelerate the decision-making processes, the act provides for qualified majority voting (in place of the previous unanimity requirement) on issues relating to the internal market.[4] Impetus for the plan has come from the business community.

Europe: By Parts and Community • 109

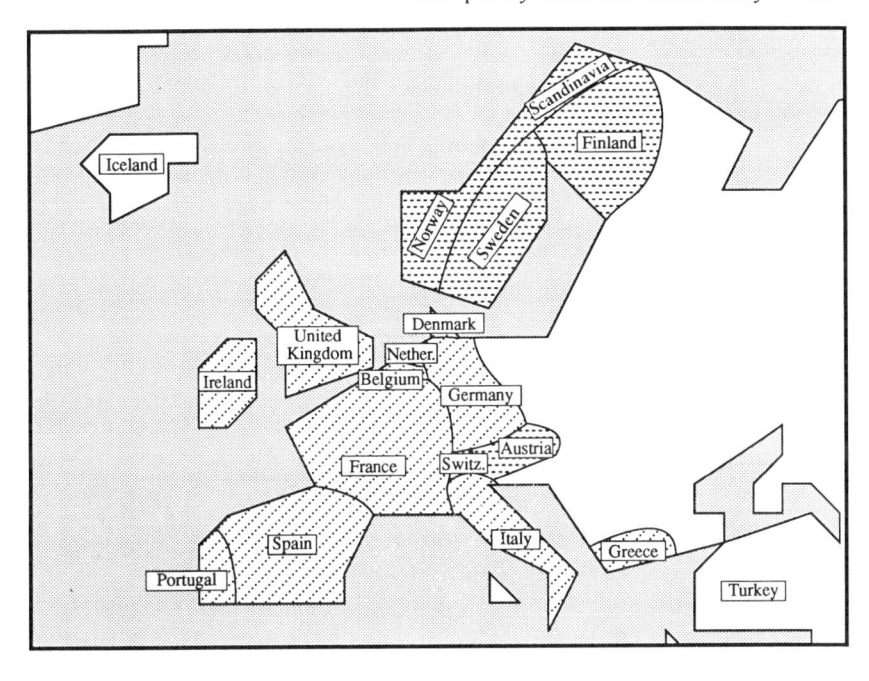

Map 7-1. Western Europe

Transfrontier Broadcasting

For advertising, the plan foresees uniform standards in television commercials. Heretofore broadcasting in Europe has been regulated primarily on the national plane. Technology today, however, offers vastly expanded opportunities with international dimensions. Thus, Europe is grappling with issues of inter-European regulation that would facilitate transfrontier broadcasting while protecting the public interest on a European-wide scale.[5]

The twenty-two member states of the Council of Europe have addressed the issues in their Convention on Transfrontier Broadcasting adopted in Spring 1989 and the twelve member states of the European Communities are debating the problems in negotiations on their draft Directive on Broadcasting.

Although having different constituencies and legal status both documents are to be closely aligned in substance. The major significance of the convention is that it provides the rules necessary to facilitate broadcasting throughout all of Europe. Although the convention is not legally binding, as a voluntary recommendation it carries moral authority and is strongly influencing the development of the directive that will become legally binding after adoption.

Table 7–1
Regulatory Profile: European Communities

Countries:	Belgium, Denmark, Fed. Rep. of Germany, France, Greece, Ireland, Italy, Luxembourg, the Netherlands, Portugal, Spain, United Kingdom (see map 7–1)
Government:	Republics and constitutional monarchies; parliamentary, multiparty, pluralist/elitist systems
Politico-economic ideology:	Liberal capitalism; social democracy
Economic system:	Free enterprise with significant European Community and national control
Legal system:	Romano-Germanic civil code prevailing
Investment policy:	Liberal under Treaty of Rome; adherence to Organization for Economic Cooperation and Development (OECD) principles
Ad regulation:	Strong community and national regulations; European Community directive merges France, Germany, Denmark, and UK types of ad regulation systems
Ad expenditure:	49 billion; per capita: $119; %GNP: .9
Consumer market:	Large; moderately expanding
Social indicators:	
Population:	350 million
Urbanization:	85%
Per capita income:	$8,800
Language:	Multilingual (English, French, and German are dominant)
Class structure:	Dominant middle class; traditional elites; growing body of foreign workers
Life expectancy:	70–75 years
Literacy:	90%

Both documents proscribe advertising that offends against prevailing standard of decency; is discriminatory on grounds of sex, race, or nationality; relies on fear; or encourages behavior contrary to the interests of health, safety, and the environment. They prohibit broadcast advertising of cigarettes and tobacco products. In addition to provisions on advertising alcoholic beverages they foresee national rules. Moreover they provide special guidelines to protect children.

Both documents seek to ration the time alloted to advertising and to determine European content quotas. They set maximum limits on the amount of advertising to 15 percent of total daily transmission time or 18 percent in any one hour (this may increase to 20 percent if teleshopping is allowed). Both documents suggest that a majority of the broadcasts be of European origin. Article 14 of the convention and Article 11 of the directive governing the insertion of advertising in programs are the most controversial. They may allow breaks in programs after twenty minutes (other than those devoted to children, the news, or religion, or are under thirty minutes) but limit breaks to two per ninety-minute film features and one additional break if the feature exceeds twenty minutes. Advertising can be inserted in natural breaks in programs with autonomous parts, for example, sports or talk shows.

Because Europe has been so divided in its traditions, the insertion of advertisements in programs and many other proposed restrictions are controversial. Compromises must be made between countries tolerating advertising, countries relying on advertising to finance broadcasting but restrictive on content, and countries with liberal advertising systems. Clarifications are needed in respect to concepts such as *broadcaster, sponsorship,* and *surreptitious advertising,* which portend regulatory loopholes. Controversy surrounds the definition of good taste and decency such as in respect to questions of nudity and sexuality. Here the question of the freedom of expression confronts potential restriction on the grounds of safeguarding public morality.

Directive on Misleading Advertising

The European Community Directive on Misleading Advertising demonstrates the kinds of accommodations the member countries will need to make in order to achieve the greater goals of the EC. The membership of the EC assembles a cross section of the major types of regulatory regimes operating in Europe. Because the work of the EC on advertising regulation is sufficiently advanced and because it was formulated to lead to consistency and harmony in regulatory policies in all European countries, the work of the EC is a central concern of this chapter.

The proposals for the EC directive reflected the variety of members' approaches toward the regulation of advertising as well as the existence of different regulatory systems operating in the community. The main task of the drafters was to reconcile the three basically different, but effective, systems for controlling advertising already operating in the community. One type places emphasis on a direct legal approach through access to the courts. The regulatory regime of France typifies this mode. French code and statutory law prohibit unfair and misleading advertising, and any individual or organization has direct access to the courts in cases of suspect violation of these laws. In the second type, the system used in Denmark and other Nordic countries, an administrative authority, the *ombudsman* (commissioner, or people's protector) plays a central role. This person is empowered to investigate all reported violations of statutory laws prohibiting unfair and/or misleading advertising and to seek court injunctions as necessary to prohibit the continuation of such advertising. The third type, represented by the United Kingdom, differs from the others in two respects: (1) in the absence of general statutory laws prohibiting misleading and unfair advertising, and (2) in the central role of voluntary self-regulation in the control of advertising abuse. This system, because of its voluntary aspects, differs significantly from the hard-law approach of its fellow members in the community.

The EC Directive on Misleading Advertising was formally adopted in September 1984 after years of long and complex negotiations. The directive is the first intergovernmental attempt to regulate advertising through binding international legislation. The directive establishes minimum standards for the regulation of "misleading advertising" in the twelve member countries of the community.[6]

The directive is intended to remove distortions in trade in the European Community resulting from differences in relevant laws and procedures and to protect the public welfare, the consumer, and competitors from the adverse effects of factual errors in advertising presentations. The directive establishes the validity of the three generally effective regulatory systems operating in the European Community and requires member states that do not have systems equivalent to one of the three models to adopt necessary laws and procedures to bring their systems into harmony with the minimum criteria, standards, and procedures provided in these models. Violations of the directive by states will be brought to the European Court of Justice, while individual violations by advertisers will be dealt with in national courts or administrations. In accordance with the EC Convention on Jurisdiction and Enforcement of Judgments in Civil and Commercial Matters, the judgments of courts in one member state will be recognized in the other member states.[7]

Areas of Contention. Debate on the draft directive centered on (1) the scope of unfair or misleading advertising and (2) the regulatory procedures that should be accepted. Final agreement depended on compromises, notably between the United Kingdom and West Germany on the procedural approach.[8]

The original draft presented in 1978 and its amended version in 1979 dealt with both misleading and unfair advertising.[9] Misleading advertising, the less complex, focused on advertising errors of a factual nature and was consumer oriented. The definition of misleading advertising in the early draft remained in the final directive.

Unfair advertising was more problematic. The concept of unfair advertising was familiar in continental Europe. Many European countries, as well as the United States, had approached advertising regulation with a view toward maintaining fair competition. However, the United Kingdom has never incorporated the concept in its laws on advertising. Unfair advertising is principally concerned with anticompetitive practice. Further, the concept of unfairness in recent years has come to embrace areas of consumer protection in many countries. At the time of negotiation, unfair advertising embraced (1) anticompetitive acts, including disparagement, passing off, tendentious arguments, and false statements that might injure the commercial reputation of another person, and (2) subjective anticonsumer acts involving moral judgments, such as appeals to fear, promotion of discrimination, exploitation of the credulity, trust, or lack of experience of the consumer, or other influence in an improper manner. It was the anticompetitive aspects of the unfair advertising concept that became a source of division in the drafting of the directive.

Unfair, anticompetitive practices are still the basic rationale for advertising regulation on the Continent, particularly in West Germany. The controversy over the acceptability of comparison advertising was one important aspect of the debate on the directive. Particularly in light of the British opposition to the inclusion of *unfair advertising* in the directive, the scope of the directive was limited to *misleading advertising*. Unfair advertising was set aside for further study and an eventual directive.[10] The British still remain to be convinced of the need for such a directive. Their position is one of wait and see; meanwhile, they point out that there is a wide overlap between unfair and misleading advertising with respect to consumer protection.[11]

Sharp differences in the regulatory systems in operation in the member countries was cause for division on proposed regulatory procedures. The main arguments focused on the prominence given voluntary self-regulatory systems by Britain as opposed to strongly enforced legal and administrative systems operating on the Continent, particularly in West Germany. In the debate the United Kingdom persistently defended its system and agreed only to the possibility of reinforcing its self-regulatory system through strengthening the office of the director general of fair trading (DGFT). It would not accept a law that would displace its self-regulatory system. According to the Department of Trade and Industry, "the government pursued this approach in the negotiations and managed to ensure that it recognized a continuing role for self-regulatory bodies and the possibility of arrangements that would not lead to this role being undermined.[12]

Text of the Directive. The directive is a relatively brief document. The preamble constitutes about half the document and covers the purposes, scope, and limitations of the directive. The *operational articles* are nine in number. They include working definitions, procedures for dealing with misleading advertising, operating principles, and provisions concerning implementation.

Preamble. In the preamble, the differences in the laws against misleading advertising in the member states are recognized. The fact that advertising's reach beyond the frontiers of the individual member states can lead to distortions in competition and have adverse effects on consumer welfare also is acknowledged. The preamble states that the differences in the laws are a sham in many cases and lead to inadequate levels of consumer protection as well as hinder the execution of advertising campaigns beyond national boundaries, thereby affecting the free circulation of goods and services.

The preamble also makes clear that the directive is intended to meet the needs of the general public, consumers, and competitors by harmonizing national provisions against misleading advertising. The directive sets out minimum standards for effective national legislation (including criteria for determinng what constitutes misleading advertising, suggests alternative authoritative machinery for proceedings against violations and possible remedies, and encourages self-regulation. Finally, the directive places the burden of proving material accuracy of factual claims on the advertiser.

Articles. Article 2 of the directive defines *advertising* as "the making of a representation in any form in connection with a trade, business, craft or profession in order to promote the supply of goods or services, including immovable property, rights and obligations."[13] It defines *misleading advertising* as that which "deceives or is likely to deceive persons (natural or legal) to whom it is addressed or whom it reaches and which by reason of its deceptive nature, is likely to affect their economic behavior or which, for those reasons, injures or is likely to injure a competitor."[14]

Article 3 sets out the criteria for determining what constitutes misleading advertising. In such questions an account would be taken of all its features particularly any information concerning (1) the characteristics of goods or services, (2) price and supply considerations, and (3) the nature, attributes, and rights of the advertiser.

The "teeth" of the directive are contained in article 4. According to this article, member states are required to set up procedures prohibiting misleading advertising and allowing interested parties to seek legal action in the courts or to bring the matter before an administrative authority. This authority must be competent to decide on the complaint itself and to enforce its decision or initiate appropriate legal proceedings. The administrative authority must meet certain criteria and give reasons for the decisions it has reached. The arrangements require provision for an accelerated procedure.

Article 4 reflects effective procedures elaborated in the most industrialized countries, including West Germany, the Benelux countries, France, and Denmark. Articles 4 and 5 provide for the recognition of effective self-regulation as an initial recourse in cases of misleading advertising. Thus, article 4.1 states the following:

> It shall be for each Member State to decide which of these facilities [judicial redress or administrative handling] shall be available and whether to enable the courts or administrative authorities to require prior recourse to other established means of dealing with complaints, including those referred to in Article 5.[15]

Article 5 provides the following:

> This Directive does not exclude the voluntary control of misleading advertising by self-regulatory bodies and recourse to such bodies by the persons

or organizations referred to in Article 4 if proceedings before such bodies are in addition to the court or administrative proceedings referred to in that Article.[16]

Article 6 calls for reversal of burden of proof.[17] In short it requires the advertiser to furnish evidence as to the accuracy of factual claims in advertising, if appropriate in light of the circumstances of the case, and confers power on the court or administrative authority to consider factual claims as inaccurate if said evidence is not furnished or is found insufficient.

Article 7 establishes the directive as a minimum standard for regulation of misleading advertising and does not preclude member states from retaining or adopting provisions with a view to ensuring more extensive protection for all concerned.

Finally, articles 8 and 9 address the directive to member states and require compliance by October 1, 1986, at the latest. Because of the number of changes required in certain regulatory systems and the slowness in parliamentary procedures, this deadline was extended to 1989. As of April 1989, some member countries had still not taken the necessary measures to implement the directive. At this point the EC has the possibility to resort to legal action to further implementation. The directive is implemented by regulations under section 2 (2) of the European Communities Act, 1972.

Directive on Product Liability

Generally, with few exceptions, the Directive on Product Liability conforms to the concepts accepted in the European Council Convention. This directive adopts the principle of strict liability for the community and holds producers and other suppliers liable for damages caused by product defects.[18] The directive became effective in August 1988. It has advanced liability legislation in Europe toward the strict liability not yet widely accepted in many legal systems, and it makes a clear link between advertising and product liability, presently blurred in national legislation. It holds the producers, importers, and any persons who, by putting their names, trademarks, or other distinguishing features on the article, represent themselves liable for damage caused by a defect in the article, whether or not they knew or could have known of the defect.

The link between liability and advertising is established in the definition of defect:

> A product is defective when, *being used for the purpose it was apparently intended*, it does not provide for persons or property and safety which a person is entitled to expect, *taking into account all the circumstances, including its presentation and the time at which it was put into circulation.*[19]

The concept of defect includes the integrity of warnings and instructions present and the absence thereof. Inadequate information, deceptive presentation, or misleading advertising can give rise to product defect if it misleads consumers' expectations about the product and causes harm.

Harmonization of National Laws

Before the provisions of the directives can be implemented, much work will have to be done to harmonize the various laws of the member nations. In practice harmonizing will consist of bringing national laws into conformity with minimum standards to avoid undesirable distortions in commerce and to protect the public welfare. In the case of misleading advertising, the directive establishes alternative systems for enforcing regulations. Countries with rules stricter than those imposed in the directive will continue to impose their laws nationally, while countries whose legislation is less stringent than the provisions established by the directive are required to strengthen their systems. Advertising practices consistent with the directives are held to be lawful throughout the European Community.

Many of the distinctions among various regulatory systems will continue to exist. In certain broad areas, however, the directives will bridge the gap heretofore created by national idiosyncracies. The directives are limited, however, only to the overall area of misleading advertising and product liability. Many more regulations exist outside the scope of these directives. Therefore, it is important to understand the basics of the individual systems as well as the provisions of the directives. The following sections review the basics of the regulatory systems of the United Kingdom, France, and the Scandinavian countries as representative of the three types of regulatory systems harmonized in the EC Directive on Misleading Advertising.

The United Kingdom

The British advertising regulatory regime is a unique combination of case law, statutory law, and self-regulation (see table 7–2). It differs from the regulatory systems of continental Europe and the United States in two major respects: (1) in the absence of general statutory laws prohibiting misleading and unfair advertising and (2) in the central role of voluntary self-regulation in the control of specific advertising abuses. These distinctions reflect the unique legal heritage of the United Kingdom.[20]

English law, fashioned in its formative years by the courts of Westminster and Chancery, originated as so-called judge-made law—also referred to as common law or case law. Until the end of the nineteenth century, statutory law was only a secondary source of law. Today, statutory law holds a primary position in the system and provides the framework for legal order in broad areas of socioeconomic relations, including advertising and economic pol-

Table 7-2
Regulatory Profile: United Kingdom

Government:	Constitutional monarchy; parliamentary system; multiparty, pluralist/elitist democracy
Politico-economic ideology:	Constitutionalism/legalism; capitalism; social welfarism
Economic system:	Mixed free enterprise with declining public ownership and regulation
Legal system:	English common law buttressed by statutory law
Investment policy:	Liberal; merging with European Community policy
Ad regulation:	Strict; heavy reliance on self-regulation
Ad expenditure:	10.3 billion; per capita: $180; %GNP: 1.7
Consumer market:	Mature; reaching saturation for many products
Social indicators:	
Population:	57 million
Urbanization:	92%
Per capita income:	$8,900
Language:	English
Class structure:	Predominant middle class
Life expectancy:	72–78 years
Literacy:	99%

icies, substantive matters largely external to traditional case law. However, the permeation of the legislative environment by common-law tradition gives rise to unique features in statutory laws.

In the legislative process, the formulation of statutes is in style, form, and terminology consistent with the language of common law. Unlike their counterparts on the Continent, British legislators shun so-called general principles of law, or formulations of behavioral norms. Instead, British legislation is replete with legal definitions and detailed prescriptions. How it actually is applied is established by a number of procedural rules. There are many acknowledged gaps in the laws left to be filled by rules emerging from court cases. For this reason British statutory law has been characterized as open-ended, left to be interpreted and developed as judges apply law to each particular case. The discretion of the judges, however, is restrained by expectations of Parliament that statutory law should be applied in the spirit of legislative intent.[21]

Advertising law is no exception to these generalities on statutory law. Particularly striking are the absences of the general principles of unfair competition and misleading advertising. However, rules restricting acts of either nature emerge in court decisions. Laws related to advertising make explicit the rights of and limits on the advertiser in specific circumstances. This approach contrasts with that of civil-code countries, where it is the duty of the courts to deduce the advertiser's precise legal obligation from considerations of general principle—regardless of the circumstances of the case. According to Peter Thomson, who served as director of Britain's Advertising Standards Authority:

> The gain in certainty the British approach offers, however, can be offset by inconvenience to the advertiser who wishes to know the full extent of his obligations and to do so must piece it together from a wide variety of sources, not all of which, to the uninitiated, have any immediate apparent relation to the advertising business.[22]

Over the years statutory laws relevant to advertising have accumulated. Today, they outweigh case law as the strongest constraints on advertising. Many of the statutory laws, however, embody common-law rules or supplant and build upon them. Likewise, contemporary case law is continually developing and interpreting existing statutory laws. Thus, both common law and case law must be taken into account in the broad picture of British regulation. Highlights of the British regime are summarized in the following discussion.

Common Law

The advertising regulatory system grew from a common-law base, which proscribes the commercial exploitation of individuals without their permission. Under the common law of contract, advertising may be established as either an *offer* or an *invitation to treat*, depending on the facts of a case. An invitation to treat, by display or advertisement, is merely a solicitation of negotiations in hope that an acceptance might materialize. The invitation to treat is distinct from an offer, which, when accepted, constitutes a contract. For an advertisement to constitute an offer (capable of acceptance and thus presenting the advertiser with a binding contract), it must spell out a promise in unambiguous terms. The classic case is *Carlill v. Carbolic Smoke Ball Co.*[23]

Rules in regard to misrepresentation of facts in advertisements also are found in common law, according to which the buyer's basic remedy is to have the contract set aside. A distinction is made, however, between innocent misrepresentation and fraudulent misrepresentation, for which damages may be exacted. An exception to misrepresentation is made for puffing. Purchasers are expected to be capable of exercising reasonable judgment and discrimination, and they cannot complain merely because their own opinion of the goods may fall far below that of the seller. Wide latitude has been given to sellers to extol the qualities of their goods, as long as advertisers confine themselves to general praise of goods.[24] A statement ceases to be a puff and becomes a misrepresentation when it assumes the guise of a credible statement of fact.[25]

Other important common-law rules emerging during the 1700s and 1800s concerned endorsements, passing off, and certain acts of unfair competition, including comparison advertising. The unauthorized use of names and faces in endorsements has given rise to suits for defamation, violation of property rights, violation of privacy, nervous shock, or breach of confidence. The temptation to push one's goods off as another's was thwarted when the courts ruled the following: "One man has no right to put off his goods for sale as the goods of a rival trader; and he cannot, therefore, be allowed to use names, marks, letters or other indicia by which he may induce purchasers to believe that the goods which he is selling are the manufacture of another person."[26,27]

In general the courts have recognized the rights of advertisers to praise their own wares and claim superiority for them over those of rivals. However, certain forms of comparative advertising may give rise to actions for slander of goods. Statements involving derogatory statements of fact about a competitor's goods risk such action. The general disposition of the law summed up by British legal scholar, L.J. Hodson is "Comparison—yes, but disparagement—no."[28] Thus, when an advertiser makes detailed and untrue disparagement about another's goods, that advertiser is fair game for an action for slander of goods.

Statutory Law

There are more than one hundred diverse statutory acts, regulations, and orders with some relevance to the practice of advertising in the United Kingdom.[29] Two-thirds of them have been adopted since World War II, and more than half since 1960.

However, many statutory laws affecting advertising already existed prior to 1900. One of the earliest recorded statutes in the modern period is the Sunday Observance Act, which made it an offense to advertise or cause to be advertised "any publick entertainment or amusement or any publick meeting for debating on any subject . . . on the Lord's Day, to which persons are to be admitted by the payment of money or by tickets sold for money."[30] The act was modified in the Sunday Entertainments Act of 1932.[31]

Many of the earlier laws were aimed at preventing certain acts and abuses. They included vagrancy acts of 1824 and 1832, which were concerned with obscene advertising and fortune tellers. The Indecent Advertisements Act (1889) was aimed at ads relating to sexually communicable diseases and complaints, while the early trade marks acts (1875, 1883, 1888, and 1905) defined trademarks and gave protection to users. Several early acts dealt with the media of the time: billboards, billposters, noisemakers, and sandwich boardmen.[32] The protection of the landscape from obtrusive advertising was the purpose of the Advertisement Regulation Act of 1907.[33]

For ease of analysis, Peter Thomson has classified British advertising laws into three broad categories.[34] The first and largest group consists of public laws setting out obligations of advertisers vis-à-vis the state. Violators are prosecuted by local authorities appointed by the state and if convicted face criminal sanctions. Statutory examples include the Trade Descriptions Act of 1968, The Consumer Protection Act of 1987, and laws in respect to the advertising of specific products, such as foods and medicines.

The second group consists of private or civil laws whereby Parliament establishes rights and obligations between different groups of citizens. Violations of these laws gives rise to civil suits between private parties. The Misrepresentation Act of 1967 and the Trade Marks Act of 1938 are examples.

The third group consists of administrative laws establishing and empowering regulatory bodies to supervise and enforce advertising laws. A principal example is the Fair Trading Act of 1973. The principal statutory laws affecting advertising are summarized in the following paragraphs.

Group 1: Public Laws with Criminal Sanctions. The Trade Descriptions Act of 1968 is the most comprehensive public law aimed at advertising.[35] It took effect in November 1968, replacing and expanding the Merchandise Marks Act of 1887, which dealt with misdescription of goods. The aim of the Trade Descriptions Act is to ensure truth in advertising about goods, prices, and services.[36] The act makes it a criminal offense to apply false trade descriptions to goods, to supply or offer to supply any goods with a false description, and to give certain kinds of false indications about the price of goods. The section of the act dealing with misleading prices has recently been superceded in the Consumer Protection Act of 1987 which devotes part III to proscriptions in matters of price information.[37]

Sections 7–10 of the act give the Department of Trade and Industry authority to make orders defining trade terms and labeling and to require the display and provision of such information. The department is required to consult with concerned organizations in carrying out this function.[38]

A trade description is an indication, direct or indirect, by any means, of a specified number of matters listed in the act. Included are quantity, size, or gauge; methods of production; fitness for purpose; other physical characteristics; and information on testing, approval, places, dates and other history.[39] To commit an offense, the indication must be false to a material degree: "A quite insignificant inaccuracy is not enough."[40] The act does not cover statements of opinion on the character of a puff. According to the Malony Report, an accepted standard for interpreting the Trade Descriptions Act, the prosecution's proof of falsity to a material degree is determined by whether the description would be fairly regarded as inducing a puchase.[41]

The Trade Descriptions Act pertains only to stated factual information specified in the act.[42] The act does not apply to claims with ambiguous contents, claims relating to the value of merchandise, claims relating to unspecified product performance, claims relating to the identity of the supplier (not the manufacturer), or claims relating to the availability of goods.[43]

A criminal offense is committed whether the false description is made deliberately or innocently. The act does not require traders and manufacturers to give information about their goods and only deals with their legal positions when they do so. Unlike U.S. law, under the act the omission of information is not a criminal offense.

The state has the authority to prosecute violations of the act and delegates this authority to the local weights and measures authorities. The local authorities have powers of entry, inspection, and seizure. Private citizens have the right to bring cases to the attention of the local authorities, who in turn have the discretion to determine whether or not to prosecute. Under the provisions of the Powers of Criminal Courts Act of 1973, consumers can recover for damages under orders from the criminal court following conviction under the Trade Descriptions Act.[44]

A purchase is not necessary, nor is damage required, in order to prosecute. Only in rare cases has a private individual gone to court as a plaintiff for violation of this act. According to R.G. Lawson, an expert on British advertising law, this has occurred only once.[45]

In addition to the Trade Descriptions Act, numerous special acts provide special instructions and restrictions on the advertising of such items as pharmaceuticals, food, cigarettes, and alcoholic beverages. For example, the promotion of medicines to the public is controlled under the Medicines (Labelling and Advertising to the Public) Regulations of 1978.[46] The advertising of prescription drugs to the public is forbidden.[47]

Important restrictions are imposed on the advertising of foods by section 6 of the Food Act of 1984.[48] Section 6 prohibits the use of an advertisement that falsely describes a food or misleads as to its nature, substance, or quality, including its nutritional or dietary value. In addition, multiple regulations have been passed affecting the advertising of specific foodstuffs.[49]

These various acts and regulations are administered by different departments. For example, central government responsibility for advertising food falls to the Ministry of Agriculture, Fisheries, and Food; for medicines to the Department of Health and Social Security.[50] All these regulations have territorial application. No explicit mention in the laws and regulations is made concerning advertisements originating outside the territorial limits of the country and received in the United Kingdom, as is the case in French legislation.

Group 2: Laws Establishing Civil Responsibilities. A prime example in the second group of laws, laws establishing civil responsibilities, is the Misrepresentation Act of 1967.[51] The act is based largely on common-law rules that are virtually codified in this statutory law.

The act gives a purchaser who has been misled into contracts by reliance on inaccurate statements the right to sue the advertiser in a civil action for breach of contract or for tort of negligence or deceit.

A misrepresentation is defined as "a false statement of a material fact made by one party to the contract or his agent which induces the other party to enter into the contract."[52] Misrepresentations may be innocent, fraudulent, or negligent. Consistent with the common law of contract, the advertising misrepresentation must be found to be an offer rather than a mere invitation to treat. As in the case of the Trade Descriptions Act, the court must draw the line between a puff, or opinion, and a material fact.

This act provides the link between civil liability and responsibility to the general public. When the inducement to enter into a contract derives from a third party, as is the normal commercial case, the plaintiff has a remedy through the court's construction of a collateral contract. According to Lawson, the necessity for the collateral contract lies in the fact that a statement or representation may induce a contract to be made with a third party. If the representation is unsound, under the privity principle, no action lies against the other party to the contract, and the representor is liable only if consideration can be shown to have moved between him and the injured party. To give the latter party a means of redress against the advertiser, the collateral contract was construed.[53] If the misrepresentation is either negligent or fraudulent, the innocent party also would have the right to resort to common-law actions for negligence or tort of deceit. In this case the burden of the proof would be on the plaintiff.

Group 3: Laws Establishing Administrative Responsibilities. Two examples of the third group of advertising laws are the Independent Broadcasting Authority Act of 1973 and the Fair Trading Act of 1973.[54,55] The former act established the Independent Broadcasting Authority (IBA), which has the responsibility to ensure that broadcast commercials conform to its Code of Standards and Practice.[56] This task is accomplished through a system of censorship, a job delegated to the ITV Association. The 1973 act was superseded by the Broadcasting Act of 1981.[57]

The Fair Trading Act of 1973 established a director general of fair trading to oversee the impact of current trading and commercial practices on consumers' interests and to recommend government action when necessary.[58] This office also makes reports on the conduct of advertising and the efficacy of self-regulation. The responsibilities of the director general are being expanded as a result of the adoption of the EEC Directive on Misleading Advertising. Recently, the director general has been given power to act through the courts in cases of misleading advertising in order to bring the British system into line with the European Community directive.

Self-Regulation

The centerpiece of the British scheme is the self-regulatory system working in harmony with common and statutory laws in an informal public/private process to regulate advertising. Both the law and self-regulation seek to confront the fundamental issues of honesty and fairness in advertising content. Most complaints about advertising content, however, are generally directed, in the first instance, to the nongovernmental Advertising Standards Authority or Independent Broadcasting Authority. The courts and the law provide legally enforceable alternatives when self-restraint does not succeed or when the abuse is beyond the scope of self-regulation. The scope of the law differs to some extent from the scope of the self-regulatory system. Self-regulation focuses principally on the content of advertisements, while the law has a much wider scope, including the behavior of the advertisers and agencies.

The core of the self-regulatory system is the British Code of Advertising Practice (BCAP), modeled on the ICC International Code of Advertising Practice (ICAP).[59] The BCAP has undergone continual scrutiny and amendment since its introduction in 1962. The BCAP, however, goes beyond the ICAP principles to provide guidance on the practical adoption of these principles in the particular circumstances of advertising in the United Kingdom. The BCAP covers all media advertising except broadcast commercial advertising (which is subject to a separate but closely related code administered by the Independent Broadcasting Authority). The BCAP also does not cover advertisements aimed outside the United Kingdom.

The BCAP establishes general rules emphasizing honesty, decency, legality, and truthfulness; responsibility to consumers and society; and principles of fair competition. Specific rules are set for various categories of advertisements, including health claims (especially for pharmaceuticals and related products), advertisements aimed at children, weight loss, hair and scalp products, and vitamins and minerals. Special appendixes treat the advertising of cigarettes and alcohol.

The administrative system of the BCAP is complex. It consists of (a) advertisers and (b) agencies. Related trade associations also play an important role. The Committee of Advertising Practice (CAP) coordinates the executive actions of the system. It is made up of representatives from the ad industry and trade associations. The system is capped by the Advertising Standards Authority (ASA).

The ASA is an independent body, financed by a surcharge on display advertising. The ASA has an independent chair, appointed after consultation with the Department of Trade and Industry. The chair then appoints the members of the ASA's council, at least half of which must be independent of the advertising business. The authority investigates complaints about advertising and publishes monthly case reports. In a typical annual report, the chair of the ASA may report that as many as four or five advertisements each week run the risk of being in breach of the BCAP.[60] A typical monthly report records about six hundred complaints, of which about one quarter require investigation. An illustration of the treatment of a complaint in a report is as follows:

BRITISH VINEGARS LTD.

Basis of Complaint: A member of the public objected to a national press advertisement which had the heading "AT LAST CHOLESTEROL-FREE OIL" and which stated "Dufrais Pure Grapeseed Oil is unique. It's entirely free from Cholesterol, high in Polyunsaturates and rich in Vitamin E." The complainant pointed out that other oils currently available on the market were cholesterol free, high in polyunsaturated fat and rich in Vitamin E.

Conclusion: Complaint upheld. The advertisers stated that as far as they could ascertain, Dufrais grapeseed oil was the only oil on the market which contained this particular combination of constituents and they submitted a review on popular oils currently available to support this. They also provided technical data which indicated the levels of cholesterol, polyunsaturates and Vitamin E found in the oil. The authority sought independent expert advice and concluded that neither the report nor the date conclusively supported the claim that the oil was "unique" and the advertisers were requested to remove the claim until such time as it could be fully supported.[61]

As a complement to statutory controls, the government has found that self-regulation offers advantages in terms of efficacy, flexibility, and economy. As an alternative to criminal law in claims concerning advertising, self-regulation is more expedient. The work load of the local courts is already excessive, causing inordinate delays. Moreover, the courts confront other obstacles. There is no centralized body of case law from which the lower courts may draw, and the burden of proof of an abuse is on the prosecutor.

The criticism of partiality often leveled at self-regulation is not valid for the United Kingdom. This is demonstrated in the record of advertising control. In addition, the ASA's constitution and system of financing mean that it is more removed from industry influence than the more common form of voluntary regulating codes—a trade association enforcing a code of practice upon its members. Moreover, operating on a nonstatutory basis, the United Kingdom's self-regulatory system can maintain more exacting standards than those that, in practice, an official, mindful of statutory limitations, could maintain.[62]

The esteem placed on self-regulation by the British government is reflected in the British position in the negotiations on the European Community directive. These negotiations were prolonged, as the United Kingdom sought compromise in the directive to protect its system of advertising regulation and, in particular, the role of self-regulation. This was achieved. However, because the directive still requires the establishment of either a legal or administrative authority with power to prohibit and enforce prohibitions on misleading advertising in each member state, certain adjustments must be made in the British system. The United Kingdom has agreed to empower the director general of fair trading with this authority. According to the Consultation Document About Implementation of the EC Directive on Misleading Advertising:

> In cases where [the Director General] sees such measures to be necessary, taking into account all the interests involved and in particular the public interest, to institute proceedings in the High Court for an order prohibiting misleading advertising. . . . he will be entitled to refer a complainant to other established means of delaying with complaints about misleading advertising (except on radio and TV already covered under statutory law and administrative authority).[63]

Thus, the United Kingdom's arrangement to bring its system into conformity with the directive is the institution of an injunctive procedure. In it the director general of fair trading will be able to obtain court orders preventing publication of advertisements likely to deceive or mislead. The working party of the Department of Trade, suggesting this innovation, has seen such power as a reinforcement to the self-regulatory system of control, rather than as a substitute for it.

The weight attached to self-regulation in no way weakens the British regulatory regime in the eyes of the business world. The British system is considered the most restrictive among the systems of major free-market countries by marketing executives surveyed by the International Advertising Association.[64] Self-regulatory systems on the British model, governed by an independent standards authority, have been established in developing Commonwealth countries, including Singapore, Malaysia, India, and Nigeria.

Advertising and Liability

Advertising as a predicate for product liability is uncommon in the United Kingdom. The privity requirement blocks any action except by direct purchaser under contract. An action for deceit founded upon the fraudulent statement of a seller as to the properties of the product to be sold may, of course, lead to recovery for product damage. Such cases are few and far between, with the classic case being *Langridge v. Levy.*[65]

The case centered on the purchase of a gun from the defendant, who falsely and fraudulently warranted the gun to have been made in a certain place and to be of certain safe quality. The defendant was found guilty of breach of duty and of willful deceit, negligence, and improper conduct in that the gun was not made in the specified location and was unsafe and of inferior quality. The defendant at the time had full knowledge and notice of the fraudulent nature of his warranty, and the plaintiff, in reliance on the warranty, employed the gun. The gun exploded, causing the plaintiff to be deprived forever of the use of his hand.[66]

Under administrative law, a legal remedy for defective advertising is offered in the Misrepresentation Act of 1967, described earlier.[67] Very few relevant advertising/product liability cases have been tried under this act thus far.

Under the traditional liability regime, it has been difficult for anyone other than a direct buyer to seek compensation for harm, injury, or loss from products whose purchase and use was based on the consumer's reliance on advertising claims about the product. With the implementation of the EEC Directive on Product Liability, the United Kingdom has been obliged to adopt a system of strict liability. The EC Directive Prescriptions were incorporated in the Consumer Protection Act of 1987. Under the new system information defects in product presentation and marketing, for example, inadequate warnings and instructions for product use, will be covered. Also, as mentioned earlier, under the Powers of Criminal Courts Act of 1973 consumers can recover for damages under orders from the criminal court following conviction under the Trade Descriptions Act.

Other Developed Commonwealth Countries and South Africa

Many countries, members of the British Commonwealth of Nations, have adopted political and legal systems patterned on the English system. Industrialized Commonwealth countries including Canada, Australia, and New Zealand have also adapted many aspects of the British advertising regulatory scheme to their national situations (see table 7–3). South Africa, which left the British Commonwealth in 1961, is included in this group of countries because its legal system and its advertising regulatory environment fits appropriately into this group of countries.

There is considerable foreign agency involvement in all four countries (see table 2–5). Billings of foreign agencies are equivalent to 20 percent of total advertising expenditure in Canada, 40 percent in South Africa, and over 50 percent in Australia and New Zealand (see figure 7–4). Per capita expenditures range from $28 in South Africa to about $200 in Canada (see figure 7–5). Media and non-measured media distribution of advertising expenditure in these countries are compared in figure 7–6. Advertising is as much an integral part of the mass market systems of these countries as is the case in all industrialized market economy countries.

Table 7–3
Regulatory Profile: Other Developed Countries

Countries:	Australia, Canada, New Zealand, and South Africa
Government:	Parliamentary systems, multiparty, pluralist/elitist democracies; common allegiance to British Crown (except South Africa which withdrew from Commonwealth in 1961)
Politico-economic ideologies:	Constitutionalism/legalism; capitalism; social welfarism
Economic system:	Mixed free enterprise
Legal system:	Common law and statutory law
Investment policy:	Liberal
Ad regulation:	Moderate to strict, heavy reliance on self-regulation (except New Zealand)
Ad expenditure:	Canada $5B, Australia $3B, South Africa $.9B, New Zealand $.5B; Per capita: $164 to $212 (except South Africa $27); %GNP 1.4 (Canada and South Africa) to 2 New Zealand
Consumer market:	Mature (South Africa has mature European market)
Social indicators:	
Population:	South Africa: 33 million (18% white, 68% black, 12% other); Canada: 25 million; Australia: 16 million; New Zealand: 3 million
Urbanization:	80% (South Africa: 56%)
Per capita income:	Range $7,500–$14,000 (South Africa: $1850)
Language:	Australia, New Zealand: English; Canada: English and French; South Africa: Afrikaans, English and Bantu
Class structure:	Predominantly middle class; (South Africa: majority low income black)
Life expectancy:	77–80 years (South Africa: 56 for blacks, 77 for whites)
Literacy:	50%/90% (South Africa: blacks 50%)

All these countries have central self-regulatory bodies somewhat comparable with the British Advertising Standards Authority except New Zealand, which has established a less extensive system of voluntary restraints.

Although advertising in Canada is closely tied to the U.S. industry, the regulatory system is independent. A pioneer in self-regulation, Canada established a system in 1957. Today, the Advertising Standards Council (ASC) is the self-regulatory arm of the Canadian Advertising Foundation (CAF). The ASC cooperates with the government. General laws and product and media specific rules are enforced and complaints are often lodged across the U.S/Canada border where controls are comparatively less stringent. The CAF is renowned for innovation in response to social issues. It was first to outline educational guidelines for sex-role stereotyping and to establish a Broadcast Code for Advertising to Children, which it jointly administers with the federal government.

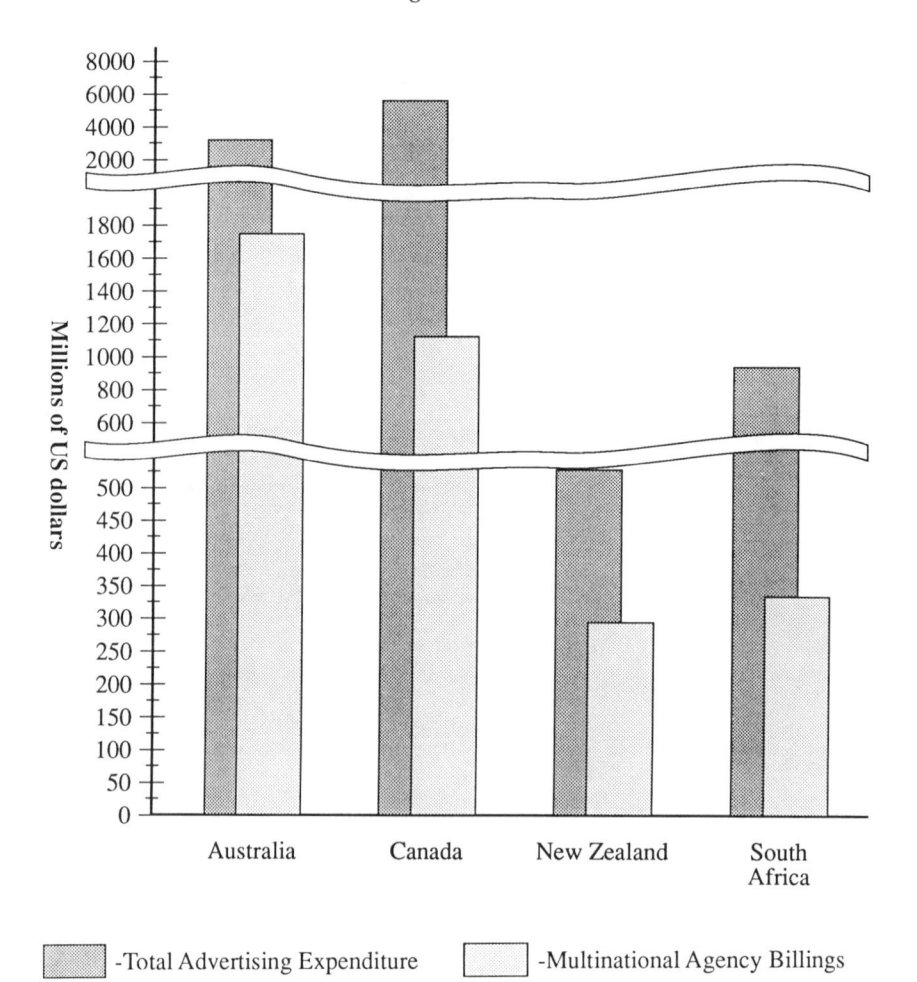

[Figure: bar chart with y-axis "Millions of US dollars" (broken scale), x-axis countries: Australia, Canada, New Zealand, South Africa; bars showing Total Advertising Expenditure and Multinational Agency Billings]

-Total Advertising Expenditure   -Multinational Agency Billings

Source: derived from *World Advertising Expenditure*, 1987, 22nd ed., Starch INRA Hooper, Inc., in cooperation with IAA; "Foreign Agency Report," *Advertising Age*, 9 May 1988.

Figure 7–4. Gross Multinational Agency Billings and Total Advertising Expenditure in Australia, Canada, New Zealand, and South Africa, 1987

There are many Federal and Provincial Acts and Regulations that pertain to advertising and the promotion and marketing of specific products. The Departments of Consumer and Corporate Affairs and Health and Welfare are two of the government bodies primarily concerned with advertising regulation. Significant legislation includes the Combines Investigation Act and the

Europe: By Parts and Community • 129

[Figure: bar chart with broken y-axis showing Per Capita GNP and Per Capita Advertising Expenditure for Australia, Canada, New Zealand, and South Africa; y-axis in US dollars]

■ -Per Capita GNP   □ Per Capita Advertising Expenditure

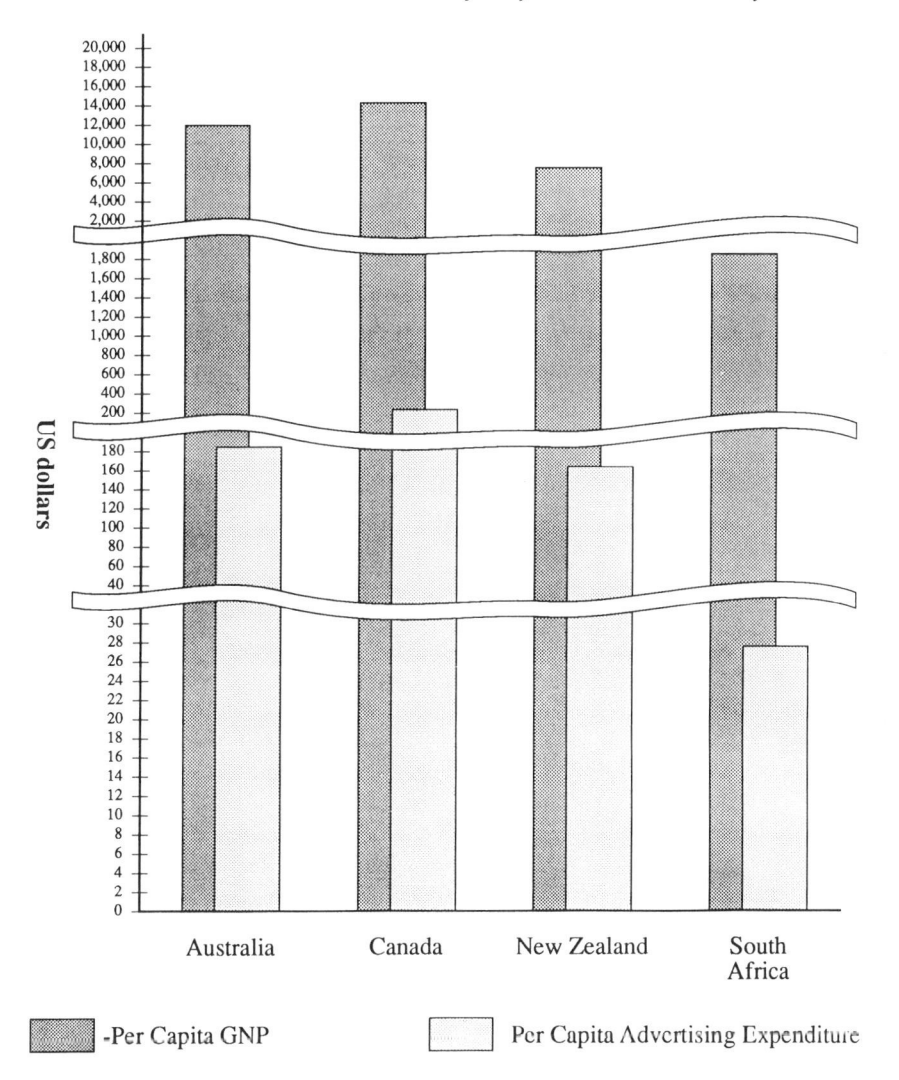

Source: derived from *World Advertising Expenditure, 1987*, 22nd ed., Starch INRA Hooper, Inc., in cooperation with IAA; *World Development Report, 1988,* World Bank.

Figure 7–5. Per Capita Advertising Expenditure and Per Capita GNP in Australia, Canada, New Zealand, and South Africa, 1986/87

Trade Marks Act, which generally forbid false and misleading advertising; more specific rules in respect to specific product advertising are specified in the Foods and Drug Act and the Consumer Packaging and Labeling Act. Broadcast Regulations of the Broadcasting Act require that advertisements for

Australia

- 48%
- 34%
- 9%
- 9%

Canada

- 36%
- 31%
- 17%
- 9%
- 7%

New Zealand

- 53%
- 27%
- 12%
- 7%

South Africa

- 64%
- 32%
- 4%

☐ -Print ☐ -T.V. ☐ -Radio ☐ -Other ☐ -Non-measured Media

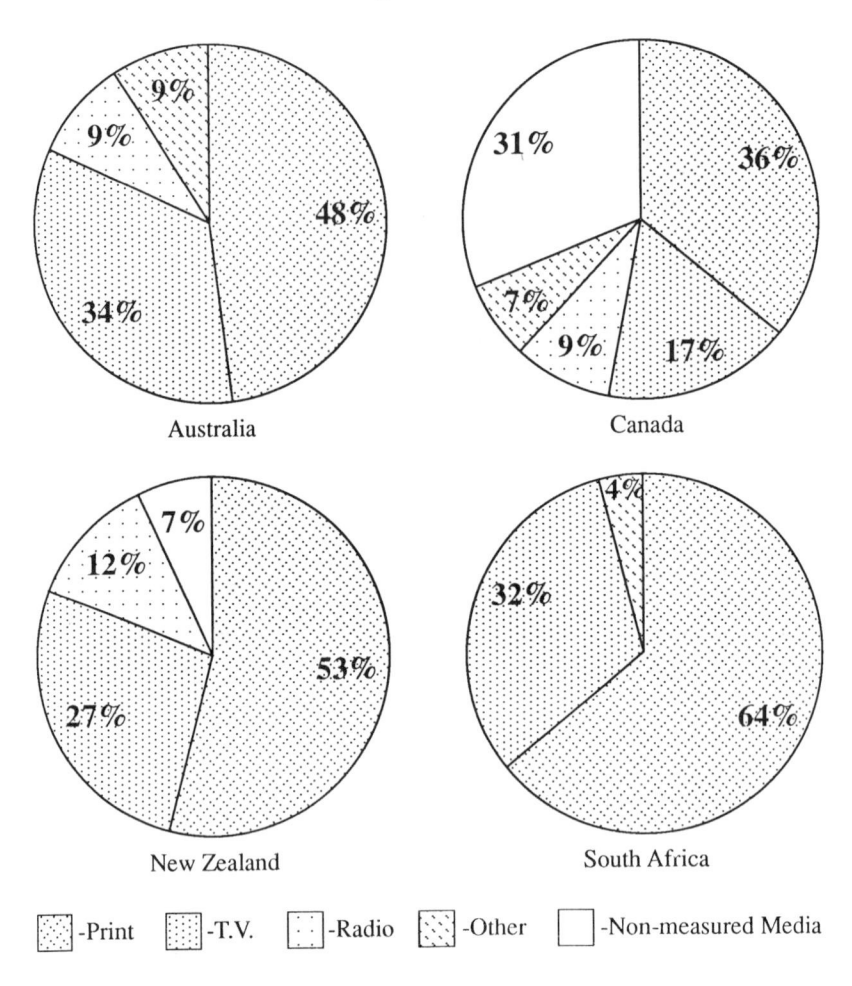

Source: derived from *World Advertising Expenditure,* 1986, 21st ed., Starch INRA Hooper, Inc., in cooperation with IAA.

Figure 7–6. Advertising Expenditure by Media and Non-measured Media in Australia, Canada, New Zealand, and South Africa (percentage shares)

foods or drugs be approved by the Minister of Consumer and Corporate Affairs and by a representative of the Canadian Radio-Television and Telecommunications Commission before they can be aired on radio or television.[68]

Self-regulation and government legislation exercise moderate control over the advertising industry in Australia. Self-regulation is the centerpiece of the system. The system has evolved from the cooperative efforts of the media, advertisers, and agencies. A number of regulatory bodies oversee the enforcement of the above codes along with a range of systems and procedures that are constantly being refined and improved. The Advertising Standards Council was established in 1974. It provides direct public access and involvement in complaints of violations of a whole system of codes. It is also concerned with interpreting advertising industry ethics and standards. The Media Council of Australia is responsible for accreditation of all advertising agencies and is the sourse of all self-regulatory codes. These Councils are complemented by the Australian Media Accreditation Authority, which is responsible for enforcing agency adherence to the Codes and to strict financial standards. Advertising codes in effect include the Advertising Code of Ethics, the Therapeutic Advertising Code, the Cigarette Advertising Code, and the Slimming Advertising Code.

In addition, advertising is regulated by various federal and state government legislation. The Trade Practices Commission is the federal government authority that oversees the strict adherence of the industry to government legislation. The Commission retains the power to undertake criminal proceedings against organizations in breech of federal legislation.

Advertising is also subject to the standards and conditions imposed by the Australian Broadcasting Tribunal. Each arm of the media maintains a clearance body that authorizes advertisements before publication or transmission.[69]

Self-regulation is the principal control on advertising in South Africa. A central self-regulatory body, the Advertising Standards Authority (ASA), was established in 1968. The Code of the Authority, to which constituent bodies adhere, is modeled on the codes of the International Chamber of Commerce and the British Advertising Standards Authority. Although there are many similarities between the South African system and that of the United Kingdom, there are also notable differences. Unlike the codes of other countries in the Western world, the South African Code of Advertising Practice covers all product and service advertising in whatever medium. In assessing an advertisement's conformity to the terms of the Code, the primary test is that of the probable impact of the advertisement as a whole on those who are likely to see it or to hear it. Where an impression is in doubt, the ASA may call for a consumer reaction test by independent research.

Government regulation is not extensive. Government departments do exercise control over advertising of certain products, for example medicines, but even in these cases the responsibility is mainly delegated to self-regulatory bodies. Nevertheless, advertisers should be aware of at least twenty-two acts of Parliament that are relevant to advertising. Among the most important are: Medicines and Related Substances Act (Act 101 of 1965), Credit Agreements Act (Act 75 of 1980), Foodstuffs Cosmetics and Disinfectants Act (Act 54 of

1972), Merchandise Marks Act (Act 17 of 1941), Price Control Act (Act 25 of 1964, amended 1984), and the Business Practices Act. Moreover, television does not allow advertising of alcoholic beverages other than beer or wine. The cigarette advertisers decided voluntarily to abstain from advertising cigarettes on television.[70]

France

In civil-code countries, of which France is a leading example, the advertising regulatory regime draws on law as contained in the code as well as on statutory law enacted as legislation or promulgated as governmental decrees (see table 7–4). For the most part, the civil-law codes of the European countries are systematic and comprehensive in their treatment of specific branches of law. They are not, however, exhaustive statements of law on any single subject. No code in any civil-law system has yet been fully integrated to contain all provisions of the substantive law relating to a given area. Many codes deal briefly or not at all with some subjects. The French code is no exception.

Because the Napoleonic code had widespread influence in Europe and elsewhere, the French legal system has many points in common with those in the other civil code countries in Europe. The backbone of the advertising regulatory regime is the French legal system. In France, as in West Germany and other civil-code countries on the Continent, the legislature and the administration protect the integrity of advertising. Both code law and statutory law are applicable to advertising. In French code law, advertising abuse may fall under provisions concerned with either the principles of unfair competition (*concurrence déloyale*) or deception or misleading advertising (*publicité mensongère*). Statutory laws, drafted since the beginning of the century, have built on the principles elaborated in the code and are both general and specific.

The French regulatory system serves as a model for other civil-code countries, notably former colonial countries. The influence of the French system also is evident in many of the provisions of the European Communties' Directive on Misleading Advertising. The directive reflects the main principles operative in the French system (for example, reversal of burden of proof, criteria of deception, and control through direct legal action).

In France advertising falls under certain articles in the civil and penal codes and has been strongly treated in statutory law. Additional sources of control are self-regulation and administrative regulations of various sorts. The law-making role of the judiciary is less clear in France as compared with the United Kingdom. The French courts, however, play a definite role in interpreting and applying the code and statutory law. Judgments are not considered a formal source of law, even though judges resort to previous cases for legal precedent. Together, government codes and statutes, administrative

Table 7-4
Regulatory Profile: France

Government:	Republic; presidential/parliamentary system; multiparty, pluralist/elitist/popular democracy
Politico-economic ideology:	Constitutionalism/legalism; social democracy; capitalism/socialism
Economic system:	Mixed free and state enterprise with significant public regulation
Legal system:	Romano-Germanic civil code buttressed by statutory and administrative law
Investment policy:	Relatively liberal; European Community policy
Ad regulation:	Significant government control; special controls on foreign advertising
Ad expenditure:	6.7 billion; per capita: $121; %GNP: .9
Consumer market:	Mature
Social indicators:	
Population:	55 million
Urbanization:	81%
Per capita income:	$10,700
Language:	French
Class structure:	Predominant middle class
Life expectancy:	74–80 years
Literacy:	99%

rules, and self-regulation combine to form a regulatory system that is general and specific concerning language, product, and media.

General Laws

Under code and administrative law, false advertising can be a civil and/or criminal offense. As a civil offense, the violation is usually treated as concurrence déloyale (unfair competition). As a criminal offense, it falls under the concept *publicité mensongère et trompeuse* (misleading advertising).

Unfair Competition. The theory of unfair competition is based on commercial usage. Unfair competition occurs in the course of business when a merchant commits a fault with the potential for causing harm to a competitor or an act with the intention of turning away the latter's customers.[71] Liability for unfair competition is jurisdictionally based on article 1382 of the French civil code, which states that any human act causing injury or damage to another is liable for compensation.[72] Unfair competition is classified as a tort, and, generally, liability is established regardless of whether the tort was deliberately or innocently perpetrated. A presumption of damage must be shown.

In advertising, unfair competition comes in two forms: (1) creating confusion or the risk of confusion between two houses of commerce and (2) denigration, including some aspects of comparative advertising. Although the theory of unfair advertising has evolved with the objective of protecting business and not the consumer, consumers often may benefit from the effects of its application insofar as it eliminates false, misleading, or confusing claims, such as imitation of advertising messages. Prosecution in cases of disparagement, however, may also work against consumers' interest in that consumers stand to lose relevant product information generated by comparison advertising, classified as disparagement. Today, certain forms of comparative advertising are becoming acceptable.

The French code concept of unfair competition has had extraterritorial application even though, in principle, French law operates on the basis of territoriality. The single-enterprise theory was applied in *Syndicat du Commerce des vins de Champagne c. Ackerman-Laurance*.[73] The French court decided that the British firm Ackerman-Laurance, in reality a subsidiary of the French firm of the same name established in Saumur, did not have the right to advertise its Saumur wine in England using the phrase, "finest champaign—imported from Saumur." The argument was that as a result of possible travel of British citizens in France or possible distribution of British newspapers in France, French consumers could confuse wine from the region of Champagne with wine from Saumur, hence damaging the reputation of the former, while implying the latter to be at the same level of reputation as champagne. This was a case of deliberate fraud. The court explicitly noted that the existence or lack of comparable laws in the United Kingdom was irrelevant. It was enough to prove that the defendant was French and that his commercial practice could have harmful effects in France for the plaintiff.

It is unclear whether this case has been used as a precedent for subsequent cases, as French civil and penal laws have been limited to territorial application. For foreign offenses, the law generally requires that the defendants be French without doubt and that both the French law and the law of the country where the act was committed regard it as an offense.[74] This is intended to obviate any cause for conflicts of law.

Misleading Advertising. The concept of misleading advertising traces its source to article 405 of the penal code proscribing fraudulent and deceitful activities.[75] Misleading advertising has been found to be an act of deceit, and the act of publishing or otherwise communicating the ad was first considered fraudulent activity in a number of cases dealing with healers and astrologers.[76] Fraudulent activity was first applied to advertising in 1885.[77]

Inspired by article 405, *La loi du 1er août 1905 sur les fraudes et falsifications* (or the law of 1905) was adopted, making it a crime to commit fraud in a contractual situation. Article 1 of the law of 1905 provides penalties for those who deceive or attempt to deceive another party through a contract concerning the qualities of goods sold. Inasmuch as this law deals with the attempt to deceive, it has been applied by the courts to false advertising.[78]

Since 1905 the development of administrative laws on advertising has been a slow process. Until the early 1960s, misleading advertising was controlled only indirectly through interpretations of penal code and the law of 1905. It was not until 1963 that French legislators decided to control misleading advertising directly through legislation by categorizing the term a criminal offense, providing that the advertiser's statements were proven to have been made in bad faith.[79] The 1963 act, in turn, was not satisfactory to consumers, as its scope was too restrictive: it did not cover all forms of misleading advertising; it placed the burden of proof of bad faith on the plaintiff; it referred only to the precise advertising statement, ignoring the effect of images and sounds; and it did not provide adequate sanctions. Only five hundred convictions were made during 1963–72, most of which concerned foods and health products, and two-thirds of these cases were tried under the earlier legislation.[80]

The 1963 act was superseded by articles 44–46 in the Royer Act of 1973. According to Article 44–1, what is prohibited is any advertising containing false or misleading allegations, indications, or presentations, as long as they affect one or more of the following elements: existence; nature; composition; substantive qualities; instructions for use; origin; quantity; method and date of manufacturing; price and selling conditions; expected results of the product or service being advertised; and name and characteristics of the maker, the seller, the retailer, the promoter, or the advertiser.[81]

The law prohibits false and deceptive or misleading advertising. The concept includes false advertising as well as truthful advertising such as would induce a mistake. It includes not only allegations, but also indications, images, and presentations. Although the law limits the scope of misleading advertising to the types of information listed in the law, the list is so comprehensive that lawyers would have difficulty imagining what type of ad would not fall under the law. Consumerist activity had brought advertising offenses to public attention in the early 1970s, and thus the 1973 act widened the scope of illegal advertising punishable under criminal law and made consumer protection, rather than competition, its main objective.

Article 44–2 of the 1973 law deals with the mechanics of applying the law. It provides that the advertiser is the principal party responsible for offenses committed, because he or she orders the advertisement. The agency and the media may be cited as accomplices if they knowingly and willingly assist the advertiser in the deception. Action against the advertiser is initiated by the director of public prosecutors on the advice of law officers and agents. Three government departments participate: (1) la Direction de la Concurrence et des Prix, (2) le Service de la Répression des Fraudes, and (3) le Service des

Instruments de Mesure. These agents are empowered to demand that the advertiser make available all elements necessary to explain the statements, information, and advertising presentations. This requirement amounts to reversal of burden of proof (in other words, the accused must prove their innocence). Failure to provide information may constitute incrimination. Private citizens also may initiate proceedings in civil actions, thereby obliging the public prosecutor to initiate prosecution.[82]

In the 1973 act, the French government also has contended with the problems of international advertising. According to article 44-II, an offense is committed when misleading or false advertising or advertising of the nature to mislead is produced, received, or perceived in France. Thus, France assumes the right to control messages broadcast on French territory from radio and television emissions, even though they may originate from outside French territory.[83]

Since the law's inception, numerous violations have been reported in the annual publications of *le Cahier du droit de l'entreprise* (the *Cahier*). At least one hundred cases of penal investigations for misleading advertising have been reported annually in the *Cahier,* and an increasing number of cases before the Cour de cassation, the highest court of ordinary jurisdiction, are published in its bulletin on criminal proceedings.[84] The application of the law has expanded and been clarified through jurisprudence, according to which:

1. The law includes the advertising of goods and services made to the public, when the advertising could mislead a potential customer.

2. The law pertains to advertising conveyed through any kind of medium by print, radio, television, posters, billboards, etc., including sound and images.

3. Acts of omission are included in the umbrella terms *publicité mensongère*.

4. Although the law is silent as to whether the misleading advertising must be found an intentional act or whether the offender would be held responsible if the prohibited advertising were made innocently or negligently, the courts have determined that intent to deceive is not necessary for an offense.[85]

5. Advertising is not explicitly defined in the act of 1973. The definition used by the courts is all commercial, industrial, or professional communication with the purpose of promoting the supply of goods or services.[86]

The cases show that under the 1973 act, all advertisers have needed to be more careful than under the earlier legislation. An illustrative case concerns a French subsidiary of General Foods accused of misleading advertising in the use of images likely to mislead the consumer, even though they were accompanied by honest texts. The case involved the advertising of the artificial orange drink Tang.[87] On the individual packages were pictures of an orange peel rolled in the shape of the orange, as if it had just been emptied. Beside it was a glass of orange-colored juice surrounded by leaves. The actual contents were printed below in small print. Posters showed the package and bore the slogan, "the taste of fresh squeezed oranges." The Cour d'appel, the regional court of appeals, held this to be misleading advertising because the illustration implied real orange juice, and overruling an earlier decision of another court, it imposed sanctions on the company.[88]

Specific Legislation

In addition to the general laws, the government has adopted laws and regulations governing the advertising of foods, alcohol and other beverages, tobacco, pharmaceuticals, cosmetics, and special foods and other health products. It has also adopted legislation on the use of the French language in advertising. Moreover, there are laws governing prices and discriminatory practices in advertising. These measures are too numerous to describe. However, specific regulations addressed to foreign advertisers are of particular interest.

The advertising of pharmaceuticals and health products is strictly regulated under the Code of Public Health and Décret 76–807 of August 1976.[89] Article R. 5046 of the *Décret,* or decree, requires that the advertising of products of foreign origin be subject to the same requirements as French-produced advertisements as long as the advertising message can be received or perceived in France.

In 1975 the French government adopted a law making compulsory the use of the French language in all written and printed advertising and forbidding the inclusion of foreign expressions when there are equivalent French terms.[90] The interpretation of the law was modified in 1982.[91] The law is applicable in all French territory. Violations are punishable under the terms provided in the 1905 act on the repression of fraud.

In the case of sales of foreign goods not conforming to the rule, the French importer or the foreign exporter selling directly into France is held responsible for infringements. The intent of the law is to ensure the protection of consumers so that they may utilize a product or take advantage of a service in full knowledge of its nature, its use, and related guarantees.[92] With respect to foreign advertising in France, there is a 9 percent tax on the importation of "printed material devoted to advertising, industrial publications, and other advertising matter."[93]

Special rules govern television advertising. In 1988 television advertising came under the authority of the Conseil Superieur de l'Audiovisuel (CSA) established in that year. The CSA administers general government laws on advertising as well as specific rules and regulations. Television ads must be precleared. In exercising its duties the CSA is aided by a special Commission consisting of government officials and representatives of professional bodies and the BVP (see below). The representatives of the CSA has the final decision-making authority. Rules proscribe advertising of alcoholic beverages and tobacco products on television. Special rules govern the use of children in ads.[94]

Self-Regulation

Self-regulation is an important instrument for the protection of the consumer and the integrity of the advertising profession. Self-regulation is largely an inner-industry affair aimed at preempting problems from the exterior. The principal self-regulatory body is the Bureau de Vérification de la Publicité (BVP) established in 1953. The BVP has roots going back to the l'Office de Control des Annonces, founded in 1935 and closed in 1940. The BVP is composed of representatives of the advertisers, the agencies, the press, and other concerned organizations. The chairperson is an independent citizen of the community. The BVP is financed and supported by the advertising community.

Rules for self-restraint are found in the Receuil de Recommendations, a collection of detailed general and product specific rules and specifications. They are elaborated in the spirit of the ICC Code. Although legally non-binding, failure to comply with the rules can mean loss of membership in the BVP.

The receuil is administered by the BVP. A recommendatory body, the BVP replies to questions, reviews complaints, and monitors ads before and after publication. In 1988, the BVP handled 4034 cases including: advise on 1046 ads before publication (of which 42 percent were cleared and 58 percent required modification); 2333 consumer complaints; 655 ads controlled after publications.[95]

Advertising and Liability

Although advertising has not been treated explicitly in French legal literature as having a specific place in liability law, neither negligence nor warranty principles are strictly confined to the inherent properties of a product. These principles also embrace the manner in which a product is marketed.[96] Today, manufacturers not only have the duty to test their products before putting them on the market, but the products also must be accompanied by instructions for use, precautions to take, and warnings of possible ill effects and risk to the consumer. The absence of information or the presence of false information would make the manufacturer liable for the ill consequences of product use by the consumer.

Consequently, the consumer or the person who purchases a product on the strength of advertising and who is consequently injured or incurs a loss as a result of the product has the choice of several legal options for redress under civil or penal law. In such cases the usual choice is between breach of warranty under civil law or violation for misleading advertising under penal law.[97]

Advertising thus has been implicated in a number of liability suits, particularly for latent defects. One such case concerned the publicity for a new car. The ads contained figures on gas consumption, which proved to be untrue. Instead of seeking redress under criminal law, misleading advertising, the plaintiff chose a civil-law remedy. The courts considered the matter one under article 1644 of the French civil code, since gas consumption was considered an important factual quality concerning an automobile.[98] Other similar cases involving advertising have been heard by the courts.[99]

Finally, advertising was mentioned in a case involving failure to provide adequate information: "The maker of a Murphy bed indicated that his product was both entirely reliable and extremely simple to handle. In spite of a previous accident, he omitted, however, to mention that the vertical part of the bed had to be secured to the wall. He therefore became liable when selling the same product." [Civ. 15 Mai 1979, D. 1979 IR. 440][100] This case, on the surface, evokes cases of strict liability or negligence for watered-down warnings decided in the United States.

Scandinavia

The Nordic systems for regulating advertising practices in Denmark, Norway, and Sweden differ from either the European continental systems or the British system (see table 7–5). They are important for two reasons: first, one who intends to advertise in this region needs to know the regulatory system; and second and perhaps more important, the Scandinavian system has influenced the EEC's development of a harmonized European regulatory system.

The original bases of law in Scandinavia are civil law and canon law. National law was taught in Sweden and Denmark from the seventeenth century. The Scandinavian legal systems developed independently after the adoption of national codes, first in Denmark in 1683, Norway in 1687, and subsequently in Sweden and Finland. These codes, predating the Napoleonic code of 1805, dealt with the whole of law. None of these countries adopted the formulation of the Napoleonic code. Today, codes no longer exist in Denmark and Norway. In Sweden and Finland, nine-part codes, extensively amended versions of the original codes, continue to be cited. Codes and statutes enjoy equal status in all these countries.

The Scandinavian legal system differs from either the civil-code or common-law regimes in its establishment of the quasi-autonomous legal office

Table 7-5
Regulatory Profile: Scandinavia

Countries:	Denmark, Finland, Norway, Sweden
Government:	Constitutional monarchies; parliamentary systems, multiparty, pluralist democracies; Finland, Iceland: republics
Politico-economic ideology:	Constitutionalism/legalism; social welfarism; capitalism/socialism
Economic system:	Mixed free and public enterprise; significant public regulation
Legal system:	Norway, Iceland, and Denmark: statutory law; Sweden, Finland: Civil code of 1734 and statutory law
Investment policy:	Conservative (Denmark under Common Market rules)
Ad regulation:	Strict; ombudsman system, no TV advertising
Ad expenditure:	Norway and Denmark $.7B; Sweden and Finland $1.4B; per capita: Denmark $143, Sweden $170, Norway $181, and Finland $298; %GNP: 1 (Finland 2.1)
Consumer market:	Mature
Social indicators:	
Population:	4-8 million
Urbanization:	60-86%
Per capita income:	$12,200-$15,400
Language:	Scandinavian national languages (secondary: English)
Class structure:	Predominant middle class
Life expectancy:	72-80 years
Literacy:	99%

of ombudsman meaning parliamentary commissioner for civil and military government administration. Legally empowered to mediate between the government and private parties, the ombudsman acts as a public watchdog. The institution of the ombudsman is comparable with the commission system in the United States; the office of the consumer ombudsman performs many of the same functions as the Federal Trade Commission in the United States.

Considerable collaboration exists in the development of administrative rules and regulations among all the Scandinavian countries. Advertising is no exception. Collaboration is evidenced in the similarity of regulatory institutions and in regulations imposed on advertising in the public media. Until recently television broadcast advertising was prohibited throughout Scandinavia. Today it is permitted in Denmark and Norway. In all countries the activities of government advertising regulation and self-regulation are fulfilled by the consumer ombudsman.

The advertising regulatory functions of the consumer ombudsman were established in Sweden in 1971, in Norway in 1973, and in Denmark in 1975. Although the ombudsman is an official but independent government functionary appointed by the government, he or she also fulfills functions that in some countries fall under self-regulation. The ombudsman and his or her staff administer the marketing-practices act in each country. The ombudsman plays the role of arbitor and investigator, exacting voluntary cooperation in the first instance.

In each country the ombudsman is complemented by a judicial infrastructure, either the Marketing Council (Norway), Marketing Court (Sweden), or Maritime and Commercial Court (Denmark). It is to one of these bodies that the ombudsman refers for matters not settled via negotiation and to which injunctions are appealed. The members of these groups are appointed by the royal heads of state and include representatives from the business community and consumer interests, as well as expert authorities from the government, judiciary, and scientific community. These bodies have legal authority to enforce provisions of marketing ads.

The consumer ombudsman and the marketing council, both financed by the state, in practice have assumed all government functions of advertising regulation. Generally, the main function of self-regulation is review prior to publication, carried out by the industry, marketing associations, or better business councils.

In Denmark it is the duty of the consumer ombudsman to ensure that proper marketing practices (as set out in relevant legislation, in particular the marketing acts in which the ombudsman is instituted) are followed. The ombudsman, either on his or her own initiative or in consequences of complaints, is expected, through negotiations, to induce marketing behavior in accordance with the law. If voluntary cooperation is not obtained, the ombudsman may institute civil procedures concerning prohibited unlawful acts. When swift action is required, interlocutory injunctions may be issued by the ombudsman. These must shortly be confirmed by the court because if the judicial support is not received, the injunction will lapse. The ombudsman is empowered to require and receive all such information considered necessary for the performance of his or her functions, including information needed to prove that the cases fall under his or her jurisdiction. The ombudsman is appointed by the government and must have the same qualifications as a judge.[101]

The principal terms of reference of the Consumers' ombudsman are outlined in the respective marketing-practices acts of Denmark, Norway, and Sweden.[102] These laws embrace all kinds of marketing practice, including advertising communications. They replace earlier laws dating from the 1920s, which concentrated on unfair competitive practices. The current market-practices acts place strong emphasis on protecting the interest of consumers, particularly as it involves truth, fairness, and sufficiency of advertising information. The emphasis of these acts is on consumer protection. The acts make it an offense to use false, misleading, unreasonable, or incomplete indications, statements, or practices likely to affect the demand or supply of goods and services. The acts also prohibit certain unfair business practices, such as the use of trade secrets to the detriment of competitors.

In addition to the marketing acts, the various broadcasting acts of the

Nordic countries contain provisions indirectly applied to advertising on radio and television. For example, the Danish Broadcasting Act of 1973 provides that Danmarks Radio (which broadcasts one national television program and three radio programs plus regional programs) is to be financed by fees levied for the use of personal radios and televisions. It leaves no scope for revenue from commercial advertising.[103] The law does not prevent advertising contained within foreign programs received in the Nordic countries.

Notes

1. See EEC, Treaty of Rome, 1957, e.g., article 3 (c) & (f), article 59, and article 62.

2. EC, Interstate Convention, *Single European Act, Official Journal of the European Communities* 30 L 169, 29 June 1987; Corrigenda L 304, 27 October 1987: 46 and L 327, 18 November 1987: 30.

3. Ibid, Article 7.

4. See European Communities, Commission, *Completing the Internal Market: White Paper from the Commission to the European Council,* Com (85) 310 Final, Brussels, 14 June 1985; European Communities, Commission, *Third Report from the Commission to the Council and the European Parliament on the Implementation of the Commission's White Paper on Completing the Internal Market,* Com (88) 134 Final, Brussels, 21 March 1988. European Community members include Belgium, Denmark, France, West Germany, Greece, Ireland, Italy, Luxembourg, the Netherlands, Portugal, Spain, and the United Kingdom.

5. For discussion of problems created by differences in advertising regulations see European Communities, Commission, *Television without Frontiers (Green Paper on the Establishment of the Common Market for Broadcasting; Especially by Satellite and Cable),* Com (84) 300 Final, CB-CO-84-270-EN-C, 14 June 1984.

6. European Communities, Council, *Directive Relating to the Approximation of the Laws, Regulations, and Administrative Provisions of the Member States Concerning Misleading Advertising, Official Journal of the European Communities-Legislation* 210 (7 August 1985): 29 et seq.

7. European Communities, *Convention on Jurisdiction and Judgments in Civil and Commercial Matters, Official Journal of the European Communities-Legislation* 304 (30 October 1978).

8. Jeremy Sheehan, Director of Consumer Affairs, Commission of the European Communities, interview with author, Brussels, Belgium 13 August 1984.

9. European Communities, Commission, *Amendment to the Proposal for a Council Directive Relating to the Approximation of the Laws, Regulations, and Administrative Provisions of the Member States Concerning Misleading and Unfair Advertising, Official Journal of the European Communities,* no. C 194/3 (1 August 1979): 3 et seq.

10. Jeremy Sheehan, interview.

11. United Kingdom, Ministry of Trade, *Consultation Document,* 11 July 1985.

12. Ibid.

13. European Communities, Council, *Directive Concerning Misleading Advertising,* Article 2.1.
14. Ibid, Article 2.2.
15. Ibid. Article 4.1.
16. Ibid. Article 5.
17. Ibid. Article 6.
18. European Communities, Commission, *Directive Relating to the Approximation of Laws, Regulations, and Administrative Provisions of the Member States Concerning Liability for Defective Products, Official Journal of the European Communities-Legislation* 210 (7 August 1985): 29 et seq. In effect as of 7 August 1988. Not included as a legislative step to complete the single internal market.
19. Ibid., Article 4.
20. For detailed analysis of the British advertising regulatory system refer to R.G. Lawson, *Advertising Law* (London: MacDonald and Evans, 1978) and Gordon E. Miracle and Terence Nevett, *Voluntary Regulations of Advertising* (Lexington, Mass.: Lexington Books, 1987).
21. Refer to Rene David and John E.C. Brierley, *Major Legal Systems in the World Today* (London: Stevens and Sons, 1978), 356–57, 360–62.
22. Peter Thomson, "Advertising Rules—Legal and Self-Regulatory Systems," *The Practice of Advertising,* ed. Norman A. Hart and James O'Connor, published by Communication, Advertising, and Marketing Education Foundation, Ltd. (CAM) and Institute of Marketing (London: Heinemann, 1983), 167. Peter Thomson has served as director of the United Kingdom's Advertising Standards Authority and as secretary of the Code of Advertising Practice Committee and is an expert of advertising ethics, control systems, and advertising law.
23. *Carlill v. Carbolic Smoke Ball Co.,* [1893] 1 Q.B. 256; Lawson, *Advertising Law,* 1–24.
24. *Dimmock v. Hallett,* [1866] L.R. 2 Ch. App. 21; Frank Patrick Bishop, *Advertising and the Law,* 2d ed. (London: Benn, 1952), 47.
25. *Carlill v. Carbolic Smoke Ball Co.,* at 261; *Esso Petroleum v. Cmrs. of Customs and Excise* [1976] All E.R. 117, at 121, per Lord Simon, cited in Lawson, *Advertising Law,* 16.
26. *Johnston v. Orr-Ewing,* [1882] 7 App. Cas. 219.
27. Lawson, *Advertising Law,* 69–73, 257–60; Miracle and Nevett, *Voluntary Regulations,* 36 37.
28. *Cellacite & British Aralite v. Robertson Co., The Times,* 23 July 1957, as cited in Lawson, *Advertising Law,* 260.
29. Refer to Lawson, *Advertising Law,* for a listing and discussion of the statutes adopted prior to 1978.
30. United Kingdom, *Sunday Observance Act,* 21 Geo. 3, c. 49 sec. 3, as cited in Lawson, *Advertising Law,* 317–18.
31. United Kingdom, *Sunday Entertainments Act,* 22 & 23 Geo. 5, c. 51, sec. S.4.
32. *Metropolitan Police Act,* 2 & 3 Vict. c. 47 (1839); *Pedlars Act,* 34 & 35 Vict. c. 96 (1871); *Uniforms Act* 57 & 58 Vict. c. 45 (1894); *Indecent Advertisements Act,* 52 & 53 Vict. c. 18 (1889); and *Public Health Acts Amendment Act* 7 Edw. 7 c. 53 (1907).

33. Miracle and Nevett, *Voluntary Regulations*, 35–39.
34. Thomson, "Advertising Rules," 168–69.
35. United Kingdom, *Trade Descriptions Act, 1968* (as amended in 1972), *Public General Acts and Measures of 1968* 1, c. 29, 659–84. The 1972 amendment concerns marking of country of origin on product label.
36. United Kingdom, Department of Trade, "The Trade Descriptions Acts, 1968 and 1972," Internal memorandum, January 1973.
37. *Trade Descriptions Act, 1968*, sec. 1; United Kingdom, *Consumer Protection Act of 1987*, 15 May 1985, 1987 c. 43.
38. John Livermore, *Legal Aspects of Marketing* (London: Heinemann, 1984), 259.
39. *Trade Descriptions Act, 1968*, sec. 2(1)–(3).
40. United Kingdom, Department of Trade, Internal memorandum.
41. Lawson, *Advertising Law*, 207–9; United Kingdom, *Final Report of the Committee on Consumer Protection* (Malony Report), Cmd. 1781 (1962). The Malony report, in paragraph 634, states, "The error must be of such a substance that it could fairly be regarded as inducing a purchase," and expresses the wish that the term "trade description" excludes "statements of opinion of the character of a 'trade puff' such as that goods are 'the best on the market'." Lawson also cites a test case (*Cadbury, Ltd. v. Halliday*, [1975] 2 All E.R. 226) where use of the term *extra value* was considered by the plaintiff as a *false description*. The court differed. "The important fact about the ten trade descriptions listed in s. 201," Ashworth J. believed, is "that they are all matters in respect of which truth or falsity can be established as a matter of fact." According to Ashworth, "valuable is a description but not a trade description." *Cadbury Ltd., v. Halliday*, at 230.
42. United Kingdom, Department of Trade, Internal memorandum.
43. Norbert Reich, *Consumer Legislation in the EC Countries, A Comparative Analysis*, study prepared for the EC Commission (London: Van Nostrand Reinhold, 1980), 44.
44. United Kingdom, *Power of Criminal Courts Act of 1973, Public General Acts and Measures of 1973* 3, c. 62, 1807–93.
45. R.G. Lawson, formerly on the faculty of law at the University of Southampton and leading expert on United Kingdom and international advertising law, interview with author in Southampton, England, 8 July 1985.
46. United Kingdom, Department of Health and Social Security, *Medicines (Labeling and Advertising to the Public) Regulation, 1978*, SI 1978/no. 41.
47. J.M. Nelson, official in the United Kingdom Department of Health and Social Security, letter to author, 18 July 1984.
48. *Food and Drug Act of 1955* 4 Eliz. 2, c 16 (as amended) now the *Food Act 1984, Public General Acts and Measures of 1984* 1, c. 30, 873–982.
49. United Kingdom, Ministry of Agriculture, Fisheries, and Food, *Legislation Governing the Labeling, Advertising, and Composition of Food*, notes prepared as a general guide by the Standards Division (May 1983).
50. B.M. Smith, United Kingdom, Department of Health and Social Security, letter to author, 11 May 1984.
51. United Kindom, *Misrepresentation Act of 1967, Public General Acts and Measures* 1, c. 7, 219–20.

52. Livermore, *Legal Aspects of Marketing*, 33.
53. R.G. Lawson, interview with author, University of Southampton, England, 22 July 1985; Lawson, *Advertising Law*, 8. See also *Shaklin Pier, Ltd. v. Detel Products*, [1951] 2 All E.R. 471; and *Carlill v. Carbolic Smoke Ball Co.*, at 271. The advertisement was constructed as an offer for contract with the public. Use of the product was the consideration. The case involved de facto collateral contract.
54. United Kingdom, *Independent Broadcasting Authority Act of 1973, Public General Acts and Measures of 1973*, 2, c. 19, 225–273.
55. United Kingdom, *Fair Trading Act of 1973, Public General Acts and Measures of 1973* 2, c. 41, 1107–1240.
56. Independent Broadcasting Authority, *Code of Advertising Standards and Practice*, September 1983.
57. United Kingdom, *Broadcasting Act of 1981, Public General Acts and Measures of 1981* 2, c. 68, 2063–2143.
58. United Kingdom, *Fair Trading Act of 1973, Public General Acts and Measures of 1973* 2, c. 41, 1107–1240.
59. Advertising Standards Authority, *The British Code of Advertising*, 7th ed., October 1985, in force since 1 January 1986.
60. Advertising Standards Authority, *Annual Report 1984/85* (London: ASA Ltd., Brook House, 1985).
61. Advertising Standards Authority, *Case Report 123* (London: ASA Ltd., Brook House, 17 July 1985), 7.
62. United Kingdom, Department of Trade and Industry, "Consultation Document About Implementation of the EC Directive on Misleading Advertising," Internal memorandum circulated by Consumer Affairs Branch 2, 11 July 1985.
63. Ibid., para 6.
64. John Ryan and James R. Wills, *Final Report on Consumerism's Impact on Advertising: A Worldwide Study* (New York: International Advertising Association, 1979), 12.
65. *Langridge v. Levy*, Exch. of pleas (1837), 7 Will. 4 519.
66. Ibid., at 519, 520.
67. United Kingdom, *Misrepresentation Act of 1967, Public General Acts and Measures of 1967* 1, c. 7, 219–20.
68. Government of Canada, Consumer and Corporate Affairs, *Guide For Food Manufacturers and Advertisers*, Consumer Products Branch, Bureau of Consumer Affairs, Department of Consumer and Corporate Affairs, Canada, 1984; James P. Neelankavil, *Advertising and Self Regulation: Concepts, Prospects and Problems, A Worldwide Study* (New York: International Advertising Association, 1988, unpublished manuscript.
69. Graham De Villiers, Executive Director of McCann-Erickson in South Africa and Australia, interview with author, Cercy La Tour, France, August 12, 1988; and letter to author, Johannesburg, South Africa, March 7, 1989.
70. Jack Siebert, Executive Director, Advertising Standards Authority of South Africa, Memorandum in response to authors request, Johannesburg, South Africa: March 14, 1989; Graham De Villiers, letter, March 7, 1989.
71. See Pierre Greffe and François Greffe, *La publicité et la loi*, 5th ed. (Paris: Litec, 1983), 151.

72. *Code civil;* Part Four, on non-contractual agreements by convention, decree of 9 February 1804, promulgated 19 February, *French Code and Common Laws,* Paris, 1889. Whatsoever human act which shall cause injury or damage to another shall render that person through whose fault the act was performed liable to compensation (unofficial translation of code article). For further discussion, see J. Calais-Auloy et al., *Consumer Legislation in France,* study prepared for the EC Commission (London: Van Nostrand, Reinhold, 1980).

73. Judgment of 15 December 1891, Cour d'appel, Angers, 1895, *Jurisprudence,* 1144–7.

74. 1985 Dalloz-Sirey, *Jurisprudence,* 1144–7.

75. Whoever, by using a false name or qualification, or through fraudulent means, attempts to convince others of the existence of a company or credit that does not exist, or attempts to create expectations regarding a success, a failure, or accident, or any other fanciful event and obtains or tries to obtain money, capital, stocks, bonds, obligations . . . and through this, steals or attempts to steal all or part of the assets of another person, shall be punished. Unofficial translation. *Code Pénal,* Article 405 from the law promulgated 13 May 1863, *Code Français et lois usuelles,* 17th ed., 1889, 75.

76. Greffe and Greffe, *La publicité,* 201.

77. Cass. crim., 6 February 1855: S, 1, 223 rapp. Poux Franklin cited in "Concurrence: Publicité et droit pénal de la concurrence et de la consommation—Publicité mensongère et trompeuse," *Le jursiclasseur: Concurrence et consommation,* sec. 670-1 (November 1982): 5.

78. Ibid., 8; Calais-Auloy et al., *Consumer Legislation,* 65; Greffe and Greffe, *La publicité,* 202.

79. *Loi des finances de 2 juillet 1963,* art. 5, 6, *Journal officiel de la République Française,* 3 July 1963.

80. *Concurrence et consommation,* 12.

81. *Loi "Royer" d'orientation du commerce et de l'artisanat* (directions for commerce and handicrafts, or Royer Act), 27 December 1973, *Journal officiel,* 30 decembre 1973: 14139–49, article 44–1. The terms of article 44 were completed by articles 39–42 of *la Loi no. 78-23 sur la protection et l'information de consommateurs* (the act on consumer protection and information), 10 January 1978, *Journal officiel,* 11 January 1978: 301–8.

82. Calais-Auloy, *Consumer Legislation,* 69.

83. *Le Lamy Commercial,* no. 2133 (1983): 668, citing cass. crim. 18 May 1982: "The fact that a catalogue came from abroad was no defense for an advertiser (*un annonceur*) in France." *Le Lamy* is a several-volume collection of commercial law and practice. It is edited each year and updated every month.

84. *Concurrence et consommation,* 4–11.

85. "Le notion de publicité trompeuse,"*Le Lamy Commercial* no. 2159 (1983): 682. See also Cass. crim. 5 May 1977 (d. 1977, 502, note Pirovano); Cass. crim. 17 October 1977 (GP 1977-2-673).

86. *Le Lamy Commercial,* no. 2130–34, 667–69.

87. Judgment of 17 May 1978, Cour d'appel, Versailles, *Louis Cohen et societé General Foods France c. U.N. des producteurs de fruits et S.N. des boissons rafraichissantes et M.P.*

88. Cited in Greffe and Greffe, *La publicité,* 209.

89. *Decree 76-807, 24 August 1976, modifying the code of public health regarding the regulation of advertising for pharmaceuticals and all products, devices, methods, presented as being beneficial to health, and regarding the labeling of pharmaceuticals.* Translation. *Journal officiel,* 26 August 1976. SP.2.253, 11406.

90. *Loi no. 75-1349 relative a l'emploi de la langue française,* 31 December 1975, *Journal officiel,* 4 January 1976: 189–90.

91. "Circulaire du 20 octobre 1982 modifiant la circulaire de 14 mars 1977 concernant *la loi du 31 decembre 1975 relative a l'emploi de la langue française,*" *Journal officiel,* 21 October 1982, N.C. 9419; "Circulaire du 14 mars 1977 concernant la loi du 31 decembre 1975, relative a l'emploi de la langue française," *Journal officiel,* 15 March 1977: 1483–84.

92. Unofficial translation of the circular of 20 October 1982 from Samuel J. Cerrato, commerical attaché, American embassy, Paris, France, letter to author, 8 June 1984.

93. United States, Department of Commerce, "Marketing in France," *Overseas Business Reports* (OBR 79-41), December 20 1979.

94. Mme Françoise Perucki, Chargé de la documentation, Bureau de la Vérification de la Publicité, Paris, interview with the author, 16 May 1989.

95. Ibid.

96. Calais-Auloy et al., *Consumer Legislation,* 29.

97. Fourgoux et al., *Principes et pratique du droit de la consommation* (Paris: T. Delmas and Co., et cie. 1983), D5–6.

98. Paris, 3 May 1967, Gaz. Pol. 1967, 2, 34.

99. T.G.I. Paris, 7 April 1976, unpublished, Cass. civ. 13 January 1982, D. 1982, I.R. 209.

100. Memento pratique, Francis Lefebvre, *Réglementation economique, concurrence consommation, 1984* (Paris: Editions Juridiques Lefebvre, 1984), sec. 3828, 788.

101. Dansk Folkting, *The Danish Marketing Practices Act,* no. 297, 14 June 1974.

102. Denmark: Ibid.; Sweden: *Marketing Law* 1975: 1418 *Sveriges Riksdag* (1988), 1097–1102 and *Consumers' Ombudsman* 1986: 629, *Sveriges Riksdag* (1988), 1096; Norway: *Marketing Act,* No. 47, 16 June 1972 *Norgesloven* (1685–1987), 1837

103. *The Radio and Television Broadcasting Act* L 421/1973, as amended 1983, (Lovforlag no. L 42, official papers of the parliament, Folketinget part 2, p. 43, section 9).

8
Japan

Japan has the second most powerful economy in the free world. Its industrial machines account for 10 percent of the world's output and generate one trillion dollars annually. Japan's population exceeds 120 million, and per capita gross domestic product is about thirteen thousand dollars. Agriculture supports about one-quarter of the population; the remaining three-quarters live in urban environments. Manufacturing and service industries are the major sources of employment.

The advertising industry shares in the economic success of the country. In 1987 total advertising expenditure amounted to $27.3 billion, an amount surpassed only by the United States, and per capita expenditure exceeded $220, a figure surpassed only by the United States, Finland, and Switzerland (see figure 8-1 and 8-2).

In many respects the advertising industry, along with its regulatory environment, is very different from that encountered in Western societies (see table 8-1). While possessing the most modern technological, economic, and management acumen, the Japanese revere many traditions rooted in ancient Eastern philosophy. The accumulated cultural, philosophical, and religious heritage of Japan influences modern commercial, political, and legal practices and institutions in ways that are foreign in thinking of the industrialized market-economy countries of Europe and North America.

Although political traditions were once markedly otherwise, today's political and legal institutions in Japan are structurally similar to those of the United States and Western European countries. Following World War II and during the U.S. occupation in May 1947, the Japanese legislature (the Diet) ratified a new constitution establishing a constitutional monarchy. Executive power is exercised by the Cabinet, headed by the prime minister, who is elected by the Diet from among its members. Legislative power is vested in the Diet, a bicameral body consisting of the House of Representatives and the House of Councillors. Of the five major parties, the Liberal-Democratic party, which is regarded as conservative, has been in power for more than thirty years and generally is supported by both the business and agricultural communities.

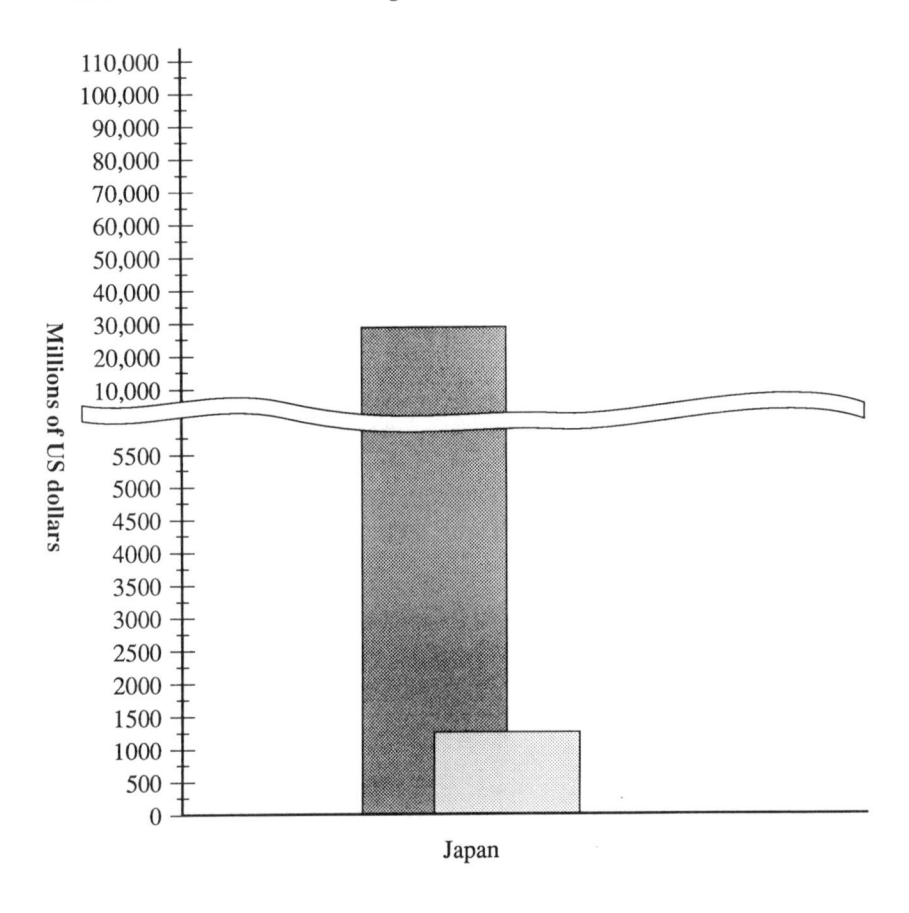

150 • *International Advertising Handbook*

[Chart showing two bars for Japan with a broken y-axis (Millions of US dollars). Total Advertising Expenditure bar reaches approximately 30,000; Multinational Agency Billings bar reaches approximately 1300.]

■ -Total Advertising Expenditure □ -Multinational Agency Billings

Source: derived from *World Advertising Expenditure,* 1987, 22nd ed., Starch INRA Hooper Inc., in cooperation with IAA; "Foreign Agency Report," *Advertising Age,* 9 May 1988.

Figure 8–1. Gross Multinational Agency Billings and Total Advertising Expenditure in Japan, 1987

Upon joining the OECD in 1964, Japan committed itself to a policy of free trade and movement of capital. In December 1980 the Foreign Investment Law was established, and the Foreign Exchange and Foreign Trade Control Law was amended to incorporate all matters related to foreign investment

Japan • 151

[Bar chart with broken y-axis showing US dollars, comparing Per Capita GNP and Per Capita Advertising Expenditure for Japan]

■ -Per Capita GNP   □ -Per Capita Advertising Expenditure

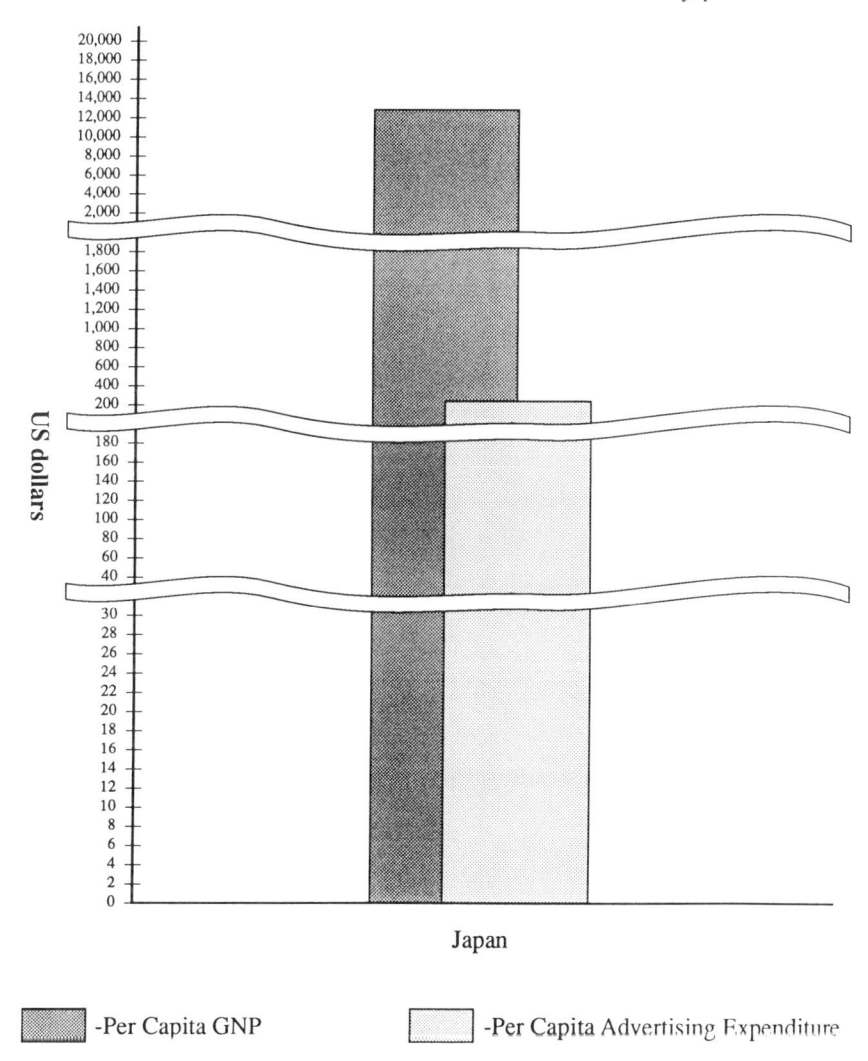

Source: derived from *World Advertising Expenditure,* 198, 22nd ed., Starch INRA Hooper, Inc., in cooperation with IAA; *World Development Report, 1988,* World Bank.

Figure 8–2. Per Capital Advertising Expenditure and Per Capita GNP in Japan, 1986/87

and foreign exchange control. Under the amended legislation, foreign trade and investments between Japan and foreign countries are free in principle, although certain procedures are required.

Despite these initiatives, Japan's current trade surplus has led to friction

Table 8–1
Regulatory Profile: Japan

Government:	Constitutional monarchy: parliamentary system; centralized multiparty, elitist/pluralist democracy
Politico-economic ideology:	Traditionalism; constitutionalism; capitalism; Confucianism/Shintoism
Economic system:	Free enterprise close cooperation with state
Legal system:	Asian Confucian tradition; adaptation of Romano/Germanic code; increasing development of statutory law; commercial law bears U.S. influence
Investment policy:	Conservative
Ad regulation:	Moderate government control; established cultural traditions
Ad expenditure:	$27.3 billion; per capita: $223; %GNP: 1.4
Consumer market:	Mature and culture bound
Social indicators:	
Population:	122 million
Urbanization:	76%
Per capita income:	$12800
Language:	Japanese
Class structure:	Predominant middle class
Life expectancy:	75–80 years
Literacy:	99%

with other industrialized countries, the United States in particular, for several reasons. Common views are that the Japanese government allows little competition from foreign corporations, that Japanese enterprises protect the interest of favored groups, and that these firms tend to favor long-term, steady dealings in the open market. Foreign business has been discouraged by tariffs, quotas, and invisible trade barriers, such as seemingly arbitrary inspection procedures. In addition, many foreign companies have faced problems entering into Japanese markets because they have failed to learn how to operate in the complex and unique distribution channels. Finally, foreign investors have found it difficult to compete with Japanese producers in their domestic markets.

Often overlooked are the high competitiveness of products and the advanced marketing skills and advertising creativity of the Japanese. Despite recent policy and trade improvements, foreign businesses, in particular American, have made insufficient efforts to understand the Japanese market. The problem, in short, is that the foreign business must appeal to the idiosyncracies of Japanese consumers and tailor their products and advertising to the demand of the Japanese market.[1] Moreover, by comparison with the other industrialized countries, Japan has a unique profile of top advertisers. While the principle advertisers in the West are the producers of processed foods, tobacco, soaps, and toiletries, the top advertisers in Japan are the chemicals, automobile and electrical appliance manufacturers.

The Advertising Industry

The advertising industry in Japan is highly concentrated. Although there are a considerable number of advertising agencies, only a handful of indigenous agencies dominates the local market. The top five Japanese agencies accounted for more than 50 percent of the Japanese billings. Among these top agencies, none is owned by foreign multinational firms. Even among the top twenty agencies in Japan, only two are subsidiaries of foreign multinationals, and one has a minority affiliation. Yet, as an educated and extremely literate country, Japan is receptive to international advertising. Foreign and Japanese themes intermingle in programming on radio and television and in the contents of newspapers and magazines.

Dentsu, Inc., in existence for almost eighty-seven years, is the world's largest advertising agency. It accounts for an approximately 24 percent share of ad billings in Japan, with 40 percent of prime-time television buying in Tokyo. The agency is involved in a wide range of commercial activities, such as marketing research, sales promotion, and event and convention planning. It seeks diversification through producing motion pictures and through arranging exhibitions. In 1987 the agency had a gross income of $884.5 million on billings of $6.2 billion.

Unlike the Western advertising giants, Japanese advertising agencies have, until very recently, restricted their operations almost entirely to the domestic market. In the early 1980s, however, Dentsu embarked on international operations. Today it has nine overseas offices and seven subsidiaries located in Europe, the United States, and Asia. Dentsu is also a partner in the international advertising network, HDM World-wide, which began operations in 1987 as a triventure of Dentsu, Young & Rubicam and Eurocom. HDM is a composite of HCM offices established in an earlier venture between Eurocom and Young & Rubicam and DYR offices established under a joint venture agreement between Young & Rubicam and Dentsu in 1981. In 1988, HDM had a network of thirty-nine offices in nineteen countries in North America, Europe, and Asia. Total billings of HDM were $1,384 million in 1987. European offices are established in many EC countries and in Sweden, Switzerland, and Austria. Asian offices are established in Hong Kong, Malaysia, Thailand, China, and the Philippines. Association agreements exist with offices in Taiwan and India. Other large Japanese agencies including Hakuhodo and Tokyu also have begun to move abroad to Europe, the United

154 • *International Advertising Handbook*

States, and to other countries in Asia. Japan is the principal home country of foreign advertising in China.

The outstanding advertising creativity of Japanese agencies has brought them numerous international awards. Dentsu won the top prize at the 1987 advertising film festival at Cannes and captured the title of *Advertising Age's* International Agency of the Year for 1987. The company's slogan Communications Excellence is the cornerstone of Dentsu's corporate identity.[2]

All modern mass media are available for advertising in Japan (see figure 8–3). Significant is the advanced development of the media. Japan publishes

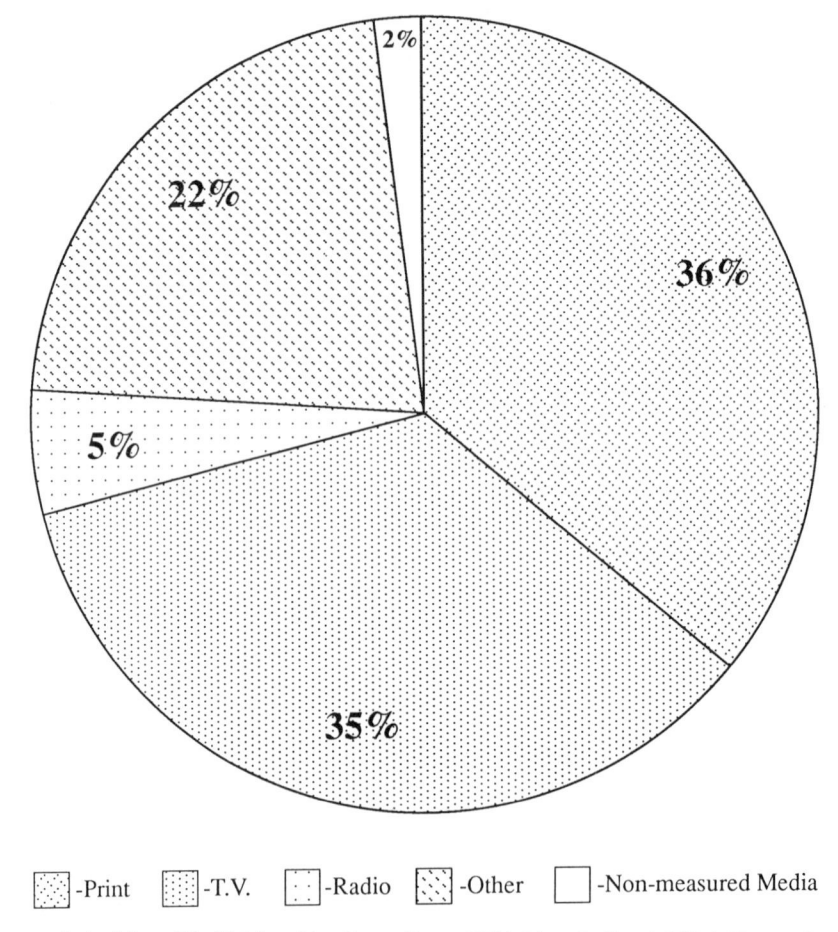

[Pie chart showing: 36%, 2%, 22%, 5%, 35%]

▦-Print ▦-T.V. ▦-Radio ▦-Other ☐-Non-measured Media

Source: derived from *World Advertising Expenditure*, 1986, 21st ed., Starch INRA Hooper, Inc. in cooperation with IAA.

Figure 8–3. Advertising Expenditure by Media and Non-measured Media in Japan (percentage shares)

more newspapers per capita than any other country. Diffusion rates for radio and television are also extremely high, reflecting wide income distribution and the advanced state of the electronics industry.

A large number of general and specialized business publications also disperse commercial information throughout the country. Transit advertising on buses and subways is particularly common because of the high degree of reliance on public transportation. Billboards and posters are also popular advertising media.[3] Direct mail has been gaining popularity in recent years.

Commercial television broadcasting, begun in 1953, has enjoyed phenomenal growth. Television has been a top advertising medium since 1975. All television stations broadcast in color, and there are five major commercial networks (NTV, TBS, CS, ANB, and TX) that combined give nationwide coverage. These stations have a number of affiliates. Competition among these networks is intense. Approximately 40 percent of households watch television daily, with that figure climbing to 70 percent during prime time (7:00 P.M.–11:00 P.M.), 10 percent of which is commercial time. The average individual watches nearly three hours daily (compared to seven hours in the United States).

Newspapers and magazines account for 47 percent of all Japanese advertising, of which newspapers are 37.8 percent and magazines are 9.0 percent (see figure 8–3). Notable features of newspaper circulation are stability, because of the high percentage of regular subscribers, and deep penetration. The dissemination rate is one newspaper for every 2.49 persons. Five papers are read nationwide, the two largest by over 7 million subscribers. Circulation of the five national newspapers (*Yomiuri, Asahi, Mainichi, Sankei,* and *Nihon Keizai*) for the latter half of 1986 exceeded 25 million (morning editions only), or 65 percent of households in Japan.

Among the mass media of Japan, magazines have the longest history. In 1986, combined circulation totalled approximately 4.1 billion for over two thousand monthly magazines and seventy-three weekly magazines. The market is segmented, splintered, and local. Magazines are divided into narrow categories corresponding to many social variables, sex, age, lifestyle, and so on.

Commercial radio broadcasting began in 1951, and with the country's economic reconstruction, achieved rapid growth following World War II. The overwhelming popularity of television forced radio into the background by the early 1960s. Today radio broadcasting is seen as a complement to television. There are at least seventy-three private radio broadcasting companies operating commercial stations. The main radio stations are most heavily concentrated in the Tokyo, Osaka, Nagoya, and Fukuoka areas, but many independent stations are distributed throughout the country. As of March 1987, there were 153 million radios in use across Japan, approximately 3.9 radios per household. Listening time is concentrated between 6 to 8 A.M. and after 11 P.M.

Environmental Influences on Advertising

Understanding the advertising phenomenon in Japan requires an awareness of many unique environmental factors. Education and training, culture, and religion all claim a part in Japan's advertising success.

The Japanese educational system has produced one of the world's highest rates of literacy. The national universities are training grounds for business and government elites. Established during the nineteenth century, they follow a tradition akin to that of European institutions in their emphasis on theory in the fields of law, history, and social sciences. Education and training are highly valued by the advertising industry. Moreover, a high percentage of the total staff participates in some on-going training activities each year.[4]

Two strong cultural traits that influence the advertising environment and set Japan apart from the Western industrialized market societies are the emphasis on the group and on frugality. Communal consciousness is a core characteristic that defines many social values. The preeminence of the group is an expression of prevailing religious tenets of Shintoism and Confucian philosophy. Social interdependence and harmony, similarities in personal taste, and cooperative living reflect this core social value.[5]

The communal orientation permeates many aspects of commercial life. Group decision making is commonplace. In the office or at play, the individual is expected to work for the good of the team, although he or she may compete to be the best team player. In sports baseball players refrain from argument with officials. Communalism even extends to advertising. Group consensus appeal is underscored, while individuality tends to be downplayed. However, in the future, with a growing emphasis on consumption and the general trend toward smaller family units, Japanese advertisers may also stress the emerging individuality of the Japanese consumer.[6]

Frugality is another strong cultural trait. The sources are historic and economic, traced in part to the samurai ethic of personal austerity and associated today with the need to save because of economic constraints and wage payment systems. In a comparison between Japan and the United States, the Japanese gross domestic savings amount to 19 percent (the second highest figure for industrialized market countries); the corresponding U.S. figure is 7 percent. Besides this bent for saving, there is a strong preference for cash purchases and minimal borrowing.

Many of these cultural traditions also are reflected in advertising. Communal spirit is solicited by having famous celebrities appear to be close acquaintances. Humorous wordplay and nonsensical content also are used to create a bond of mutual feelings. Consistent with social harmony, priority is placed on company trustworthiness, rather than on product-quality advertising. In general, the Japanese believe that if they can trust a company, they can trust its products.

Cultural traditions also are reflected in the process of business negotiations. Bargaining with the Japanese requires patience and preparation. Western executives often confront negotiating teams of ten or fifteen well-informed Japanese. The negotiation process is time consuming, with one goal being the consensus of all concerned. Unlike the legalistic approach to business relations in the United States, successful negotiations in the Japanese business environment require the cultivation of personal trust, trustworthiness, and a desire to cooperate on a project. Lawyers frequently are unwelcome in the negotiating process.[7]

Profit considerations in business dealings include quantified economic benefits and estimates of the nonquantifiable social costs. Important for the Japanese is the effect of agreements on business associates and other members of society. Language and semantic differences have led to serious misunderstandings and require skill to avoid problems. Hands-on negotiating, often delegated to the middle-level executives, is common in Japan. The formal role of high-level officials is to arbitrate decisions recommended by the middle-level executive.[8]

Religious beliefs also are highly relevant to commercial relations. Over the years the Japanese have evolved a continuum of opposing religious and philosophical ideals and practices from major Asian religions and to a lesser extent from Christianity. From Shintoism they have obtained the foundations of their theology; from Buddhism, their philosophy; from Confucianism, their ethics; and from Christianity, an understanding of other modes of thought. The prevailing element is Shintoism, to which other beliefs have had to adapt. The Japanese faith is empirical, emphasizing the visible world and explaining man's nature as he appears. Religion also perpetuates the belief that man is able to find spiritual fulfillment in nature. The basic feature of Japanese religion has been defined by noted observers as the *michi* (*tao* in Chinese), or way. Nobel laureate Yukawa Hideki describes the way as "thorough going passiveness [in which one] submits to the irrationalities omnipresent in the universe by regarding them as inevitable."[9] The concept of the way transcends many cultural practices and activities (such as the way of judo, the way of making and using tea, and even the way of advertising). By following any of the ways, one achieves not only technical proficiency, but also harmony, peace, integration with nature, and possibly enlightenment.[10]

These religious beliefs have a strong, but subtle, effect on advertising. Soft sell is the way of advertising in Japan. It is evidenced in advertising's aesthetics, its art, and its use of emotional appeal. Emotional responses are elicited through beautiful scenery, touching short stories, or sentimental dialogues. Reverence for nature and the aesthetic is also the way in advertising. The sea, the blue skies, the sun rising and setting, and flowers as symbols appear frequently in Japanese ads. There is little material relevance between ad content and product. Through belief dialogue or narrative, with minimal explanatory content, Japanese advertisers resort to image-building symbols. In summary the three distinctive characteristics of Japanese advertising are the use of imagery, product demonstration, and nonsense non sequitor humor and these stem from the unique culture and philosophy of Japan.

Regulation of Advertising

The Japanese legal system is eclectic. It is an amalgam that combines formal laws inspired by the German civil code, Anglo-American common-law concepts, Chinese public law, Confucian teachings of local customs, and old commercial codes. On paper the formal system resembles Western systems, yet the manner and extent to which the formal machinery is applied are peculiarly Asian in the Confucian tradition and uniquely Japanese in practice.

Japan shares with most Asian countries a philosophy inherently averse to law and legalism. The general public still tends to regard law as the means whereby the state's political leaders can exercise arbitrary powers; further, they associate law with inevitable punishment and imprisonment. Going to court—even in a civil or private law case—is cause for shame, embarrassment, or loss of face.[11]

Basic to understanding the spirit of law and its application is a knowledge of the Confucian philosophy, which still strongly influences legal practices in Japan. Interpersonal relations in the Confucian tradition stress a ritualistic and harmonious social order leading to customary rules of behavior for each type of interpersonal relationship. According to tradition, to claim rights in any relationship depersonalizes human relations and places all men on an equal footing without regard to the harmonious social hierarchy imposed by the natural order. Law, according to Confucius, is the embodiment of the natural social order. Thus, apart from contracts between artificial legal persons (such as business and enterprises), it is uncommon for an individual to seek his or her rights in court, even though such a suit would be permitted according to modern legal codes.[12]

All these legal attitudes affect the application of commercial laws. The preferred methods for dispute settlement are mediation and conciliation, of which there are several types. In domestic business contracts, dispute settlement is provided in clauses stating that parties will seek solution through mediation.

There are two forms of advertising regulation: administrative law and industry self-regulation. The earliest government regulation, the Police Regulations of 1908, prohibited exaggerated and false advertising, coercion of advertising publication, and demand for payment for any nonsubscribed advertisement. In 1911 this law was superseded by the adoption of the Advertising Control Law.

Self-regulation had its beginnings in 1885, when the press established its Outlines for Advertising Service, (later superseded by the 1938 adoption of its Particular Limits to Advertising Publications and Principal Laws Concerned). In 1914 the advertising club Kokoku Kurabo began discussion of general voluntary restraints on the industry. It was joined by other groups in this long-term effect. The first actual code, the Japanese Advertising Statute, was adopted in 1940.[13]

The most far-reaching administrative laws affecting advertising practice are the *Act Concerning Prohibition of Private Monopoly and Maintenance of Fair Trade of 1947* as amended and supplementary legislation including the *Act Against Unjustifiable Premiums and Misleading Representation of 1962* and the *Fair Trade Commission Notification on Unfair Trade Practices, 1982*. These measures have been amended and supplemented by additional legislation over the years.[14] These laws are enforced by the Premium and Representations Division of the Fair Trade Commission. These antimonopoly laws, specifically the sections dealing with unfair trade practices, forbid unjust and deceptive consumer inducement through misrepresentation and coercion. The Act against Unjustifiable Premiums and Misleading Representations establishes stringent provisions to prevent unjust inducements to customers by means of an unjustifiable premium and misleading representations of a certain good or service. This act protects the general interest of the consumer and maintains fair competition. Unfair trade practices forbid descriminatory pricing, unjust low price sales, and so on. It also forbids deceptive consumer inducement by competitors so as to cause consumers to misunderstand the substance of commodities or services offered, or to miscomprehend the terms of the transactions or other matters that fool consumers into thinking they have better deals than they have or that other competitors can offer.

The FTC takes steps against misleading advertising through abatements and warnings. When advertisers are given orders for abatement of their ads, they must make public that their ads have violated the law and at the same time must report the violation to the FTC. Moreover, the advertisers have a special obligation to submit subsequent advertisements to the FTC for the duration of one year. Despite the penalties set by the FTC, it does not publicize the names of the violators nor fine them.[15] Consumers are protected also under the Consumer Protection Fundamental Act of 1968.

Produce-specific regulations also exist but are not generally severe. Tobacco and cigarette advertising occur on the public electronic media, but must not suggest that smoking is harmless. It cannot encourage young people to smoke. Every cigarette packet must include a government health-warning label. Alcoholic drinks and food advertising is also covered under Japanese competition laws. However, pharmaceutical advertising is permitted but strictly controlled. In many cases the Ministry of Health and Welfare must give the pharmaceutical advertising special clearance. Advertisements directed to children are entrusted to the self-restrictive rules of the advertising agencies' organization and of individual mass media companies.

Overall the regulatory system is not severe. As noted, the Japanese tend to avoid legalism and disputes. To sue or to be sued is dishonorable. For this reason the Japanese prefer self-regulation laws to national laws. Moreover, the trend toward governmental action has obliged the Japanese advertising industry to establish a self-regulatory center to obviate the need for undesirable governmental regulation. The Japan Advertising Review Organization (JARO), established in 1974 as a self-regulatory body for the advertising trade, sets standards and settles complaints and disputes outside the framework of the government. JARO works in close connection with governmental administrative agencies.

Notes

1. Ohio State University, East Asian Studies Program, *Business and Society in Japan; Fundamentals for Businessmen,* ed. Bradley M. Richardson and Taizo Ueda (New York: Praeger, 1981), 236–44.

2. Roy Sekigahama, "Madison Avenue Goes Shinjuku," *AsiAM,* January 1988. See also David Kilburn, "Diverse Dentsu," *Advertising Age 59,* 9 May 1988.

3. Information concerning the media was obtained from a research contribution by Li-Mei Yang, Boston University, May 1988, in connection with an unpublished work on the establishment of a joint venture between two advertising agencies Young & Rubicam and Dentsu; and also "A Comparison of Four Mass Media in the U.S. and Japan 188," (Tokyo: Communications Excellence Dentsu, 1988).

4. Ohio State University, *Business and Society,* 236–43.

5. Ibid., 244–47.

6. Barbara Mueller, "Reflections of Culture: An Analysis of Japanese and American Advertising Appeals," *Journal of Advertising Research* 27, (June/July 1987).

7. Ohio State University, *Business and Society,* 152–55.

8. Yoshi Tsurumi, *Multinational Management* (Cambridge, Mass.: Ballinger, 1977).

9. Ohio State University, *Business and Society,* 224–26.

10. Ibid., 225.

11. Rene David and John E.C. Brierly, *Major Legal Systems in the World Today* (London: Stevens and Sons, 1978), 477–505.

12. Ibid., 492.

13. Toshio Yamaki, "Advertising Regulation in Japan," (Paper presented to the Fourteenth Advertising Congress (Seoul, Korea, 18–21 June 1984).

14. *Act Concerning Prohibition of Private Monopoly and Maintenance of Fair Trade (Act No. 54 of April 14, 1947)* was amended in 1949, 1953, 1958, and 1977.

Supplementary legislation includes *Act Against Unjustifiable Premiums and Misleading Representations (Act No. 134 of May 15, 1962),* and *Unfair Trade Practices (Fair Trade Commission Notification No. 15 of June 18, 1982).*

15. Fair Trade Commission of Japan, *Legal Framework of Japanese Competition Policy,* Tokyo, April 1986.

Part III
Socialist Countries

9
Advertising in Socialist Countries

Of the world's population, 25 percent live in centrally planned socialist countries. These include the Soviet Union, the industrialized Eastern European countries, China, and several small developing countries in Southeast Asia, Africa, and Central America (see map 9–1).

Drawing on Marxism/Leninism, the socialist countries have adopted legal and economic systems, institutions and rules distinct from those of market-economy countries. In market economies the law sets limits on private economic activities that are otherwise allowed. In theory under the socialist system, wherein the state has traditionally controlled the vast majority of the economy, private economic activities are eschewed unless officially sanctioned.

The centrally planned countries generally adhere to principal socialist law. The distinctions in socialist law as compared with civil and common-law practices in the Western industrialized countries evolved from Marxist theory after the socialist revolution. Socialist law is subordinate to the task of creating the economic structure. Its architects are the legislators in obedience to popular will as guided by the Communist party. Because the socialist economy is a collective society wherein the state owns the means of production, there is limited scope for private legal relationships. Thus, compared to legal systems in the Western countries, private law has limited relevance; generally, all law in socialist countries is public law.

Significantly, socialist law is not uniform among centrally planned countries. Socialist law in Europe differs from socialist law in Asia because of fundamental differences in legal history, culture, and tradition. The legal systems of Eastern Europe, originally based on civil-code law, still maintain many characteristics of this legal system. A legalistic approach to social order is maintained. General rules of conduct are prescribed by law, and the terminology and classification of areas of law remain consistent with civil-code practice.

A very different approach has been taken in China. Traditionally, the Chinese have had an aversion to rule by law, associating law with the exercise

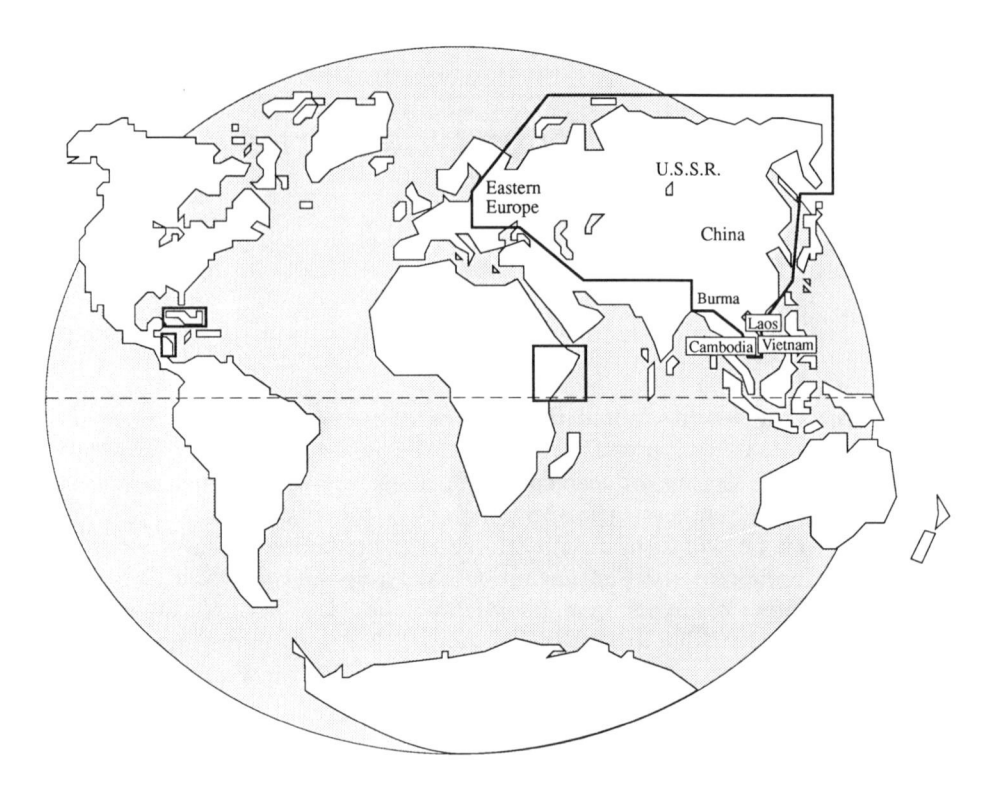

Map 9–1. Second World

of arbitrary power. The conduct of individuals has been governed by extra legal methods emphasizing the search for harmony and peace in interpersonal relations, which are based on a hierarchy of relationships and duties according to the individual's position in the hierarchy. The expansion and penetration of written law and legal processes in the social and commercial life of China have been minimal. Written law governing commercial relations has only recently been developing.

Centrally planned countries all vary considerably in the substance of their laws, and in particular in the degrees to which these laws permit private market operations. Often deviations from socialist principles involve pragmatic policy decisions to widen the scope for private market operations and foreign participation as a means to accelerate the modernization and industrialization of the socialist state.

Liberalization varies among Eastern European countries. Geography, culture, history, leadership, and the nature of relations with the Soviet Union are determining factors. Yugoslavia, Poland, and Hungary have adopted systems with significant decentralization and have accepted elements of private market economies. China and, most recently the Soviet Union have gone the farthest in adopting a deliberate policy of liberalization in the interest of rapid development. These countries have established relations with many private foreign enterprises. East Germany, Bulgaria, and Rumania consistently have followed a relatively more orthodox policy.

The role of foreign advertising in each country also varies inversely with the concentration of economic power. The more decentralized the production and distribution systems, the more consumers participate in buying decisions, and the more likely is advertising to influence purchasing decisions.

Commercial advertising is practiced to some extent in all socialist countries, liberal and orthodox alike. The total volume is much less, and the manifestation may be quite different, from that commonly seen in market-economy countries. The differences reflect not only ideology and public policy, but also the relative dearth of consumer goods. Less than enthusiastic attitudes toward advertising as practiced in the West reflect Marx's heavy emphasis on material products and his views on marketing. Although apparently never making explicit reference to advertising, Marx held that the only activities benefiting society were those that embodied labor value. "Costs of circulation which originate in a mere change of form of value, ideally considered, do not enter into the value of commodities."[1] Such costs, according to Marxist disciples, include market research, sales promotion, and advertising.[2]

Despite Marxist principles, the necessity for advertising of a limited nature has always been apparent to public administrators. Advertising policy in centrally planned countries was outlined at the first Conference of Advertising Workers in Socialist Countries held in December 1957 in Prague and at the first All Soviet Conference held in August 1958. The recommendations adopted in Prague are enshrined in the current policies of Eastern European countries. Accordingly, socialist advertising's aims are to form demand for goods by educating consumers' tastes and shaping their needs, to help consumers by giving them information about the most rational forms of consumption, and to improve service to consumers in the retail trade.[3]

In accordance with public policy, advertising promotes the achievement of socioeconomic objectives. The informational role of advertising is emphasized in contrast to advertising practices in market economies, where image and impression are highly important. Thus, foreign advertisers are advised that in socialist countries, they should emphasize a product's advantageous qualities rather than its prestige, value, or price. Such emphasis on information rather than on image reflects not only the limited decision-making power of the ordinary consumer, but also the fact that advertising is not necessarily intended to generate immediate sales. Traditionally, in socialist countries, state agencies and state media are the only channels for advertising and the biggest advertisers are the public enterprises. Advertising continues to be heavily concentrated on industrial products. Since industrial equipment is the major item sold by foreign firms in Socialist European countries, these firms advertise primarily in scientific, technical, trade, and industrial journals. Advertising has limited use in stimulating demand for consumer goods that are in relatively short supply. While imported consumer goods are generally in demand, they are lower on the priority lists of state import agencies. Limited supplies concentrate in hard currency stores. Strong demand in excess of supply has prompted little call to promote these products.

But radical changes are in the air. Within the last few years the governments of China, Hungary, and the Soviet Union have invited and approved the establishment joint ventures with foreign advertising agencies. Foreign agencies are even permitted to have majority ownership of the ventures. Moreover, radio, television, and print media including newspapers have become available for foreign advertising. Even foreign consumer products from the West have begun to be advertised directly to the general public.

Notes

1. Karl Marx, *Capital* (Moscow: Foreign Languages Publishing House, 1957), 136.

2. Marshall I. Goldman, "Product Differentiation and Advertising: Some Lessons from Soviet Experience," *Journal of Political Economy* 68 (August 1960): 346.

3. Everett M. Jacobs, "New Developments in Soviet Advertising and Marketing Theory," *International Journal of Advertising* 5, no. 3 (1986): 243–46; V.E. Demidov and I.P. Kardashidi, *Reklama v Torgovli: Teoria i Praktika* (Moscow: Ekonomika, 1983), 5.

10
Eastern Europe

Although Eastern Europe countries have a market of 300 million consumers, their commercial advertising budgets are miniscule compared with the advertising expenditures of the United States, Japan, Western Europe and even the advanced Latin American countries. The trend today, however, is toward increased outlays for advertising in many of these Eastern European countries, as socialist marketing theorists recognize the need for direct advertising to consumers and for reflection of consumer interest in product development.

Over the last two years, Supreme Soviet Presidium Chairman and Communist Party General Secretary Mikhail Gorbachev has been working to achieve revolutionary changes in the Soviet economic system. *Perestroika, glasnost,* and overall new thinking in the international arena have been translated into a number of reforms that for advertising mean foreign goods, including consumer products, can be expected to be advertised on the mass media, joint ventures with foreign advertising agencies may be negotiated directly between state commercial organizations including advertising enterprises and media organizations, and foreign advertising agencies may retain majority ownership of the venture. These changes in the Soviet way of doing business with the outside world will undoubtedly spill over to other Eastern European countries. Such is the case already in Hungary where multinational agencies have concluded joint venture agreements.

The recent changes are significant. Prior to 1988, advertising contracts in most of Eastern Europe were made through foreign trade organizations (FTOs). This is still the practice in the more conservative countries in Eastern Europe. These organizations, commonly subordinate to ministries of foreign trade, are independent legal entities with the right to make contracts subject to government approval. They were established by the government to deal exclusively in a particular economic area in accordance with the policies and plans of the ministries to which they are attached. These state agencies also act as intermediaries between foreign sellers and domestic end-users.

170 • *International Advertising Handbook*

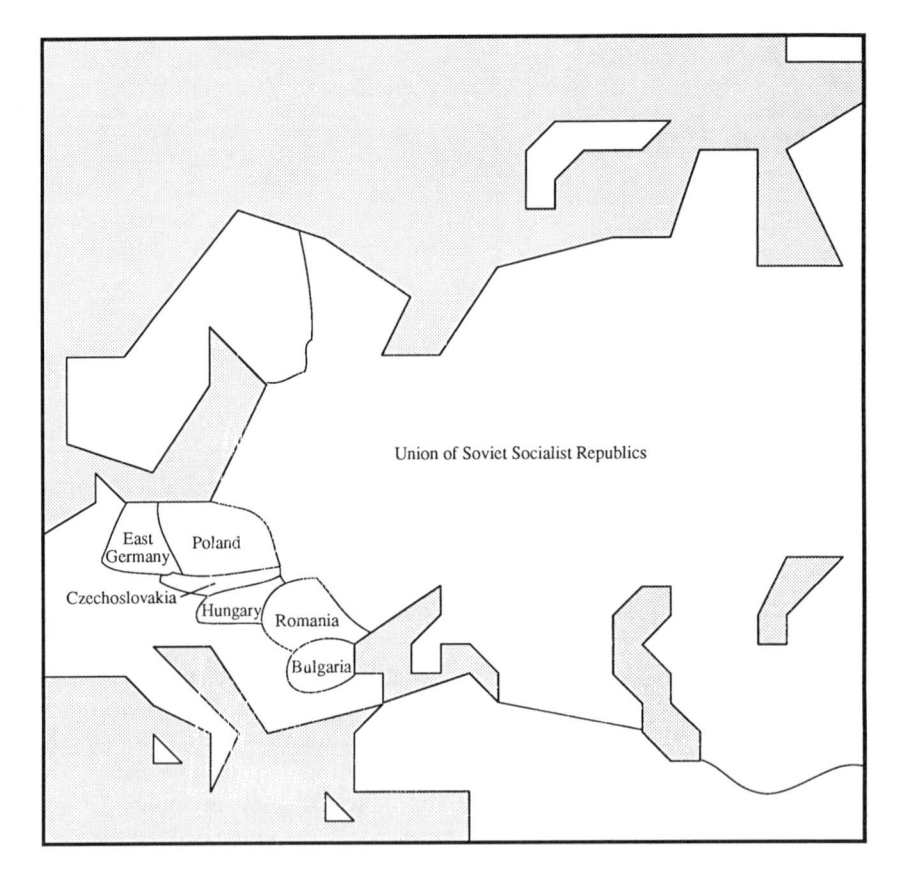

Map 10–1. Eastern Europe

This chapter focuses on the largest market in Eastern Europe, the Soviet Union, as the ideological leader in this part of the world, and provides short summaries for general Eastern European countries (see map 10–1).

The Soviet Union

The development of advertising in the Soviet Union has been cautious. Lenin permitted the practice in the mid-1920s along with some free enterprise. During this period, according to author Marshall Goldman, "Newspapers carried ads, poets wrote copy, and advertising was not too different from that in the rest of Western Europe."[1] When Stalin came to power and introduced the Five-Year Plan, commercial advertising and free enterprise were virtually swept out. After Stalin's death advertising began to enjoy a limited renaissance. The change came about slowly. Even in Stalin's time, there was recognition of the need for product labeling to facilitate administrative controls on output. As production increased, planners introduced trademarks to encourage repeat sales and to save on inspection costs. In the post-Stalin period, self-service shops were introduced, and advertising began to fulfill the information function of the salesperson. With increased production advertising also was needed to encourage sales of newly introduced products and to clear overstocked inventories.

Today, although Soviet theory has advanced along more liberal economic lines, advertising is still underplayed, carefully orchestrated according to public policy and operated under many constraints (see table 10–1). Control over advertising is virtually assured because it is a state economic activity. Soviet economic policy, although moving in the direction of decentralization since 1986, has not fully adopted a system of economic management based on market mechanisms. Central planners continue to oversee advertising and consumption so that demand is not stimulated beyond what is thought to be rational. Political theory remains paramount in advertising practice; advertising must accord with the Communist party's political and economic objectives

Table 10–1
Regulatory Profile: Soviet Union

Government:	Union of Socialist Republics: consisting of 15 sovereign republics, 20 autonomous republics, and 128 oblasts (division largely on ethnic lines); single communist party rule
Politico-economic ideology:	Democratic centralism and socialist pluralism
Economic system:	Centrally-planned state enterprise system; under restructuring with increasing sectors opening for cooperatives
Legal system:	Socialist law superimposed on Romano/Germanic code base
Investment policy:	Joint-ventures with foreign agencies are permitted
Ad regulation:	Significant dispersed government controls; foreign advertising permitted through state advertising enterprise or through the media
Ad expenditure:	Actual figure not available ($.3 billion-estimated)
Consumer market:	Growing, many scarcities
Social indicators:	
Population:	281.7 million
Urbanization:	66%
Per capita income:	Not available
Language:	Russian plus many national languages, 18 of which are spoken by more than 1 million.
Social structure:	Workers, collective farmers, and intelligentsia
Life expectancy:	65–74 years
Literacy:	About 90%

for society. Socialist advertising is based on the psychology of socialist materialism and emphasizes the systematic spending of family incomes on consumer necessities. The general paucity of advertising reflects the widespread scarcity of consumer goods. Consumer advertising has been concentrated on goods in relative abundance that may or may not be desirable to consumers. Nevertheless, the role of consumer interest in product design is increasing.[2]

Compared with advertising in the West, advertising in the Soviet Union is relatively discreet and generally rare, especially when it comes to consumer goods. When it occurs generic rather than brand-name advertising is more typical. For example, ads state "Drink Milk" or "Buy Radios." However, this is consistent with the organization of production and trade in the Soviet economy. Even though production of goods has expanded and standards of living are improving, the need for advertising remains limited because heretofore manufacturers have not competed. Each individual organization produces a unique line of equipment or series of items that is not replicated elsewhere in the economy. Word of mouth is effective when an item is found in the marketplace. Although considerable progress has been made, the limited supply of consumer goods remains the most serious constraint on the growth of advertising.[3]

Emphasis in the Soviet Union is on the information content of advertising. Advertising copy and message content are quite different from that produced in advanced market-economy countries. Speechlike texts are common in Soviet ads. At the opposite extreme, other commercials use little text, relying on slogans employing such terms as *special* or *indispensable*. The absence of brand-name advertising and special model names for many products also has an impact on the nature of the message. All these factors have given rise to criticisms that the advertising is bland, lacking in central ideas, either too general or confusing, and received with public indifference. There are strong hints that as more emphasis is given to the production of consumer goods and the need to respond to consumer needs, advertising will be given more attention and will become increasingly appealing and sophisticated.

Total annual advertising probably amounted to about $300 million in 1987, about 200 million rubles. The share of foreign advertising from the United States, Western Europe, and Japan in the Soviet industry has been very small. Recent figures value the total advertising of products from the West at about $7.5 million or about 2 percent of total Soviet advertising expenditure in 1987.[4] The media distribution of foreign advertising is shown in figure 10–1.

Prior to 1988, the government financed advertising through plan allocations. The government accumulated financial resources for advertising on the basis of planned assignments. One assigned figure commonly used was .05 percent of the wholesale price of goods oriented for public needs. Such deductions may create funds for shops, supermarkets, and enterprises. In

Eastern Europe • 173

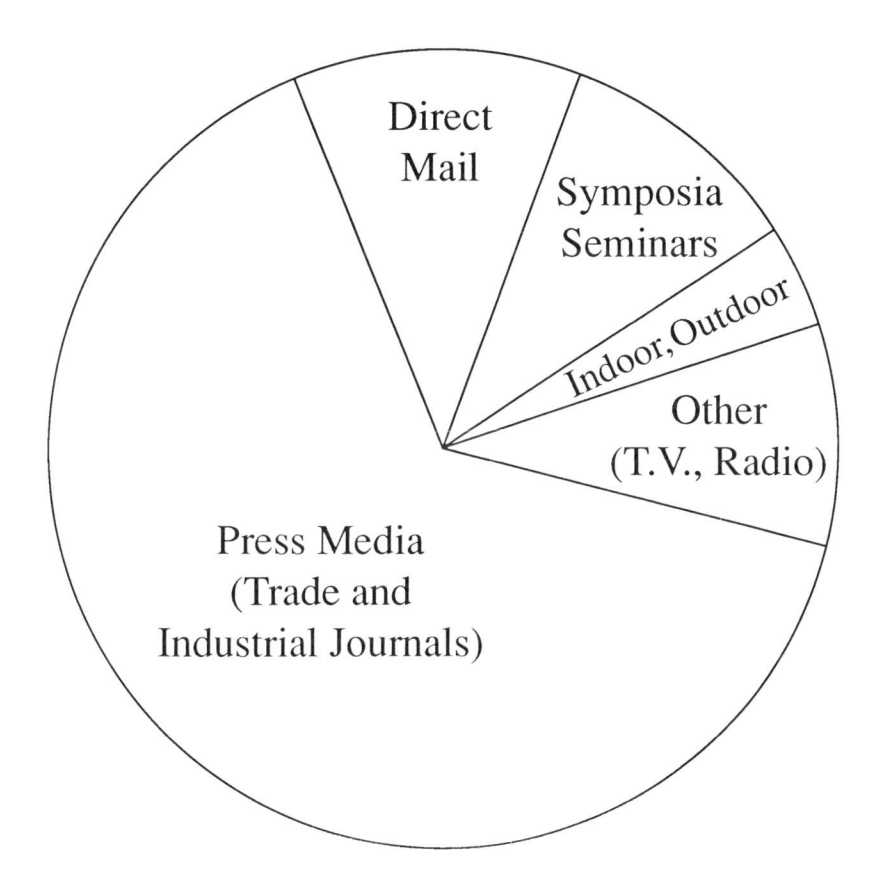

Source: Alexander Mudrov, Veneshtorgreklama, Amtorg Trading Co., New York, New York.

Figure 10–1. Distribution of Media Used by Foreign Advertisers in the Soviet Union, 1988

addition, advertising was financed by voluntary allocations from local and central ministries.[5] Since 1988, the financing system has been decentralized. This means that each state enterprise, exporter, or manufacturer can allocate their funds for advertising as they perceive the need.

Advertising in the Soviet Union is organized and coordinated on several administrative levels. On the national scale there is the Interdepartmental Council of Advertising, directed by a Deputy Minister of Foreign Trade. The Council has consultative status, and its membership consists of representatives from the major ministries (including the ministries of trade, civil aviation, health, and culture) and those responsible for the production of specific goods. Beyond this point domestic and foreign advertising today will be handled by independent legal entities including state enterprises, cooperatives, and other amalgamations.

Domestic Advertising

On the national level, the state advertising agency Soyuztorgreklama, under the direction of the Ministry of Trade, has had responsibility for all commercial advertising in the Soviet Union and between the Soviet Union and the COMECON, that is the Soviet Union and the Eastern bloc. Since 1988 Soyuztorgreklama is handling advertising with the Western countries as well. This agency incorporates a number of advertising enterprises and workshops. Its functions include the transmission of advertising to technical journals and newspapers; the distribution of commercials on television; and the production and distribution of films, posters, catalogues, displays, and so on. Below the state echelon each Soviet republic has its own agency. Two of the most important agencies are Rostorgreklama and Ukrtorgreklama, handling domestic advertising for the Russian Republic and the Ukrainian Republic, respectively.

Various media are available for domestic advertising. The largest amount of sophisticated advertising is transmitted through technical journals, of which there are hundreds. There are nearly seven hundred newspapers, each with a circulation of over 1 million, that publish advertisements. However, about 95 percent of Soviet newspapers do not run retail or wholesale advertising. There are two primary television stations: Channel 1 reaches 92 percent of the population, and Channel 2 about 50 percent. In addition, there are local stations in major cities. There is some commercial television advertising. Also available are billboards and neon signs connected with major events, such as international sporting events. Outdoor boards recently have been mounted on buses.

In recent years there has been increasing advertising of Soviet consumer goods on television in the form of one-minute to two-minute films in half-hour programs transmitted several times weekly. Items advertised include some foods and beverages, fashion items, home appliances, electronic toys, movie cameras, portable battery-operated televisions, video machines, and so on, the vast majority of which are produced in the Soviet Union. Many of the goods advertised are not yet readily available to the average consumer, or if available, they are sold at prices often beyond the reach of average consumers. Although the films cannot always sell products, they do indicate that improvements in the material lives of Soviet citizens may be expected in the near future and that the Soviet Union can produce the same caliber of sophisticated goods found in Western countries.

Foreign Advertising

Up until 1988 foreign advertising in the Soviet Union and the advertising of Soviet goods and services abroad has been centered in Vneshtorgreklama, the state foreign-trade advertising agency, and its foreign-trade advertising arm, Sovero.[6] Sovero was established in 1964 to promote Soviet goods abroad and to publicize foreign goods and services within the Soviet Union. Sovero issues *Soviet Export* magazine (from January 1990 Soviet Export will be titled *Business Contact*) and consists of six specialized firms. Among these, Komplexreklama handles export advertising, and Inoreklama deals with foreign advertising using Soviet media.

Inoreklama, a division of Sovero, puts foreign advertisers in contact with representatives of potential buyers and acquisition decision makers. Its services also include launching comprehensive advertising campaigns (from concept to management); advertising in Soviet trade and technical journals and magazines; advertising via indoor and outdoor advertisements, radio, technical symposia and seminars, direct mail; and coordinating with other advertising services available in the Soviet Union.

Foreign advertisements appear mainly in trade, technical, and industrial magazines and journals that are published by respective branch ministries or other state commercial organizations. Traditionally, Soviet foreign trade organizations, individual Soviet firms or similar organizations, and firms from COMECON countries, members of the Council for Mutual Economic Assistance (CMEA—other Eastern European countries) have had priority in obtaining advertising publication space in Soviet publications. Space for Westerners has generally been scarce with the exception of *Soviet Export* (as of 1990 *Business Contact*) published by Vneshtorgreklama and *Technical Trends* published by West Germany's Messemagazin International in cooperation with Vneshtorgreklama, the USSR State Committee for Science and Technology and the USSR Chamber of Commerce and Industry.[7]

Soviet journals enjoy wide circulation in the Soviet Union and in Eastern Europe. Because these journals were not designed originally for advertising, printing facilities, and space for advertising are limited. Moreover, ready-made ads are sometimes unacceptable because, in addition to printing limitations, translation and editing are necessary. Hence, advertisers have been warned of time lags and the need to submit materials at least three months in advance of intended publication. They are also advised to run ads frequently and to use several journals and newspapers. Prospectuses and pamphlets are requested from advertisers and are mailed to appropriate Soviet companies and organizations.

A positive indicator of the USSR's intention to move in the direction of more advertising and more cooperation with the West is the appearance, for the first time ever in a Soviet daily newspaper, of advertisements of multinational enterprises. On 3 January 1989, the Soviet newspaper *Izvestia* ran two full-page advertisements for Pechiney and Occidental Petroleum, respectively. Previously, these heavy industrial enterprises advertised only in technical journals and occasionally on television.[8] The Soviet newspaper *Trud* is also seeking one or two pages of foreign advertising a week as is *Nedelia* the weekly supplement of *Izvestia*.

Primarily since 1988, advertising of Western industrial equipment and some consumer goods is also appearing on a very limited scale on Soviet television. Recently Gostelradio, the Soviet state television network, established Sovtelexport to sell ad time on selected Soviet television broadcasts. Gostelradio is engaged in joint program production projects with Global American Television, Inc., a small Massachusetts firm that sells time on Soviet television to foreign advertisers. On all the joint productions Global American has rights to sell advertising time within the context of the programs of which there were four in 1988. On the last such program, November 17, 1988, for example, Coca-Cola, Combustion Engineering, and R.J. Nabisco bought billboard ads that were flashed on the screen during the broadcast of a joint concert of the New York Philharmonic Orchestra and the Soviet State Symphony.[9]

While many foreign companies are allowed to promote their industrial products, foreigners are also beginning to advertise consumer goods. Permission to advertise Pepsi Cola in the Soviet Union was obtained in exchange for the promotion of Stolichnya Vodka in the United States. Pepsi ads have been seen on transit boards affixed to buses in Moscow. As mentioned above other foreign consumer products are also beginning to appear on Soviet television. For the next few years most foreign advertising will be concentrated on industrial products. As the economy becomes more prosperous over the next two or three years, and consumer products appear in much greater supply, it is expected that foreign consumer goods will also be advertised more frequently in all the mass media.

Although several foreign advertisers have long operated in the Soviet Union, until 1988, apparently only one Western foreign advertising firm, Finnav, operated there. Finnav had the concession to handle advertising at sporting events in the Soviet Union. Today, three multinational advertising firms, Young & Rubicam, Ogilvy & Mather, and Saatchi & Saatchi, are also operating in the Soviet Union and it is only a matter of time before firms such as McCann-Erickson and J. Walter Thompson join them.

Regulatory Environment

In the Soviet Union, general legal principles and much legislation are embodied in fifteen separate codes. Each code is divided into general provisions and special rules, as are the codes of many Western European countries. Unlike the codes of France and Germany, however, socialist codes contain no separate commercial code. Industrial property and copyright laws are incorporated in the civil code. Although not a formal source of law, guidance to the interpretation of the code is provided by the courts in the form of *rukovodia shchie raz"iasmeviia* (guiding explanations) frequently used by the Soviet Union and the Union Republic supreme courts. They summarize court practice on specific legal issues, resolve errors, and clarify legal points. These explanations are binding on lower courts.

Each Soviet republic has its own series of legal codes. There currently are fifteen codes, including a constitution. The codes elaborated in the Russian Soviet Federative Socialist Republic (RSFSR), the largest of the republics, provides the standard model for other republics, whose codes are all virtually the same.[10]

The substantive content of the Soviet codes differs substantially from codes of the Western market-economy countries. The Soviet codes regulate legal relationships in a centrally owned socialist society. Thus, the criminal code contains several chapters outlining crimes, most of which are perpetrated against the collective rights of society (for example, crimes against the state, against socialist ownership, or against the system of administration); economic crimes and official crimes also are covered. Three chapters alone detail crimes against the individual: life, health, freedom, and dignity; political and labor rights; and personal ownership rights.

Advertising abuse might be covered by several chapters in the criminal and civil codes. For example, advertising judged illegal may involve an economic crime in that it may have deceived purchasers and consumers or committed other marketing acts forbidden under article 156 of the code.[11] Conviction may result either in no more than two years' loss of freedom to the advertiser, one year or a correctional task, or loss of the right to occupy offices in commercial enterprises. Crimes against the health of the individual are committed by the advertising of pornographic writings; conviction is punishable by no more than three years deprivation of freedom, and so on.[12] Advertising abuse also may fall under articles in the criminal code forbidding defamation;[13] passing off (violations of another person's political and labor rights);[14] or swindling (acquiring another's possessions [money] through deception or abuse of trust).[15]

A number of articles in the civil code also may be relevant to advertising practice. Chapter 21 on contracts of sales, and chapter 24 on supply contain several articles concerning obligations of sellers or suppliers to buyers in terms of the delivery of goods as promised according to the contract and the need to make good when the contract has been breached. Under chapter 11 on liability for torts, advertisers who cause harm to individuals may be obligated to make good in full measure for harm or damage they may cause unless they can prove that the harm caused was not their fault. Organizations must make good the faults of their work.[16]

Because all advertising has been channeled through state agencies in accordance with state policy, there has been little need to adopt general statutory advertising laws. Statutory rules and regulations exist, however, in the context of administrative regulations governing products and the media. In addition to controlling both the product and the advertising media, authorities in various ministries also set out specific requirements regarding information about particular products. For example, the Ministry of Trade is responsible for organizing food-product advertisements. The Ministry of Food Industry, in turn, transmits that consumer information via written data on labels or packaging. Such information includes the name, manufacturer, price, date of production, preservation dates, and cooking instructions. These data are established according to a set of standard regulations complying with the Soviet Union Health Authority rules. All foods and other products coming into close contact with foods imported from foreign countries also are submitted to scrutiny of the Ministry of Health and can be used in the Soviet Union only with the approval of the Health Authorities.[17]

Future Outlook

In the future, expectations are for a greater role for advertising in the Soviet economy and for a significant increase in joint ventures with foreign firms in the production of goods and services. These expectations have been encouraged initially by the 1987 decree of the Presidium of the USSR Supreme Soviet and the decision of the USSR Council of Ministers on the establishment of joint ventures with foreign firms and even more so by the December 1988 Decree of the Council of Ministers on foreign trade and joint ventures.[18]

The 1987 legislation stipulated that agreements drawn up by the involved parties have appropriate ministerial approval and cover matters of management, capital formation, public sharing, and dispute settlement. The limit on foreign ownership was set at 49 percent and all agreements were required to have government approval. It also specified the matters that might require unanimous decisions, thereby giving the minority partner equal control. Disputes would be settled in local courts or through local or foreign arbitration arrangements. The number of foreign employees allowed to work in the Soviet operations of the venture was limited to a small number and the law required that the chairman of the board and the director general of the venture would be citizens of the Soviet Union. Moreover, the joint venture guidelines stipulated that ventures would have to meet their own hard-currency requirements.

For Western businesses, the 1987 law raised a number of problems in several areas. Ambiguity surrounded the procedures for government approval. There was uncertainty as to which government body would be the final approving authority. Hard currency matters also caused concern as did a number of other problems related to minority shares, government involvement and daily management.[19]

Many of these objections were intended to be met by the wide ranging December 1988 decree of the Council of Ministers. As of April 1, 1989, foreign trade was opened to all Soviet business organizations, including state enterprises and cooperatives so long as their activities were self-supporting. This decree ended fifty years of virtual state monopoly over foreign trade whereby all foreign trade was in the name of the state and the state would assign certain organizations responsibility for specified trade functions.

The State Foreign Economic Committee of the USSR Council of Ministers, however, has not given up all controls on international trade or business, and reserves the right to suspend trade in cases involving unfair competition or where activities are found to harm the interests of the state. It also required registration of all organizations engaged in trade. The Council of Ministers established a list of items that cannot be imported for economic or political reasons. Moreover, the right of enterprises to import consumer products is limited to 10 percent of their hard-currency reserves.

Specifically with respect to joint ventures, the December 1988 decree lifted the 49 percent limit on foreign ownership. Today a foreign business may, in principle, establish majority or even virtually wholly owned joint ventures in the Soviet Union provided Soviet partners retain a minimum 1 percent share of the joint venture. Moreover, the chief executive officers as well as the chairman of the venture's board of directors may be foreign citizens. The Soviet partner however, retains the right to veto important decisions by virtue of the requirement of unanimous consent for all key board decisions. The joint venture has also been given sole discretion in matters of hiring, firing, and remunerating its own employees.

The decree offers a number of other incentives including tax breaks for producers of particularly desired goods. Foreign personnel are also free to arrange for their own housing and services and to pay for them in rubles.

By virtue of this legislation, the Soviet Union has demonstrated serious intention to open its economy on a wide scale to foreign manufacturers and service enterprises. Specific objectives are the attraction of new technology, managerial experience, product expansion, and the promotion of trade. The newest investment regulations open the way to a wide array of business opportunities in the Soviet Union. Increasing numbers of joint ventures are being established in a number of sectors including advertising. As noted above Young & Rubicam and Vneshtorgreklama have concluded negotiations to establish Young & Rubicam Sovero. Also mentioned above is the joint project between Gostelradio and Global American Television, Inc. Moreover, Saatchi & Saatchi has become the advertising and marketing consultant for Gostelradio. In addition, Soyuztorgreklama has established a joint venture called

Tisza with the Hungarian agency Mahir and Ogilvy & Mather which is the majority joint venture partner of Mahir in Budapest.

The overall future impact of the joint venture law on foreign advertising is difficult to predict. Attitudes toward advertising are still influenced by socialist ideology and the Soviets are relative newcomers to joint ventures with advertising agencies in the West. Because of the general inexperience in the area of foreign joint ventures, project success may depend on considerable flexibility, patience, and imagination.

A further development enhancing optimism over the future is the recent decision of the state's domestic advertising agency, Soyuztorgreklama, to join the International Advertising Association as an organizational member. This reflects the intention of the Soviet government to advance advertising in the Soviet Union as rapidly as possible. Organizational membership could be a step toward the establishment of an IAA Chapter in the Soviet Union, and it gives the Soviet national agency access to the IAA's worldwide network of advertising professionals and information.[20]

Other Eastern European Countries

Among other countries in Eastern Europe, there are some variations in the restrictions on advertising and in the role of consumers in purchasing decisions. Hungary, Poland, and Yugoslavia are the most liberal in this respect. In the German Democratic Republic (East Germany), Bulgaria, and Czechoslovakia, target audiences are more restricted. There are several advertising agencies, and they use all forms of media. In all countries the government maintains control over foreign advertising, as state advertising agencies have a monopoly over all foreign advertising in their respective territories.

Hungary

Hungary is the so-called window of the West in the centrally planned countries. The advertising scene in Hungary appears most similar to that in Western Europe. The state agencies Hungexpo and Magyat Hirdeto (Mahir) and Interpress are the main channels for advertising services. Mahir has sixty-two subsidiaries and its own television station. Mahir has established a joint venture with Ogilvy & Mather as the majority partner. Together they have established a joint venture, Tisza in Moscow with Soyuztorgreklama. McCann-Erickson has established a joint venture with Interpress.

Advertising is possible through all print, electronics, and other media (such as cinema and outdoor advertising, including neon signs and billboards). Although acceptable, the advertising of consumer goods on radio and television is subject to restrictions; tobacco and alcohol advertisements, however, are proscribed, as is advertising for Western imports that use energy or that may be considered luxury products. Advertising is conceived as an arm of the state in Hungary, as in all centrally planned countries.

Advertising in Hungary is an integral part of the social reproduction process. Its tasks include reordering proper economic information and product instructions for use throughout the production chain to the consumer. It is a tool to assist enterprises in the fulfillment of their roles. Advertising must be pursued with a strong sense of political and social responsibility, as it contributes to the building of society and the predominance of the society's socialist character and to sustaining the priority of collective interests.[21]

Legislation adopted in respect to advertising includes the Uniform Compliance Act of 1923, which remains valid in large measure, and the Home Trade Law of 1978. The earlier law emphasizes the interests of business, the latter those of the state and the consumer.

Hungary is the only centrally planned country that has adopted a self-regulatory system in the style of Western countries. It is inspired partly by the ICC's code. The first advertising code of ethics issued by the Hungarian Advertising Federation took effect in May 1981. Complementing the regulations of the Home Trade Law, the self-disciplinary code of conduct establishes professional guidelines to stimulate higher ad standards. Ads must be "legal, honest, truthful, and decent" so that consumers will not lose confidence in advertising.[22] The code emphasizes respect of human personality, the correct use of Hungarian language in ads and complete and precise information on products (including full disclosure of charges and conditions in credit and premium ads). It rejects abuses in advertising to children, pornography, violence or crime in ads, marketing for unnecessary products, and fostering need of goods that are not available. The code places more responsibility on member agencies, media, and advertisers' representatives and imposes sanctions for violating the self-regulatory provisions.

Czechoslovakia

In Czechoslovakia there are two state advertising agencies. One is an FTO, the other an organ of the Czechoslovak News Agency. Advertising is permissible through all the traditional media. On radio and television, it is limited to a specific number of time blocks. These limitations are less stringent on radio, where it is permitted in five-minute blocks three times an evening, than on television.

Poland

In Poland foreign investment is invited in the handicraft sector (which includes twenty-five different types of production and service activities, such as clothing) and food and food purveying industries for the home market and export. Of the 144 foreign firms established now in Poland, most produce clothing, small technical instruments or components, construction materials and equipment, and decorative articles.[23]

As a rule all advertising is to be coordinated or licensed through the government agency Agpol (the Foreign Trade Publicity and Publishing Enterprise, an FTO). This agency handles advertising in Poland for both foreign and domestic firms. The publicity division of Agpol programs and executes complex or individual advertising campaigns on behalf of its clients, including advertising in the press and television and organizing symposia, conferences, and individual and collective displays.[24]

Thus, the government bureaucracy maintains formal control over foreign advertising campaigns in Poland. However, the Polish government has recognized that these procedures are not particularly attractive to foreign investors and is in the process of changing them in light of Poland's economic needs.

Bulgaria

All foreign advertising in Bulgaria is channeled through Bulgarre Klama, the FTO with the state monopoly in this area. Advertising is available on all media, but the electronic media are rarely used. Law prohibits advertising of cigarettes and alcohol. No private marketing in Bulgaria by foreign concerns is allowed. Foreign-produced consumer goods (both food and drugs) are available, mainly in so-called hard-currency shops. Some imported consumer goods can be found on an erratic basis in regular retail outlets for local currency, but at very high prices.

Advertising promotes domestic products and takes the form of short television spots (during a designated period once each night) or of ads in newspapers and periodicals. As there is no private production, all advertising, which is limited, is for the output of state-owned enterprises.

Notes

1. Marshall I. Goldman, "Product Differentiation and Advertising: Some Lesons from Soviet Experience," *Journal of Political Economy* 68 (August 1960): 348.

2. Everett M. Jacobs, "New Developments in Soviet Advertising and Marketing Theory," *International Journal of Advertising* 5, no. 3 (1986): 243–46; V.E. Demidov and I.P. Kardashidi, *Reklama v. torgovli: Teoria i praktika* (Moscow: Ekonomika 1983), 6–7.

3. "Russia," *Advertising Age,* 6 January 1986; "Ads Make Marx on Buses," *Advertising Age,* 25 August 1986; "Soviet TV—Only One Commercial Message," *Advertising Age* 56, 18 February 1985.

4. Stephen J. Simurda, "Primetime 'Peristroika': Soviet TV Looks to the West," *Adweek,* 16 January 1989, 37.

5. V.P. Shestakov, "Structure and Organization of Advertising in the USSR," in *Mass Communications and the Advertising Industry* (Paris: UNESCO, 1984), 17.

6. Information obtained from Alexander Mudrov of the office of Veneshtorgreklama, Amtorg Trading Co., New York, New York.

7. George Black, "Tactics for the Russian Front," *Business Marketing,* January 1989, 43–4.

8. *Le Monde,* 5 January 1989, 5.

9. Simurda, "Primetime 'Perestroika'," *Adweek,* 37.

10. William B. Simons, ed., *The Soviet Codes of Law,* in *Law in Eastern Europe,* series of publications issued by the Document Office for East European Law, University of Leyden, No. 23 (The Hague: Martinius Nijhoff, 1984).

11. Ibid., chap. 6 ("Economic Crimes"), art. 156.

12. Ibid., chap. 10 ("Crimes against Public Security, Order and Health of Population"), art. 228.

13. Ibid., chap. 3 ("Crimes against Life, Health, Freedom and Dignity of the Person"), art. 130.

14. Ibid., chap. 4 ("Crimes against Political and Labor Rights of Citizens"), art. 141.

15. Ibid., chap. 5 ("Crimes against Personal Ownership of Citizens"), art. 147.

16. *The Civil Code of the RSFSR,* pt. 3 ("Law of Obligations"); idem, chap. 21 ("Contract of Sale"), chap. 24 ("Supply"), chap. 15 ("Obligations Resulting from the Infliction of Damage") (tort).

17. B.B. Orlovski, expert in regulations affecting food products imported into the Soviet Union, Ministry of Food Industry, letter to author, 28 June 1984.

18. *Decree on issues relating to the establishment in the territory of the Soviet Union of joint ventures and the activities of those joint ventures, international associations, and organizations where there is participation of Soviet and foreign organizations, firms, and administrative bodies,* adopted by the Presidium of the USSR Supreme Soviet, 13 January 1987; *Decision on procedures regulating the establishment in the Soviet Union of joint ventures and their activities where there is participation of Soviet organizations and firms of capitalist and developing countries,* adopted by the USSR Council of Ministries, 13 January 1987; *Resolution on future development of the foreign economic activity of state cooperatives and other socialist enterprises, amalgamations, and organizations,* adopted by the USSR Council of Ministers, 2 December 1988, effective 1 April 1989.

19. Ivan D. Ivanov, "Joint Ventures in the Soviet Union," *CTC Reporter,* no. 23 (Spring 1987): 48–51.

20. International Advertising Association, Press Release, Spring 1988.

21. Hungarian Advertising Association, *Hungarian Code of Ethical Advertising,* Budapest, 1981, 8.

22. Ibid., Clause 4.

23. Inter-Polcom (Polish-Polonian Chamber of Industry and Commerce), *Doing Business in Poland,* March 1982, 3.

24. Polish Chamber Foreign Trade, *Information for Businessmen Trading with Poland,* Warsaw, 1980.

11
China and Socialist Asia

The socialist countries of Asia run the gamut from the colossus China to the comparatively small states of Burma, Laos, Kampuchea, and Vietnam. China boasts an established sociopolitical and economic infrastructure, a government reaching out for trade relations and foreign investment, a high rate of literacy, and a vast urban population manifesting a growing appetite for consumer goods. The doors to the markets of the other countries are virtually closed to the Western industrialized world.

China

Although China is a low-income country, it is potentially the largest consumer-goods market in the world (see table 11–1). China has almost five times as many people as the United States. Of the more than 1 billion population, almost two-thirds are between the ages of fifteen and sixty-four, the prime spending ages. Although 80 percent of the population is rural close to 500 million people live in near urban areas, where transportation facilities enable easy access to growing consumer markets. Rural consumers are also the recipients of increased incomes and provide a growing market for ready-made consumer goods. Although increasing consumption is the trend, savings remain high (20 percent in urban areas, 12 percent in rural areas), suggesting potential for increased consumption as relatively scarce consumer products become more abundant.[1]

Within the last decade, a virtual revolution in economic thinking and commercial relations with the outside world has occurred in China. Vast changes in attitudes, institutions, and economic structure have taken place. With the injection of market elements into the economy and with the solicitation of direct foreign investment, the Chinese have begun to set aside centuries of aversion to legalism and have started to give prominence to long-neglected service industries, including advertising.

Table 11-1
Regulatory Profile: China

Government:	People's Republic; single Communist party rule
Politico-economic ideology:	Democratic centralism: Marxist socialism undergoing modernization
Economic system:	State-controlled enterprise system with extensive decentralization and increased opportunities for private entrepreneurs
Legal system:	Socialist law superimposed on Confucian legal traditions; undergoing extensive revision on European-U.S. code models
Investment policy:	Strictly controlled, but all types of foreign investment arrangements considered
Ad regulation:	Significant government control; foreign advertising permitted
Ad expenditure:	310 million; per capita and %GNP insignificant
Consumer market:	Underdeveloped; rapidly expanding
Social indicators:	
Population:	1.1 billon
Urbanization:	22%
Per capita income:	$300
Language:	Modern Chinese plus many regional dialects and minority languages
Class structure:	Predominantly low income
Life expectancy:	68–70 years
Literacy:	85%

Attitudes toward foreign economic relations have shifted with historical epochs, but they have never been more favorable than at present.[2] Following the death of Chairman Mao, Chinese economic thinking underwent a striking change. In a dramatic effort to remedy substantial weaknesses in the Chinese economy, policy makers announced in 1978 the Four Modernizations Program and put it into operation in 1979. The major characteristics of the program included structural reform and readjustment of the economy. Although socialism and self-reliance were not abandoned, the class struggle was set aside, and the market was rediscovered. Consistent with the program was the adoption of a policy favorable to foreign investment.[3] Today China boasts over 5,000 enterprises jointly managed by foreigners and Chinese and 120 companies managed exclusively by foreigners.

Significantly, services have lost the traditional stigma of servitude, and advertising, long considered a politically inappropriate service, has gained public acceptance. The new policy stresses advertising's important place in China's modernization drive. As a form of socialist publicity, advertising is to help achieve objectives of growth in the socialist commodity economy. This recognition stems from the increasing willingness of decision makers to rely on market forces for the distribution of goods and services, to guide consumption, and to serve consumers. In so doing, advertising is to promote awareness of new products, awaken brand consciousness, and introduce trademarks.

Recent official policy on the purpose and content of advertising was outlined in a speech by the State Administration for Industry and Commerce's director of management for industry and commerce in April 1987:

> [Advertising] should adhere to four cardinal principles—following the socialist road, and guided by the people's democratic dictatorship, leadership of the Communist Part of China, and Marxism-Leninism and Mao Zedong Thought. Attention should be paid to the unity of ideological content and artistic quality. It shall also serve to promote both sound socialist material development and socialist ethics and culture. An advertisement shall also pay attention to economic efficiency and social results and have a lively and vivid artistic form.[4]

The Chinese share some significant cultural characteristics with other Asian societies, notably Japan, which are important for foreign advertisers to understand. Unlike Western societies, which stress individuality, privacy and diversity, the Chinese culture places emphasis on the group and on frugality. There is, for example, no simple language equivalent for the concept of privacy. *Self* carries the connotation of selfishness as contrasted with *public*, inferring the public good. As is also true in Japan, the concept of rights is alien, and society emphasizes the idea of duty in interpersonal relations of all kinds. Little wonder that the Japanese are the top foreign advertisers in China.

Consistent with their culture and the government's official position that advertising is primarily a means of promoting product and service awareness, the Chinese tend to favor advertising that is straightforward and informational, rather than persuasive in nature. Aesthetics have importance; well-designed, full-color ads are appreciated. Tending to take advertising more seriously than Western consumers, the Chinese appreciate campaigns using factual rapport for selling messages. Campaigns that are avant garde, too subtle, or too ironic are not appreciated.

Cultural and political sensitivities are to be taken into account as well. Care must be taken that any idiom, analogy, humor, cultural symbolism, or translation is consistent with the local vernacular. Models are to be well clad; sexual undertones and emotional appeals are considered decadent. Maps and flags indicating the global reach of a multinational firm are ill-advised. Also, caution is suggested in the translations of global messages into Chinese or in the pronunciation of brand names or company names.[5] Successful ads relate the company or product to the national goals of the country.

Advertising's role in modernizing the economy is reflected in the distribution of products advertised. In 1986, 32 percent of all advertising billings were for industrial goods, intermediate goods, and electronic equipment; foods and pharmaceuticals each accounted for about 9 percent. The share for pharmaceuticals was almost the same as for foods. Daily necessities, including watches, clothing, and cosmetics, amounted to 21 percent. Culture and arts received 6 percent of the billings. The preponderance of foreign advertising is for technical goods, including small electronic equipment, machinery, and industrial goods.[6]

Significant constraints on the growth of advertising still abound in the economy's overall low level of development. Advertising foreign consumer products should always be weighed in relation to the availability of the product in the public distribution system. For the vast majority of the population, incomes are exceedingly low and supplies of consumer goods in short supply. Too often goods advertised are unattainable by the general public. Generally, it is the government's policy to discourage expenditure of foreign exchange on imported consumer products. Official concern is voiced periodically about the materialistic influence of attractive product advertising and the rising expectations stemming from increased awareness of the outside world's higher standards of living. These concerns, however, have not been translated into specific restrictions.

Thus, many foreign consumer products have penetrated the economy, but only as far as the hard-currency stores. The general availability of consumer goods is in flux; supplies become abundant or scarce in accordance with the availability of foreign exchange and with government decisions on quantities of consumer goods (for example, beverages, watches, cosmetics, televisions, and recorders) allowed to be imported or produced locally. The most successful foreign advertisers of consumer products are those engaged in joint ventures, producing the products locally. Local foreign exporters fair even better.

National Advertising Structure

Advertising in China has developed along two lines: (1) directly through the media and (2) through advertising agencies. Compared to western countries advertising expenditure in China is relatively insignificant, but growing rapidly. In 1987, advertising billings totalled $310 million an increase of 36 percent over the preceeding year (see figure 11–1). Per capita advertising as compared to per capita GNP amounts to only 0.1 percent and total advertising expenditure as a percentage of GNP is neglible (see figure 11–2). Direct expenditure to the media for advertising is still the main approach to advertising. In 1986, advertising agencies accounted for only 25 percent of all advertising billings; by contrast, direct placements of ads with newspapers, television, magazines, and the radio accounted for more than 50 percent of total billings. The remaining 25 percent was placed by people engaged in wirebroadcasts, billboards, and other media (see figure 11–3).[7]

Among the media newspapers and periodicals account for the greatest portion of advertising billings. Over 1,300 newspapers and 3,000 periodicals serve the Chinese, providing one copy for every five citizens. Radio reaches virtually 100 percent of the population and is very inexpensive. Television is

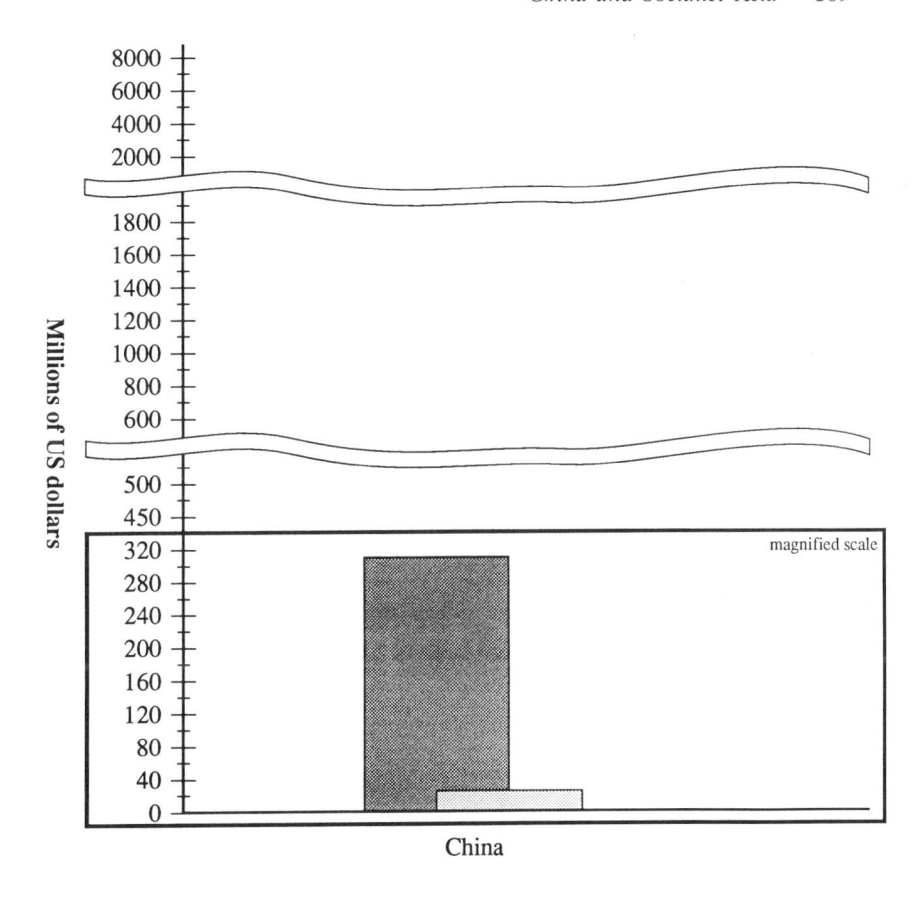

Figure 11-1. Gross Multinational Agency Billings and Total Advertising Expenditure in China, 1987

[Chart showing Total Advertising Expenditure and Multinational Agency Billings for China, with y-axis "Millions of US dollars" using a magnified scale. Legend: ■ -Total Advertising Expenditure[a]; ☐ -Multinational Agency Billings]

Source. Advertising Office of State Administration for Industry and Commerce.
[a]Total Advertising Billings

the fastest-growing medium: over 65 million sets reach 250 million people; eight out of ten urban households own a television set. Cinema and lighted display cases are popular media in urban centers. Lighted display cases (light boxes) are typically found in tourist areas, hotel lobbies, and airports and are used for cosmetic, cigarette, and alcohol advertising.[8]

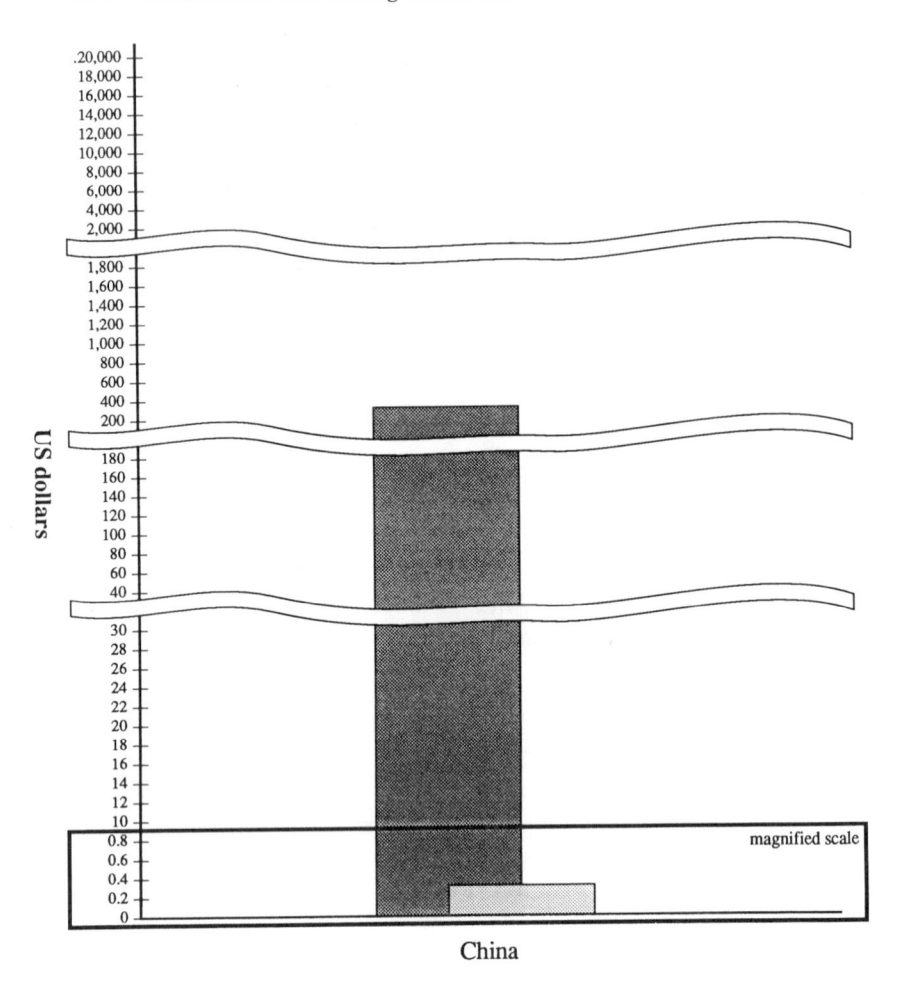

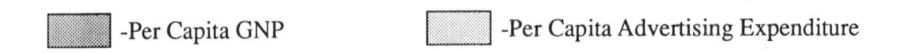

Source: derived from *World Advertising Expenditure*, 1987, 22nd ed., Starch INRA Hooper, Inc. in cooperation with IAA; *World Development Report, 1988*, World Bank.

Figure 11–2. Per Capita Advertising Expenditure and Per Capita GNP in China 1986/87

Currently, there is debate on the structure of the advertising industry in China. Proponents for the agencies argue that the media have been overstretched in the ad business, thereby curbing the growth of the ad agencies. In

[Pie chart showing percentages: 34.5%, 25.5%, 22.1%, 4.2%, 13.6%]

▨-Print[a]   ▦-T.V.   ⋮-Radio   ▩-Other   □-Non-measured Media[b]

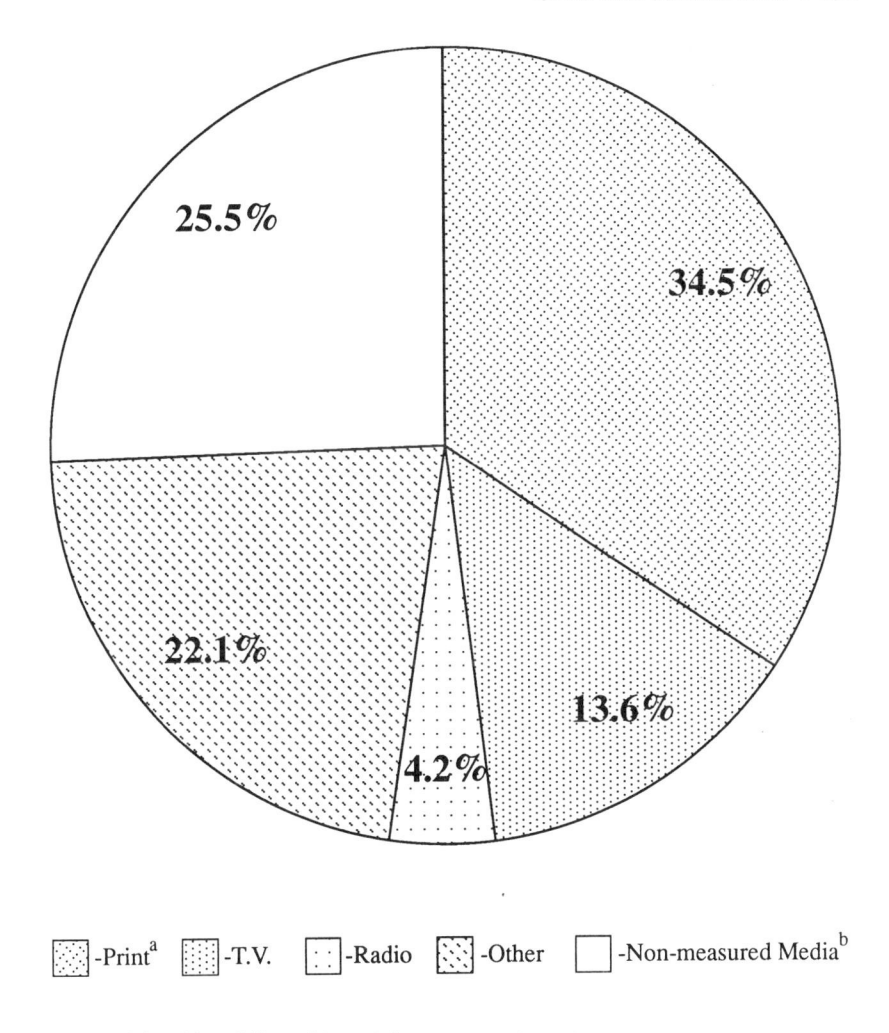

Source: Advertising Office of State Administration for Industry & Commerce.
[a]Newspaper and magazine ads.
[b]Ads handled by advertising companies.

Figure 11–3. Advertising Expenditure by Media and Non-measured Media in China (percentage shares)

the future, they argue, the media should provide time and space and the agencies should provide all-around services. The media respond that under current conditions, they are better equipped and more experienced than the agencies. They decry attempts to curb them.[9]

An estimated 680 major advertising companies operate in China, along with thousands of small workshops or studios. Among the major agencies, some operate on a national scale and others on a regional or local basis. China also has established national and provincial international advertising agencies for the promotion of Chinese exports and imported foreign products in China. They may operate in cooperation with or in joint ventures with foreign agencies.[10]

Two state agencies oversee and coordinate the work of all agencies in China. The first is China National United Advertising Corporation, established in 1981. It operates under the aegis of the State Administration for Industry and Commerce (SAIC), the institution responsible for the licensing and registration of all enterprises in China. One of SAIC's major functions is to bring under control, through its licensing authority, all local corporations (over 1,500) dealing in advertising.[11]

Later in 1981 the Ministry of Foreign Economic Relations and Trade (MOFERT) established the China National Foreign Trade Advertising Association. This organization, functioning as both a trade association and agency itself, is charged with coordinating, regulating, and overseeing the more than 20 Chinese foreign-trade advertising corporations—the agencies of principal interest to foreign advertisers.

Another corporation, China International Advertising Corporation, a specialized enterprise in foreign economic relations and trade advertisements, is concerned with opening up international advertising business, performing market research for domestic and overseas clients, and designing advertising. It is authorized by the Ministry of Foreign Economic Relations and Trade to organize local foreign-trade advertising agencies.

Foreign Advertising Activity

The Chinese experiment in liberalization has created a positive environment for foreign investors, advertisers, and their agencies. No longer limited to trade in goods, relations with foreign enterprises take many forms, including joint ventures, coproduction arrangements, and wholly owned subsidiaries. Joint ventures are formed under joint laws and regulations requiring a minimum foreign contribution of 20 percent of the capital and permitting foreign majority ownership. Coproduction arrangements entail partnerships between Chinese and foreign enterprises in which the foreigner assumes the principal role at the outset but fades out within a specified time. Foreign advertising is accepted as a source of foreign exchange and is charged reasonable but higher rates as compared with local enterprises.

Foreign advertising and the promotion of foreign products is conveyed through foreign advertising agencies operating in China, through direct operations between advertisers and the media, or through other arrangements. Foreign advertising agencies are doing a limited but growing business (at a growth rate of 15 percent per annum). In 1986 foreign advertising accounted for about 6 percent of total advertising billings, equivalent to $15 million.[12] The Beijing Advertising Corporation has the task of monitoring these foreign advertising activities. Thus far, Japan is the leader among foreign advertisers in China, accounting for more than 80 percent of foreign billings.

China is the only socialist country in which advertising agencies have reported income in the annual "Foreign Agency Income Report" of *Advertising Age*. Currently, at least eight multinational advertising agencies are doing business in one form or another in China. Among them, Dentsu, Interpublic Jardine China, and HDM have established joint advertising arrangements with Chinese partners. Ogilvy and Mather has opened an office in Beijing and has a nonequity arrangement with the Beijing Advertising Corporation. Needham Harper and Steers also operates in the China market.

Foreign advertising also is conveyed through arrangements made directly through the media. A number of joint publishing arrangements have relied on advertising sales to repay the foreign partner. For example, *Discover Magazine*, published in a Chinese-language edition through an agreement between Time, Inc., and China Popular Science Press, sells ads to Western firms (including Philip Morris and Rolex) to generate income. In an agreement with Chinese authorities, CBS has purchased advertising time on Chinese television in exchange for CBS programs shown in China.[13]

To encourage further its relations with foreign advertisers and agencies, China hosted the Third World Advertising Congress in Beijing on June 16–20, 1987. The congress was cosponsored by the China National Advertising Association for Foreign Economic Relations and Trade and by *South Magazine*. Moreover, the China chapter of the International Advertising Association was formally established in Beijing on May 12, 1987.

Regulation of Foreign Advertising

In the regulation of advertising in China, as throughout nearly all of Asia, tradition continues to exert a strong influence. Indeed, an antipathy toward formal legal systems exists and has deep roots in Chinese history and culture. Until the end of the nineteenth century, legalism was associated with the exercise of arbitrary autocratic power and criminality.[14] The dominant legal philosophy in China is based on Confucian teachings and philosophy. At its heart is a dichotomy between the concepts of *li* and *fa*. *Li* is associated with the Confucian concept of the natural order in society, while *fa* refers to written law, developed by the despotic Qin dynasty.[15]

The concept of *li* refers to rules of conduct in a system of natural order, the basic units of which are human beings in certain fundamental social roles. Each role carries with it rules of behavior—how the individual is to fulfill his or her own role and how he or she is to act in relationships with others in their roles. Good social behavior is maintained by moral force, perpetuated through example and education. Concrete prescriptions under the *li* concern private social relations.

Fa, recognized by Confucius and originally formulated by the legalists in the third and fourth centuries, is written law to be applied when *li* is inadequate to the maintenance of order.[16] In essence, *fa* is penal law, based on the governing of human behavior through the pleasure/pain principle. Under *fa* order is maintained by imposing fear of punishment and sanctions of force. Later extended as the instrument for government reform and despotic rule, *fa Zhiu* (rule by law) was discredited in the centuries following the Qin dynasty and the reign of the legalists.

The permeation of generations of society with Confucian thought and the heavy reliance on *li* have shaped legal thought and slowed formal legal development over the centuries. There has been some growth in written law, including a detailed criminal code and an accumulation of administrative rules. Some traditions for legal interpretation also have emerged.

The most significant changes have occurred in the twentieth century. In the early years of the twentieth century, the Chinese imperial government adopted a series of codes based on the European model: a civil code in 1929–31 (encompassing private and commercial law), a code of civil procedure in 1930, and so forth. With the advent of the People's Republic of China in 1949, more changes were introduced as the principle of socialist legality was superimposed on tradition. Existing laws, decrees, and court systems were shelved, and a series of fundamental laws was gradually adapted from the Soviet model as an aid to social reorganization. The People's Supreme Court and local people's courts were established, along with a codification commission for the drafting of codes of socialist law. The trend toward building a socialist legalist society came to a halt with the Cultural Revolution, and until the late 1970s, the role of law was downplayed.

Since 1979 there has been a new movement toward reliance on legal institutions and a rule of law. A major impetus has been the desire to attract foreign commercial relations and direct foreign investment. Technical assistance in the development of commercial laws has been sought from the United Nations and from Western industrialized countries. Chinese students of law have come to study in the United States and Western Europe in order to become more familiar with Western systems of law. In only a few years, China has promulgated several series of laws, regulations, and notices, over seventy of which address relations with foreign enterprises.[17]

Nevertheless, Confucian tradition remains strong and continues to be reinforced by doctrinal Marxism, which also emphasizes a political process of mediation in dispute settlements and the extralegal solution of disputes as a means of promoting the success of socialist objectives. Today, there are no more than ten thousand to fifteen thousand lawyers in China. With so few legal specialists, China's legal system is simple in structure, method, and content, permitting relatively untrained officials and the general public to participate in legal processes. Court trials are relatively new. A traditional antipathy toward clear-cut legislative statements persists. There is only a small body of judicial decrees, and the concept of binding judicial precedents remains alien.[18]

Despite the body of law now in place, traditional preference for nonlegal settlement of disputes prevails. The Chinese aversion to confrontation is reflected in the insistence on friendly consultations and conciliation in preference to litigation. The concept of individual rights is alien to *li;* self-interest is suppressed in a society governed by *li.* Conflicts of interests are solved by the willingness of the conflicting parties to make concessions. In those few cases that actually come to the courts, Confucian standards are used to achieve a settlement.

A similar preference is expressed in provisions for dispute settlements in bilateral treaties and in the Foreign Contract Law. The purpose is the saving of face and the maintenance of friendly relations. Damage to friendly relations would be costly to all parties and is inevitable when breaches of trust result in litigation. Arbitration and litigation are considered last resorts. Moreover, foreign lawyers are not allowed to practice before Chinese people's courts. In addition Chinese lawyers are duty bound to serve the interest of the state above interests of their clients if there is conflict.[19]

Among existing commercial laws and regulations, three are directly or particularly relevant to advertising: (1) the Joint Venture Law, (2) the Regulations of the People's Republic of China on the Registration of Joint Ventures Using Chinese and Foreign Investment, and (3) the Regulations for Advertising Management.[20] The first two laws, adopted in 1980, permit foreign companies, advertisers, and agencies to be incorporated in China. According to these laws, when negotiations between Chinese and foreign partners conclude in a legally binding contract, all documentation, including feasibility studies and the like, must be submitted to the Ministry of Foreign Economic Relations and Trade (MOFERT) for initial approval and to the State Council for final approval. Thereafter, the joint venture must be registered and licensed to operate with the State Administration for Industry and Commerce.

Since December 1987 advertising has been governed in accordance with Regulations for Advertising Management. These regulations supersede the Provision Articles on Control of Advertising, in effect since May 1982.[21] In two brief pages and twenty-two articles, the government in the new regulations outlines the purpose of advertising in the socialist state, states official requirements for licensing and certification of contents, defines permissible contents, lists acceptable fees, makes suggestions for self-regulation, establishes some limitations on media, and provides remedies for violations.

These regulations are similar in substance to the earlier regulations in effect from 1982. The language of the new regulations is clearer, less detailed, and less ideological in formulation. Although the new regulations supersede the 1982 rules, it is perhaps useful for the foreign advertising agency to continue to preserve the earlier set of regulations as one guide to possible official interpretation of the rules. A major innovation in the new legislation is the absence of any distinction between foreign and domestic advertising enterprises. Both sets of regulations are compared and discussed below.

Objective. As stated in article 1, the new (1987) regulations are formulated to strengthen advertising management, to promote the development of the business, and to ensure the effective use of advertising as a means of developing the Chinese socialist economy. This reflects a strong shift in emphasis. The earlier statement of purpose, also in article 1, set a stronger ideological tone and emphasized the establishment of effective control over the industry in order to ensure that the advertising tool would be effectively used "so as better to serve the socialist material civilization and spirit."[22]

Scope. The new regulations simply extend to advertising on all media. The earlier text was more detailed (see article 2 in both regulations).

Licensing and Control. Articles 3 and 4 of the 1982 text specifically stated that the organization responsible for advertising was SAIC. The language in the new text (see article 6) is more general, indicating a higher degree of decentralized supervision. Administrations for industry and commerce at state and local levels are responsible for management. Registration and licensing are still required for anyone engaging in advertising. In contrast to the earlier regulation forbidding private individuals from engaging in the advertising business, licenses to advertise may now be granted to self-employed individuals engaged in advertising. Different licenses are issued according to whether the business specializes in advertising, is engaged in advertising, or consists of self-employed individuals. In all cases approval by relevant industrial and commercial departments is a prerequisite to the operations of advertising agents.

Substance and Content. Under article 3 of the 1987 regulations, all advertisements must be truthful, healthy, and clear. Deception of any kind is forbidden. This resembles the formulation in article 6 of the 1982 document in substance in many respects. The insertion of the word *healthy* in the 1987 regulations should be noted. The recent statement of the director of SAIC stressed the prohibition of false advertising and the need to supervise strictly the advertising of foods, medicines, and durable goods that have an impact on human lives.[23] Moreover, the new text has dropped reference to the advertising of substandard goods. The content of ads must be consistent with the terms of reference of the agency or the range permitted by the state.

In accordance with state policy and similar earlier regulations, no advertisements are released if they are contrary to state laws and regulations; demean the dignity of the Chinese nation; use any official symbols or the tune of the national anthem; or contain reactionary, obscene, superstitious, or absurd content. Unlike the earlier regulations, the new make no reference to slanderous propaganda, and the phrase "Chinese nation" is employed instead of "the dignity of China's various nationalities."[24]

Both regulations prohibit monopolization and unfair competition. A major change is the inclusion of a constraint on comparison advertising: "An advertisement shall not be released if it . . . belittles other products of the same kind."[25]

The new regulations forbid cigarette advertisement on radio and television broadcasts and in newspapers, while they permit the advertising of certain high-quality (prize-winning) liquors (see article 10). Earlier regulations were silent on these issues.

As in the earlier regulations, appropriate certification requires the satisfaction of a long list of criteria regarding substance, inluding quality standards, awards, quality titles of advertised products, patent rights, registered trademarks, production licenses, and culture and education or health claims. The list is open-ended, concluding with the requirement, "for other advertisements which need references, advertisers must provide references from related government departments."[26] The earlier regulations provided a shorter list that was closed-ended and more specific.

Self-Regulation. Reference to self-regulation may be inferred from article 12 of the 1987 regulations. Advertising executives or agents must check the content of advertisements and related certificates. Ads violating the rules should not be released. Self-regulation is of growing importance in China, which is a member of the IAA, which promotes self-regulation.

Penalties and Sanctions for Violation of Regulations. The SAIC continues to supervise advertising, advertisers, and advertisements' conformity to regulations (see articles 18–21). Advertisers or advertising agents will be punished for violating regulations in accordance with the seriousness of the offense. The new regulations allow for appeal by defendants to higher levels of administration or to the people's courts. In addition, victims may file suit with the people's courts.

Future Outlook

In light of the relative novelty of law in Western sense and the absence of legal precedents, it generally is realized that considerable time will pass before a full code of law and formal legal system will take root in China. In the meantime there are many uncertainties among foreigners concerning the role of law, its application, and its interpretation. In contrast with the laws of Western countries, Chinese written laws are brief and imprecise. Even though detailed administrative regulations fill gaps in the laws, they do not guarantee certainty for foreigners. Although the Chinese consider the substance of their laws self-evident, for foreigners there is uncertainty regarding the spirit and application of the law. To them official interpretations of laws appear to differ from what is written in the official text. And in unpredictable circumstances, administrative authorities may cite internal rules that deviate from the explicit formulation of promulgated laws and regulations. Moreover, such internal laws may not have been published. The dearth of actual court cases reinforces a high degree of uncertainty about legal applications.

A gap between rules, regulations, and practice is illustrated in the actual registration process and the process as outlined in the Regulations on the Registration of Joint Ventures. On paper the process is straightforward; in practice, it is labyrinthine and involves many intraministerial negotiations at various levels. Heavy emphasis is placed on achieving consensus among all interested parties. In the course of negotiations, it may be difficult, if not impossible, to determine which Chinese organizations are involved and how important a role they play. Chinese government organizations have complex hierarchies, and the links of authority sometimes intersect among several distinct groups.

Other Low-Income, Centrally Planned Asian Countries

In other poor, centrally planned countries in Asia, such as Burma and Laos, advertising and foreign investment are practically nonexistent. These countries generally are isolated from international advertising activity. What consumer goods that are sold have been found on the black market.

Laos does not have a constitution or code of law. There are no edicts dealing with the advertising of domestic or international food or drug products. Such advertising is not conducted here. In cases when government action might be taken against foreign investors or importers and distributors of consumer products, decisions involving fines or penalties are made on an ad hoc basis in lieu of regulations. Laos has no consumer protection movement.[27] These characteristics of Laos also apply to Vietnam, Mongolia, Kampuchea, and North Korea.

Burma provides a similar example. For years Burma has enjoyed its own brand of socialism. Officially, there is little or no foreign investment. Because joint ventures have been strictly limited, there are no advertising regulations affecting foreign investors. There is no well-developed law on product liability, advertising, and marketing.

A shadow economy or black market accounts for three-quarters of Burma's pharmaceuticals, consumer necessities, and luxury-goods trade. Private advertising as well as trade of these goods has existed outside government trade and payments channels.[28] Following the recent political upheavals in Burma, considerable changes are expected, including the opening up of the economy to foreign investors.

Notes

1. United States, Department of Commerce, Bureau of Census, "China's Escalating Consumer Markets," *Statistical Brief,* 5B-3-87, August 1987.

2. Prior to the Opium War, foreign goods were unnecessary. In the interim until the beginning of World War II, foreign investment was linked to foreign imperialism, privilege, and extraterritorial control and caused widespread resentment. During the Maoist regime, this xenophobia was reinforced by Marxist ideology, increased animosity toward the Western countries, and fear of the Soviet Union. According to political dogma, foreign enterprises were vehicles of capitalist imperialism, exploitation, and unfair competition; many were expropriated or eliminated. N.T. Wang, *China's Modernization and Transnational Corporations* (Lexington, Mass.: Lexington Books, 1984).

3. For a discussion of these developments see Wang, *China's Modernization.*

4. Summarized and reprinted in *Advertising in China* 1 (June 1987): 5-6.

5. Tom Gorman and Jeffrey S. Muir, *Advertising in the People's Republic of China* (Hong Kong: China Consultants International, 1979); Wang, *China's Modernization,* 134-35; Ace Dalton, "Views on Advertising in China," *International Advertiser,* March/April 1988, 23.

6. "Structure of China's Advertising Industry," *Advertising in China,* April 1987 (test issue). Statistics obtained from Advertising Office of the State Administration for Industry and Commerce, Beijing, China.

7. "Structure of China's Advertising Industry," *Advertising in China,* April 1987, 2-4.

8. *Advertising in China* 1 (July 1987): 15-19.

9. *Advertising in China* 1 (September 1987): 1-2.

10. China National Advertising Association for Foreign Economic Relations and Trade, *China's Infrastructure Facts and Figures,* Beijing, 1987.

11. Seligman, Scott D., "China's Fledgling Advertising Industry," *China Business Review,* Vol 11 no. 1 January/February 1984, 12-17.

12. *Advertising in China* 1 (April 1987): 2.

13. Seligman, "Fledgling Advertising," *China's Modernization,* 135.

14. N.T. Wang, *Chinese Legal Framework for Foreign Investment and Its Implications* (New York: China-International Business Series, Columbia University, 1986).

15. Benjamin Schwartz, "On Attitudes toward Law in China," in *Government under Law and the Individual,* ed. Milton Katz (Washington, D.C.: American Council of Learned Societies, 1957): 27-39.

16. During this dynasty the Chinese world was ruled under the control of a centralized bureaucratic empire in the third century B.C.

17. Wang, *Chinese Legal Framework.*

18. Rene David and John E.C. Brierley, *Major Legal Systems* in *The World Today* (London: Stevens and Sons, 1978), 477–91; Barton et al., "Chinese Law," *Law in Radically Different Cultures,* (St. Paul, Minn.: West Publishing Co., 1983).

19. Wang, *Chinese Legal Framework,* 16–20.

20. *The Law of the People's Republic of China on Joint Ventures Using Chinese and Foreign Investment,* adopted at the 2d session of the Fifth National People's Congress, 1 July 1979, effective 8 July 1979; *Regulations on the Registration of Joint Ventures Using Chinese and Foreign Investment,* adopted at the fifteenth session of the National People's Congress Standing Committee and formally issued and made effective on 26 August 1980; People's Republic of China State Council, *Regulation for Advertising Management,* adopted 26 October 1987, effective 1 December 1987.

21. People's Republic of China State Council, *Provisional Articles on Control of Advertising,* promulgated 17 February 1982, effective 1 May 1982.

22. Ibid., Article 1.

23. Summarized and reprinted in *Advertising in China* 1 (June 1987): 5–6.

24. *Regulation for Ad Management* 1987, Article 8, *Provisional Articles on Control of Advertising,* Article 8.

25. *Regulation for Ad Management,* 1987, Article 8.

26. Ibid., Article 10.

27. American embassy, Vientiane, Laos, letter to author, 19 July 1985.

28. American embassy, Rangoon, Burma, letter to author, 22 May 1984.

Part IV
Third World Countries

12
The Third World: Special Considerations

The Third World is an aggregate term referring to some 120 multi-varied and culturally diverse countries in the Middle East, Latin America, Asia, and Africa and represents two-thirds of the world's population (see map 12-1). Despite dramatic differences that exist in socioeconomic, political, and legal institutions among these countries, the traditional definition of the Third World is expressed in a composite of commonly shared socioeconomic indicators: varying rates of low GNP, low levels of industrialization, high rates of population growth, high incidences of infant mortality and disease, low levels of literacy, and unequal income distribution.

Such socioeconomic conditions as these indicators reflect are inextricably linked with overriding political and economic problems plaguing, in varying degrees of intensity, most Third World countries. Problems include general political instability, underdeveloped political institutions, embryonic or ineffective systems of laws and legal machinery, and competing ideologies (among which are liberalism, nationalism, socialism, and religious fanaticism). Political institutional weaknesses expose many countries to frequent political upheavals and to economic and political dependency on First World and Second World countries.

Historical circumstances have led to dependency or peripherality, the most distinctive complaint common to the Third World. This complaint, in the view of many political scientists, summarizes the economic condition of the Third World and sets it apart from the First and Second World in comparative politicoeconomic analyses. The multivaried countries of the Third World, partially united in efforts to remain politically non-aligned, share subordination to the dominant economic forces of Western Europe, the United States and/or the Soviet Union. The emergence of the Third World as a player in world commerce and politics is a phenomenon of post–World War II.

In international commercial relations, the Third World provides a relatively untapped market for industrialized nations' advertisers of low-priced, high-volume manufactured consumer products. Faced with growing saturation in their own markets and with advertising restrictions, advertisers are

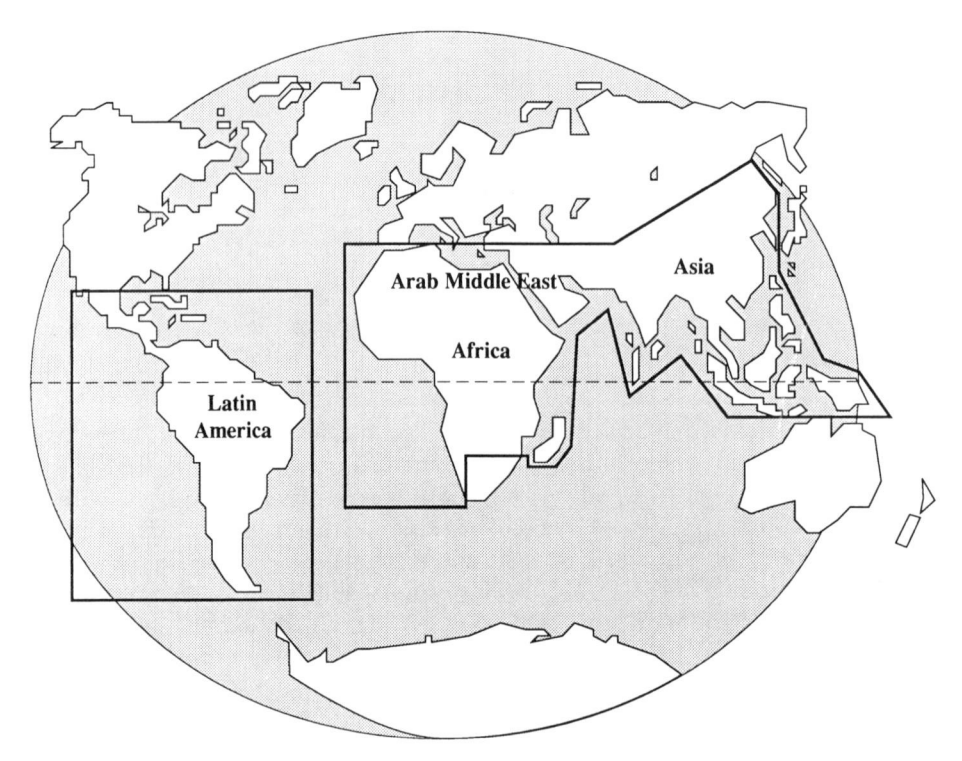

Map 12–1. Third World

finding the Third World increasingly attractive. Impotent to effectively mobilize and organize the resources necessary to augment independently the economic power, income, and security of their states, economic and political leaders in many developing countries employ political wit and wiles to control for their greater benefit foreign investment and assistance.

In the postwar period and largely since the independence of Third World countries in the 1950s and 1960s, the growth of advertising and the involvement of multinational business in Third World countries have varied (see figure 12–1). Urbanization, industrialization, and prevailing political and economic ideologies determine the extent of foreign advertising involvement in Third World countries. Growth has been slower where currents of nationalism and socialism run strong and discourage foreign investment in consumer industries. It has been most rapid where capitalist enterprises and multinationalism have been encouraged.

Mohammed Mansour, a consultant for the UN Centre on Transnational Corporations, has classified consumers of developing countries into roughly three categories.[1] The first group includes rural peasants and handicraft pro-

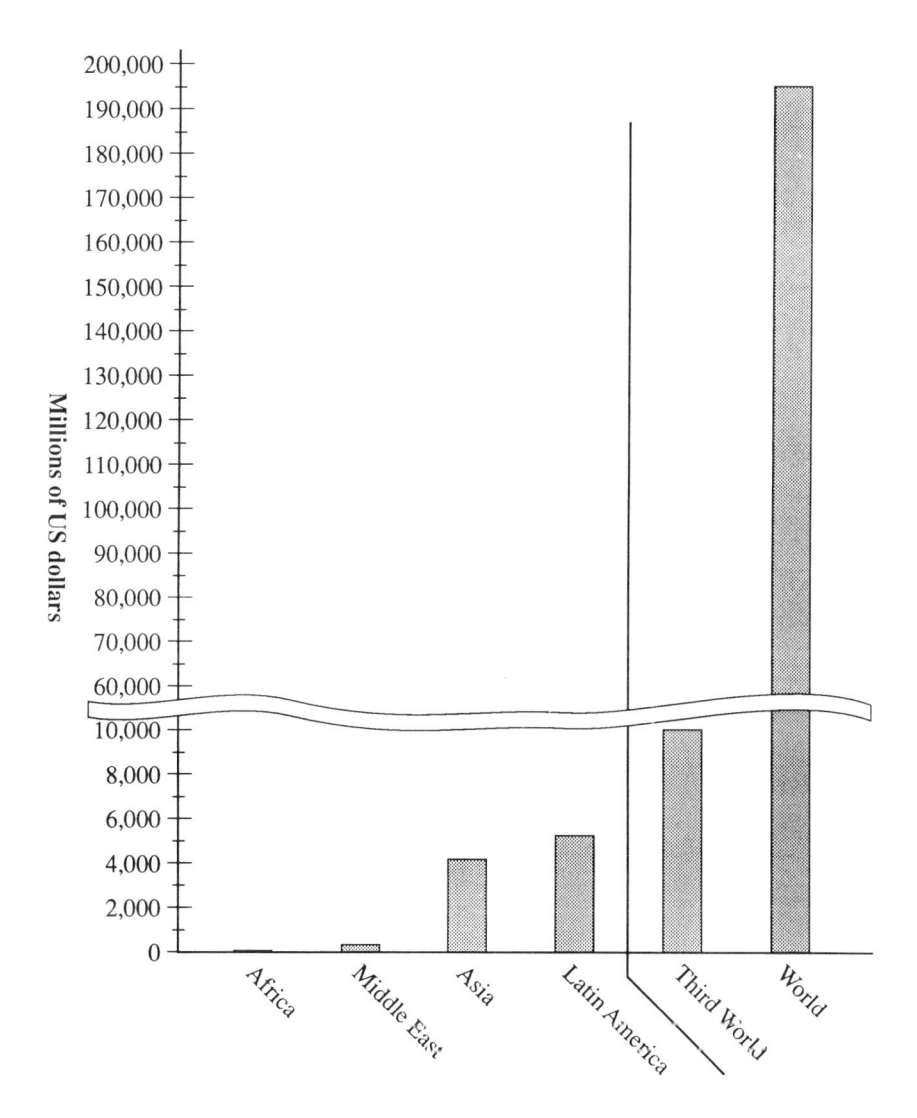

Source: derived from *World Advertising Expenditure,* 1987, 22nd. ed., Starch INRA Hooper, Inc. in cooperation with IAA.

Figure 12–1. Total Advertising Expenditure in the Third World, 1987

ducers earning subsistence or slightly above subsistence-level income. Market access for this group is generally limited to small self-contained markets operated by small-scale wholesalers and retailers of traditional staples and/or semi-processed milk and dried meats and fish. Some government-supported corporations supply this group additional manufactured consumer goods. However, many manufactured goods and consumer services are physically and financially unattainable by these consumers. The government's role is largest in meeting essential needs for drugs and grains when subsistence supplies fail and/or as supplements to traditional supplies. This group composes the majority of the population in many low- and low–middle-income developing countries, particularly in Asia and Africa.

The second group consists of the urban poor, low-income employees and worker groups also served by numerous small-scale wholesalers and retailers, but dependent on low wages and local retail markets for basic food and health needs. They have an advantage over the rural poor in that they have access to processed and manufactured goods, on better terms, and in larger quantities.

The third and comparatively smallest group in all developing countries is composed of the urban middle class and the upper class, which include foreign residents. Their numbers vary. In absolute terms the size of this group can exceed the population of many Western countries. For example, the middle-class market in India is estimated at somewhere over 100 million upwards to 200 million. In Latin America, the middle class is comparatively larger than in most other Third World countries. Needs of these consumers provide attractive opportunities for foreign enterprises. Their tastes follow those of people with comparable income in the developed countries.

Those countries with the largest middle class attract the highest concentrations of multinational advertisers and advertising agencies. Significant foreign activity is found in few more than a dozen developing countries that are generally heavily populated or have densely populated urban centers. Many of these countries are among the most advanced in the Third World. Of these countries, presently fourteen—including eight high-income countries: Argentina, Brazil, Colombia, Mexico, Venezuela, Turkey, Nigeria, and Korea; four middle-income countries: Egypt, the Philippines, Indonesia, Thailand; and two low-income countries: India and Pakistan—accounted for more than two-thirds of the markets for the multinational food, drug, and advertising agencies during the 1970s.[2]

Within this group, the five Latin American countries (12 percent of Third World population) provide markets for an estimated 54 percent of total processed foods and beverages, 43 percent of pharmaceuticals, and more than 40 percent of the gross income earned by advertising agencies in developing countries. These countries have relatively high female literacy rates (ranging from 73 to 82 percent); high levels of urbanization (65 to 83 percent); and comparably long average life expectancy (63 to 70 years).

The two most populated countries of Africa—Nigeria south of the Sahara and Egypt part of the Middle East—provide the largest potential Third World markets for multinational firms on the African continent. However, access to these markets has periodically been limited by strict government restrictions on foreign operations. Nigeria and Egypt account for more than 25 percent of the population of the African continent. These countries combined with other Third World African countries account for less than 10 percent of the sales of foreign processed foods and beverages, less than 10 percent of the consumption of pharmaceuticals and less than one percent of foreign advertising in the Third World. Nigeria, with almost double the population of Egypt, is 30 percent urbanized. Egypt is about 56 percent urbanized. Egypt is an Islamic country; Nigeria has a large Moslem population. Oil-exporting Nigeria has a relatively small but affluent modern sector, a growing middle class, and an extensive traditional sector; Egypt has an extensive middle class.

Among the Asian countries, India, Pakistan, Indonesia, and Thailand are largely rural (urbanization ranging from 18 percent in Thailand, to 20 percent in Indonesia and India, to 26 percent in Pakistan). From one-half to two-thirds of the population are engaged in agriculture while a significantly smaller percentage of the gross national product is derived from this sector. Literacy rates are quite low in India but somewhat higher in Indonesia. In India, Pakistan, and Indonesia average life expectancy is about 52 years. By contrast average life expectancy is 63 years in Thailand, Korea, and the Philippines. Relatively high rates of literacy also prevail in these countries. Taken together these Asian countries account for the largest share of the remainder of foreign advertising and manufacturing activity in the Third World.

Consumer participation in controlling the abuses of advertising dissolves as one moves from industrialized free-market economies toward less developed regions in the Third World. Today, however, there is an increasing number of consumer organizations in developing countries. An IAA study noted the presence of consumer groups in Brazil, Mexico, Venezuela, Nigeria, India, Indonesia, the Philippines, Korea, and Malaysia.[3]

On the whole, in developing countries there is a lack of consumer representation in governments, and what exists may be relatively weak when weighed against support for the economic interests including those of manufacturers, wholesalers, and retailers—often foreign, as well as domestic. Health ministries are sympathetic to consumer interests but more often their concern is outweighed by the larger problems of underdevelopment.

There are significant gaps between industrialized market-economy countries, centrally planned countries, and developing countries in the elaboration and application of restrictions as they impinge on foreign and domestic advertising. In the application of rules to foreign enterprises, the gaps are attributed to the relatively weak bargaining power of Third World countries in international commercial relations. To strengthen this power, many Third World governments have sought support in international organizations, thereby presenting a unified front. Organized as the Group of 77, they have gained leverage to claim larger shares of world resources, respect for their sovereignty, and more cooperation from multinational enterprises.

Although the gaps between the industrialized countries and the Third World countries will not be closed in the near future, the concerns of each will increasingly affect advertising regulation. Through historical, colonial, and present commercial links, the influence of the stronger on the weaker in the regulatory field is undeniable. The effects of former colonial ties and traditional marketing relations is undeniable in the development of advertising regulatory systems. The impact is most visible in Commonwealth, Francophone, and Latin American countries, where legislation reflects traits of legal systems of the United Kingdom, France, and the United States, respectively.

Whereas most industrialized market-economy countries and socialist countries have developed effective advertising regimes, relatively few developing countries with free-enterprise economies have comparably effective regulatory systems. Among developing countries, strong government controls over advertising are exerted in relatively few countries, including Saudi Arabia, Mexico, Peru, Malaysia, Thailand, and Singapore. Moderate control is exercised in Colombia, the Philippines, Pakistan, Sri Lanka, Kenya, Zambia, and Zimbabwe. Effective control through investment codes is intended in the Andean countries, Ghana, Indonesia, and India.

Developing countries tend to rely more on government regulation than on industry and media codes. Control over advertising through foreign investment regulations and taxation also is common. Many Third World countries have adopted legislation concerning the advertising of foods and drugs. The most common requirement is clearance or government approval of commercials prior to broadcast on radio or television. The advertisers bear the burden of defending their claims (reversal of burden of proof) in about half of these countries. At least five countries exercise restrictions on nutritional claims. The current trend is toward more regulation as a result of varying attention being given in the United States, some European countries, and the Codex Alimentarius Commission to health and nutrition claims in advertising of food products.

Practically every developing country has adopted some legislation on drugs. The minimum is to assign the responsibility for the pharmaceutical sector to a division of a ministry of health and to prohibit claims that are false, misleading, or deceptive. Some governments go beyond this first step and require that part or all pharmaceuticals marketed locally be registered. The sale of home remedies and herbal medicines is often exempted, as in Sudan and Burkina-Faso. In some countries, the drug sector has been nationalized, and legislation on commercial advertising is obviated. Very few former French colonies report any legislation on the advertising of pharmaceuticals. This sector is generally a government monopoly, French style, whereby academically qualified pharmacists have the exclusive right to prepare, stock, distribute, and sell pharmaceuticals. Thus, legislation on advertising in these countries is considered unnecessary.

Many Third World countries, notably in Latin America and Asia, require licenses for advertising and the registration of all pharmaceutical specialties sold in their country. Advertising of prescription drugs to the medical profession is often exempted from these restrictions and from most prohibitions with respect to claims.

The existence of regulations, however, does not mean these regulations are effectively applied. Implemental problems abound. First, markets for processed, brand name foods and pharmaceuticals in the poorer developing countries are small and fragmented. Supplies of these commodities range from limited to nonexistent. Communications and marketing infrastructure rarely extend beyond a few urban centers. The penetration of regulation in such cases is minimal, reaching a relatively small proportion of the population. Significant also to the effectiveness of regulation is that advertising regulation itself is a low-priority concern for most Third World governments.

Other impediments exist. Government action is hampered by inordinate delays due to cumbersome procedures, imprecise interpretations, and overall bureaucratic inefficiency. Moreover, the administrative machinery, even when overstaffed, often lacks experience. Thus, consistency and capacity to follow through is often missing. In addition, advertising law, where a significant amount exists, is often decentralized, which has resulted in no central authority to monitor the activity, to coordinate, and to administer the laws that few people realize exist. These are well-known problems notably in larger, more advanced developing countries, such as India and Mexico.

Other difficulties are encountered where reliance is placed on traditional antilegalist sociopolitical systems for social order. Absolutism, favoritism, and corruption are commonplace in such regulatory settings. All these factors are reflected in the lack of consistency in applying laws. Smuggling is rife when borders are unguarded, and sales of illegal goods are easy when there is laxity in controlling the marketplace.[4] Despite the problems, rule by law is very much in existence in developing countries and should not be underestimated. It is, in fact, the uncertainty as to how and when it is to be applied that is the problem facing foreign business.

Notes

1. Mohammed B. Mansour, "Consumer Protection in Developing Countries: Problems and Issues," April 1976, United Nations Centre for Transnational Corporations Subject File 72 (typewritten).

2. UN, *Transnational Corporations and the Pharmaceutical Industry,* ST/CTC/9 (1979); and UN, *Transnational Corporations in Food and Beverage Processing in Developing Countries,* ST/CTC/19 (1981).

3. James P. Neelankavil, Albert B. Stridsberg, *Advertising Self-Regulation: A Global Perspective,* Report for International Advertising Association, (New York: Hastings House, 1980); James P. Neelankavil, *Advertising Self-Regulation: Concepts, Prospects and Problems,* sponsored by the International Advertising Association, Draft IV, June 1987, unpublished.

4. F. Johnson-Romuald, "Some Factors Influencing the Regulation of Pharmaceuticals in Developing Countries, with Particular Reference to Africa," *International Digest of Health Legislation (IDHL)* 31, no. 3 (1980): 459–60.

13
The Arab Middle East

In the aggregate income statement of international sellers, advertising expenditure in the Middle East is a relatively small item. This does not imply that the Middle East market is inconsequential. On the contrary, advertisers find this region an intriguing challenge. Despite its dual economic societies, fluctuating oil revenues, and frequent political turmoil, there is vibrance in Middle East markets. Middle to high average per capita incomes, a sophisticated urban middle class, a sizable Western-educated elite, and increasing numbers of urban consumers fuel demand. Yet, with certain exceptions, the region has been reluctant to allow the types of advertising associated with the Western consumer affluence. The fundamental reason for this reluctance lies in the pervasive influence of Islam.

The Arab Middle East, with a population of nearly 150 million, is the heart of the Islamic world, whose boundaries extend south of the Sahara and east as far as Indonesia and wherein abide some 800 million Muslims.[1] Twenty countries in the Near East and North Africa combine to form the Arab Middle East, a contiguous geographic area stretching from Morocco on the west to Iraq in the east (see map 13–1). All are members of the Arab League.

In this context the label *Arab* has no single meaning. Over time, the term has accumulated different meanings. An early definition refers to nomads, some Semitic people of the Arabian peninsula. Later the term also denoted those who spoke the Arab language.[2] The broad notion of Arab peoples and Arab nations emerged in the 1950s as a political concept in the course of Gamal Abdul Nasser's efforts to create an Arab confederation. Today, a common view of Arabs is of an emotional people expressing well-defined attitudes toward social justice and honor according to certain fundamental religious tenets and having pride in their common bonds of language and religion.

Although similarities among Arab countries are strong, this region is hardly monolithic (see tables 13–1 and 13–2). Politically, ideologically, economically, socially, and legally, these countries are heterogeneous. While strong centralized leadership generally characterizes political rule in the

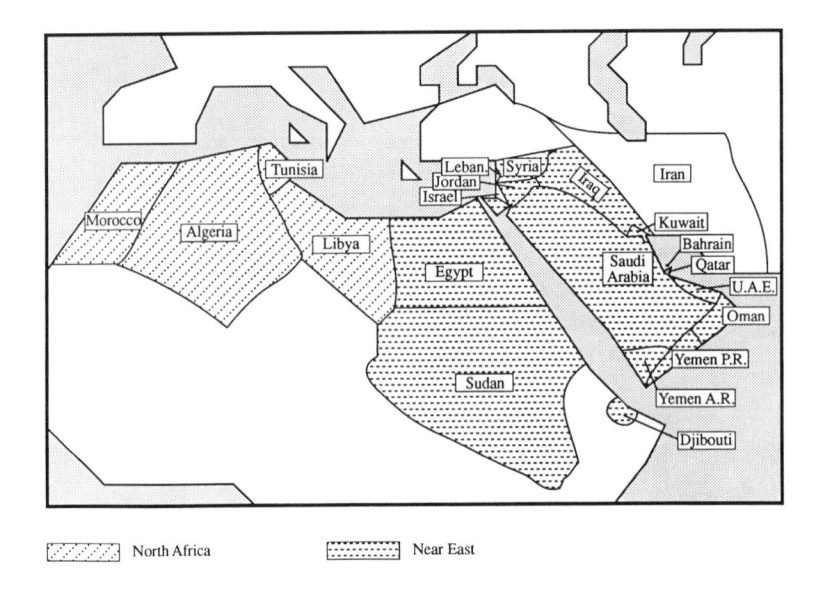

Map 13-1. Arab Middle East

majority of Arab countries, notable differences exist in the institutional structures of government; in turn, these differences also affect the nature of government intervention in the marketplace. Many countries have adopted republican forms of government structured along the lines of continental European models, with a separation of power between head of state and head of government. In these countries heads of government are addressed as prime ministers, while the heads of state may be constitutional monarchs (as in Morocco, Jordan, Sudan, Kuwait, Bahrain, and the United Arab Emirates [UAE]) or elected presidents (as in Egypt, Tunisia, Lebanon, Federal Republic of Yemen, and Algeria). In most cases secular power is concentrated in the office of head of state. Traditional hereditary regimes rule in Saudi Arabia, Oman, and Qatar, led by a king, a sultan, and a caliph, respectively. Strong militant socialist regimes control the governments of Iraq, Libya, Syria, and People's Republic of Yemen.

Ideologically, Arab Islamic countries adhere neither to communism nor to capitalism but are fundamentally democratic. Marxism, an atheistic philosophy, is alien to Islam. However, many elements of capitalism and socialism are consistent with many tenets of Islam. Most governments have adopted economic policies that combine concepts of capitalism and socialism while also upholding Islamic values. Central to the prevailing interpretation of Islam is the right of all individuals, male or female, to own property. Usury is to

Table 13–1
Regulatory Profile: Near East

Countries:	Bahrain, Djibouti, Egypt, Iran, Iraq, Jordan, Kuwait, Lebanon, Oman, Qatar, Saudi Arabia, Sudan, Syria, United Arab Emirates, Yemen, P.R., and Yemen, A.R. (see map 13–1)
Government:	Republics; presidential systems; dominant party rule; traditional hereditary rule
Politico-economic ideology:	Islamism; capitalism/socialism; pan-Arabism
Economic system:	Free enterprise with significant government involvement; relevant Islamic principles and moral rules respected
Legal system:	Islamic law; strong influence of French civil code and some traces of English common law in administrative and commercial laws of liberal Islamic countries
Investment policy:	Nationalistic; foreign control or ownership discouraged
Ad regulation:	Culture bound; strong moral and religious codes, particularly in conservative countries under traditional rule
Ad expenditure:	Less than $100 million in any country; per capita: under $22; %GNP: less than .20
Consumer market:	Small to moderate; affluent in oil-exporting countries; expanding
Social indicators:	
Population:	Ranging from 10–45 million (with exception of some ministates)
Urbanization:	Average 70%
Per capita income:	Oil exporters: $6,500–$15,000; others $750 (Egypt)–$1,600 (Jordan, Syria)
Language:	Arabic; secondary French and English
Class structure:	Small wealthy elite; growing middle class; predominant low/middle income
Life expectancy:	50–60; 69–74 years
Literacy:	Males: 60–70%; females: 30–40%

be avoided. Excessive profits are redefined. Surplus wealth is redistributed for the collective benefit through the giving of *zakat* (alms), one of the five principles of Islam.

Democracy is inherent in the tribal heritage of the nomadic populace and is God ordained. According to Islam, each individual is a godly being, simultaneously surrounded by and integrated into all social structures: the general public, organizations, groups, and families. Individualism and interpersonal relationships traditionally transcend public and commercial life. However, the more traditionally Islamic the setting, the more difficult it is to separate personal from business relationships. Many times job performance is evaluated in terms of social behavior and personality. Often direct appeals to the employee's "person" are the most effective means of accomplishing a task conveying an idea.[3] In modern-sector enterprises, however, Western standards of professionalism are being adopted.

Table 13-2
Regulatory Profile: North Africa

Countries:	Algeria, Libya, Morocco, Tunisia (see map 13-1)
Government:	Republics; presidential systems; single-party rule; Libya: military rule; Morocco: monarchy
Politico-economic ideology:	Islamism; socialism; Morocco and Tunisia: capitalism
Economic system:	Mixed; heavy state control; limited but growing free enterprise
Legal system:	Islamic law; strong influence of French civil code on secular law
Investment policy:	Strongly regulated; foreign control or ownership restricted in most countries
Ad regulation:	Strict moral codes; advertising of foreign products generally discouraged
Ad expenditure:	Generally very low; Morocco: $19.7 million
Consumer market:	Small and moderately expanding
Social indicators:	
Population:	Ranging from 4-19.7 million
Urbanization:	Average 40-60%
Per capita income:	Oil exporters: $7,700 (Libya); others $590 (Morocco), $2,600 (Algeria)
Language:	Arabic; French; secondary English
Class structure:	Small wealthy elite; growing middle class; predominant low/middle income
Life expectancy:	50-74 years
Literacy:	Males: 60-70%; females: 30-40%

Among other factors, economic distinctions among countries reflect relative differences in wealth gained, in particular from oil exports, as well as variations in economic ideology. The big oil exporters are Iraq, Libya, Saudi Arabia, Kuwait, and the UAE. In these relatively sparsely populated countries, per capita incomes are about $5,000 higher than in the other Arab countries and at least fourteen times greater than in Egypt, which has the largest population among Arab countries. Socialist policy in Algeria, Libya, and Syria is expressed in government intervention in the marketplace and in controls on the availability of consumer goods.

Social conditions and religious traditions in Arab countries also vary. Depending on the country, secular societies have lived according to customs or laws that, while more or less based on principles of Islamic law embodied in the Shari'a, have deviated from orthodoxy in multiple variations according to time, country, and subject matter. The Shari'a is the embodiment of law of Islam. Literally translated it means "the way to follow" or "the duty of man." There are dramatic differences between the traditionally conservative Islamic countries, such as Saudi Arabia, Qatar, and Oman, and the more liberal countries, such as Egypt and Lebanon. In the conservative countries, the influence of Islam continues to affect directly many aspects of social and economic life. In Egypt, Sudan, and Lebanon, which are ethnic melting pots, the separation between state and religion is most clear and the influence of religion on secular life is least pronounced.

Western advertisers, accustomed to women playing an active role in the economy, often find Arab countries confusing. In the exercise of the individual's divine rights, the male is the more privileged. The rights and status of women vary from country to country. As a rule, men and women are segregated in traditional societies. Nevertheless, women have opportunities to pursue higher education on equal terms with men in many countries, including those in North Africa, Iraq, Syria, Jordan, Lebanon, and Kuwait. In all Islamic countries, the woman is revered as a "sacred temple" and thus is well protected; in conservative societies she often is confined to a world of internal family concerns.

The legal systems of each country also differ greatly. The basis for these differences is the fact that no country is exclusively governed by Islamic law, even though its authority may be proclaimed in principle. Thus, while the Shari'a provides a common cornerstone for the legal systems of Islamic countries, each country has superimposed on this base its unique codes of public, commercial, and private law. Moreover, in all Arab countries, distinctions must be drawn between Islamic law and the modern secular laws of the country.

In the area of secular laws, the differences among countries are most striking. The conservative countries of the Arabian peninsula have been slowest to adopt modern commercial laws. In other societies, such as those of Egypt, Lebanon, and the countries of North Africa, Islamic law has been amalgamated with custom and remains valid, primarily in interpersonal relations, and modern private and administrative laws govern the public and the commercial life of the country. Other than in the Sudan, all Arab countries have developed their modern legal systems according to the blueprint of the French civil code.[4]

In short, the unique ethnic origins, histories, political, and economic circumstances of each country contribute to defining different national attitudes and policies toward foreign commercial relations. All too often, conflicts between some or all of these factors work against the development of a modern consumer society. For example, in the wealthiest Arab countries, religious conservatism and small populations discourage the development of a large consumer-goods market. Where population and public policies would appear to favor a thriving consumer market, economic conditions often are unfavorable. Likewise, political ideology is a dampening factor where incomes and population size are favorable. These elements and their repercussions on foreign commercial advertising activity and on regulation in the Middle East are discussed in the following sections.

Characteristics of Advertising

Modern commercial advertising, foreign and domestic, is relatively recent in the Middle East. It began in the 1950s with Cairo as its center. Total expenditures were on the order of $5 million per year at that time. After Egypt nationalized the Suez Canal, Beirut became the hub of international marketing activity. Until the period of political unrest in the 1980s, Lebanon was the principal international marketplace for seven Middle Eastern countries. Currently, a number of international advertisers channel their advertising through agencies in Dubai, the United Arab Emirates, and Bahrain. Increasing foreign activity also takes place in Saudi Arabia, and renewed impetus is being given to advertising in Egypt.[5] Current estimates of advertising expenditure for the region differ, but according to a local source, it hovers between $350 and $400 million (excluding Israel: $450)—well below 1 percent of the world total.[6] According to the same source, Kuwait and Saudi Arabia vie for first place in the overall total, accounting for 20 percent and 22 percent of total in 1987, respectively. Egypt and the UAE follow, spending 16 percent and 12 percent, respectively (see figure 13–1). Estimates of per capita advertising expenditures range from $1 to $4 in Egypt, Jordan, Morocco, Oman, and the Yemen Arab Republic, and $7 to $22 in Saudi Arabia, Bahrain, Qatar, the United Arab Emirates and Kuwait (see figure 13–2). With the exception of Egypt, per capita expenditure on advertising is very low compared with other countries with similar GNP per capita figures, for example, Jordan and Lebanon, as compared with Chile, Colombia, and Costa Rica; Saudi Arabia, as compared with New Zealand and the United Kingdom; and Kuwait, as compared with Norway. On the basis of available data, it is not feasible to distinguish public sector from commercial sector activity, but a high percentage of expenditure is reportedly on public advertising, notably in Egypt and North Africa.

In many countries the print media are the principal channels for advertising. Traditionally, most advertising has been placed in local and national newspapers, which are circulated to local communities. Such advertising is national in character, and a large percentage is classified or public. Close to 80 percent of all advertising expenditures is directed to newspapers and magazines in Saudi Arabia and Oman. The strong position of the print media reflects the relatively small scale of the advertising industry and reflects the government restrictions on advertising in the electronic media.

Of total expenditure 16 percent is attributed to what are known as the pan-Arab print media. These magazines and journals circulate throughout the Middle East. They range from business and current-affairs journals to general illustrated women's magazines. They are published in Beirut, Paris, London, and Kuwait. The success of the pan-Arab journals occurs in large measure because their international character enables them to avoid many local restrictions.

The Arab Middle East • 217

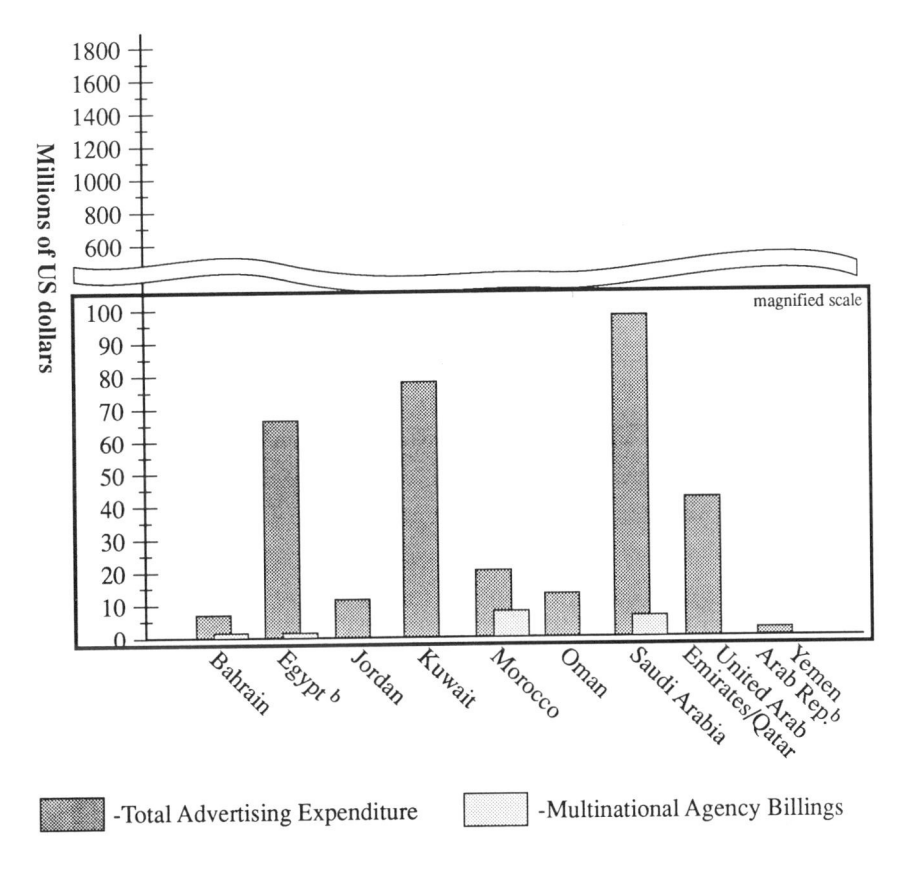

Figure 13–1. Gross Multinational Agency Billings[a] and Total Advertising Expenditure in the Middle East, 1987

Source: derived from *World Advertising Expenditure*, 1987, 22nd ed., Starch INRA Hooper, Inc. in cooperation with IAA; and Park Monitoring System and Arab AD, *Advertising Expenditure in the Arab World*, 1986.

[a] Foreign advertising expenditure in many Middle Eastern countries is reported "not available." However, foreign companies do operate in many Middle East countries through contract arrangements, and through pan-Arab media beamed in from third countries. These arrangements are not reflected in generally available data.

[b] Estimate projected from 1986 figures provided by Park Monitoring System and Arab AD. Park estimates of advertising expenditure in the Middle East in 1986 are as follows, in millions of dollars; Kuwait 71.8, Saudi Arabia 67.3, UAE 41.1, Bahrain 10.4, Qatar 8.0, Oman 6.0, Jordan 11.8, Egypt 54.5, Yemen Arab Republic 1.8, Lebanon 9.7, and Pan Arab Media 52.5.

On the average television absorbs 19 percent of total advertising expenditures. Increasing use of the television medium is found in Egypt, the Gulf countries (Bahrain, Qatar, and the UAE), Lebanon and Jordan. Only since 1986 has television advertising been permitted in Saudi Arabia. In Egypt

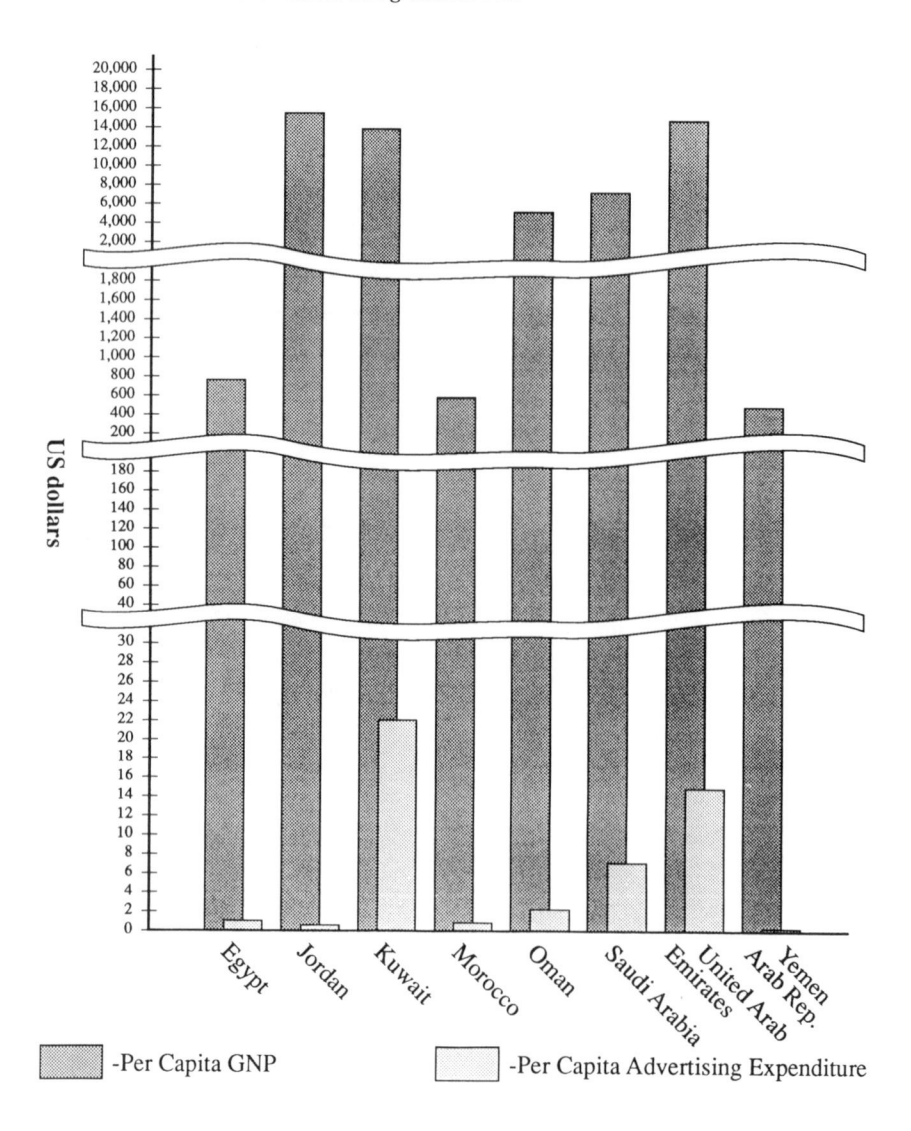

218 • *International Advertising Handbook*

■ -Per Capita GNP   □ -Per Capita Advertising Expenditure

Source: derived from *World Advertising Expenditure,* 1987, 22nd ed., Starch INRA Hooper, Inc. in cooperation with IAA; *World Development Report, 1988,* World Book; Park Monitoring System and Arab AD, *Advertising Expenditure in the Arab World,* 1986, see note "b" to figure 13–1.

Figure 13–2. Per Capita Advertising Expenditure and Per Capita GNP in the Middle East, 1986/87

perhaps as much as 50 percent of expenditure is spent on television advertising. Its cost, per thousand inhabitants, is relatively lower than the cost for advertising in most newspapers and magazines. Nevertheless, the cost of a single television spot exceeds that of a four-color page in *October,* the region's most expensive magazine. Despite generally limited use, television is the primary medium for consumer-product advertising, and it is the most effective medium for largely illiterate populations.

Use of national radio in Egypt and other countries generally is limited because of governmental restrictions and the audience's low-income status. The majority of radio transmissions are noncommercial. Of exceptional interest to advertisers, however, are pan-Arab public and private stations that transmit from Egypt, Jordan, and Cyprus, offering penetration into several more affluent markets. These include Egypt's government-controlled Radio Middle East, Jordan's Radio Hashemite, and Radio Monte Carlo (transmissions amplified through Cyprus).[7]

The principal products advertised in the Middle East reflect a growing demand for products and services supplied by international marketers. Processed foods and beverages accounted for 11 percent of total advertising in 1986, followed by cosmetics and beauty aids (10 percent); tobacco products and accessories (8 percent, the single largest group of advertisers); automobiles and road vehicles (7 percent); travel, hotel, and resorts (7 percent); and financial services (6 percent).[8] Generally, the same advertisers use television and print media. Foodstuffs, cosmetics, and household products split their budgets, 30 percent each to television, newspapers, and magazines.

Regulation and Advertising

In Islamic economies society's position on the control of business activity generally is consistent with the Shari'a, which permits and encourages commercial activity as long as the business acts in the overall interest of society. While no comprehensive laws govern advertising per se, specific rules and restrictions govern the marketing and treatment of particular products, the use of the media, and foreign investment and trade. All countries have, as a minimum, written regulations governing the advertising of specific products. Consistent with Islam, advertising restrictions on foods and alcoholic beverages conform to strict moral codes. Alcohol advertising generally is banned (except in Lebanon, with its large Christian population). Pork and pork products cannot be advertised. In Saudi Arabia certain products may not be advertised because it is believed the products would jeopardize the consumers' safety and morals.[9]

All countries restrict the advertising of pharmaceuticals. There are many forms of restrictions. In Bahrain, for example, particulars contained in advertisements of pharmaceuticals must indicate the exact composition and properties of the products. Terms contrary to public morals or liable to mislead may not be used, and advertising texts must be approved by the medicaments commissioner of the Ministry of Health.[10] In Egypt only governmentally authorized scientific departments may permit advertisements for foreign or domestic medicinal products. Advertisements for prescription drugs are conveyed through professional journals.[11,12] In Saudi Arabia only doctors and pharmacists may advertise drugs—through medical scientific offices regulated by the Health Department.[13] Likewise, in other North African countries, pharmaceuticals are strictly controlled by the government, and advertising is limited to scientific journals aimed at professionals. By law in Libya, no medicaments may be advertised in newspapers or other news media. Pharmaceutical products may be advertised in scientific journals, provided that the product in question is duly registered with the Ministry of Health. Advertisements for pharmaceutical products may not use terms or statements that are untrue or that may harm in any way the prestige of the medical profession.[14]

In most countries regulations also govern the advertising of tobacco. Jordan has imposed a total ban on tobacco advertisements. Tobacco and/or cigarettes are banned on television in all countries except Lebanon. In Lebanon health warnings must accompany all tobacco-product advertisements. Nevertheless, in all countries of the Arab Middle East, the consumption of tobacco is high by international standards.

Media controls on advertising are common in the Arab Middle East. The strongest controls are exercised in the most conservative Islamic countries. Advertising through the television media is restricted in many countries. Oman television does not accept advertising and Saudi Arabia has only since late 1986 allowed commercial television advertising, including the promotion of international products. In Kuwait and Qatar, commercial airtime is confined to specific segments of the day. Most radio stations in the Middle East are publicly owned and noncommercial. In Syria radio commercials must be substantiated and cleared for broadcast. Many governments restrict the creative content of commercials on all public media. One area that escapes these tight restrictions is the pan-Arab journals. As previously noted, the ability of these journals and magazines to circumvent local restraints partly explains the large amounts of advertising found in them.

In some North African countries and in many Middle Eastern countries, general economic policy and foreign investment laws also pose additional obstacles to foreign advertising. Government decrees restrict foreign ownership and control over local agencies and the affiliates for foreign agencies. The most restrictive controls are exercised in North Africa. In Algeria and Libya, the socialist-oriented government controls the marketplace. The import, manufacture, and sale of consumer goods are centralized in the public sector. In general, little or no advertising of consumer products exists. Algeria encourages local industry and discourages the importing of consumer goods. Foreign investment is permitted only in partnership with the government. Thus, there is little incentive to the multinational advertising firms to operate in these countries.[15]

Perhaps the fewest written laws exist in the poorest countries in this region. There, relatively low levels of development make advertising a low priority. For example, advertising in Morocco is not big business, nor are most Moroccan consumers accustomed to product choices or even a differentiation between products. Moroccan advertising and consumer law, therefore, are in early stages of development.[16] Djibouti is also illustrative. Currently, no regulations control promotional activity other than setting the price of an advertisement in the weekly newspaper or on local television. Some citizens have attempted to persuade the government to take action against companies whose advertisements have offended Muslim traditions of decency, but their complaints have not attracted any official concern. The extent of consumer protection in the Republic of Djibouti is the establishment of a base price on staple food articles.[17]

Above and beyond the law is the influence of Islam on national cultures, resulting in unwritten codes of behavior for social relations and commercial comportment. According to some interpretations of Islam, any enterprise—advertising or otherwise—may be viewed as an act of devotion, if approached according to God's will. Thus, the social responsibilities of business organizations are part of the moral obligations of the managers in an Islamic society.[18]

In gauging the types of appeals to use in marketing, advertisers generally will remember that obligations to family, tribal traditions, and public morality weigh heavily in the behavior of Islamic audiences. Effective advertisements stress family roles and parental advice and approval; they avoid allusions to children as decision makers. The advertising of certain products may be ill-advised, such as items containing forbidden ingredients and food for pets or other lower forms of life. Marketing methods that rely on idolatry, hero worship, or the use of credit also may be frowned on, especially in the more conservative countries.

Given the Arab sensitivity to the appearance of women in advertisements in conservative countries, sexual allusions, immodest dress, or even female models in advertisements may arouse official concern.[19] In Saudi Arabia, for example, visual images of women have been banned in the press. It is also difficult to interview women for market-research purposes. When and where females are permitted in advertisements, careful attention to their attire and overall impression is required to ensure conformity with the prevailing interpretation of the Islamic moral code. The special status of women demands special marketing techniques in the most conservative countries. Access to female consumers is most easily gained through women's magazines and other print media, directly through female salespeople, and in specialty shops for women.

Because few Islamic countries state many of their socioreligious guidelines officially, marketers may produce offensive or counterproductive advertisements without being aware of having transgressed any code. Offenses may be identified during the censorship process, in which ads are screened before being permitted on the public media. The limits regarding what may or may not be stated or shown depend on the discretion of the members of the screening committee. Such discretion is directed by personal interpretations of the Shari'a and the socioeconomic market's prevailing culture.

In sum, cultural and religious differences create variances in attitudes and legal permissiveness toward commercial advertising in liberal and conservative countries. In light of these differences, advertising firms should pay particular attention to such issues as women in advertising, censorship (criteria and administration), target audiences and customs relating to selling, and sense of humor, all of which are particularly idiosyncratic.

Notes

1. Over 80 percent of the populations of the following predominantly non-Arab countries are adherents of Islam: Afghanistan (20 million adherents), Iran (40 million adherents), Indonesia (136 million adherents), Pakistan (77 million adherents), Turkey (44 million adherents), and Bangladesh (74 million adherents).

2. *Arab* meant "those who speak clearly," as contrasted with *Ajan,* which meant "those who speak indistinctly," (i.e., Persians).

3. Peter Wright, "Doing Business in Islamic Countries," in *Selling in Foreign Markets,* Reprints from *Harvard Business Review 1974–1981* (Boston: The Review, 1981), 19.

4. Rene David and John E.C. Brierley, *Major Legal Systems in the World Today,* 2d ed. (London: Stevens and Sons, 1978). See also Majid Khadduri and Hebert J. Liebesny, eds., *Law in the Middle East,* vol. 1 of *Origin and Development of Islamic Law* (Washington, D.C.: Middle East Institute, 1955).

5. Michael Hook, "Making Your Market in the Middle East," *Advertising World,* February/March 1984, 21–23.

6. The combined figure for eleven Middle East countries for which figures are readily available. Park Monitoring System and Arab Ad, *Study: Advertising Expenditures in the Arab World,* 1986. Park is a comprehensive data bank for the advertising industry. It tracks commercial advertising transactions and classified information in about 700 product categories.

7. Hook, "Making Your Market," 23.

8. Park and Arab Ad, *Advertising Expenditures,* 1986.

9. Zaki S. Hindi, acting Director General of Medical Licenses and Pharmacies, Ministry of Health, Riyadh, Saudi Arabia, letter to author, 10 May 1984.

10. Bahrain, *Decree-Law No. 26 Regulating the Profession of Pharmacy and Pharmaceutical Centers,* 1975, in *International Digest of Health Legislation (IDHL)* 30, no. 2 (1979): 50.

11. Egypt, *Law No. 212 Organizing the Trade in Medicines, Chemicals, and Medical Accessories,* 14 July 1960, in *Repertoire Permanent de Legislation Egyptienne,* 12.

12. United Arab Republic, *Regulations on the Quality Control and Advertising of Pharmaceutical Preparations in the U.A.R.,* 14 July 1960, in *IDHL* 12, no. 3 (1961): 582.

13. Hindi, letter.

14. Libya, Ministry of Health, *Order No. 654 Prescribing Regulations for the Implementation of the Health Law,* 1975, 1 September 1975, *Al-Jaridah al-Rasmizah,* sec. 541, 24 June 1976; and *Provisions Concerning the Advertising of Pharmaceutical Products,* translated and condensed in *IDHL* 31, no. 1 (1980): 77; Algeria, *Decree No. 76-139 Regulating Pharmaceutical Products,* 23 October 1976, and Ordinance No. 69-14 *Establishing Exclusive Rights of Importation of Pharmaceutical Products,* 25 March 1969, in *Journal officiel de la République Algérienne démocratique et populaire* 29 (4 April 1969): 226; Morocco, *Decree No. 2-76-266 on the Approval of Licenses for the Sale of Pharmaceutical Specialties and the Approval of Advertising for Specialized Medicaments Sold in Pharmacies and Pharmaceutical Specialties,* 6 May 1977, in *IDHL* 29, no. 2 (1978): 408.

15. American Embassy, Algiers, Algeria, letter to author, 28 May 1984.

16. American Embassy, Rabat, Morocco, letter to author, 6 June 1984.

17. American Embassy, Djibouti, letter to author, 26 July 1984.

18. M.A. el Araby, *Islam and Economy* (Cairo: Cairo University, 1973), 14–17; R. el Mallakh, *Saudi Arabia: Rush to Development* (Baltimore: Johns Hopkins University Press, 1982), 188–245.

19. Mushtaq Luqmani et al., "Marketing in Islamic Countries: A Viewpoint," *MUS Business Topics,* Summer 1980, 20–21.

14
Latin America and the Caribbean

Latin America and the Caribbean extend from the southern borders of the United States to Cape Horn, to just north of the Antarctic Circle. The geographic area embraces thirty-three independent countries grouped in three broad geographic areas: the twelve republics of continental South America, the eight Central American republics, and the thirteen Caribbean Island republics (the West Indies) (see map 14–1). Their combined population approaches 350 million, or about 6 percent of the world's total population. Latin America offers significant attractions to foreign advertisers. One is the familiarity, and especially the European character, of language, religion, and the political and legal systems. Familiarity also has been bred by geographic proximity and two hundred years of close relations with the United States.

Originally inhabited by Indians descended from ancient, highly developed Incan, Mayan, and Aztec civilizations, the region was "discovered," conquered, and settled in the 1500s by adventurers of Spanish and Portuguese empires. The legacy of the ensuing colonial period, which ended in the early 1800s, is a veneer of homogeneity in ethnicity, language, and religion, as well as similarities in formal approaches to education, politics, and law.

The populations of almost all countries fall into three major groups: Europeans (mainly of Spanish or Portuguese descent), mestizos, and Indians. The relative proportions vary with each country. Argentina is predominantly European. Portuguese, Africans, and mulattoes make up the vast majority of Brazil. Mestizos and Indians constitute the majorities in the countries bordering the Pacific, in Mexico, in most Central American countries, and in Venezuela.

With few exceptions, notably Brazil and the Caribbean republics, Spanish is the official language of all countries. Moreover, except for a few island republics, all countries are essentially Roman Catholic. The inhabitants of the Caribbean republics, mainly of African descent, have English or French as their official languages, and most inhabitants are Protestant.

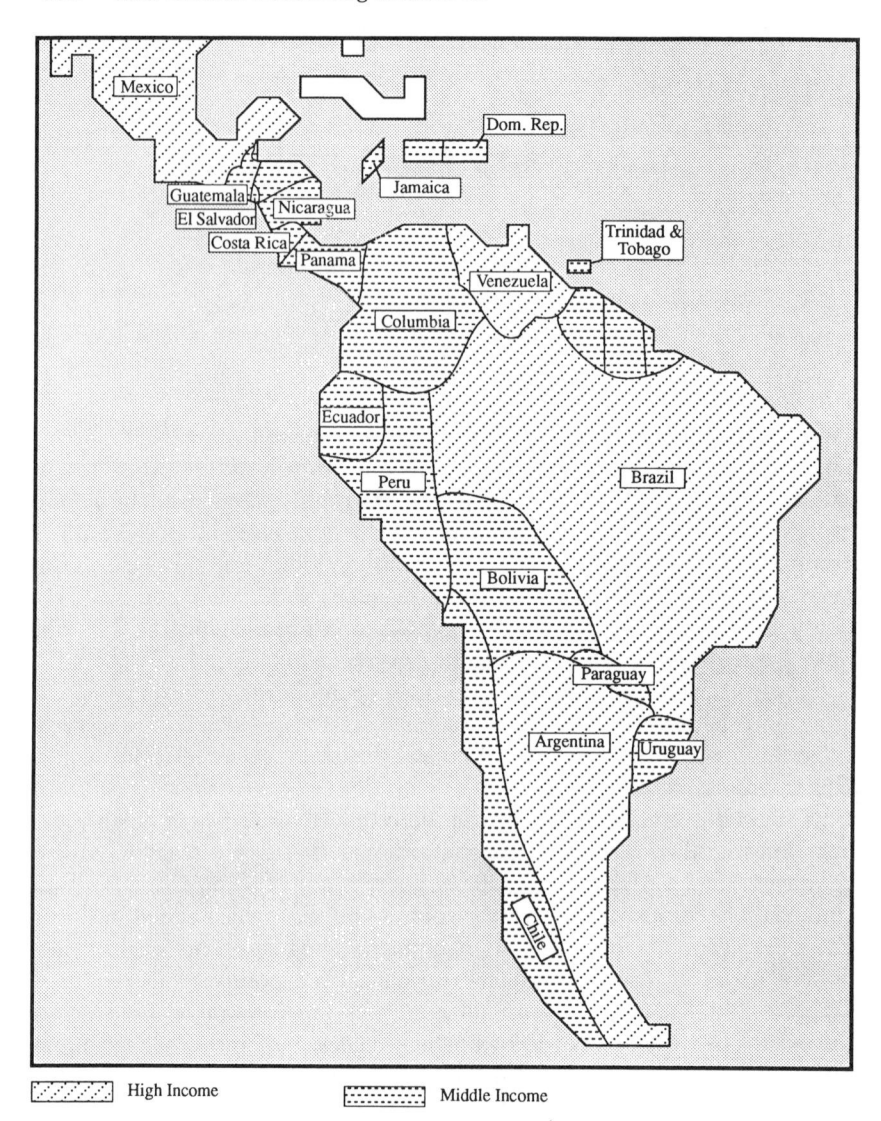

Map 14–1. Latin America

The political, administrative, and educational institutions of most Latin American countries are patterned on models that emerged in nineteenth-century Europe, when the republics superseded the monarchies. Most countries have maintained a representative form of government, with a strong executive president, a bicameral legislature, and an independent judiciary.

With few exceptions all countries have legal systems modeled on the French civil code.

Urbanization and widespread literacy in urban areas are additional attractions. With few exceptions over 60 percent of the population of Latin American countries is urban, and at least as high a percentage of the population is literate. In terms of GNP and per capita income, the vast majority of countries fall within the middle and upper-middle income ranges, with per capita incomes rising from $700 to $2,000. Education has generally conformed with the nineteenth-century European tradition's emphasis on the humanities. Despite the economic influence of the United States, many middle-class and upper-class people of the more-southern countries send their children to Europe to be educated.

In 1987 Latin America attracted more than half of all foreign investment in Third World countries and an even larger share of the expenditures of foreign advertising agencies. Total advertising expenditure approached $5 billion, about 3 percent of the world total (6 percent excluding the United States). The average per capita advertising expenditure was $14 (see table 2–6).

However, the picture is not altogether favorable. The business environments of Latin American countries create a mosaic of different levels of development and political and economic problems. The most acute problems include uncontrollable inflation influencing and being influenced by widely fluctuating exchange rates, blocked funds, uncontrolled debt, and price controls.

As is often the case in Third World countries, there is a high degree of public-sector involvement in many countries. Measured in terms of state-generated GNP, it ranges from 35–40 percent in the lesser developed countries, such as Honduras and Guatemala, to 50–55 percent in the Dominican Republic, to 65–70 percent in Mexico and Brazil, to 92 percent in Bolivia.[1] Correspondingly, there is a high degree of bureaucracy in most countries. For advertising this means (1) that the public sector is often the largest client and (2) that there may be considerable delays in obtaining necessary approvals in respect to advertising.

Moreover, Latin American attitudes toward foreign investors and international advertisers are ideosyncratic and ambivalent. Recognizing the benefits to be gained from foreign capital, technology, and know-how, these countries simultaneously reject the different forms of political, cultural, and economic intervention that foreign involvement often brings. Many leaders remain wed to the prejudices and policies of the 1960s and 1970s, inspired by the assumption that foreign direct investment is a form of economic exploitation and a threat to the national security.[2] The ideological *dependencia* (dependency) school of development theory in Latin America argues that multinational corporations are fundamentally exploitative and growing more so.[3] Others disagree. They are confident in the increasing economic bargaining power of Latin American countries. Also aware of the enormity of their economic problems, they have resisted discriminatory policies toward foreign investors and have found weakness in the multinational enterprise's vulnerability to shifts in policy by public officials controlling prices, credit, foreign exchange, and trade.[4]

A principal factor in the development of these attitudes is the special relationship Latin America enjoys with the United States, the principal foreign economic influence in the region. The relationship is a complex of political, strategic, economic, and institutional links. Politicians have characterized this relationship in generalities and rhetorical expressions. The nature of the relationship was first described in the Monroe Doctrine and later formulated in such terms as "good neighborliness," "nonintervention," "hemispheric solidarity," an "alliance for progress," and the "inter–American family." In the family relationship, the United States is portrayed at various times as good father, rich uncle, and big brother, with responsibilities to protect and/or to chastise the junior Latin American members.[5]

Resentment among Latin American political leaders at being assigned the inferior role in the United States/Latin America relationship has grown with the increasing gap in economic wealth and power, particularly since World War II. To offset the imbalance, several countries have pursued different avenues: first, self-reliance through economic cooperation among themselves and with other developing countries; second, the pursuit of foreign investment under controlled conditions; and third, the use of their positions as economic leaders in the Third World to build support for international measures to control and direct the activities of investors in the public interest.

Self-reliance and mutual cooperation are voiced in the Acuerdo de Cartagena, among others, the treaty that resulted in the formation of the Andean Common Market (ANCOM).[6] Other earlier integration initiatives included the Latin America Free Trade Area (LAFTA), Central American Common Market (CACM), and the Central American integration programs, which did not have the same objectives. ANCOM, a regional economic organization, includes Bolivia, Colombia, Ecuador, Peru, and Venezuela. The goal of the group is accelerated, balanced, and integrated development through economic and social harmonization. The agreement works mainly through internal tariff liberalization, common treatment of foreign capital, and common rules of corporate organizations. Decision 24 of the Andean Group establishes the group's common policy on foreign involvement in their economies in the form of a Code on Foreign Investment commonly referred to as the Andean Code.[7]

The design of policies and regulations toward foreign commercial activities reflects not only individual national experience with foreign commercial interests, but also prevailing social and economic conditions and shifting ideologies of the national leadership. Foreign investment has been accepted and even encouraged in most countries, but only according to specific rules. Particularly welcome have been projects that contribute needed capital and technology for development.

Frequently, however, nationalism and pride seem to override economic rationality in the prescription of restrictive policies on foreign business. Many Latin American countries have enacted local content and management requirements and offer weak protection of intellectual property through patent and copyright laws. Further, through direct regulation or foreign-exchange controls, most limit foreign earnings, imports, interest payments, and fees. Foreign ownership restrictions have been imposed in a number of countries, notably in Mexico, Bolivia, Colombia, Ecuador, Peru, and Venezuela. Such ownership restrictions are built into the agreements establishing the Andean Common Market.

In accordance with the Andean Foreign Investment Code, new foreign investments (investments made after July 1, 1971) are prohibited in advertising enterprises, telecommunications, the print media, or any domestic marketing enterprises of products of any kind. Decision 24 told foreign enterprises operating in any of these sectors prior to its adoption to convert themselves into national enterprises. They were given three years to sell a minimum of 80 percent of their shares to national investors. In addition to 80 percent ownership, the appropriate national authority had to be satisfied that the 80 percent proportion also was reflected in the technical, financial, administrative, and commercial management. The term *national* refers essentially to citizens, but also to foreign nationals with a minimum one year's residency in the recipient country. These foreign nationals must renounce the right to reexport capital or to transfer profits abroad.

In the ANCOM countries, however, treatment of foreign investment and ownership has been more liberal than the letter of the law permits. As a general rule, most countries make exceptions for all foreign investments found favorable to the public interest and contributory to the development of the country.

Moreover, consumer protection is by no means unknown in Latin America, although modern initiatives to establish formal organizations are relatively recent. More than five hundred years ago, in Tenochtitlán in the Aztec market of the Tlatelolco, there existed a consumers' protection council with full powers to punish abusive tradesmen. In recent history the government of Mexico has taken the lead. The first private organization for consumer protection (Asociación Mexicana de Estudios por la Defensa del Consumidor) was created in Mexico in 1970. A federal law for consumer protection was passed in 1975. More recently, Brazil, Venezuela, and Colombia have enacted laws for consumer protection, which provide for government surveillance of advertising activity.[8]

Given this background it is not surprising that Latin America has led the Third World in the articulation of host-country policies toward foreign investment. As the first group of developing countries to operate as a regional bloc in international organizations, the Latin American countries continue to provide political leadership for developing countries in the regulation of multinational corporations. Since the beginning of the nineteenth century, in reaction to the U.S. diplomatic protection of foreign investment in Latin America, these countries have challenged the theoretical foundations and practical implications of customary international law in its application to foreign investment. The basis of their objection has two elements. First, the countries maintain that a nation state has the right to complete freedom from interference by other states. Second, they contend that foreigners are entitled to no greater rights and privileges than those available to nationals. These elements are the principles embodied in the Calvo Doctrine, which enjoins aliens from seeking redress for investment disputes anywhere other than in national courts. Because of this position, Latin American countries have rejected, with few exceptions, the International Convention for Settlement of Investment Disputes sponsored by the World Bank. Further, many of these countries oppose the formation of bilateral investment treaties.[9]

The Latin American group also has opposed the industrialized market-economy countries on many issues in the development of the United Nations' Charter of Economic Rights and Duties of States and in ongoing intergovernmental negotiations on the United Nations' Code of Conduct for the Transfer of Technology, the revision of the Paris Convention on Industrial Property sponsored by the World Intellectual Property Organization, and the United Nations' Code of Conduct on Transnational Corporations. The main objective of the charter is to ensure that foreign investment in developing countries is consistent with and subordinate to the development needs and public interests of each developing country.[10]

Latin America's comparative homogeneity and apparent political unity must not obscure striking economic, social, and political differences among these countries. These differences influence foreign commercial activity in general and foreign advertising in particular. Among thirty-three countries, only four account for nearly 75 percent of the Latin American population, foreign investment, and foreign advertising billings: Brazil, Argentina, Mexico, and Venezuela (see figure 14–1). Brazil and Argentina alone account for well over 50 percent of total foreign and domestic advertising in Latin America. The remainder of this chapter examines the region's contrasting policies toward foreign advertising. First reviewed is advertising regulation in the large, upper-middle income countries (referred to as *high-income Latin America*). The policies of countries in the middle-income group are summarized thereafter.

Latin America and the Caribbean • 231

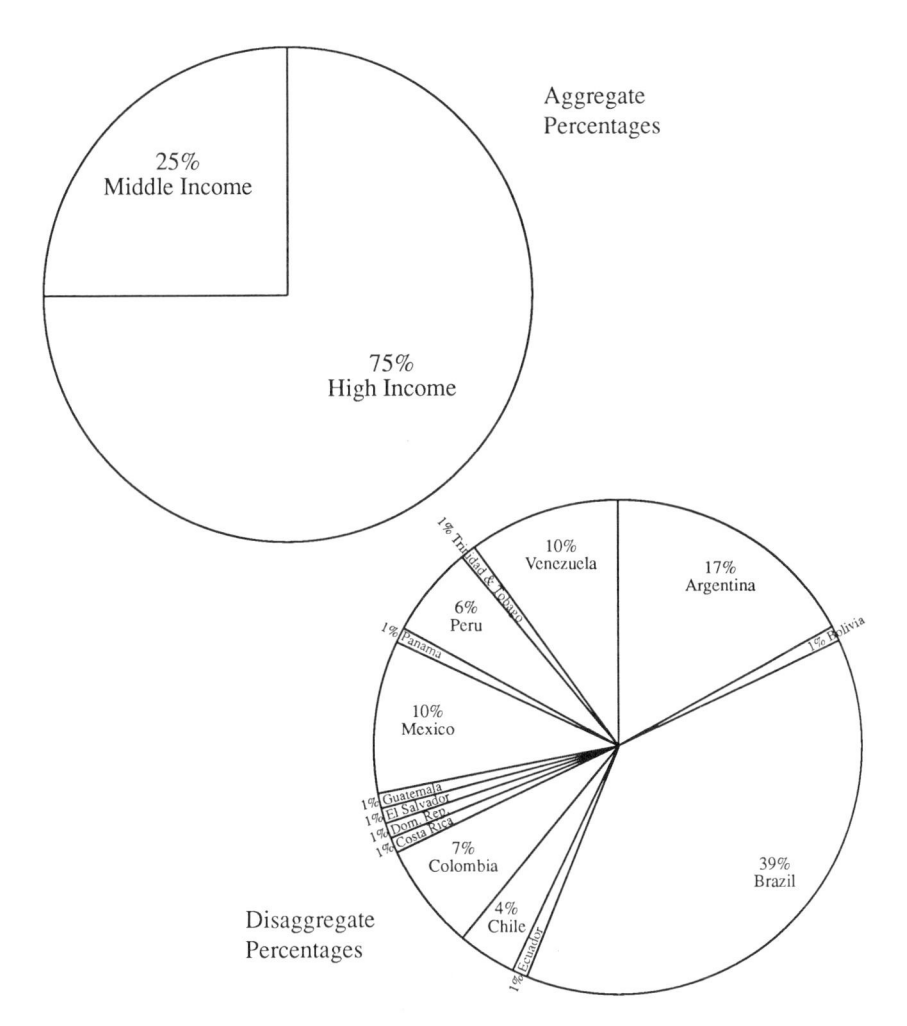

[Pie chart: Aggregate Percentages — 25% Middle Income, 75% High Income]

[Pie chart: Disaggregate Percentages — 10% Venezuela, 17% Argentina, 1% Bolivia, 1% Trinidad & Tobago, 6% Peru, 1% Panama, 10% Mexico, 1% Guatemala, 1% El Salvador, 1% Dom. Rep., 1% Costa Rica, 7% Colombia, 4% Chile, 1% Ecuador, 39% Brazil]

Source: derived from *World Advertising Expenditure*, 1987, 22nd ed., Starch INRA Hooper, Inc. in cooperation with IAA.

Figure 14–1. Comparison of Advertising Expenditure in High- and Middle-Income Latin American Countries, 1987

High-Income Latin America

Mexico, Argentina, Brazil, and Venezuela are the largest and wealthiest Latin American countries (see table 14–1). They account for at least two-thirds of

Table 14–1
Regulatory Profile: High-Income Latin America

Countries:	Argentina, Brazil, Mexico, Venezuela (see map 14–1)
Government:	Republics; presidential rule; dominant party; elitist systems; significant military presence
Politico-economic ideology:	Constitutionalism/legalism; capitalism; state corporatism
Economic system:	Free enterprise with government control
Legal system:	Romano-Germanic civil code
Investment policy:	Moderate to strong controls on foreign ownership and control
Ad regulation:	Significant regulation
Ad expenditure:	$480 million (Venezuela)–$2 billion (Brazil); per capita: $6 (Mexico)–$27 (Argentina); %GNP: .3 (Mexico)–1.1 (Argentina)
Consumer market:	Moderate with long-run expansion
Social indicators:	
Population:	18 million (Venezuela)–141 million (Brazil)
Urbanization:	75%
Per capita income:	$1,800 (Brazil)–$3,000 (Venezuela)
Language:	Spanish; Portuguese
Class structure:	Dominant low/middle class; traditional elites; Indian minorities
Life expectancy:	65–70 years
Literacy:	80+%

recorded advertising expenditures in Latin America and for about 2 percent of the world's total expenditure. Argentina and Brazil rank among the world's top twenty countries in total advertising expenditure. A comparison of foreign agencies' billings with national advertising expenditure suggests that foreign agencies play a different role in each country, accounting for about 17 percent of the industry activity in Argentina as compared with a near 50 percent of total expenditure in Mexico (see figure 14–2). With the exception of Mexico, per capita advertising expenditure—falling in a range between $14 and $27—is well above the average for developing countries (see figure 14–3).

All media are available for advertising in each country. Characteristic of many advanced developing countries is the heavy concentration of advertising through the electronic mass media. Television and radio absorb close to 60 percent of advertising expenditure. Film and outdoor media also are relatively important advertising media in Argentina and Mexico (see figure 14–4).

A number of economic problems plague these countries, creating considerable uncertainty for foreign investors and leading to policies that would tend to discourage consumption, imports, and foreign investment. During the 1980s declining or stagnant growth rates faced each country. Most countries have been adversely affected by deterioration in their terms of trade and by continuing debt-servicing problems. Moreover, currency exchange rates fluctuate strongly and are unpredictable.[11]

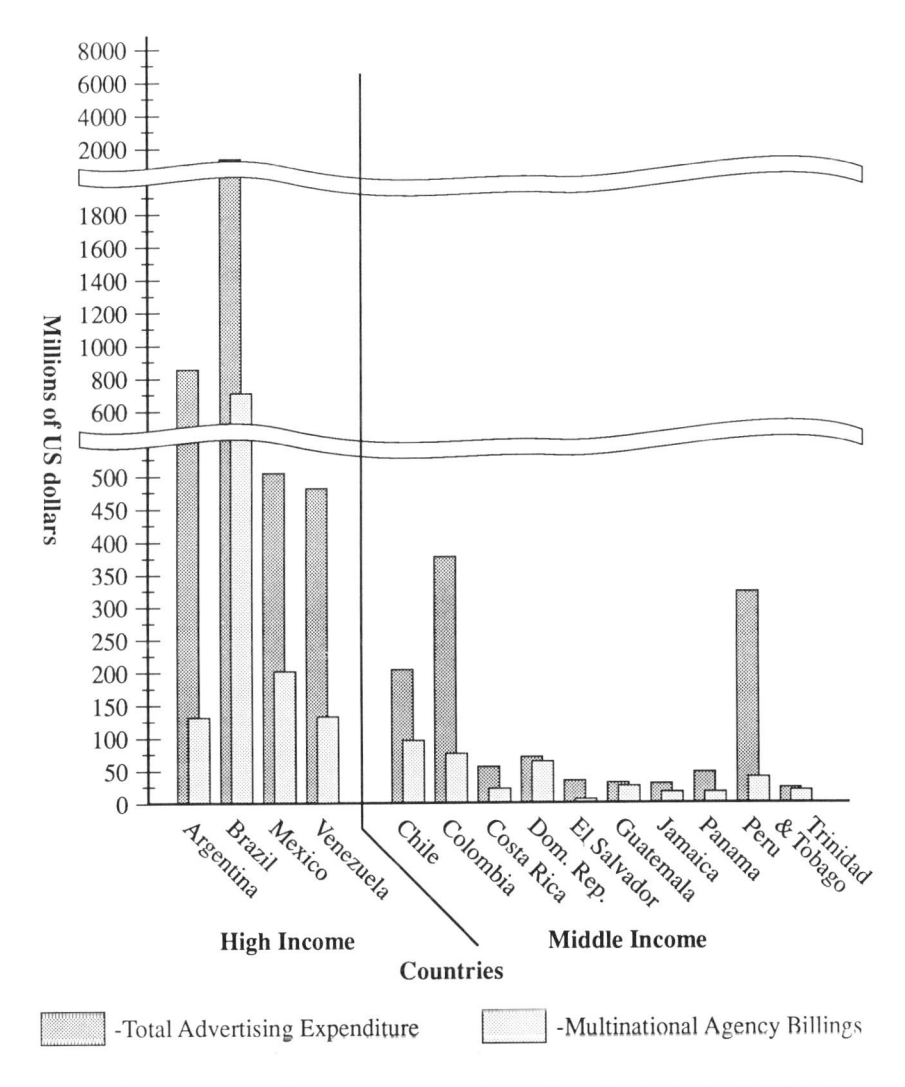

Figure 14–2. Gross Multinational Agency Billings and Total Advertising Expenditure in High- and Middle-Income Latin America, 1987

Source: derived from *World Advertising Expenditure*, 1987, 22nd ed., Starch INRA Hooper, Inc. in cooperation with IAA; "Foreign Agency Report," *Advertising Age*, 9 May 1988.

To encourage domestic growth in their advertising industry and to contribute to efforts to stem the outflow of foreign exchange, Brazil and Venezuela have adopted restrictions on the importation and use of foreign-

234 • *International Advertising Handbook*

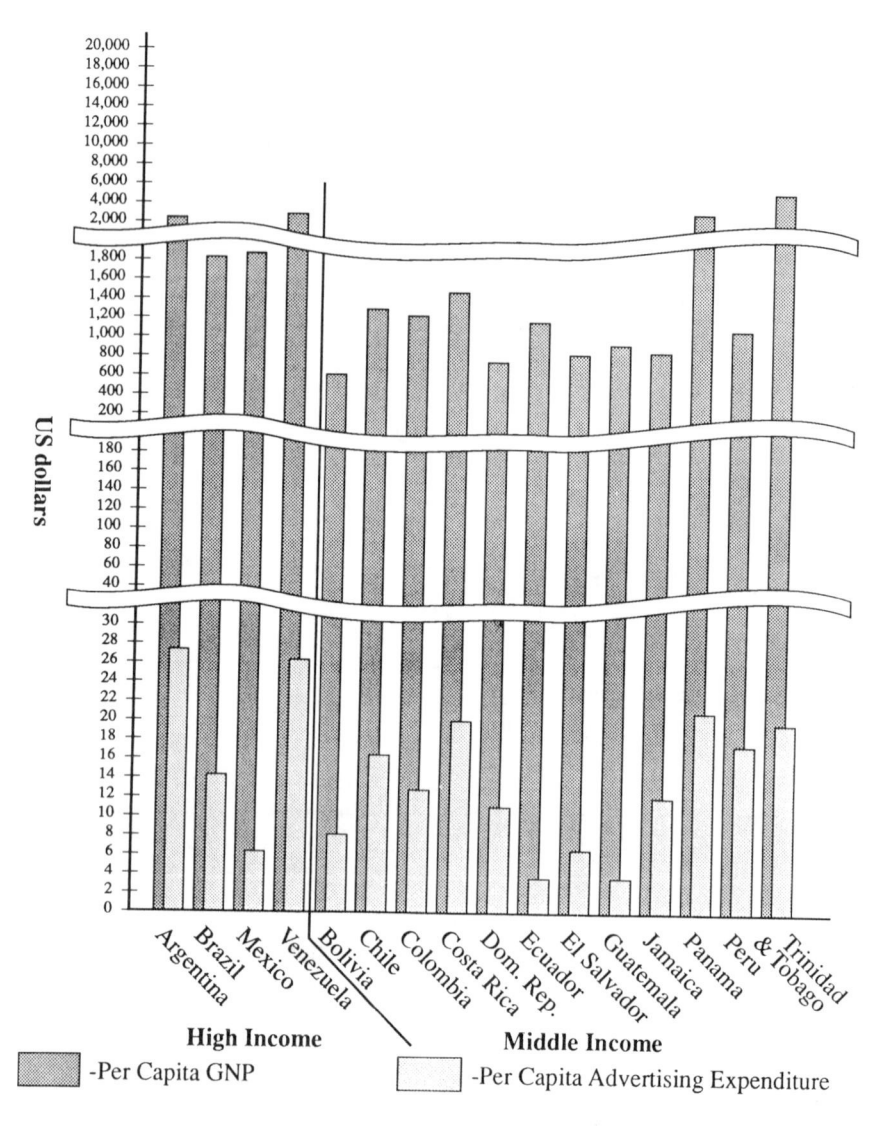

Figure 14–3. Per Capita Advertising Expenditure and Per Capita GNP in High- and Middle-Income Latin America, 1986/87

Source: derived from *World Advertising Expenditure*, 1987, 22nd ed., Starch INRA Hooper, Inc. in cooperation with IAA; *World Development Report, 1988*, World Bank.

produced advertising materials. Brazil imposes high import duties on all materials and quotas on films. Venezuela prohibits imports of all materials except for print materials. Both countries impose duties on tools-of-trade materials.

High Income

10%
7%
26%
10%
48%

Middle Income

5% 4%
16%
26%
50%

▨ -Print　▦ -T.V.　▫ -Radio　▨ -Other　☐ -Non-measured Media

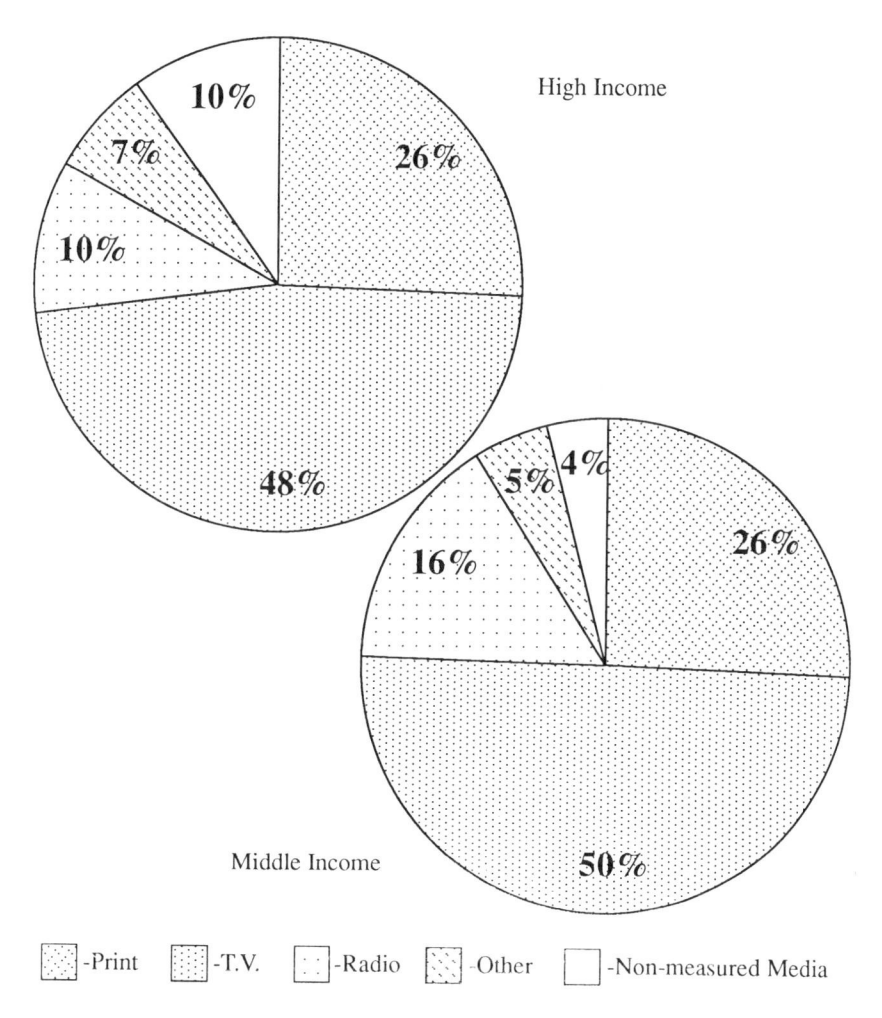

Source: derived from *World Advertising Expenditure*, 1986, 21st ed., Starch INRA Hooper, Inc. in cooperation with IAA.

Figure 14–4. Advertising Expenditure by Media and Non-measured Media in High- and Middle-Income Latin America (percentage shares)

All four countries have requirements favoring the use of local personnel. Argentina and Venezuela prohibit the use of foreign films unless they are shot and produced by national crews. Local actors and musicians must be used in Venezuela. Brazil sets a ceiling of 30 percent as the maximum allowable footage of foreign content in television commercials, and it prohibits foreign payments for advertising films.[12] Moreover, the Brazilian government, the country's largest advertiser, has withheld public advertising accounts from foreign-owned agencies.

Advertising regulatory regimes differ from one country to the next. The most extensive government control of foreign advertising, direct and indirect, is exercised by the Mexican government. In the late 1970s, Mexico ranked tenth among free-market countries, in a study by fifty-eight marketing executives of leading transnational advertisers, as having the most restrictive advertising regulations.[13] Self-regulation is particularly noteworthy in Argentina and Brazil. Venezuela relies heavily on foreign-investment laws and trade policy as strong indirect control limiting foreign activity according to economic conditions.

Mexico

Mexico offers the international business community an immense challenge. Any foreign firm doing business here must become involved in Mexico's aspirations to make the best use of its human and natural resources toward the achievement of its socioeconomic development goals.[14]

The foreign advertising industry in Mexico has kept pace with the increase in commercial manufacturing and industrialization. Before World War II, there were few foreign advertising agencies. By 1964 many of the top multinational agencies were already established in Mexico City. Today, of the top twenty agencies in Mexico, thirteen are subsidiaries of multinational agencies, three are minority affiliates, and four are indigenous firms. Billings of the foreign agencies may equal 50 percent of the total advertising expenditure in Mexico. The indigenous industry also has grown; two of the top five agencies in the country are national firms.

Consistent with its nationalist spirit and left-of-center social policies, the Mexican government has restrained foreign imports or local production of goods and services by foreign subsidiaries. Advertising by MNEs has been attacked by government functionaries, labor leaders, consumer agencies, and universities.

A complex regulatory regime with a strong emphasis on government control has been adopted. The regulatory system consists of a consumer protection law, product-specific advertising rules, media restrictions, and indirect laws governing investment. Self-regulation is developing in Mexico but lacks adequate government encouragement and support.

At the end of 1975, Mexico enacted the Federal Consumer Protection Law, establishing basic principles applicable to contracts between consumers and merchants.[15] One principle requires suppliers to provide consumers with adequate and truthful information in the Spanish language. Consequently, misleading advertising, labeling, and marking are all illegal. The law empowers the Department of Industry and Commerce to make the necessary administrative rules for implementation. To remove doubt as to the accuracy of ads, suppliers may submit ads for advanced ruling or approval. No response within forty-five days implies approval, and the supplier is usually relieved of civil liability for misleading information. All principles and rules apply to imported goods and impose joint and individual liability on the foreign parent company as well as on its local affiliates.

In December 1974 the Mexican government adopted extensive regulations governing the advertising of health-related products.[16] The regulations extend to advertising material prepared abroad and intended for dissemination in Mexico. In general, they provide that the advertising of these products be authorized by the Secretariat for Health and Welfare. To assist in this work, a Joint Advisory Committee on Advertising was established in 1976. The regulations forbid advertising that is misleading in regard to quality, origin, purity, preservation, and so on; or advertising that contains offensive or defamatory statements concerning competitive products; causes corruption of the language and is contrary to good morals; denigrates civic values; contains emotion-evoking ideas and images; uses subliminal methods; or uses such adjectives as *pure* and *natural* for products that have undergone any processing modifying their biological, physical, or chemical characteristics.

Separate chapters of these regulations outline specific rules governing advertising of foodstuffs, nonalcoholic beverages, alcoholic beverages, tobacco, medications, perfumes, beauty products, and toiletries. Of concern are the integrity of content and the substance of messages. For example, food advertisements will not be authorized if they depict some heroic qualities to be gained by consuming the product, if they assert that the food can satisfy the nutritional requirements of an individual, if they attribute therapeutic properties to a product, or if they indicate behavioral changes attributed to the consumption of a product. Regulations on pharmaceuticals are even more complex. Alcohol and tobacco products face the strongest restrictions. Advertisements of alcoholic beverages must be limited to information on product characteristics, quality, and manufacturing techniques; tobacco ads must be limited to the quality, origin, and purity of the products.

Advertising also is controlled through the media. Tobacco and alcohol advertising are permitted on television only after 9 P.M. and 10 P.M., respectively. Alcohol advertisements are banned in cinemas and on government-owned television and radio stations. Regulations governing advertising directed to children proscribe mention of collectible promotional items or discounting. No comparative advertising is allowed on any media.[17]

No effective central or coordinated self-regulatory system operates in Mexico. However, a number of separate organizations administer sectoral activities, including those formed by advertisers, advertising agencies, and media groups. These organizations deal with complaints and answer inquiries.[18]

Brazil

Brazil, the fifth-largest country in the world, covers almost one-half of South America. Its GNP is equal to 30 percent of the total GNP for Latin America. The economy of Brazil, unlike that of its neighbors, enjoyed strong growth in 1986. The population of over 140 million has an average per capita income exceeding $2,000; higher figures are attained in urban sectors, where markets for foreign goods are concentrated. Brazil provides bountiful opportunity for foreign advertisers. The Brazilian public welcomes foreign brand names, and foreign products command a premium price over competing national products.

In 1914 the first advertising agency was established in Brazil when a businessman and a journalist joined forces to introduce American techniques of mass advertising. Following its success, four other agencies were established. During the 1920s and 1930s, advertising flooded the newspapers. Foreign agencies first moved in during the 1930s and 1940s, beginning with N.W. Azur and Son, followed by J. Walter Thompson and McCann-Erickson. The advertising industry of Brazil experienced its greatest growth during the decade of 1950–60, when the number of agencies increased from 126 to 239.[19]

Brazil has the largest national advertising industry among Third World countries. Per capita advertising expenditure also exceeds that of most large Third World countries. The growth of the industry has been favored by the government policy of commissioning all public advertising through locally owned agencies.[20] Today, the top three agencies in the country are nationally owned. Of the top twenty-four agencies in the country, only twelve are foreign subsidiaries. There are two minority foreign affiliates and three local agencies with nonequity arrangements with multinational firms. In 1986 the billings of these agencies were equivalent to 40 percent of Brazil's total advertising expenditure of $2 billion for that year.

Television is the most widely used medium for advertising. Television/radio advertising accounts for more than 50 percent of advertising expenditure. Three commercial television channels broadcast advertising through a regional network of stations, and twelve independent local stations also carry advertising. There is no commercial advertising on any of the eight government stations. A large proportion of the urban population receives advertising, while about half the rural population experiences little or no exposure to commercial television advertising. Print media account for less than one-third of the total figure. Print media are regional in character, and low levels of literacy among large segments of the population pose a problem to this method of communication. About one-quarter of the population reads a daily newspaper. Magazines are faced with distribution problems.

Unlike many Third World countries, Brazil harmonizes comprehensive governmental and self-regulatory systems. Self-regulation in Brazil dates back to 1957, when the Code of Ethics for Advertising Professionals was established. It was modeled on the 1955 version of the ICC Code.

A second self-regulatory code was presented at the Twenty-sixth IAA World Congress in Copenhagen in May 1978.[21] This code was modeled on the 1973 ICC Code of Advertising Practice and on the British system of self-regulation, with adaptations to fit Brazilian market conditions. It is comprehensive and product specific. It incorporates the ethical principles established in the first code and adds sixteen appendixes covering such product categories as alcoholic beverages, cigarettes, foods, and pharmaceuticals and focusing on target audiences, in particular children. This code also deals with comparative advertising and protection of privacy.

The National Commission for Advertising Self-Regulation (CONAR) was established to administer the 1978 self-regulatory code. The commission deals with complaints and makes recommendations on remedial measures. Although the commission does not have legal authority to enforce its decisions, its powers of recommendation are considerable. The commission may act directly against the offender or by requesting the media to suspend an ad. Moreover, it refers serious violations to public authorities.

Brazil's 1957 code served as a basis for comprehensive govermental regulation on advertising.[22] In the basic legislation, the public authorities prescribe general ethical principles for advertising.[23] Through law, the government also regulates agency remuneration. Agencies operate with 20 percent over gross media costs and a minimum of 15 percent over production costs.[24]

Indirect controls on advertising are not excessive. In many respects the government policy is favorable to foreign enterprise, and aside from local-import requirements and foreign-charge controls, there are few restrictions imposed specifically on foreign activities. The law does require that two-thirds of employees in foreign operations be Brazilian. As in many countries, the law forbids foreign ownership of the public media, including newspapers and radio and television networks.

Consumer organizations have been in place since 1976. Small private organizations for consumer protection began to appear in 1976 in Rio de Janeiro and Rio do Sol. In 1985 the federal government created the National Council of Consumer Protection, which has been promoting various kinds of consumer organizations in the country. The media occasionally promote exposé-type investigations of products and services. Awareness and concern on the part of the great majority of consumers as to their rights and the means of enforcing them are rapidly increasing. Although general provisions are found in the law on the social responsibility of manufacturers and sellers concerning the safety of their products, product liability litigation is uncommon.

Argentina

Argentina boasts the oldest established modern commercial advertising industry in Latin America. The most European of the Latin American countries, Argentina also is the most open to foreign investment. The growth of advertising, foreign and domestic, has closely paralleled the economic growth of the country. The first local advertising industry was established in 1889. The growth of the industry was strongly influenced by three U.S. multinational agencies: J. Walter Thompson, which began operating in Buenos Aires in 1929; McCann-Erickson, beginning in 1935; and Grant Advertising, which arrived in 1943. Local agencies patterned their structures after these foreign agencies.[25]

Commercial advertising in Argentina is heavily regulated. Over the last three decades, numerous specific codes and regulations have been adopted relating to product standards and to the advertising content of certain health-related products, including foods, drugs, and cosmetics.[26] They require review and authorization by government authorities prior to broadcast or publication. Media restrictions limiting commercial time and certain content on broadcast media also have been imposed. The government also has passed a law specifying that the costs of advertising cannot be added to the costs of finished products, with the exception of drugs and medicines. In addition to product-specific and media-specific federal regulations, there are numerous local and provincial regulations. Argentina is in the final stages of adopting a comprehensive consumer protection law.

Argentina followed Brazil in the establishment of a formal system for self-regulation. In 1969 the Tripartito Comisión Inter-Societaria was formed to govern radio and television advertising.[27] The organization was created in response to growing criticism from public-interest groups and concerned consumers.

In 1976 the impact of self-regulation on the advertising industry spread to the other media, and a broader organization was established, the Comisión Inter-Societaria de Autoregulación Publicitaria (CIAP). The new commission has issued a code of ethics along the lines of the 1969 Argentine Standards of Ethics for television and radio. The code emphasizes conformity with the law and avoidance of irreverence for traditional national concepts regarding patriotism, religion, and customs; avoidance of immorality, sexuality, truculency, and crudeness; and avoidance of disloyalty to competitors, testimonials lacking veracity, and professional endorsements. Special attention is given to advertising directed to children and that associated with prizes.[28]

Venezuela

Despite existing restrictions on foreign ownership and control of industries, there is considerable foreign advertising activity by MNEs in Venezuela. There is no general law governing advertising. Consumer protection laws are applied almost exclusively by means of price control. Advertising regulation is decentralized and both product-oriented and media-oriented. Foreign advertising also is limited by controls on foreign investment, foreign exchange, and imports of consumer goods. There is no self-regulation system in the Venezuelan advertising industry, and consumerism is not well developed.

In the absence of general governmental advertising policy, the regulation of advertising is determined by a number of different ministries. All advertising through radio and television media is regulated by the Ministry for Transport and Communication.[29] The advertising of foods, drugs, and cosmetics is governed by the Ministry of Health. The law on pharmaceutical products prescribes that advertising through print media avoid false, misleading, or exaggerated claims that would harm the consumer. The law also requires that advertisements be submitted for written approval by the Division of Pharmaceutical Inspection in Caracas. Regulations governing the promotion of cosmetics prohibit the use of confusing or doubt-provoking terms and graphic representations in labeling, packaging, and advertising messages, by whatever media, as to quality, nature, origin, and utility of the goods.

The Ministry of Justice deals with advertising for cigarettes and liquor, for which prior clearance must be obtained. In this way limitations on showing people drinking alcoholic beverages, on using status symbols, on presenting testimonials, and so on, are enforced.[30]

The superintendent of foreign investments applies the foreign-investment laws of Venezuela, which conform to Decision 24 of ANCOM. In general, the media industries, as well as the advertising and publicity industries are reserved for local ownership and management. However, many exceptions are made. Today, of the eleven of the largest agencies operating in Venezuela, seven are majority-owned by foreign companies (refer to table 2–5).

The state of its economy determines the Venezuelan government's inclination to enforce its foreign-investment restrictions. Currently, with depressed oil prices, treatment is becoming increasingly liberal. The areas reserved for national investment have been reduced, and the government is granting more favorable conditions to foreign investors. Moreover, bureaucratic delay and legal loopholes have weakened the otherwise strict foreign-investment codes. For example, foreign advertising agencies, including Young & Rubicam (which returned to Venezuela in 1985 after leaving in 1978 to avoid conforming with the stringent 19.9 percent ownership restriction), have been able to circumvent the restrictions through loopholes permitting 100 percent ownership of nonequity voting stock. Other agencies, such as J. Walter Thompson and Leo Burnett, have consistently maintained ownership of their Venezuelan agencies because the government has been slow to act on their divestment plans or has lost interest in so doing.[31]

Otherwise, trade policies periodically limit opportunities for multinational exporters of consumer goods. Faced with periodic foreign exchange and economic crises, the government may impose or lift strict import-substitution policies, including prohibitions on the importation of finished consumer products.[32]

Middle-Income Latin America and the Caribbean

In many respects the advertising environment of middle-income Latin America and the Caribbean is similar to that of the high-income countries (see table 14–2). However, everything is on a smaller scale. Although multinational advertising agencies operate in all countries, minority affiliations and non-equity arrangements are more frequent than in the larger-market countries (see table 2–5). Strong nationalist sentiments and weaker economic environments oblige many governments to apply significant limits on foreign investments. Moreover, Peru, Colombia, Ecuador, and Bolivia belong to ANCOM, and thus subscribe to limitations of foreign investment prescribed in the Andean Code mentioned above.

Among the middle-income countries, relatively significant advertising activity occurs in most Central American republics; in Trinidad, Jamaica, and Barbados in the Caribbean; and in Peru, Ecuador, Colombia, Paraguay, and Chile. With the exception of Peru, Chile, and Colombia, the three largest countries in the group, total advertising expenditure is less than $100 million, and per capita expenditure on advertising hovers around $10 (see figures 14–2 and 14–3). The use of the media for advertising in this group of countries is very similar to the high-income countries (see figure 14–4).

The problems facing advertisers and agencies in these countries vary. In general, the advertising industry is relatively small and employs basic procedures and tools. Sophisticated modern techniques tend to be difficult to use because of generally low disposable incomes, widely distributed populations, and a dearth of modern consumer goods. In Ecuador, Bolivia, and Peru, large Indian populations with multiple languages complicate operations.

Product-specific advertising regulations are common everywhere. The number and comprehensiveness of regulations vary directly with the volume of advertising in the countries. Most countries have adopted regulations concerning the marketing of pharmaceutical products. These often include dietetic foods, cosmetics, toiletries, and other health products intended to cure disease and to make people healthier and more beautiful.

These countries, like many other countries in the world, have been partic-

Table 14–2
Regulatory Profile: Middle-Income Latin America

Countries:	Bolivia, Chile, Colombia, Costa Rica, Dominican Republic, Ecuador, El Salvador, Guatemala, Jamaica, Nicaragua, Panama, Paraguay, Peru, Trinidad and Tobago, and Uruguay (see map 14–1)
Government:	Republics; presidential rule; dominant party; elitist systems; military role important
Politico-economic ideology:	Constitutionalism/legalism; capitalism; state corporatism
Economic system:	Free enterprise with government control
Legal system:	Romano-Germanic civil code
Investment policy:	Moderate to strong controls on foreign ownership and control
Ad regulation:	Moderate regulation
Ad expenditure:	24 million (Trinidad and Tobago)–$320/$375 million (Peru and Colombia); per capita: $10–$20; %GNP: .8–1
Consumer market:	Growing from relatively limited middle-class base
Social indicators:	
Population:	Average under 10 million (Peru 21 million; Colombia 30 million)
Urbanization:	Average 40–50% (Peru and Colombia 67%; Chile and Uruguay 85%)
Per capita income:	$820 (El Salvador)–$1200 (Colombia); average $1,000+
Language:	Spanish
Class structure:	Dominant low/middle class; traditional elites; Indian minorities
Life expectancy:	55–60 years
Literacy:	80+%

ularly concerned about excessive self-medication and consumption of drugs and medicines. This is particularly true where superstitions are strong among large groups of Indian and African descent. Here, medicines for preventing hair loss, improving the bust, slimming, treating constipation, and curing sexual impotence find innumerable dupes. Thus, the most frequent restrictions on advertising inevitably relate to pharmaceuticals.

Government regulations, orders or decrees require that advertisements of medicaments, cosmetics, and toiletries to the public be licensed or otherwise officially authorized by public-health authorities.[33] In all countries prescription drugs may not be advertised to the public. Advertising to professionals directly through journals intended for medical professionals is usually free from regulation.[34]

Jamaica, Trinidad, and Tobago have adopted comprehensive Food and Drug Acts based on the U.S. model. In Jamaica regulations have been established for the advertising of foods, drugs, and cosmetics. Regulations require authorization from the minister of health before advertising any drugs. Advertisements of food and cosmetics also must be in accord with the provisions of the regulations implementing the act.[35] The advertising of food is controlled in Guatemala, where advertisements for food products must be licensed or approved.[36]

Many countries also have special regulations governing the advertising of cigarettes and alcoholic beverages. Ecuador, Nicaragua, and Peru have adopted legislation governing the advertising of tobacco. Legislation prohibits advertising of tobacco products in the electronic media or in the press when and where the ads would be most accessible to children.[37]

Advertising agencies are affected by foreign-investment codes and other nonspecific regulations.

Local-input requirements also are frequent in these countries. As in Brazil and Argentina, economic development considerations have motivated countries, including Colombia and Paraguay, to adopt restrictions on the use of foreign materials or films produced by foreigners.

Nationalism (the desire to keep or forge a national identity, as well as the intention to protect cultural traditions and names) appears to be the compelling force in Peru's development of restrictions on the use of foreign languages and materials in advertising. Peru's regulations stress the protection and enhancement of national culture, epitomized in the slogan "Peruvian man and his way." No foreign-language ads or advertising commercials prepared abroad are permitted. Only Peruvian residents can take part in advertising products in Peru.

Finally, in the absence of specific advertising laws, various articles in general-trade laws govern advertising. In Bolivia advertising is regulated under the Commercial Code of Bolivia. According to this code, advertising fraud is not tolerated. Fraud also is dealt with under pertinent regulations of the civil and penal codes.[38]

Notes

1. Harold J. Wianda, "Economic and Political Statism in Latin America," *Latin America: Dependency or Interdependence* (Report of conference sponsored by the American Enterprise Institute for Public Policy Research, Washington, D.C., 1985).

2. William Brock, "Trade and Debt: The Vital Linkage," *Foreign Affairs* 62 (Summer 1984): 1040.

3. For more information on this subject, refer to "Multinational Corporations and Third World Investment," *Latin America: Dependency or Interdependence* (Report of conference sponsored by the American Enterprise Institute for Public Policy Research, Washington, D.C., 1985). See also: Fernando Henrique Cardoso and Enzo Faletto, *Dependencia and Development in Latin America* (Berkeley: University of California Press, 1979); Thomas J. Biersteker, *Distortion or Development: Contending Perspectives on the Multinational Corporation* (Cambridge, Mass.: M.I.T. Press, 1978); Theodore H. Morán, "Multinational Corporations and Dependency: A Dialogue for Dependentistas and Non-Dependentistas," *International Organization* 32, no. 1 (Winter 1978).

4. Roberto Campos, "A nova demonologia," *O Estado de Sâo Paulo,* 22 May 1984. Campos is a former minister of finance.

5. D. Ypsilón, "A Note on Inter-American Relations," *Latin American Issues: Essays and Comments,* ed. Albert B. Hirshman (New York: Twentieth Century Fund, 1961).

6. Andean Group established by *Agreement of Cartagena* (Colombia) 26 May 1969 (effective 26 October 1969), as modified by *Protocol of Lima,* 30 October 1976; Decision 117, 14 February 1977; and the *Arequipa (Peru) Protocol,* 21 April, 1978.

7. Commission of the Cartagena Agreement, *Decisión No. 24, Common Regime of Treatment of Foreign Capital and of Trademarks, Patents, Licenses, and Royalties,* 31 December 1970, as amended in articles 3 (c), 17, 28, 30, and 35 by *Decisión No. 37* (24 June 1971) and in article 1 by *Decisión No. 37-1* (17 July 1971).

8. *Consumer Protection for Latin America and the Caribbean* (Report of the Seminar on Consumer Protection for Latin America and the Caribbean, Montevideo, 9–11 March 1987. Organized by the Deparment of International Economic and Social Affairs, United Nations Secretariat, in cooperation with the United National Development Program.

9. UN, Economic and Social Council, *Work on the Formulation of the United Nations Code of Conduct on Transnational Corporations,* E/C.10/1985/S/2 (22 May 1985), par. 38–42.

10. See, for example, Robert F. Meagher, *An International Redistribution of Wealth and Power: A Study of the Charter of Economic Rights and Duties of States* (New York: Pergamon Press, 1979).

11. United Nations, *World Economic Survey: Current Trends and Policies in the World Economy* (New York: United Nations, 1987).

12. For more information, see International Advertising Association, *Foreign Languages, Materials, Trade and Investment in Advertising: Regulation and Self-Regulation in 46 Countries,* prepared by J.J. Boddewyn (New York: IAA, 1985).

13. International Advertising Association, *Final Report on Impact of Advertising: Reply to Questionnaire,* Report by John K. Ryans and James R. Willis, IAA internal document (1980).

14. See Susan K. Lefler, ed., *Doing Business in México* (New York: Matthew Bender, 1987).

15. *Consumer Protection Law,* 16 December 1975, in *Diaro officio,* 22 December 1975.

16. *Regulations on Advertising of Foodstuffs, Beverages, and Medicaments,* 16 December 1974, in *Salud pública de México* 17 (1975): 107–17, trans. in IDHL 27, No. 2 (1976): 163.

17. Incorporated Society of British Advertisers, *Advertising Conditions and Restrictions* (London: ISBA, 1981), sec. México.

18. James P. Neelankavil, *Advertising Self-Regulation: A Global Perspective* (New York: International Advertising Association, 1980), 99–102.

19. Eliezer Burla, "Brazil," *International Handbook of Advertising,* ed. S. Watson Dunn (New York: McGraw-Hill, 1964), 289–90.

20. Peat Marvick (Auditores Independientes), *Investment in Brazil* (Rio de Janeiro: Peat Marvick International, 1983), 1, 19.

21. *Brazilian Advertising Self-Regulatory Code,* Brazil Association of Advertising Agencies, 1978.

22. It was appendixed to the "Standards for Advertising Agency Service" section of *Law No. 4680* (18 June 1965) and its implementing *Decree No. 57690* (1 February 1966).

23. Geraldo Alonso (director of Inter-Associative Commission of Brazilian Advertising), "Exposé on Reasons for Self-Regulation in Brazil" (Paper delivered at the Twenty-Sixth IAA World Congress, Copenhagen, May 1978).

24. ISBA, *Advertising Conditions and Restrictions,* sec. Brazil.

25. Frank E. Johnson, "Argentina," *International Handbook of Advertising,* 282–83.

26. See, for example, *Decree No. 2126 Embodying the Argentina Food Code,* 30 June 1971, in *Bolletin oficial de la República Argentina,* 20 September 1971, and *Ministerial Resolution No. 4 26/65 Concerning Pharmaceutical Advertising,* 21 January 1965, in *IDHL* 20 (1969): 177; and *Law No. 16463 on the Control of Pharmaceutical Products,* 23 July 1964, in *IDHL* 16 (1965): 617.

27. Composed of the Argentina Association of Advertising Agencies, the Argentine Advertisers' Chamber to the Argentine Television and Radio Stations Association.

28. IAA, *Advertising Self-Regulation,* Neelankavil, 51.

29. Teolinda Galicia de Nuñez, director de la oficina de salud pública internacional, Ministerio de Sanidad y Asistencia Social, letter to author, 30 September 1985. The letter cites *La Ley del Ejercicio de la Farmacia y su reglamento,* art. 56 and *El Decrete No. 1.118 sobre productos cosméticos,* art. 15.

30. IAA, *Advertising Self-Regulation,* Neelankavil, 140.

31. See, for example, Mary Farquharson, "Y and R Coming Back to Venezuela in '85," *Advertising Age,* 10 September 1984, 56.

32. U.S. State Department, *U.S. Exports of High-Debt LDCs,"* State 115435/ Caracas 4788, sec. 3, 10.

33. Bolivia, *Regulations on Pharmacies and Laboratories,* 15 March 1982, in *IDHL* 34, no. 3 (1983): 590–96; Ecuador, *Supreme Decree No. 188 on the Sale of Foods and Drugs,* 4 February 1971, in *Registro oficial* 158 (February 1971): 1–15, and *Order No. 8022 on Regulations Governing Medicaments, Cosmetics, and Toiletries,* 20 July 1977, in *Registro oficial* 391 (1 August 1977): 4–10; Guatemala, *Decree No. 45-79 on Health Code,* 9 August 1979, in *Diario de Centro América* 212, no. 1 (6 September 1979): 1–9.

34. Colombia, *Decree No. 2228 on the Manufacture and Sale of Pharmaceutical Preparations: General Provisions,* in *Diario oficial* 30.877 (12 August 1962): 427–52, and *Decree Concerning the Office for Control of Pharmaceutical Preparations and Biological Products,* 29 May 1964, in *Diario oficial* 31.391 (17 June 1964): 1138; Dominican Republic, *Regulation No. 2648 on Control of Advertising and Publicity Material for Pharmaceutical Products,* 17 April 1957, in *Gaceta oficial* 8114 (24 April 1957): 14–15; El Salvador, *Decree No. 96 with Regard to Pharmaceutical Specialties,* 19 November 1959, in *Diario oficial* 185, no. 217 (27 November 1959): 9224–26; Peru, *Supreme Decree Regulating and Authorizing of National and Foreign Pharmaceuticals,* 31 December 1960, in *El Peruano* 5915 (9 January 1961): 2, and *Special Decree No. 104 on Advertising of Pharmaceuticals,* 26 April 1962, in *El Peruano* 6306 (4 May 1962): 2.

35. Jamaica, *Food and Drug Act No. 46-1964,* 27 July 1964, and Food and

Drug Regulations, March 1974, in *Jamaica Gazette Supplement: Procedures, Rules, and Regulations* 98, no. 18 (3 March 1975): 129–62.

36. Guatemala, *Order No. SP-6-65-78 Prescribing Regulations on Food Registration and Control,* 5 September 1978, in *Diario de Centro América,* no. 68 (25 September 1978): 1361–65.

37. IAA, *Tobacco Advertising Restrictions Around the World* (New York: International Advertising Association, 1983).

38. Bolivia, *Decree Law No. 14379 on the Commercial Code,* 25 February 1977, *Decree Law No. 12760,* 7 August 1975, and *Supreme Decree No. 10426,* 23 August 1972, effective subsequent to *Supreme Decree No. 10772,* 16 March 1973.

15
Third World Asia

Third World Asia presents foreign advertisers with a challenging opportunity. The challenge is to expand, to adjust, or to survive in countries where changing public policies respond to fluctuating tides of nationalism, periodic surges of religious conservatism, and shifting development strategies that alternatively favor or discourage promotion of consumption and foreign commercial activities. In most countries demonstrable market potential exists. In countries encouraging foreign investment, the transnational agencies have flourished. Elsewhere, strong nationalist sentiment has led to policies restricting foreign participation in industry, irrespective of the country's level of development. India, Indonesia, and South Korea are examples of this. The influence of conservative Islamic values on public policy directed toward commercial advertising is illustrated by the restrictive laws of Indonesia, Malaysia, and Pakistan.

Clearly, the advertising environments of Third World Asia present many contrasts. Economically, countries fall into three distinct income groups. Populations range from 800 million to less than 20 million. Many societies are multicultural. In such societies advertisers confront a variety of languages and dialects, vastly different attitudes and capacities to enjoy material life, and a full range of religious values and ethical standards. Religious influence on public policies varies among countries; secularism generally prevails, except where Islamic majorities exert political influence.

Freedom to operate within these economies without the uncertainty of shifts in public policy depends, to some extent, on the nature of the governments. Although all governments in this region are classified as republics, they take different forms. Many countries have adopted parliamentary democracies, with a separation of powers between heads of state and heads of government. Prime ministers and ceremonial presidents govern in India, Sri Lanka, and Singapore. Constitutional monarchs serve as heads of state in Nepal, Malaysia, and Thailand. Strong power is centralized in the chief executive in other countries, exercising few checks and balances over presidential authority. Strength is lent to the powers of the prime minister in Thailand by the military's involvement in the government. Presidents wield authoritarian power in Pakistan and Korea, which also elect prime ministers. In Indonesia, Taiwan, and the Philippines, executive powers are concentrated in the authority of a president, who serves both as head of state and head of government. In Bangladesh executive power is virtually absolute under the current system of martial law. The more centralized the authority, the greater the facility to enact sudden changes in the law to offset increasing political and economic tension.

To facilitate further analysis, Third World Asia is divided into three groups of countries corresponding simultaneously to the level of development, the per capita GNP, and the per capita expenditure on advertising. The low-income countries are the first group and include India, Pakistan, Bangladesh, Sri Lanka, and Nepal—all located in south-central Asia. Middle-income countries, the second group, are Malaysia, the Philippines, Thailand, and Indonesia. The so-called Four Tigers, Singapore, Taiwan, Hong Kong, and South Korea, the high–middle-income countries, constitute the third group (see map 15–1).

Low-Income Asia

India, Pakistan, Bangladesh, Sri Lanka, and Nepal together account for over 20 percent of the world's population and for less than 1 percent of the world's total advertising expenditure (see table 15–1). With a population approaching 800 million, India is the second most populated country in the world. Pakistan and Bangladesh each have populations nearing 100 million; the populations of Sri Lanka and Nepal each approach 17 million. Although these two smaller countries differ in many respects from the others, their approaches to advertising regulation reflect the influences of commercial ties with India and a common heritage of British colonialism.

Characteristics of advertising in low–income Asia include extremely low per capita expenditure and relatively limited foreign-advertising involvement. Print is the dominant advertising medium, as it is in most countries, followed by television and then radio (see figures 15–1, 15–2, and 15–3).

These countries offer foreign advertisers vastly different market opportunities. As the principal advertising spender in the group and as a major spender among Third World countries, India merits special attention.

India

The Indian market is a paradox. The epitome of the dual society, India is at once one of the poorest countries in the world and one of the most commercially and industrially advanced countries in the Third World. About 200

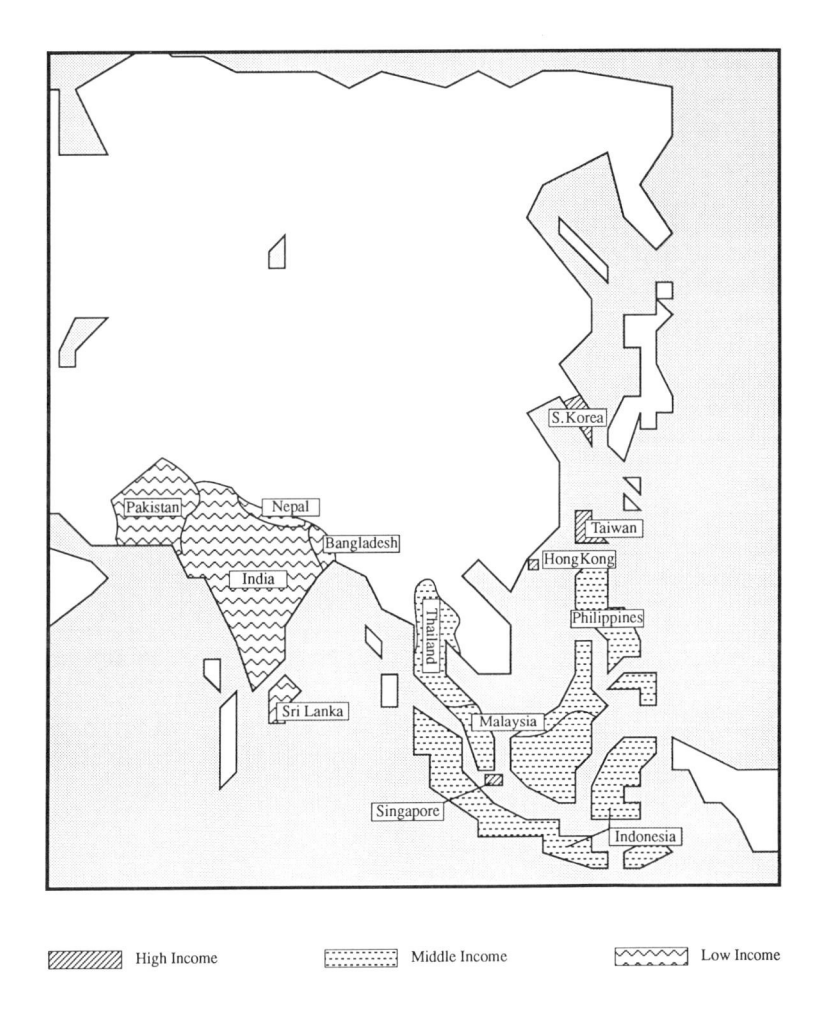

Map 15-1. Asia

million citizens participate in the modern sectors of the rural and urban economies and enjoy access to television, energy from oil or atomic power, opportunities for higher education, and the material fruits of an advanced consumer society. About 400 million impoverished and illiterate Indians live beyond the limits of development in densely populated, rural settlements, where for centuries the cow, the ox, and the water buffalo have fueled and powered the subsistence economy. The remaining population, 200 million people, survives in a state of transition between urban and rural life. These people belong neither to the poor subsistence economy nor to the affluent

Table 15–1
Regulatory Profile: Low-Income Asia

Countries:	Bangladesh, India, Nepal, Pakistan, Sri Lanka (see map 15–1)
Government:	Republics; parliamentary systems; dominant party; semi-pluralist/elitist systems (Nepal: constitutional monarchy); Commonwealth members (except Nepal, Pakistan)
Politico-economic ideology:	Constitutionalism/legalism; nonalignment; capitalism; state corporatism
Economic system:	Free enterprise with government control
Legal system:	English common law; Hindu law; buttressed by parliamentary legislation (Pakistan: Islamic law)
Investment policy:	Moderate to strong restrictions on foreign ownership and control
Ad regulation:	Moderate regulation modeled on British system
Ad expenditure:	$18 million (Sri Lanka)–$800 million (India); per capita: $.90–$1.10 (Nepal negligible); %GNP: .3
Consumer market:	Moderate; potentially large in India and Pakistan
Social indicators:	
Population:	16 million (Sri Lanka)–800 million (India)
Urbanization:	30% with numerous densely populated urban centers in India numbering 36% and Pakistan 7%
Per capita income:	$270–$380
Language:	Many official languages; English common second language
Class structure:	Majority low income; remainder of traditional caste system; significant middle class in India and Pakistan
Life expectancy:	57 years
Literacy: 50%	

and educated middle and upper classes. Moving back and forth between rural and urban sectors, they are the primary source of unskilled and semiskilled labor in the economy. These people earn small wages, have access to primary education, and provide a vast, emerging market for low-priced consumer products.

The commercial advertising industry has been growing since the 1920s, when foreign agencies began operating in India. Local agencies began to appear during World War II, when it was necessary to appeal to many segments of the population in the many local vernaculars to gain sympathy for the war effort. Today, in total advertising expenditure, India is second in Asia and fourth in the Third World after the Republic of Korea, Brazil, and Argentina. There are over 450 local advertising agencies of various shapes and sizes in the five principle urban centers of India, an increase of 480 percent since 1980. Total advertising expenditure was $802 million in 1987, equivalent to $1 per capita.

The role of foreign advertising in the local industry has changed over the years. In the 1960s the top agencies were owned and managed by multi-

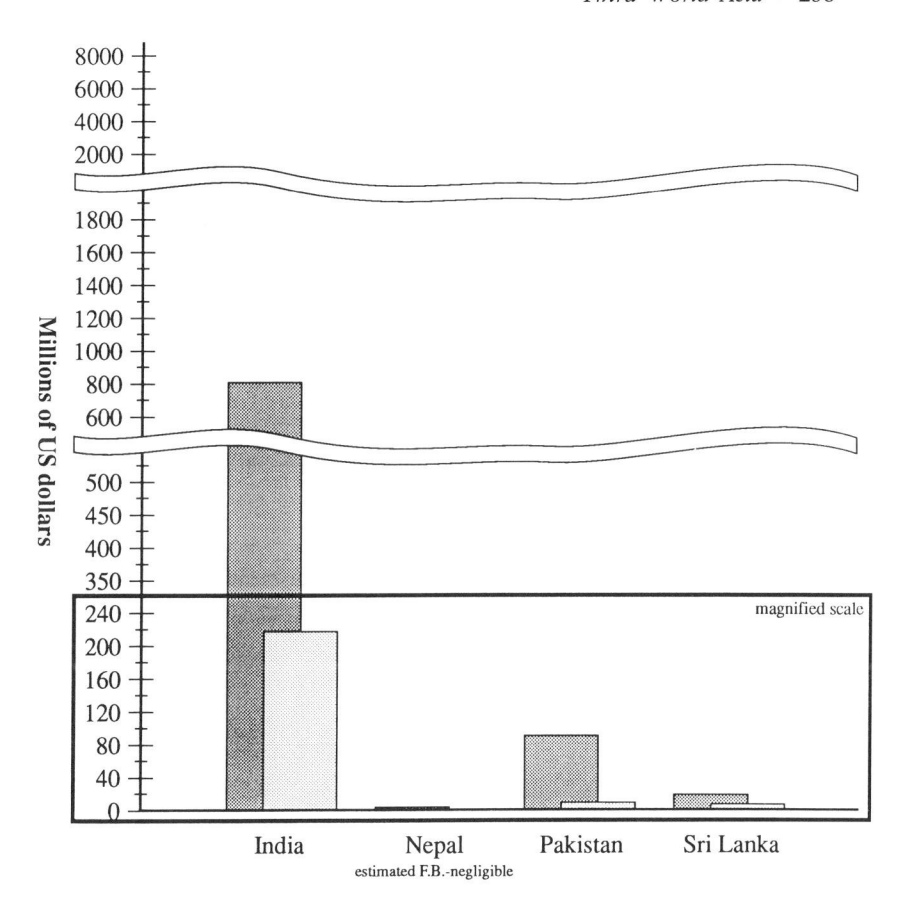

Figure 15–1. Gross Multinational Agency Billings and Total Advertising Expenditure in Low-Income Asia, 1987

Source: derived from *World Advertising Expenditure*, 1987, 22nd ed., Starch INRA Hooper, Inc. in cooperation with IAA; "Foreign Agency Report," *Advertising Age*, 9 May 1988.

national corporations. Today, all nineteen of India's largest agencies, accounting for 65 percent of total expenditure, are locally owned. Only three local agencies have minority foreign ownership, and five have nonequity affiliations with foreign agencies. The multinational agencies including Lintas Worldwide, Ogilvy & Mather, and Saatchi & Saatchi Advertising Worldwide have minority shares in three of the top five local agencies and handle the sig-

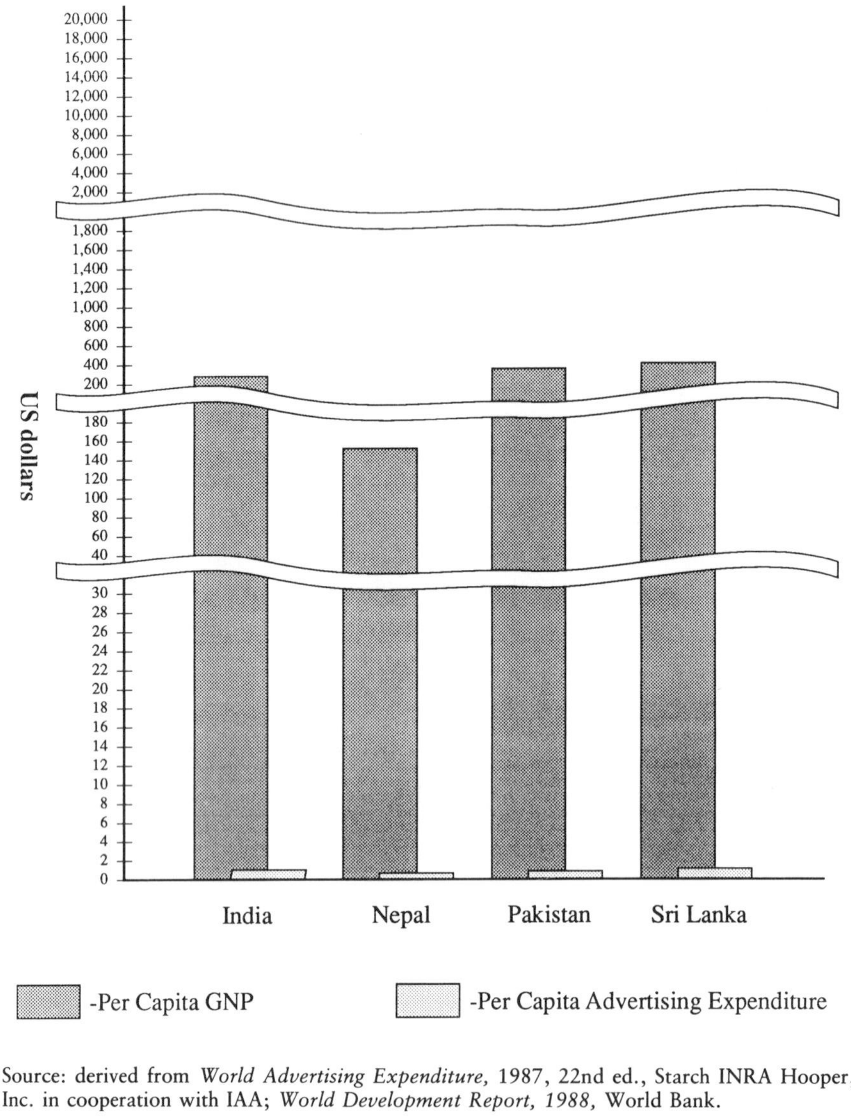

Source: derived from *World Advertising Expenditure,* 1987, 22nd ed., Starch INRA Hooper, Inc. in cooperation with IAA; *World Development Report, 1988,* World Bank.

Figure 15–2. Per Capita Advertising Expenditure and Per Capita GNP in Low-Income Asia 1986/87

nificant foreign accounts.[1] Two Eastern-bloc agencies, Vneshtorgreklama and Zabranreklama from the Soviet Union, and Agpol International, from Poland, are operating in association with Interads Advertising, the eighth-largest agency in India.

Third World Asia • 255

[Pie chart showing: 43%, 19%, 10%, 8%, 20%]

☒ -Print   ☒ -T.V.   ☒ -Radio   ☒ -Other   ☐ -Non-measured Media

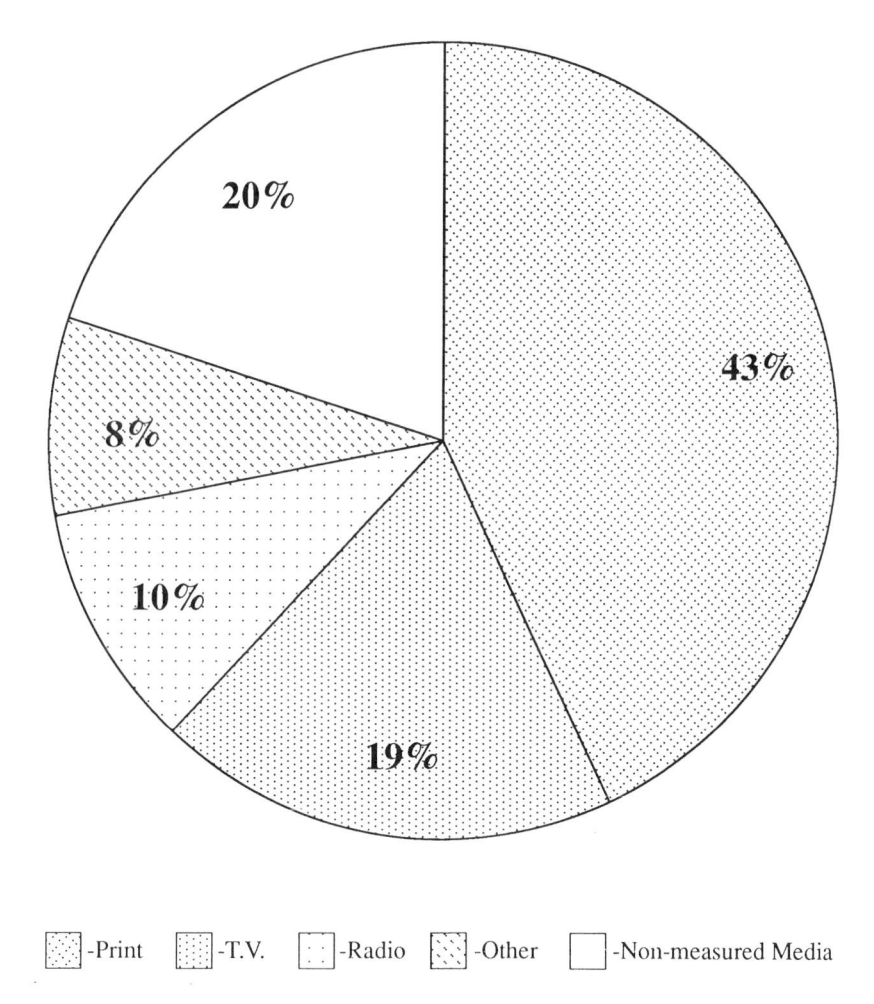

Source: derived from *World Advertising Expenditure*, 1986, 21st ed., Starch INRA Hooper, Inc. in cooperation with IAA.

Figure 15–3. Advertising Expenditure by Media and Non-measured Media in Low-Income Asia (percentage shares)

Socioeconomic conditions, public policy, and investment laws strongly influence the extent of foreign advertising activity in India. Although there is a large consumer market, activity is slow, and there are relatively few multinational clients. Production of consumer goods generally lags behind demand, and scarcity obviates demand for large-scale advertising campaigns. Moreover, widespread poverty places both ethical and economic limits on advertising.

Another barrier to foreign participation in the Indian advertising industry is the large group of educated elites who are nevertheless unemployed because of numerous bottlenecks in the economy. This group provides a pool of relatively inexpensive advertising talent for the government and for indigenous suppliers in the economy. The relative ease with which these individuals can form a local agency, with low costs and rates, appropriate to the needs of the local producers and sellers, makes it difficult for higher-profit-seeking foreign agencies to compete effectively, even in the absence of government discrimination.

Given India's current stage of development, the most effective medium in terms of reaching consumers is the press. There are 20,000 regularly published newspapers and 500 magazines (with their own readership of 50 million) that together reach the greatest number of people. Radios, cinema, television, and outdoor displays follow in descending order. Over 75 percent of total expenditure in 1986 was directed to the press; television was a distant second, accounting for 17 percent of the total. The more than 10 million television sets reach perhaps 50 million inhabitants through the two nationally owned channels transmitted from Bombay and New Delhi. For all of India, only thirty commercial stations with over 160 transmitters serve the country.

Regardless of the medium, to penetrate large segments of the population requires overcoming numerous language barriers. Fifteen languages are officially recognized, and there are hundreds of dialects. Newspapers are published in a total of eighty-four languages; 4,000 are published in English, and 5,000 in Hindi. About 50 percent of all advertising is in English, the preferred business language because opinion makers in the affluent upper echelons of society speak it. While some prefer English, others feel that ads should be presented in the vernacular of the popular audience. The translation of ads into many different languages is a difficult process requiring considerable research and increased expenditures.

Advertising is a controversial subject, and government attitudes have been ambiguous. Recent development strategies stress increased levels of demand for consumer products, leading to enhanced competition in the marketplace and a larger role for advertising. At the same time, statements of government officials deplore the harshness, wastefulness, and unproductive virtues of advertising. Competing Marxist, socialist, religious, and capitalist sentiments add uncertainty to the government's position.[2]

Nevertheless, public funds finance the largest share of advertising in the print media. The public sector includes central and state governments, as well as public corporations. Public advertising includes classified ads and announcements, as well as institutional and product/service ads. The latter includes social marketing campaigns (for family planning, national savings, public-health programs, and national integration) that seek to inculcate new habits, attitudes, and values in the society. Government policy requires that all public advertising be channeled through indigenous agencies.

The public sector tends to discriminate against foreign agencies. Agencies wishing to carry public-sector ads must by wholly locally owned and accredited by the Directorate of Audio-Visual Publicity (DAVP), a department of the Ministry of Information and Broadcasting, which oversees the advertising industry. This policy encourages nonequity arrangements by foreign advertisers wishing to expand into India in particular; local companies benefiting from contracts with foreign agencies tend to attract foreign accounts.

Unlike other low-income developing countries, India has a complex regulatory system, modeled to a large extent on the British system. The system includes federal and state statutes and common-law precedents that are both general and specific in scope, media and product-specific restrictions, and an industrywide self-regulating code. Regulatory machinery exists at the federal, state, and industry level. A consumer organization also has been formed.

General legislation includes the Monopolies and Restrictive Trade Practices Act of 1969, amended in 1984. The act proscribes unfair practices, including misleading advertising and false representation; bargain prices and bait advertisement; the offering of gifts, and prizes; and the use of promotional contests, lotteries, and games of chance or skill. The act is enforced by the government's Monopolies and Restrictive Trade Practices Commission. The 1984 amendment extended the scope of the act beyond anticompetitive practices to provide consumer protection.

There are numerous product-specific measures. For example, the Drugs and Magic Remedies (Objectionable Advertisements) Acts and Rules of 1954 (as amended in 1963) ban the advertising of cures for the treatment of certain diseases and disorders, the use of misleading advertisements, and the import and export of certain advertisements. The Prevention of Food Adulteration Act of 1954 (as amended in 1978) contains provisions governing advertising and labeling.[3] According to the Ministry of Health, there has never been a court case implicating an advertisement of a foreign drug company. Other specific acts include the Emblem and Names Act of 1950 (proscribing improper use of registered names and organizations), the Price Competitions Act, 1955, and the Weights and Measures (Enforcement) Acts. Finally, individual states have imposed restrictions on product advertising in various media and have enforced weights and measures acts according to individual standards.

The government imposes media restrictions on publicly owned radio and television stations and has stipulated that commercial breaks must not occur during program time. Advertising tobacco is prohibited in the electronic media, and advertising alcoholic beverages and infant formula to the public is proscribed on all public media throughout the country.

Indirectly, government measures to control foreign exchange, to protect domestic industry, and to earn revenue for development have had a strong impact on the advertising industry. Periodic import levies on newsprint have increased costs for media and consumers, thereby reducing demand for advertising. Particularly unacceptable to the advertising industry has been the introduction of a 20 percent tax disallowance on advertising expenditure in excess of $10,000, introduced by the Ministry of Finance in 1983.

India's Foreign Investment Law of 1973 discourages the entry of foreign advertising agencies. The law limits foreign-equity ownership to a 40 percent ceiling. It requires branch and foreign companies established before 1970 to convert to Indian companies unless eligible for an exception.[4] The rule led to the exit of IBM and Coca-Cola in the mid-1970s and to the reduction of equity holdings of the transnational agencies Ogilvy & Mather and Lintas Worldwide from 100 percent to 40 percent. The continuing impact of the law is reflected in the relatively small role of foreign agencies in India's advertising industry.

The idea of self-regulation has been entertained in India since the 1950s. The first code was adopted in 1965, but it was not implemented. In the meantime, public media, private advertisers, and agencies have adopted individual codes. In the mid-1980s, industrywide efforts focused on the development of a comprehensive code. Guidance was given by the British Advertising Standards Authority. On October 21, 1985, the all-industry self-regulatory body was officially regrouped and came into existence as the Advertising Standards Council of India (ASCI). Supporting organizations included the Indian Society of Advertisers, the Advertising Agencies Association of India, the Council for Fair Business Practices, the Consumer Guidance Society, and a host of media associates.

The Advertising Standards Council of India adopted the Code of Advertising Practice, modeled on the British code, at its first meeting on November 20, 1985. The purpose of this code is "to control the content of advertisements, not to hamper the sale of products, whatever their impact on society, provided that the ads themselves are not offensive."[5] The code upholds standards of high integrity and decency in advertising.

The nucleus of a consumers' movement also has formed. In 1984 the first consumer legislation was adopted. Although only a state law, many officials regard it as a model for replication at the federal level. The Madhya Pradesh (Bhopal) Consumer Protection Act of 1984 provides supportive legal measures needed for building a consumer movement, including a State Consumer Protection Board and a consumer ombudsman to implement the policies and programs set by the board, programs that will include consumer education. Recognizing the growing consumer movement, the ASCI also has worked for the establishment of a Consumer Complaints Council (CCC), composed of six ASCI members and eight members from nonrelated fields. The CCC operates independently in dealing with complaints. All CCC decitions are binding on the ASCI.

Other Low-Income Asian Countries

Overall advertising expenditure in other low-income Asian countries is insignificant. In 1987 per capita expenditure in Nepal was about $.10 and totaled $1.6 million. In Sri Lanka and Pakistan, per capita expenditures were about the same as India's, and total expenditures amounted to $18 in Sri Lanka and $94 million in Pakistan (see figures 15–1 and 15–2). Regulation is product and media specific, with objectives of maintaining consumer health and safety and protecting public standards of decency. There are no advertising self-regulatory bodies. Television and cinema commercials are subject to prescreening, and access to television for advertising is restricted. Some examples of regulations in effect are provided in the following paragraphs.

In Bangladesh advertising regulations exist only for specific products (for foods and drugs). Development of policy on the sale of drugs has been stimulated by activities in the World Health Organization. In 1982 Bangladesh revised its policy in a new law, Drugs (Control) Ordinance No. 8, the main purpose of which was formulated in an official report published by WHO. The law stipulated the removal from the marketplace of all but essential drugs and that those drugs be provided to the population at affordable prices. The ordinance also required prior approval by the drug licensing authorities of all advertising concerning the use of drugs and claims about therapeutic value. In general terms, the Bangladesh Penal Code, section 499, provides for punishment and penalty for defamation.[6]

In Pakistan Islamic codes have a strong influence on government policy toward advertising. Advertising found to be obscene or immoral is censored. Authorities are sensitive to the portrayal of women in advertising. Advertising of alcoholic products is forbidden in all the public media.

Other product-specific regulations also exist. False or misleading statements in food advertisements are prohibited, and advertisers must substantiate their claims once they are challenged. The Drugs (Generic Names) Act of 1972 prohibits advertising drugs purporting to cure or mitigate disease or conditions and advertising drugs in a manner that is false, misleading, deceptive, or likely to create an erroneous impression regarding character, value, quality, quantity, composition, and so on. Authorities are sensitive to the use of women in advertisements.

Legislation concerning advertising in Nepal and Sri Lanka is also product and media specific. In Nepal there is no advertising on television, and restrictions are imposed on cinema and outdoor advertising. In Nepal the Pharmaceutical Act of 1978 prohibits the dissemination of false or misleading publicity concerning pharmaceuticals.[7] Likewise, the Food Act of 1966 prohibits persons from selling or distributing any foodstuffs by falsely asserting it to be something else or by falsely describing it as of high quality.[8] Other relevant acts include the Libel and Defamation Act of 1959 (as amended in 1981) and the Nepal Standards (Certification Mark) Act of 1980.[9, 10]

The government of Sri Lanka allows advertising in all media. It has adopted an act to regulate and control the manufacture, importation, sale, and distribution of foods, cosmetics, devices, and drugs. The Food Act provides that "no person shall label, package, treat, process, sell, or advertise any food in a manner that is false, misleading, deceptive, or likely to create an erroneous impression regarding its character, value, quality, composition, merit, or safety."[11] The Cosmetics, Devices, and Drugs Act of 1980 established similar prohibitions for drugs, devices, and cosmetics.[12]

Middle-Income Asia

The middle-income Asian countries are clustered in geographic proximity, directly east of the Asian subcontinent. They include Malaysia, Thailand, the Philippines, and Indonesia. A higher average level of development distinguishes this group from the low-income subcontinent. Advancing developing and rapidly growing consumer markets attract foreign advertising enterprises to these countries. Economic, cultural, and historic factors shape attitudes toward foreign advertising, influence the role of advertising in each economy, and direct regulatory approaches to the advertising activity (see table 15–2).

Notable historical differences also exist. These explain divergencies in attitudes and public policies toward the participation of foreign enterprises in the countries' economies. For example, Indonesia, a former Dutch colony, fought violently for independence in 1949. Public attitude toward foreign investment and advertising oscillates from negative to cautiously pragmatic. After nearly a century, British rule in Malaysia ended peacefully in 1962. The government considers foreign commercial activities important to this rapidly growing economy. The Philippines, dominated for four hundred years by the Spanish, came under U.S. control at the turn of the century. Independent following World War II, the Philippines generally has maintained strong economic ties with the United States. Shifts in public policy following the ousting of the U.S.-supported Marcos regime reflect changing attitudes toward U.S. involvement in the economy as the country embarks upon a policy of so-called Filipinization. Thailand has no colonial history. Exercising astute diplomacy and shrewd political strategies, Thailand repeatedly countered attempts at domination and maintained its independence. Foreign investment in Thailand is consistent with public-development policies.

Strong cultural differences exist among countries in this part of Asia. The populations of Indonesia and Malaysia are ethnically heterogenous; those of Thailand and the Philippines are relatively homogenous. Indonesia is populated by peoples of various Malay, Chinese, Javanese, and Indian descent. They communicate in 362 distinct languages or dialects. Malay,

Table 15-2
Regulatory Profile: Middle-Income Asia

Countries:	Indonesia, Malaysia, Philippines and Thailand
Government:	Republic/presidential systems (Indonesia, Philippines); constitutional monarchs/parliamentary systems (Malaysia and Thailand); dominant parties; predominately elitist systems (Malaysia is member of Commonwealth)
Politico-economic ideology:	Constitutionalism/legalism; nonalignment; Islamism; Buddhism; capitalism; state corporatism
Economic system:	Free enterprise with government control
Legal system:	English common law and Islamic law (Malaysia); Asian Confucian tradition (Thailand); Islamic law and Romano-Germanic civil code (Indonesia); Anglo-American law and Romano-Germanic civil code (Philippines)
Investment policy:	Moderate to strong restrictions on foreign ownership and control
Ad regulation:	Moderate to strict regulation (Indonesia)
Ad expenditure:	Thailand $244M, Malaysia $177M, Indonesia $107M, Philippines $103M; per capita: Malaysia $11, Thailand $5, Philippines $2, and Indonesia $.60; %GNP: .1% to .6%
Consumer market:	Predominant low/middle income
Social indicators:	
Population:	17 million (Malaysia)–170 million (Indonesia)
Urbanization:	Less than 40%
Per capita income:	$500–$800 (Malaysia $1,800)
Language:	Multiple languages and dialects
Class structure:	Majority low-middle income
Life expectancy:	60+ years
Literacy:	75+%

Chinese, and Indian ethnic groups vie for power in Malaysia. Each group maintains its own language, although Malay is the single official language. In the Philippines, by contrast, over 90 percent of the population is Malay. There is a common language bond, as most of the people speak Filipino. English also is an official language. Thailand is 70 percent Thai and 14 percent Chinese. Thai is the single official language; other dialects are spoken in the rural areas.

Diverse religious philosophies prevail in each country. Over 90 percent of Indonesian profess the Islamic faith. In contrast the Philippines is over 80 percent Roman Catholic and over 90 percent Christian (though a strongly militant Islamic minority is found in the southern area of the islands). Thailand is over 90 percent Buddhist. The Malaysian population is divided in its religious philosophy. Close to 50 percent of the population adheres to Islam. The strong Islamic influence in Indonesia and Malaysia is apparent in advertising regulations.

Total advertising expenditure in 1987 was roughly similar for all countries and ranged from $103 million in the Philippines to $214 in Thailand. High per capita expenditure in Malaysia and low per capita expenditure in Indonesia mirror differences in the size of these countries populations. In general, overall per capita expenditure is low by Western standards; only Malaysia spends more than $5 per person on advertising. Per capita advertising expenditure in Malaysia is $11. However, with the exception of the Philippines, which currently is beset by economic hardship, the advertising industry is growing. Print and television prevail as the principle media for advertising in all countries except Indonesia, where television advertising has been prohibited for a number of years (see Figures 15-4, 15-5, and 15-6).

Foreign agencies operate through one mechanism or another in each country. Investment laws in Indonesia exclude foreign ownership of advertising companies; therefore, the six foreign agencies reporting activity in Indonesia have nonequity arrangements with the local firms. Foreign-agency contribution to total expenditure is not extensive. In Malaysia foreign firms have minority ownership in local firms. In 1986 sixteen minority-owned foreign agencies reported earnings. These included the ten largest agencies in the country and accounted for a large share of total advertising expenditure. More than ten majority-owned subsidiaries of foreign agencies operate in the Philippines and Thailand. In the Philippines these agencies account for a high percentage of total advertising expenditure. In Thailand they appear to account for about half of total expenditures.

Each country has a unique experience in relation to foreign-advertising regulation. Strong nationalist pride and sentiment, a bitter colonial experience, and Islamic philosophy converge in Indonesia's policy. Politics and religion combine to explain the regulatory environment in Malaysia. The impact of government change and economic turmoil is demonstrated in changing attitudes toward foreign advertising in the Philippines. Thailand may be the foreign investor's choice. Traditional independence and generally favorable relations with Western countries are reflected in the relative freedom allowed foreign advertisers and agencies in Thailand.

Thus, while relatively complex regulatory environments exist in all countries, the countries tend to emphasize control in different areas of the activity. Indonesia's concern has been to limit foreign involvement to priority development sectors of the economy. The strongest regulations are at the point of entry. Malaysia's policy emphasizes public morality and decency consistent with Islamic custom, law, and practice. Thailand and Malaysia also are mindful of protecting the local culture. The Philippines and Thailand are concerned with more general objectives of regulation. Their regulations tend to emphasize fair competition and consumer safety. Formal or informal self-regulation exists in all countries to protect competition and to forestall additional government involvement.

Figure 15-4. Gross Multinational Agency Billings and Total Advertising Expenditure in Middle-Income Asia, 1987

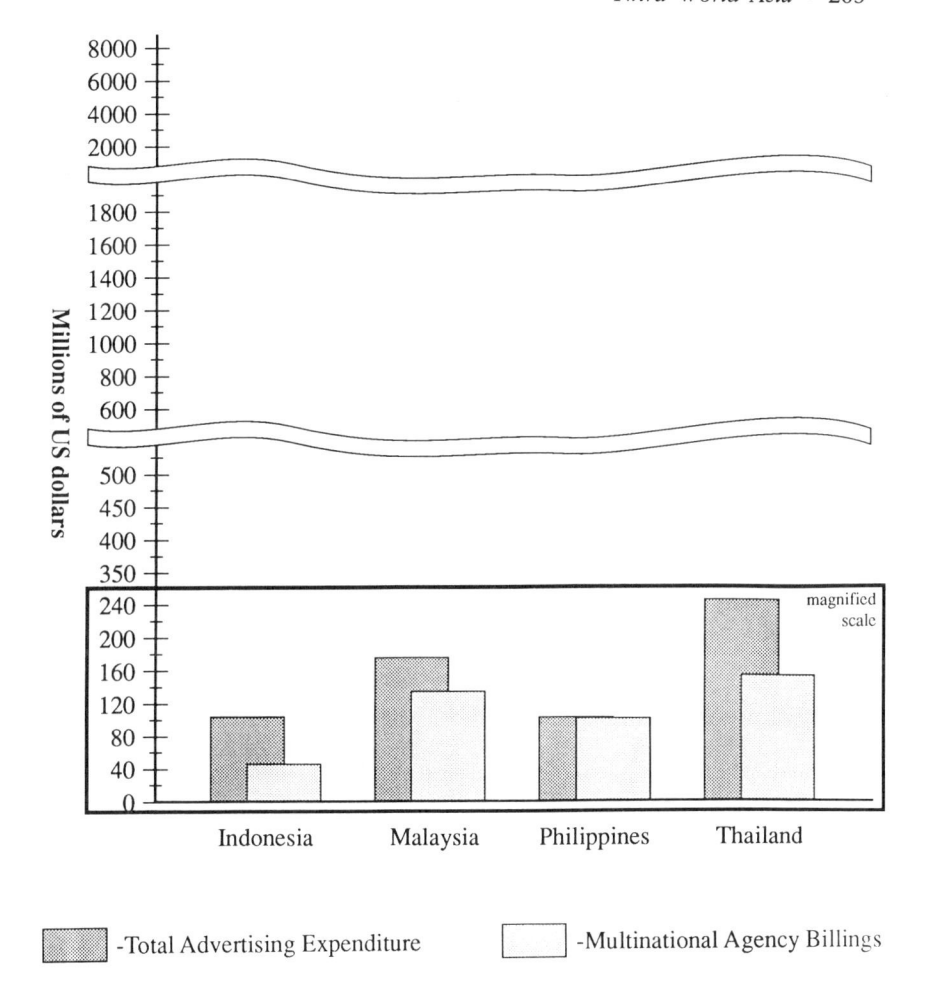

Source: derived from *World Advertising Expenditure,* 1987, 22nd ed., Starch INRA Hooper, Inc. in cooperation with IAA; "Foreign Agency Report," *Advertising Age,* 11 May 1987.

Indonesia

The modern Indonesian society is in a state of flux. It has adapted Western influences deemed necessary to attract needed foreign investment and to promote economic development. At the same time, the government continues to seek to increase national consciousness and pride. This dichotomy has been

264 • *International Advertising Handbook*

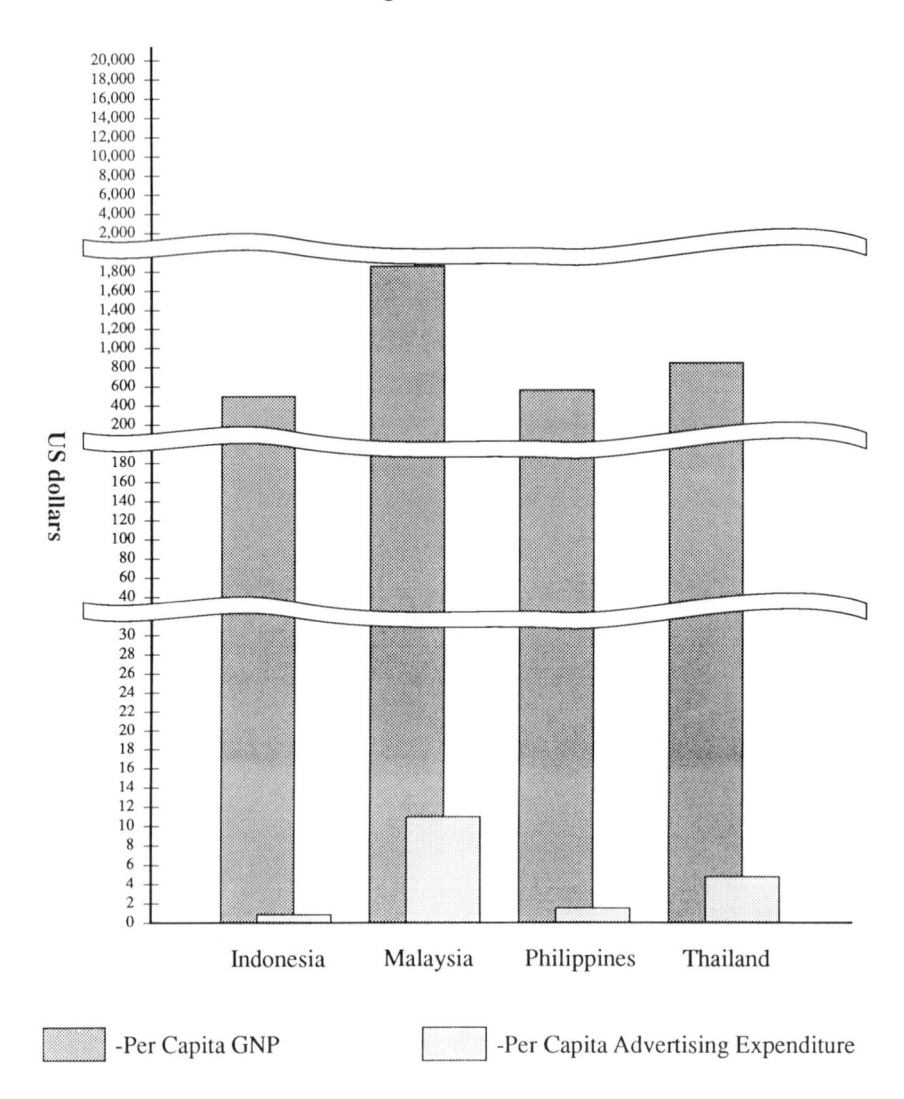

Source: derived from *World Advertising Expenditure*, 1987, 22nd ed., Starch INRA Hooper, Inc. in cooperation with IAA; *World Development Report, 1988*, World Bank.

Figure 15–5. Per Capita Advertising Expenditure and Per Capita GNP in Middle-Income Asia 1986/87

present in the development of the advertising industry since 1938 and is reflected in shifting policies toward foreign involvement.

Advertising was introduced to Indonesia in 1938, during the colonial era,

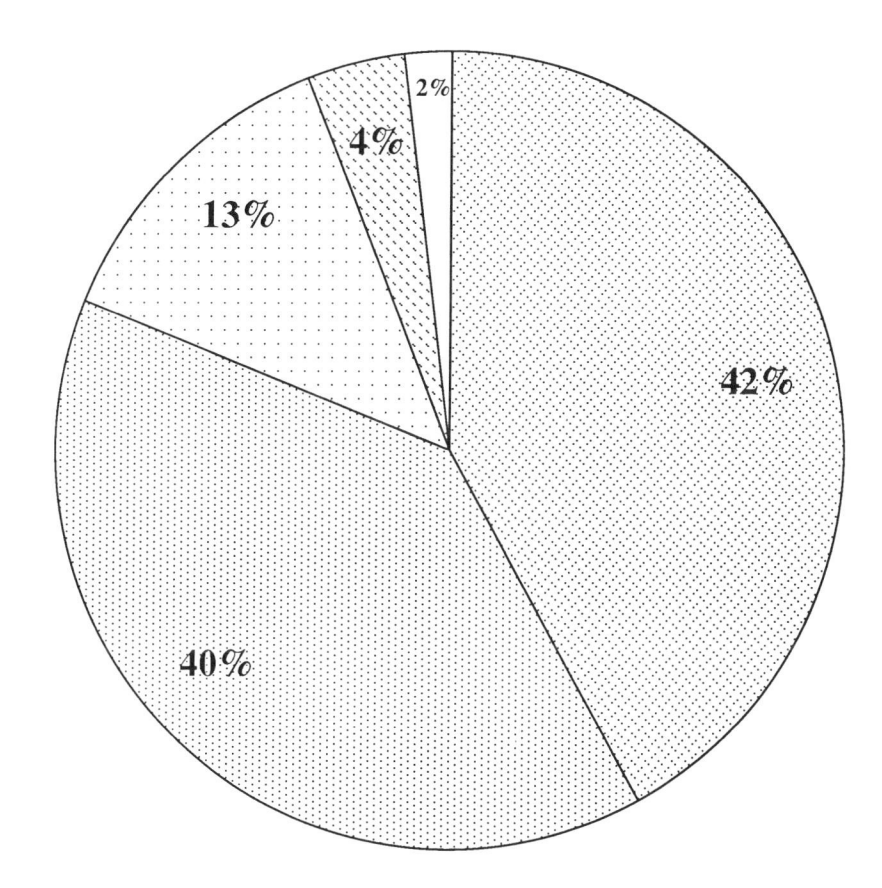

Indonesia is the exception where there is no commercial advertising on television.

▨-Print ▦-T.V. ▢-Radio ▨-Other ☐-Non-measured Media

Source: derived from *World Advertising Expenditure*, 1986, 21st ed., Starch INRA Hooper, Inc. in cooperation with IAA.

Figure 15–6. Advertising Expenditure by Media and Non-measured Media in Middle-Income Asia (percentage shares)

by Unilever/Lintas. The development of the industry was uneven and troubled. In 1963 Inter Vista Advertising, the first indigenous agency, was licensed to conduct business. Throughout the Sukarno regime, foreign businesses were harassed, and highly visible ad campaigns were politically, as well as commercially risky.[13]

In 1968 the new Suharto government adopted a liberal foreign-investment policy, returning expropriated businesses to original owners and permitting the licensing of nongovernmental commercial radio stations. These decisions contributed to the rapid expansion of foreign advertising. By 1975–76 advertising revenue accounted for about 34 percent of the national television budget, and the nation's central station in Jakarta was using advertising to finance more than 90 percent of its production and operation costs. In 1976 75 percent of all ads were either for imported products or products of joint ventures with foreign advertisers, such as Coca-Cola in Indonesia. Commercials came in almost equal proportion from Holland, Japan, and the United States. Less than 20 percent of the commercials were Indonesian.

Considerable tension arose between the Indonesian people and foreign investors during the later part of the 1970s. The tensions were attributed to increasing pressures on the economy requiring restraint in consumer expenditures, while commercials in the mass media continued to promote consumer purchases.[14] Consequently, measures were adopted to curb advertising by foreign agencies. The government implemented an earlier decree of the Ministry of Trade to limit the number of expatriates and required foreign companies to terminate their domestic trade and service activities as of December 31, 1977.[15] In 1981 the government banned all commercial advertising on television. In 1983 limitations were imposed on print-media advertising. Foreign ownership and media restrictions remain in force, and combined with difficult economic conditions, have slowed the growth of the industry.

There is no advertising on television. The print medium accounts for 75 percent of total advertising expenditure, and radio for 18 percent. Advertising in the print medium is restricted to 35 percent of total print space available in the medium. About 7 percent of advertising expenditure is allocated to cinema and outdoor display. Penetration of national newspapers is limited to urban areas, and it is estimated that these newspapers have an adult readership of 5 million—less than 1 percent of the population. The greatest penetration is made through radio. It is estimated that 80 percent of the population has access to radio commercials. Advertising on the radio is limited to twenty-one minutes per hour.

Currently, efforts are underway to simplify and standardize law and court procedures complicated by the existence of three sources of law: *adat* (customary law), the Islamic Shari'a, and civil-code law from Europe. The Shari'a is embraced by orthodox Muslims, especially in interpersonal relations under private law, such as marriage and divorce. Commercial laws are modeled on the Dutch civil code implanted in Indonesia in 1848. These laws are applied in all areas where *adat* is vague. They also are applied to foreign business.

Recommendations to the advertising community concerning advertising direction and management appear in Indonesia's Code of Ethics and Code of

Practice of Advertising. The Ministry of Information Press Council is responsible for its implementation. The code is voluntary and has been subscribed to by various professional associations involved in advertising. The principles stressed are truthfulness and harmony with current legal requirements; respect for decency and conformity with the dictates of religious faith, moral ethics, traditions, culture, and racial equality; and healthy competitiveness. The code suggests obedience to the dictates of the Department of Health in respect to the promotion of drugs, vitamins and minerals, and cosmetics and suggests moderation in the promotion of alcohol and tobacco products. Numerous recommendations in the code reflect only a moderate interpretation of the Islamic moral code of behavior.[16]

Despite the curtailment of foreign ownership of advertising agencies through foreign-investment rules and laws (stipulating in part that all advertising of foreign products be placed by local firms), foreign agencies continue to operate in Indonesia through technical assistance, management contracts, and foreign consultants. Their influence is strong and sometimes controversial. Effective regulation of advertising is hindered by lack of expertise, stringent business laws, and regulatory institutions. In the absence of effective policies and machinery enforcing national policies that might otherwise hamper their activities, foreign agencies nevertheless have been frustrated. Poor communication facilities, corruption, unclear and unenforceable government policies, and inadequate market information about the media and consumers outside the major cities have made Indonesia less attractive to advertisers.

These problems are not unique to Indonesia. Similar frustrations have been encountered in Latin America and elsewhere in the Third World. They explain the slow growth of foreign advertising in many Third World countries.

Malaysia

Malaysia's thriving advertising industry operates in a crosscurrent of liberal economic policies and conservative religious and nationalist sentiment. A strong liberal element welcomes the economic growth accompanying urbanization, affluence, and growing consumption. At the same time, the conservative element emphasizes protection of the unique Malaysian multicultural identity and strives to minimize Western-style consumerism and foreign advertising. The preamble to the Advertising Code, published by the Ministry of Information, provides that "advertisements must project the Malaysian culture, identity, (and) reflect the multi-racial character of the population."[17] Moreover, advertisements must advocate the philosophy of *Rakunegare,* which means "belief in God, loyalty to king and country, upholding the constitution, rule of law, and good behavior and morality."[18]

Reflecting nationalist sentiment, Islamic conservatism, and the desire to maintain control of its economy, the government's new economic policies encourage all companies, local and foreign, to divest 30 percent of their shareholdings to *Bumiputras* (natives of the soil) and 40 percent to other Malaysians. Many foreign companies have succumbed to increasing pressure to divest their majority holdings since the policies were enacted in the mid-1930s. Today, all foreign advertising agencies in Malaysia have minority shares, most of which are 30 percent or less.[19] Nevertheless, these laws do not inhibit creative freedom and the production of high-quality, innovative advertising.

Overall, economic conditions in Malaysia favor growth in the ad industry. Malaysia is the most economically advanced of the four countries in this group and among most Third World countries. A relatively high percentage of the population, about 40 percent, lives in urban environments. Per capita income exceeds $1800. Agriculture accounts for less than 30 percent of the GNP, while service industries exceed 50 percent. Total advertising expenditure in 1987 was $177 million, exceeding $10 per capita, more than twice the amount in other countries in this group. Of total advertising expenditure, 56 percent is spent on the print media, compared with 36 percent on television. The most heavily advertised product categories include, in order of importance, cigarettes and tobacco (despite the ban of advertising them on television), banking and financial services, airlines, entertainment, corporations, watches, clocks, and radios.

The regulatory system is complex and includes general laws, specific rules, self-regulation, and indirect law (such as the investment laws described above). General administrative rules governing advertising on television and radio are established in the Ministry of Information's Advertising Code. The code is enforced by the Ministry of Information's Radio Television Malaysia, which supervises the country's electronic media. Officially, the standards are designed to ensure social responsibility in advertising on the electronic media and also to protect the rural village population and children. Politically, the code also appeals to conservative Islamic factions supported by the largely rural Muslim population. Authority figures may not appear in ads, nor may superlatives be used. Advertising of pork and alcohol is prohibited. Advertising of tobacco products also is proscribed. Women should not seem to be the principal object of an ad nor attract sales of products other than those used by them. Males must not be used as sex objects to attract sales. A man and a woman alone in an ad must be shown to be married. The code effectively bars nudity, disco dancing, seductive clothing, and blue jeans. To preserve cultural integrity, all ads must be filmed in Malaysia, use Malaysian actors, and project the Malaysian culture and identity.[20] Directives established by the Ministry of Home Affairs spell out restrictions to be applied to photographs used in print media. These restrictions focus on sexism, cigarette ads, and medical devices.[21]

Other controls include specific regulations to prevent advertising abuses that could be dangerous for health and safety reasons. Control measures on pharmaceutical advertisements were first promulgated in 1953 under the Indecent Advertisements Ordinance, prohibiting advertisements relating to sexually transmitted diseases except in publications sent out to doctors and pharmacists. The Medicine (Advertisement and Sales) Ordinance was promulgated to prohibit publication of advertisements referring to any article in terms calculated to led to the use of that article as a treatment for diseases or conditions explicitly identified in the act. Advertisements to professionals were again excluded.[22] Responding to the negative impact of aggressive advertising and harmful effects of indiscriminate and uncontrolled advertising of medicine, the government adopted an amendment to the Ordinance of 1956, establishing a Medicine Advertisement Board to screen all advertisements.[23] The advertising of food is governed by the Food Act of 1983.[24] This act makes it an offense punishable by fine and/or imprisonment to publish a food advertisement that is likely to deceive a purchaser with regard to material facts about the product.

Based on the British sysem of self-regulation, the Malaysian advertising industry's Advertising Standards Authority has adopted a self-regulatory code, Malaysian Code of Advertising Practice, which closely parallels the government code issued by the Ministry of Information. Major restrictions cover testimonials; portrayal of male and female models; children's advertising in Malaysia; production requirements, and medical, alcohol, and tobacco advertising.[25]

Thailand

A rapidly developing country, Thailand is a constitutional monarchy with a long tradition of independence. With an open economy, Thailand has adopted economic policies favorable to foreign investment. The Thai Buddhist religious tradition is conservative, nonpolitical in character, and generally not actively involved in promoting or guiding social and cultural change. Thus, unlike Malaysia, there are no effective pressures from religious leaders to curb or influence advertising messages.

Although current foreign-investment laws prohibit majority-owned foreign firms in the advertising industry, the Thai-U.S. Treaty of Amity and Economic Relations has meant that U.S. firms have been exempt from restrictions under the Alien Business Law.[26] The U.S. multinational advertising agencies play a major role in Thailand. At least seven of the ten largest firms are locally managed and majority-owned by foreign agencies.

Thailand boasts a mature advertising industry with a total expenditure of $244 million in 1987, almost 30 percent greater than Malaysia, its nearest competitor in the group. While per capita expenditure is low compared to the United States, at $4.6 it is high relative to many other developing countries in Asia. Advertising expenditure is strongly concentrated on radio and television. The high concentration of expenditure on the electronic media in part overcomes constraints in disseminating advertising through the print media beyond urban settlements to the 62 percent of the population living in rural areas. The products attracting the greatest amount of advertising include, in order of importance, home appliances, watches and clocks, soaps, pharmaceuticals, cosmetics, automobiles, beverages, shampoos, and baby products.

The ad industry is moderately regulated in consideration of public health and safety. While all media are available to advertising, censorship exists on advertising over the electronic mass media. There are also a number of restrictions or requirements on the advertising of foods, drugs, tobacco, alcohol, cosmetics and beauty aids, and products for children. Finally, there are significant restrictions on the use of foreign language; foreign language in commercials is prohibited in television, cinema, and sales-promotion materials.

The most comprehensive legislation is in the Consumer Protection Act of 1979.[27] The act prescribes that consumers are entitled to correct and sufficient information concerning goods and services, safety in their use, and compensation for damages. Section 23 prescribes that advertisements must not be carried out "by means that may be hazardous to the health of consumers," or "by means that may cause nuisances" to consumers as defined in ministerial regulations.[28] Section 24 impowers the Ad Hoc Committee on Advertisements to require certain ads to be accompanied by warnings and instructions or to ban or restrict such advertisements.

Advertising of foods and pharmaceuticals also is governed by separate legislation. The Food Act of 1979 prohibits false or misleading advertising of the qualities or benefits of foods. All food ads must be submitted to the licensing authority for approval.[29] Advertising of medicines is governed by the Drugs Act (No. 3) of 1979.[30] The act prescribes that advertisements for drugs by radio, television, cinema, or printed matter must be licensed and must satisfy the conditions laid down by the licensing authority.[31]

In addition to government regulation, the Advertising Association of Thailand has adopted a self-regulating code. This code emphasizes four main principals: honesty and legality, social responsibility, fair competition, and preservation of public confidence in advertising as a service to the industry and the public.

The Philippines

The Philippine advertising industry is in a state of transition. Until the change in government in the mid-1980s, historic ties and commercial relations with the United States were predominant influences on the development of the industry. Today, economic turmoil and strong nationalist sentiments portend change in relations with foreign advertisers.

Because of political and economic unrest, the advertising industry has stagnated over much of the 1980s. Total expenditure in 1987 was $103 million (slightly more than $1.80 per capita), down from a peak of $108 million in 1983.

The role of foreign advertising agencies in the Philippine industry also is expected to change. Proposed investment laws attempt to limit foreign ownership in local firms. Nevertheless, five of the ten top agencies in the Philippines remain majority owned, including the top three firms. Their market share is 40 percent to 50 percent. Although advertising is a low priority, proposals before the government suggest banning foreign-equity participation in media and communications establishments. This restriction is intended to protect Philippine cultural identity. This objective was expressed in a resolution that all communications media promote, strengthen, and protect the cultural identity; foster constructive values, customs, and traditions; and afford respect to the culture of national minorities.[32] These resolutions and similar ones are part of the campaign for Filipinization and were stimulated by fears of cultural domination, particularly via Western material values. The proliferation of the import of cultural and consumer products is seen as a danger.

The influence of the United States on the Philippine economy is evident in the earliest regulations on advertising. Advertising in the Philippines has been governed by law since 1914, when by the authority of the United States, the Philippine legislature established an act prohibiting untrue, deceptive, or misleading advertisements.[33] This act was further amended in 1930, when a general act prohibited advertising that misrepresented the value, properties, or condition of the article advertised or of which it was composed.[34]

In 1971 the Philippine government issued detailed administrative orders for information and guidance in the implementation of the earlier acts. These orders were revised again in 1975. They define and distinguish advertising from sales-promotion campaigns and otherwise detail restrictions on sales promotion.[35] In addition to general legislation, there are product-specific governmental restrictions on the advertising of tobacco and pharmaceutical products.

Self-regulation has, until recently, been favored by the government. The central organization, the Philippine Board of Advertising (PBA), was formed in 1974 and is composed of a number of national trade organizations, including agencies, advertisers, and the media. In 1976 the PBA promulgated a general code of ethics rules and regulations. An ethics committee oversees the implementation of the code and examines alleged violations or complaints initiated by advertisers, the government's Fair Trade Board, and the PBA Screening Committee. The code imposes voluntary restraints on the advertising of alcoholic beverages, food, children's products, and health and beauty aids. These ads are subject to approval of the Screening Committee of the Philippine Board of Advertising.

High–Middle-Income Asia

The Four Tigers—South Korea, Taiwan, Hong Kong, and Singapore—form a group apart from other Asian countries. The expression "Four Tigers" refers to their rapid development and their aggression in international trade. They are among the wealthiest of the Third World countries, with per capita incomes ranging from $2,000 to $7,400. Over 60 percent of the Korean population is urban, while over 90 percent of Singapore, Taiwan, and Hong Kong is urban. All these countries have positive trade balances with the West and are strong competitors in the electronics and textile industries. These open economies, with their relatively affluent populations, have a healthy appetite for consumer products (see table 15–3).

All four countries have adopted some form of republican government. The governments of Korea and Taiwan have strong centralized rule under a dominant party leader. They all adhere to a capitalist economic policy. Ethnically, with the exception of Singapore, these countries are relatively homogeneous in comparison with other Asian countries. Also with the exception of Singapore, all have adopted a single official national language. English also is an official foreign language in Hong Kong and Singapore.

Total advertising expenditures in 1987 ranged from $157 million in Singapore to 1.2 billion in South Korea (see figure 15–7). Expenditures in Korea and Taiwan individually exceed those of either Mexico, Venezuela, or most small countries in Western Europe. Per capita expenditures range from a low of $28 in South Korea and $39 in Taiwan to highs $60 in Singapore and $66 in Hong Kong (see figure 15–8). The per capita expenditure figures for these four countries exceed virtually all other Third World countries.

All media are available for advertising, and penetration is over 90 percent, given the high percentages of urban populations and relatively high level of economic development, particularly with an established communications infrastructure. Print media accounts for an average of 45 percent of advertising expenditure in high income Asia. Television advertising accounts for about 38 percent of total advertising expenditure in all countries and exceeds total expenditure in the print media only in Hong Kong (see figure 15–9).

Table 15-3
Regulatory Profile: Upper-Income Asia

Countries:	Hong Kong, Singapore, South Korea and Taiwan
Government:	Republic; presidential systems; British Crown Colony (Hong Kong); dominant parties; predominantly elitist systems; Singapore is member of Commonwealth
Politico-economic ideology:	Free enterprise with government control
Legal system:	English common law; Asian Confucian tradition; supplemented by body of legislated law
Investment policy:	Liberal to moderate restrictive (S. Korea)
Ad regulation:	Moderate
Ad expenditure:	S. Korea $1.2B, Taiwan $785M, Hong Kong $361M, Singapore $157M; Per capita: S. Korea $28 to 40+ (all others); %GNP: .8% to 1.0%
Consumer market:	Predominant middle class
Social Indicators:	
Population:	3–5 million (Singapore and Hong Kong; 5–20 million
Urbanization:	90+% (S. Korea 64%)
Per capita income:	$2,000–$7,400
Language:	Chinese dialects and English (Hong Kong and Taiwan); Korean; Malay, Chinese, Tamil, English (Singapore)
Class structure:	Majority middle income
Life expectancy:	70 years
Literacy:	85+%

Directly or indirectly (through nonequity affiliations in the case of Korea and, to a large extent, Taiwan), the top ten multinationals play major roles in the advertising industries of these four countries (see table 2–5). The total billings of agencies with foreign participation account for close to 90 percent of all advertising expenditures in all countries except the South Korea, where the figure may be closer to 50 percent. The explanation of Korea's significantly lower figure lies in its foreign-investment law and regulations.

The Foreign Capital Inducement Law (FCIL), the basic statute governing foreign investment in Korea, provides that all foreign investment be approved by the Ministry of Finance.[36] The July 1984 revision to the law established a set of guidelines for reviewing investments. The guidelines include different categories of industries that may be approved and under what specific conditions. Advertising agencies are on the prohibited list, while ad production and other related services are omitted projects and treated de facto as part of the negative list.

In addition to the FCIL, the Korean government has erected a barrier to entry into the field of broadcast advertising. By law, all advertising on the broadcast media must be placed through the government-owned corporation, the Korea Broadcast Advertising Corporation (KOBACO), established in 1982 under the Korea Broadcast Advertising Corporation Law. KOBACO

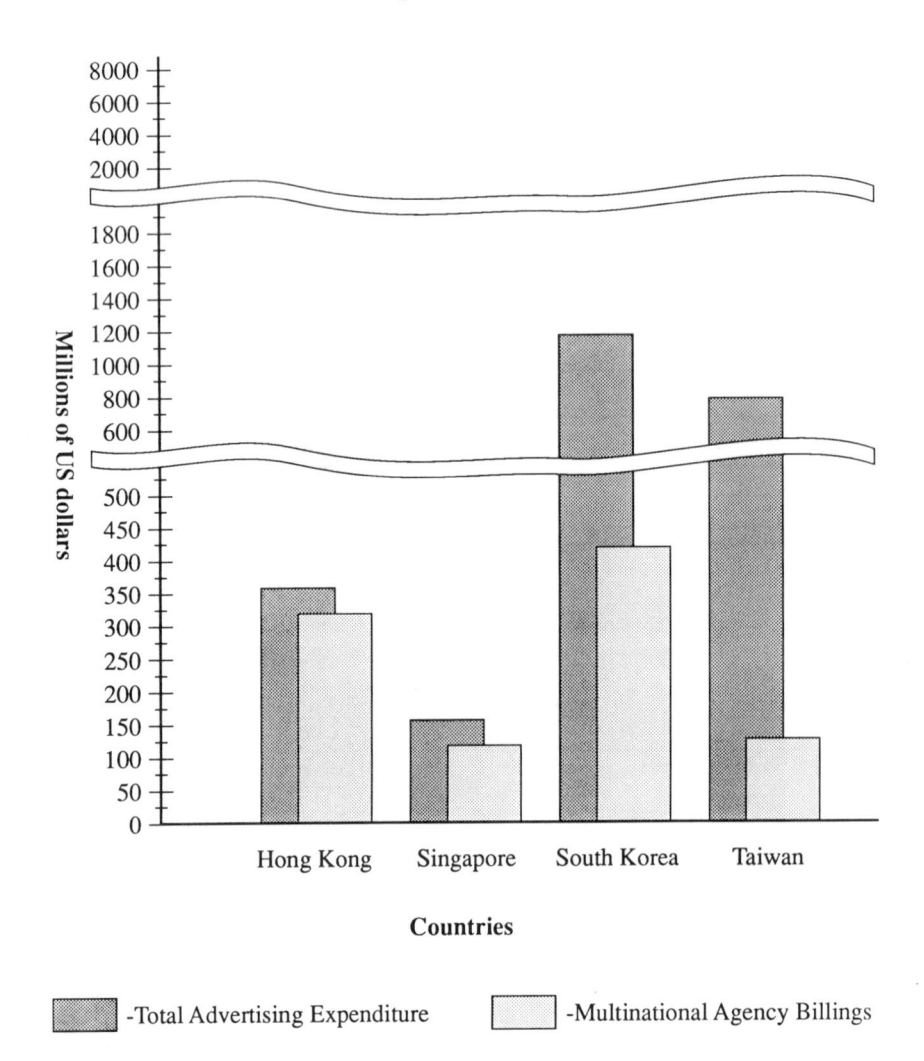

[Bar chart showing Total Advertising Expenditure and Multinational Agency Billings in millions of US dollars for Hong Kong, Singapore, South Korea, and Taiwan]

Source: derived from *World Advertising Expenditure*, 1987, 22nd, ed., Starch INRA Hooper, Inc. in cooperation with IAA; "Foreign Agency Report," *Advertising Age*, 11 May 1987.

Figure 15–7. Gross Multinational Agency Billings and Total Advertising Expenditure in High-Income Asia, 1987

recognizes and shares its 20 percent commission on all ads with only four of the sixty advertising agencies in Korea.[37]

Controls also exist on advertising content. Two self-regulating bodies operate in Korea. These include the Korean Newspaper Ethics Committee and the Korea Broadcasting Ethics Committee (KOBEC). These have been

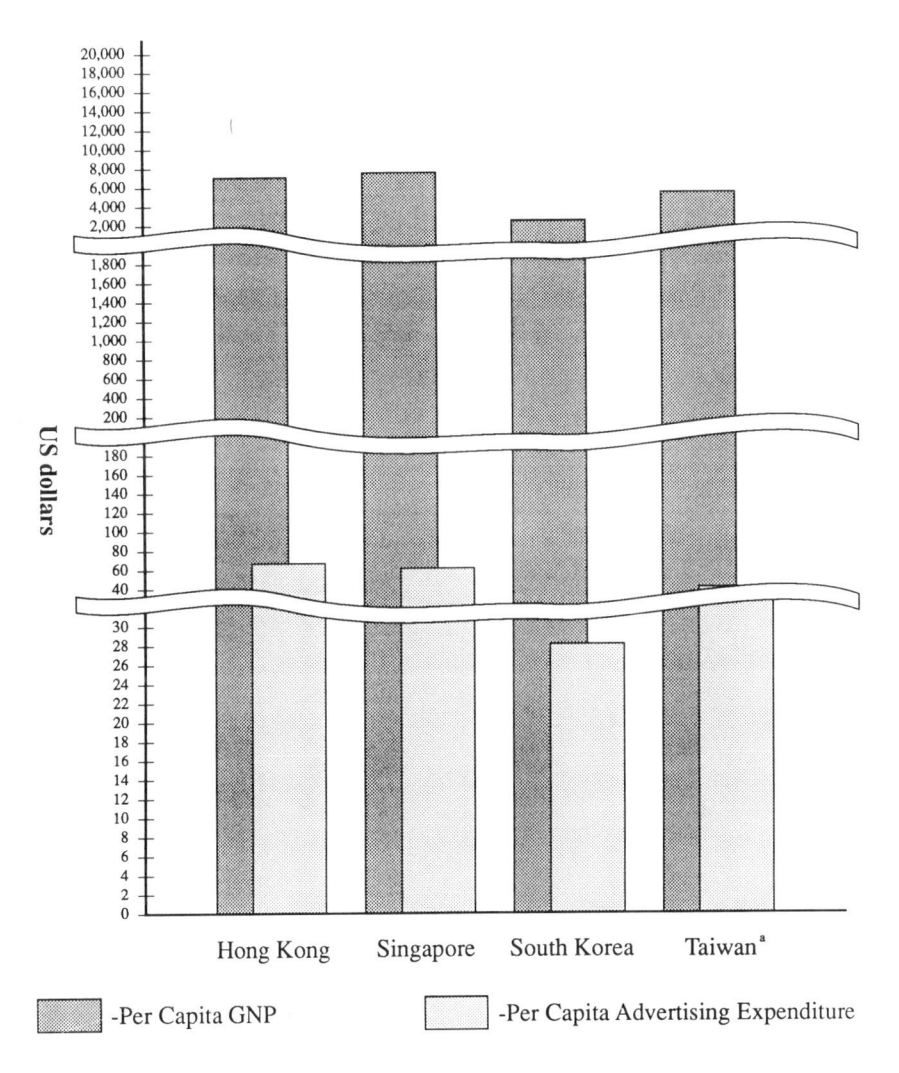

Source: derived from *World Advertising Expenditure*, 1987, 22nd ed., Starch INRA Hooper, Inc. in cooperation with IAA; *World Development Report, 1988*, World Bank.
[a]Estimated.

Figure 15-8. Per Capita Advertising Expenditure and Per Capita GNP in High-Income Asia 1986/87

in operation since the 1960s. Aside from sponsoring KOBEC, government involvement is limited. The ministries of culture and health, however, review ads and control some messages in cinema ads and foods and drug ads in the interest of public safety.

276 • *International Advertising Handbook*

[Pie chart showing: 45%, 38%, 9%, 4%, 4%]

☐-Print ☐-T.V. ☐-Radio ☐-Other ☐-Non-measured Media

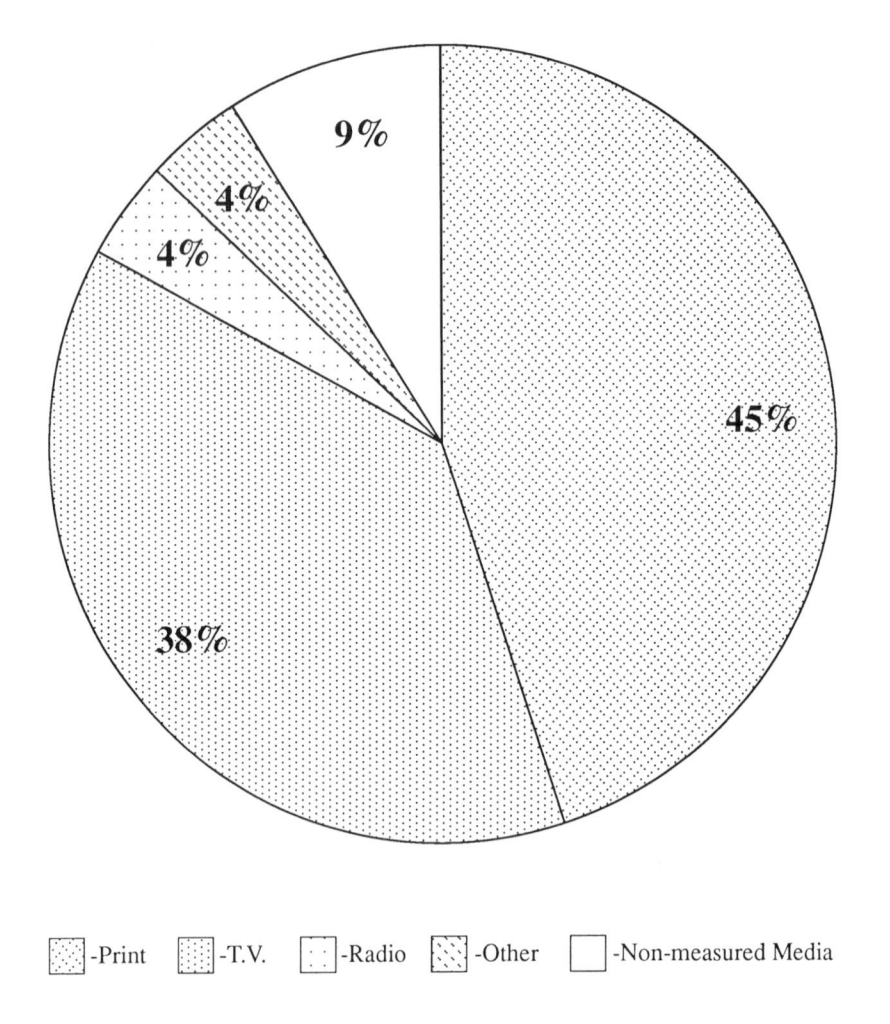

Source: derived from *World Advertising Expenditure,* 1986, 21st ed., Starch INRA Hooper, Inc. in cooperation with IAA.

Figure 15–9. Advertising Expenditure by Media and Non-measured Media in High-Income Asia (percentage shares)

Strict investment restrictions do not exist in Taiwan, Hong Kong, or Singapore. However, these governments exercise control over advertising activities and content. For example, the government of Singapore has adopted a set of regulations that resembles those of the United Kingdom. In 1975 the government adopted the Consumer Protection (Trade Descriptions and Safety Requirements) Act.[38] The act prohibits all false trade descriptions in advertisements. The act defines a false trade description as one that, by omission, commission, adulteration by addition, and so on, is false or likely to mislead in a material respect in regard to the goods to which it refers.

The Singapore government also has adopted laws in regard to advertising specific products, including foods, drugs, and tobacco products.[39] The Sale of Food Act of 1973 forbids the sale of any food that is advertised in a false, misleading, or deceptive manner or that might create an erroneous impression regarding value, merit, or safety. The Medicines (Medical Advertisements) Regulations require permits for all advertisements of medicines from the licensing authority of the Ministry of Health.[40] The Prohibition on Advertisements Relating to Smoking Act of 1970 makes it a criminal offense to publish or take part in the publishing of any advertisement containing any express or implied inducement to purchase or to smoke tobacco products.[41] Further acts require warnings on ads and labels.

Singapore also has a self-regulatory system, following the British model. Both the advertising industry and the government, to a significant extent, rely on the Advertising Standards Authority to perform this function.

Finally, in Taiwan, the Government Information Office (GIO) controls all advertisements. This organization administers Taiwan's advertising code of standards. In addition, ads for cosmetics, medicines, and food are subject to the review of the Government Health Administration, which rejects ads with exaggerated claims, comparative or discriminatory claims, and excessive use of foreign language terms.

Notes

1. Ogilvy & Mather: Unilever, Beecham, Boeing, General Foods, Johnson & Johnson, Mattel, Mercedes Benz, and Philips; Lintas Worldwide: R.J. Reynolds, Sony, and Unilever.

2. Gurchuran Das, "A Case for Advertising in India," *Financial Express of India,* 31 October 1983.

3. A.S. Biswas, Under-Secretary to the Government of India, Ministry of Health, letter to author, 27 June 1984.

4. *The Foreign Exchange Regulation Act 1973* (FERA) (Act 46 of 1973), reported in UN Center for Transnational Corporations, *National Legislation and Regulation Relating to Transnational Corporations,* ST/CTC/6 (1978).

5. Advertising Standards Council of India *Code of Advertising Practice,* Bombay, 20 November 1985, 1.

6. Bangladesh, *Drug Control Ordinance No. 8 of 1982,* in *Bangladesh Gazette,* Extraordinary (12 June 1982). Sigma Huda, advocate for chancery chambers, Dacca, Bangladesh, memo to American embassy, Dacca, Bangladesh, 9 August 1984.

7. Nepal, *Pharmaceutical Act of 1978,* in *Nepal Rajapatra* 28, no. 43A, (Extraordinary), Kartik (25 October 1978): 2035.

8. Nepal, *Food Act of 1966,* in *Nepal Gazette* 16, no. 23A, (Extraordinary) Bhadra 24, 2023 (9 September 1966): 2023.

9. Nepal, *Libel and Defamation Act of 1959,* in *Nepal Gazette,* Ashadh 15, 2016 (28 June 1960): 2016.

10. Nepal, *Standards (Certification Mark) Act of 1980,* in *Nepal Rajapatra* 30, no. 33, (Extraordinary) Bhadra 26 (11 September 1980): 2037.

11. Sri Lanka, *Food Act No. 26 of 1980,* in *Gazette of the Democratic Socialist Republic of Sri Lanka* 2, supp. (25 July 1980): 1–19.

12. Sri Lanka, *Cosmetics, Devices and Drugs Act No. 27,* in *Gazette of the Democratic Socialist Republic of Sri Lanka* 2, supp. (19 September 1980): 1–20.

13. Michael A. Anderson, "Transnational Advertising and Politics: The Case of Indonesia," *Asian Survey* 20 (December 1980): 1253–70. In 1977–78 Anderson conducted field research in Southeast Asia on advertising and national communication policy issues.

14. Mochtar Lubis, "Between Myths and Realities: Indonesia's Intellectual Community Today," *Asian Affairs,* September-October 1977, 45. Lubis was one of the sixteen members of the UNESCO MacBride Commission. The Commission was appointed in 1976 to prepare a study on world communications and society. The work of the Commission is described in chapter 18 below.

15. Indonesia, *Decree No. 314/Kp/13/1970,* cited in Anderson, "Transnational Advertising and Politics," 1265.

16. Republic of Indonesia, *Code of Ethics and Code of Practice of Advertising in Indonesia,* Directorate General for Press and Graphic Promotion, Department of Information, 1982–83.

17. Malaysia, Ministry of Information, *Advertising Code,* 1982 cited by Steven Howard, "Advertising in Malaysia," *International Advertiser,* (July–August, 1983): 13.

18. *Ibid.*

19. Basic legislation affecting investment is the *Investment Incentives Act of 1968* (as amended) and the *Industrial Coordination Act of 1975* (as amended). These acts do not restrict foreign equity participation. UN Center for Transnational Corporations, *National Legislation and Regulations Relating to Transnational Corporations,* vol. 3 (New York: United Nations, 1983), 82–93.

20. Steven Howard, "Advertising in Malaysia," 14.

21. Issued by the Publications Department of the Malaysian Ministry of Home Affairs, 1981.

22. These conditions were (a) prevention or treatment of the diseases and conditions of human beings as specified in the schedule (twenty diseases and conditions are listed in the schedule); (b) practicing contraception among human beings; and (c) improving the conditioning or functioning of the human kidney or heart or improving the sexual performance of human beings.

23. The Malaysian *Medicine Advertisement Board Regulations 1976* was gazetted in September 1976 and came into force in July 1977. Yeap Boon Chye, Director of Pharmaceutical Services for the Secretary General, Ministry of Health, Malaysia, letter to author, 3 May 1984.

24. Malaysia, *Food Act of 1983, Law No. 281,* in *Government Gazette,* 10 March 1983. This act repeals *Sale of Food and Drugs Ordinance, 1952, Law No. 280 of 1952,* in so far as it deals with food. Advertising of food was not covered in the earlier act.

25. International Advertising Association, *Intelligence Summary,* no. 36 (10 November 1983): 2, 3.

26. *Alien Business Law National Executive Council Announcement no 103 of 1972* and *Investment Promotion Act B. E. 2520* (1977), described in UN Center for Transnational Corporations, *Transnational Corporations,* vol. 4, 34–35.

27. Thailand, *Consumer Protection Act,* in *Royal Thai Government Gazette* 33, no. 24 (30 August 1979): 345–61.

28. Ibid.

29. Thailand, *Food Act 1979,* in *Royal Thai Government Gazette* 33, no. 25 (10 September 1979): 363–81, sec. 40–42.

30. Thailand, *Drugs Act (No. 3), 1979,* in *Royal Thai Government Gazette* 33, no. 26–27 (30 September 1979): 383–415.

31. Ibid., sec. 88 bis.

32. Republic of the Philippines, Constitutional Commission of 1986, *Resolution Providing That Media of Communication Shall Promote, Strengthen, and Protect Our National Cultural Identity, Foster Constructive Values, Customs, and Traditions, and Afford Respect to the Culture of National Minorities,* Proposed Resolution No. 164, introduced by Hon. Rosario Braid, Quezon City, Metro Manila, 1986; Republic of the Philippines, Constitutional Commission of 1986, *Resolution Providing That Employers of Any Media Corporations or Associations Shall Enjoy the Right to be Part-owners Thereof or to Purchase Shares of Stock Therein,* Proposed Resolution No. 49, Introduced by Hon. Foz, Quezon City, Metro Manila, 1986.

33. Philippine Legislature, *An Act Relative of Prohibiting Untrue, Deceptive, and Misleading Advertisements., No. 2333,* enacted 26 February 1914.

34. Philippine Legislature, *An Act to Penalize Fraudulent Advertising, Mislabeling, or Misbranding of Any Product, Stock, Bonds, Etc., No. 3740,* approved 22 November 1930.

35. Republic of Philippines, Ministry of Trade, *Rules and Regulations Governing the Conduct and Promotion of Sales of Goods, Services, and Securities;* Department of Trade Administrative Order no. 1, series of 1975.

36. Republic of South Korea, *Foreign Capital Inducement Law* Law No. 2598, 1973, Cited in UN Center for Transnational Corporations, *Transnational Corporations,* vol. 4, 198.

37. American Chamber of Commerce in Korea, *Barriers to Entry in the Korean Advertising Industry,* prepared by Trade Expansions Committee, 10 December 1984.

38. Singapore, *Consumer Protection (Trade Descriptions and Safety Requirements) Acts, Act No. 18 of 1975,* in *Government Gazette,* Acts Supp., no. 10 (25 April 1975): 37–83.

39. Singapore, *Sale of Food Act of 1973. Act No. 12 of 1973,* in *Government Gazette,* Acts Supp., no. 17 (6 April 1973): 318–37; *Food Regulations of 1974,* in *Government Gazette,* Subsidiary Legislation Supp., no. S 183/74 (28 June 1974):

348–428; *Medicines (Medical Advertisements) Regulations of 1977,* in *Government Gazette,* Subsidiary Legislation Supp., no. S 289/77 (n.d.): 682–84.

40. Yee Shen Kuan, Director for Licensing Authority Medical Advertisements, Ministry of Health, Singapore, letter to author, 17 May 1984.

41. Singapore, *Prohibition on Advertisements Relating to Smoking Act, Act No. 57 of 1970,* in *Government Gazette,* Acts Supp., no. 8 (5 February 1971): 27–32.

16
Africa, South of the Sahara

In the realm of international advertising, Africa south of the Sahara, is on the periphery. Combined, African countries account for much less than 1 percent of total world advertising expenditure. That the advertising industry is in its very early stage of development in African countries is indicated by the dearth of figures on advertising activity. Total advertising expenditure statistics for 1987 are only available for a few countries (see figure 16–1) and show expenditures of less than $50 million dollars, even in Nigeria, the most heavily populated country south of the Sahara. Per capita expenditures on advertising are also correspondingly low. With the exception of Zimbabwe, they are less than $1. throughout Third World Africa (see figure 16–2). Few foreign companies report billings in Africa, and overall statistics are available for only four countries. South Africa, included among First World countries in this study, stands out in stark contrast as the only country on the African continent with a mature advertising industry. For this reason, and because of the commonalities of its regulatory system with that of the United Kingdom, South Africa has been covered in chapter 7.

The marginality of Africa in world advertising reflects the dearth of urban centers, low levels of economic development, widespread illiteracy, and splintered societies. Government policies and ideological currents of nationalism periodically reinforce social and economic deterrents to foreign advertising in a number of countries. They may limit imports of foreign goods and otherwise protect domestic producers by restricting direct foreign investment in consumer goods and service industries.

Some 450 million people in forty countries live south of the Sahara.[1] Individual country populations range from 97 million to less than 1 million. Only nine countries have populations exceeding 10 million; of these, three have more than 30 million inhabitants. About half of these countries, with a total of 200 million inhabitants, are classified by the World Bank as low-income countries (defined by an average per capita income of less than $400). The remaining countries are in the middle-income range with average per capita incomes ranging from $450 to $1200 (see map 16–1).

282 • *International Advertising Handbook*

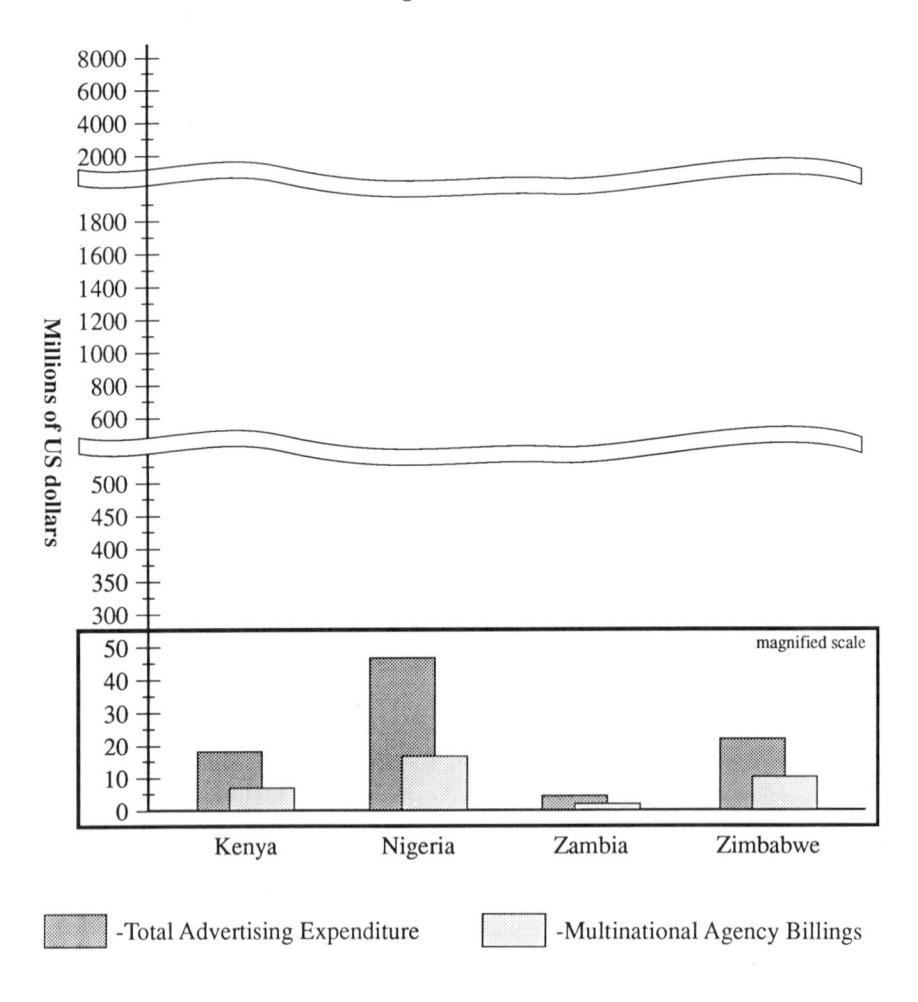

Source: derived from *World Advertising Expenditure*, 1987, 22nd ed., Starch INRA Hooper, Inc. in cooperation with IAA; *World Development Report, 1988*, World Bank.

Figure 16–1. Gross Multinational Agency Billings and Total Advertising Expenditure in Africa, 1987

Most African countries have dual economies—small, modern industrial and market sectors and large subsistence sectors. Over 70 percent of sub-Saharan Africa is agrarian, much of which is at a subsistence level. With the exception of a few middle-income countries, urbanization is less than 30 percent. Only Zaire, Ghana, and Nigeria have more than one urban center with a population in excess of 500,000; half the countries have no such centers. Illiteracy is widespread. This picture, reinforced by reports of political

Africa, South of the Sahara • 283

[Figure: bar chart with broken/magnified scale showing Per Capita GNP and Per Capita Advertising Expenditure for Kenya, Nigeria, Zambia, and Zimbabwe, in US dollars]

-Per Capita GNP   -Per Capita Advertising Expenditure

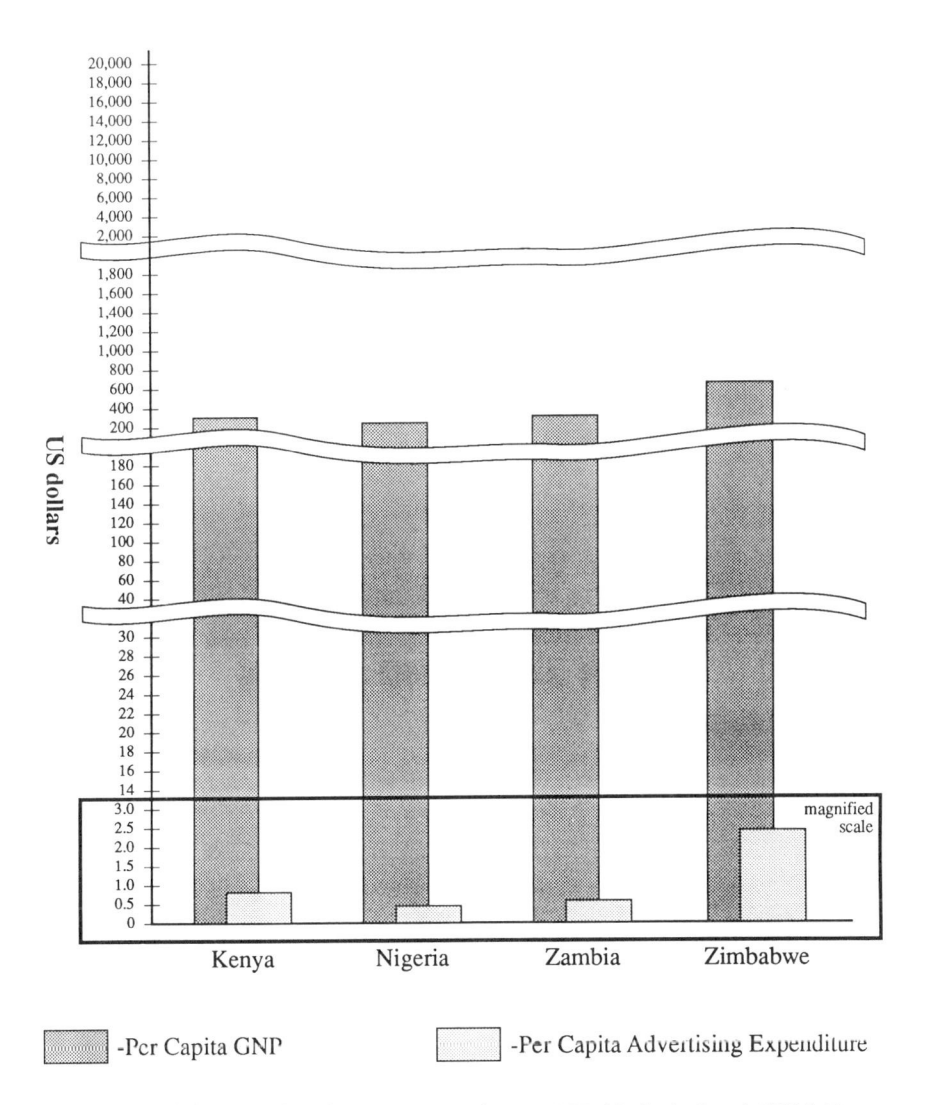

Source: derived from *World Advertising Expenditure*, 1987, 22nd ed., Starch INRA Hooper, Inc. in cooperation with IAA; *World Development Report, 1988*, World Bank.

Figure 16–2. Per Capita Advertising Expenditure and Per Capita GNP in Africa, 1986/87

upheavals, famine and droughts, social unrest, corruption, and general instability, further explains the low level of foreign commercial activity in Africa.

Given this socioeconomic picture, the foreign advertiser legitimately

284 • *International Advertising Handbook*

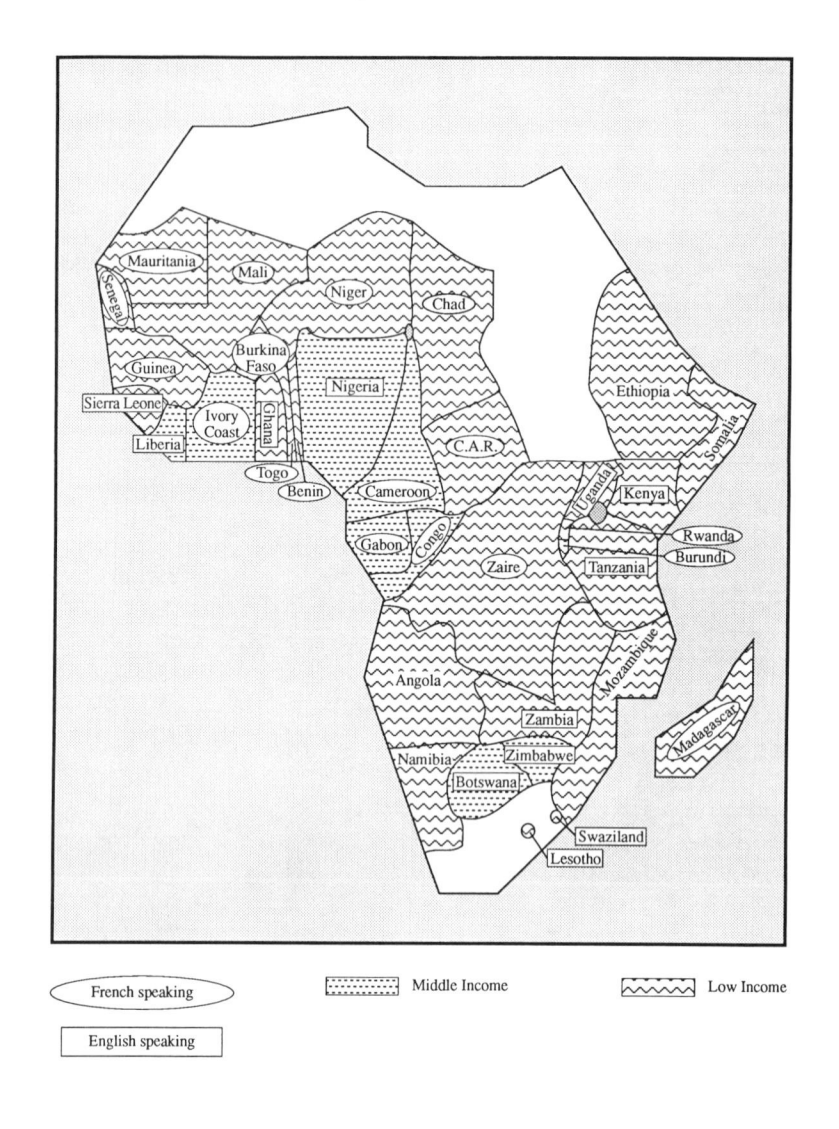

Map 16–1. Africa

asks, "What kind of market exists in Africa for foreign products if, at all?" John Spencer, notable and long-time African specialist, has given some interesting observations of this question.[2] Broadly speaking he separates African societies into four market segments describing what appears to be the quintessential illustration of the Third World market segmentation, which was outlined by Mansour as typical of the Third World (refer to chapter 12). The smallest but wealthiest segment consists of European-educated elite, wealthy landowners and foreign residents whose demands correspond to those of the elite markets in the Western world. On the second level is a larger but still relatively small (rarely exceeding 5 to 10 percent of the population) group of middle- and upper–middle-income classes. This group provides the largest market for a wide variety of foreign consumer products sold in retail stores in the national capitals and largest urban centers.

The third group consists of the low income, urban dwellers. They include many youth from the rural sectors who migrate seasonally or permanently to the urban areas where many are underemployed. They form a large nucleus of poor but aggressive consumers, each of whom would figuratively sell his own mother's shirt to own a pair of "jeans." Other prestige items such as Michael Jackson tapes or rock video cassettes are also prized items sought by this group of consumers. The more expensive and generally unattainable complements such as tape recorders, VCRs, or television sets are not as vital to these consumers as owning the easily obtainable and affordable "prestige" packaged in the cassette or tape. For other people in this broad category of consumers, low priced cosmetics, red lipsticks, mascara, etc, and perfumes are in strong demand. Powdered milks and low-priced convenience foods are also sought.

The fourth and largest group (60 to 80 percent of the population) consists of the rural poor. Peasant households seek cooking utensils, pails, flashlights, cheap cloth, sandals, and similar items. Prestige-lending items such as a Parker pen for the village elder and "dark glasses" are popular luxury items whose demand is explained not so much for need, but for sake of identification with local and foreign elites.

The latter two classes of consumers, which combined make up the vast bulk of the population, share some important characteristics. First, many exhibit common symptoms of hypochondria and are enthusiastic pill swallowers, whether or not they have an actually diagnosed or even apparent need for any kind of drug. Therefore, the markets for pharmaceutical products, particularly analgesics and vitamins, flourish. Second, brand consciousness is widespread. Product quality and composition are much less important than the label attached to goods. Thus, Reebok shoes of all grades and quality are popular in African markets. Third, these groups are most profitably serviced by black market profiteers operating through peddlers and traders in the open markets. These sellers, like the peddlers of Gucci watches on New York Avenues, with low overhead, are, practically speaking, the only ones who can afford to provide the right types of goods at prices the poor market segments can afford. The African consumers' fervent attachment to brands and labels perpetuate the profitability of the black market and the production of product look-alikes and counterfeits sold in many African markets.

Beyond the market segments, foreign advertisers must consider other distinctive features of the African market. Cutting across the class structure is a loose collage of tribal groups with distinct languages or dialects and with unique customs and religious taboos. Tribal cultures provide social, moral, and political security, as well as guidelines for accepted behavior. Within the tribal structure, there is strong respect for authority. Age is regarded as an asset as it evokes wisdom. Tribes are broken down according to kinship lines, on which are based the concepts of individual rights, duties, and prosperity. Trust and confidence requiring a high degree of sincerity are the foundations of interpersonal relations.

Tribal communalism presents formidable obstacles to advertising efficiency. For example, in Kenya commercials messages may be written in nine languages. In addition, according to one foreign advertising agent, when advertising a particular food ingredient, such as cooking fat, one must make the recipes fit tribal eating habits. In Kenya one would not give the Kikuyu recipes for fried fish—they regard fish as snakes. The tribal structure can also be beneficial to advertisers. Group consciousness has a magnifying effect on any new product coming into the community. Because there are no conflicts of interests and everyone is interrelated through extended family ties, the product that is attractive to one is attractive to all. Thus African markets may be said to be made up of family consumers rather than individual consumers.

In general, the tribal culture also suggests guidelines for advertisers. Advertising addressed to children may not be advisable. Deference should be made to authority figures. The decision-making role of women should be recognized, as women often play a strong role in African societies. In the network of commodity marketing and trading, the woman's role is extensive.

In light of all the above considerations, it is not surprising that significant advertising activity is confined to urban environments in African countries with important foreign populations, a growing indigenous middle class, and close commercial ties with the United Kingdom, France, or the United States. This picture should not, however, obscure the strong economic potential of Africa revealed in statistics that show increasing levels of literacy and industrial development. Africa produces 40 percent of the world's hydroelectric power, a significant percentage of its oil, uranium, and other vital resources. Moreover, the most recent World Bank study reveals renewed growth trends in many countries including Nigeria, Ghana, and the Ivory Coast.[3]

And, whatever the economic picture, mass media convey advertising messages in almost every African country. Billboards, newspapers, magazines, and radio are the most common channels. Television and cinema are used in urban centers. Direct advertising by word-of-mouth and through loudspeakers dominate in the open marketplaces and along road sides. The effectiveness of each media varies depending on communications infrastructures, population distribution, education levels, and the size of markets. Generally, modern communications media, with the exception of radio, do not reach the majority of populations scattered throughout the national hinterlands. In the remote areas word-of-mouth and individual consumership examples are the most common advertising tools followed in some countries by radio.

Political and economic structures vary among countries. Zimbabwe and Botswana characterize their governments as parliamentary democracies. The vast majority of countries are republics headed by a president, who is elected or chosen by the ruling elite of the dominant nationalist party. Military regimes govern in at least eight countries, including Nigeria and Ethiopia. Authoritarian regimes preside in Ghana and Uganda. Socialist one-party rule is established in the former Portuguese colonies of Angola and Mozambique. Although characteristically structured according to a constitution many governments have an autocratic, neopatrimonial style of leadership. Leaving aside the socialist states, most countries have adopted some form of mixed capitalist economic system, and considerable public involvement in the management of national resources is typical. Foreign advertising is most predominant in the republics and parliamentary democracies where socioeconomic conditions also are favorable.

The legal systems of Africa are evolving.[4] In the process, lawyers, legal scholars, and others deal with two fundamentally different sources of law: (a) customary or traditional law and (b) Western law. Throughout Africa for centuries, societies with ancient customary law prevailed. It commanded spontaneous obedience and gained its potence from superstitious fears of the supernatural and group pressure. Because each tribal group observed different customs and practices, customary law has had many diverse expressions. Despite the differences there are some notable shared myths related to order in the universe and ancestor worship. To disobey custom is to unleash evil forces. Customary law tends to reject progress; values the concept of the "group" in deference to the individual as the basic social unit, and stresses personal obligations (as opposed to individual rights). The objective of the law is the perpetuation of harmonious relations and the promotion of reconciliation where there is discord.

With the advent of colonialism, European law, notably English common law, and Romano/Germanic civil code law were introduced, the former in British colonies and the latter in the French, Belgium, and Portuguese colonies. European law was concerned with ordering the activities of state; it provided basic public laws, constitutional law, administrative law, and commercial law with nationwide scope. Since the scope of customary law was limited to intratribal relations there was no basic conflict with the introduction of alien systems.

Thus, in the post-colonial era, European law, either common law or code law systems, have been retained as the basis for national legal systems in all African countries. Today, most African countries have unitary court systems in which customary and modern national public law is applied as demanded by the facts of each particular national case. National legislation, adopted since independence, is in style and procedure similar to its colonial precursors.

Efforts have been made to codify customary law and to unify national systems through the gradual assimilation of customary laws and the adaptation of foreign law and legal machinery to the peculiar needs of African societies. In strongly nationalist countries, strong commitment is made to finding uniquely indigenous solutions to conflicts by looking to traditional legal values. But, because of the multiplicity of customary laws, each with limited tribal application, efforts to define customary law acceptable to the country as a whole have generally been futile.

This is not to say that customary law is obsolete. Quite the contrary. Given the relatively low level of development of many African countries, the extension and penetration of public laws and administrative regulation is largely limited to urbanized areas. The lives of the vast majority of African populations in rural settings are still ordered according to traditional values and customs. And, even many government rulers themselves cannot divorce themselves from the biases and attitudes of their tribal heritage. Hence, the importance for foreign advertisers and agents to be aware of customary traditions and public laws.

The degree and effectiveness of advertising regulation vary widely among these countries. In many of the smaller countries, the extent of government involvement is minimal, owing to the insignificance of the activity in the overall economy and to weaknesses in the legal and institutional infrastructure. Minimal government regulations do include controls on the marketing of drugs. Consumers generally have no voice, and any consumer organizations that might exist are in early stages of development. The small size of the industry and the lack of government interference generally have obviated any need for the industry to embark on self-regulation.

In countries experiencing involvement with multinational advertising agencies, more extensive regulations have been adopted. Having experienced foreign control over their economies, participating in international organizations, and becoming aware of their increasing bargaining strength in terms of foreign business, these countries have adopted policies restricting ownership of advertising agencies or otherwise favoring the development of an indigenous industry. The most extensive regulatory systems combine food and drug laws, media controls, measures to restrain foreign investment activities in the retail and service industries, and codes and machinery for self-regulation. The application of these regulations changes with the socioeconomic conditions and with the capacity and will of the administrative and legal infrastructure responsible for monitoring activities and enforcing the law.

To facilitate analysis of the regulatory environments in the sub-Sahara Africa continent, the region is divided into three groups of countries: Anglophone Africa, Francophone Africa, and low-income Africa. The classification distinguishes among African countries according to two sets of criteria: (a) the amount of foreign advertising activity and (b) commercial and language ties. The first two groups, low- and middle-income Francophone and Anglophone countries, have had a significant relationship with foreign advertisers. The third group includes countries whose foreign advertising experience is so marginal that no significant policies on the subject have been developed yet. In these low-income African countries, poverty and political ideology are the major determinants of the advertising environments. Commercial and language ties distinguish countries that have experienced significant foreign activity. In these countries past colonial ties and current commercial links with Western countries are the principal influences on advertising patterns and regulations. This is particularly evident in certain low- and middle-income Francophone and Anglophone countries as described below.

Low-Income and Middle-Income Anglophone Countries

Anglophone Africa includes the Commonwealth countries and Liberia. The principals are scattered throughout Africa—in West Africa: Ghana, Nigeria, and Liberia; in East Africa: Kenya; inland: Zambia and Zimbabwe (see table 16–1). The greatest concentration of foreign advertising activity has occurred in this group of countries.

Multinational agencies operate through local affiliates in many countries. In 1987 New York-based BBDO Worldwide, McCann-Erickson Worldwide, Lintas Worldwide, Young & Rubicam, Ogilvy & Mather, and London-based Saatchi & Saatchi Advertising Worldwide, reported activity in one or more Anglophone African country. Relatively small accounts in all these countries correspond to the size of the consumer market and reflect deteriorating economic conditions. In a few countries regulations on foreign investments also limit foreign participation in advertising (table 16–1).

Among individual countries the amount of foreign and domestic advertising activity varies, and strong fluctuations occur within countries. In no country does the advertising industry play a significant role in the economy. Moreover, the increasing dearth of statistical information indicates problems in the advertising industry in many Commonwealth countries. For 1987 international data were available only for Kenya, Nigeria, Zambia, and Zimbabwe, where total advertising expenditure, including foreign agencies' billings, ranged from less than $5 million in Zambia to nearly $50 million in Nigeria (see figure 16–1). Per capita advertising expenditures ranged from less than $1 to $3 (see figure 16–2). Information on media expenditure is sparse.

Table 16–1
Regulatory Profile: Low-Income and Middle-Income Anglophone Africa

Countries:	Ghana, Kenya, Nigeria, Zambia, Zimbabwe (see map 16–1)
Government:	Republics; presidential systems; single (nationalist) party rule; elitist democracies; Commonwealth members
Politico-economic ideology:	Constitutionalism; state capitalism; socialism/capitalism (Zambia, Tanzania); socialism/militarism (Ghana); pan-Africanism
Economic system:	Mixed public and free enterprise
Legal system:	English common law; customary tribal law; supplemented by growing body of national law
Investment policy:	Moderate to restrictive (Ghana, Nigeria); stresses Africanization; members of European Community*
Ad regulation:	Developing; mainly product specific; partly modeled on British system
Ad expenditure:	Zimbabwe: $21 million; per capita: $2; %GNP: .4; information for other countries not available; estimated to be under $20 million
Consumer market:	Small middle class, growing urban low-income group
Social indicators:	
Population:	Average range 6–20 million, 107 million (Nigeria)
Urbanization:	30–39%
Per capita income:	$300 (Kenya and Zambia)–$640 (Nigeria) (declining since 1982 except Zimbabwe)
Language:	Local languages; English
Class structure:	Majority low income or subsistence
Life expectancy:	48–55 years
Literacy:	45–50% (somewhat higher for males)

*African, Caribbean, and Pacific countries (ACP) affiliated with the EEC under the Lomé Convention.

Figure 16–3 shows the distribution by media expenditure only for Zimbabwe. In this country an estimated 82 percent is spent on billboards, loudspeakers, cinema and the like. Small percentages are also devoted to print and television.

Public policy, economic conditions, commercial links with Western markets, and geographic location are significant determinants in foreign advertising activity. Fluctuations in activity result from unstable economic climates and changes in public policy. The situations in Nigeria, Kenya, and Liberia are illustrative. Nigeria, the most populous country in Africa, has over 97 million inhabitants and several large urban sectors made wealthier during the recent period of high oil prices. The Nigerian advertising industry is one of the oldest and largest in sub-Saharan Africa.

The British agency Lintas established West Africa Publicity (WAP) in 1928 as the first advertising agency in West Africa. In the 1940s and 1950s, the Nigerian Bureau of Publicity was the principal competitor of WAP. Other

Africa, South of the Sahara • 291

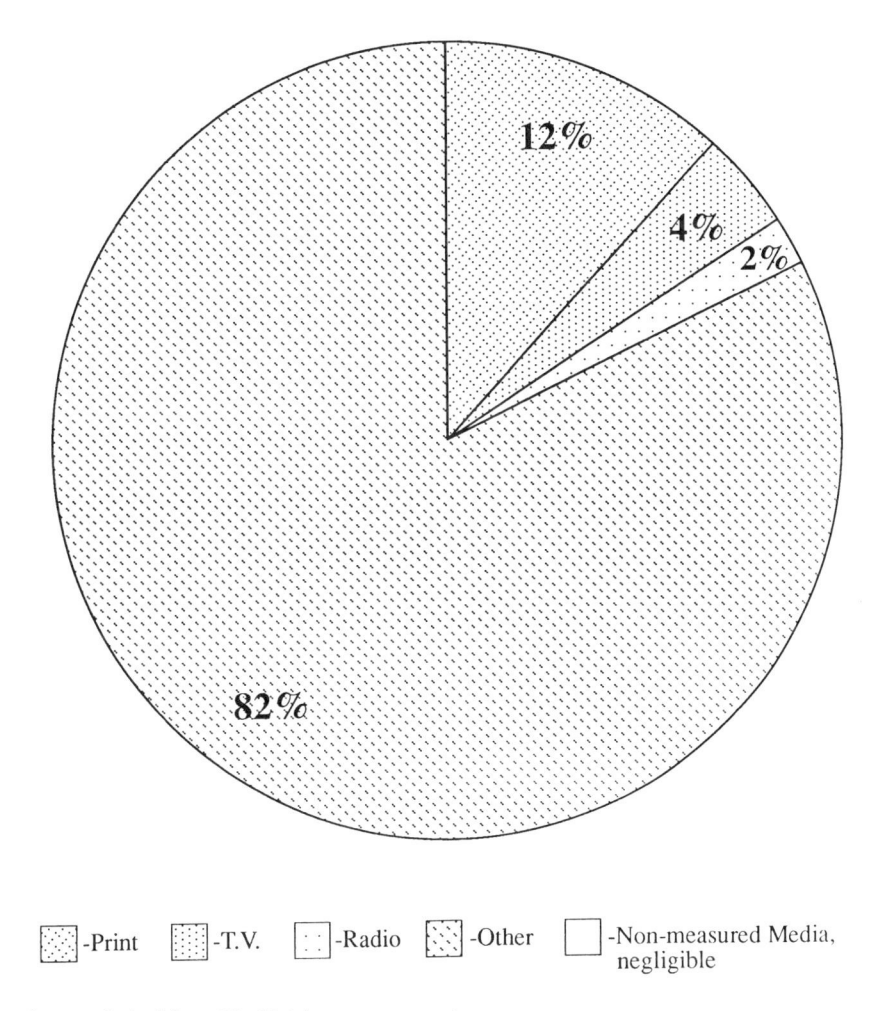

☒-Print ☒-T.V. ☒-Radio ☒-Other ☐-Non-measured Media, negligible

Source: derived from *World Advertising Expenditure*, 1986, 21st ed., Starch INRA Hooper, Inc. in cooperation with IAA.

Figure 16–3. Advertising Expenditure by Media and Non-measured Media in Zimbabwe (percentage shares)

British firms opened Nigerian agencies in the late 1950s and early 1960s. In 1971 Nigeria adopted indigenization rules to enhance local participation in advertising. The number of local agencies proliferated. Presently, sixty agencies belong to the national Association of Advertising Practitioners in Nigeria (AAPN), and some one hundred smaller agencies exist outside the organization.

In the early 1980s, estimates of Nigerian total advertising expenditure exceeded $100 million (less than .1 percent of the GNP).[5] After 1983 figures for advertising expenditure did not appear in international reports, and Nigerian sources indicated that the industry fell on hard times in 1984, with billings down by 50 percent compared with 1982.[6] Today, prevailing socioeconomic conditions are improving with fewer food shortages, reduced inflation, and diminishing unemployment. The advertising industry appears to be recovering as well. Total advertising expenditure was again reported for Nigeria in 1987 (see figure 16–1).

Kenya's drawing cards have been easy market access and its location as the commercial hub of East Africa. Nairobi, its capital and only urban center, is centrally located in both Kenya and East Africa. Much of the region to the south and west is sparsely populated and offers little attraction for foreign marketers or advertisers. In the prosperous farming districts to the north and east, an affluent European population and densely populated settlements of Africans earning cash incomes represent significant purchasing power. The relative affluence of Nairobi's civil servants and of business and industrial workers has fostered the development of a relatively sophisticated retail sector in the city. Foreign advertising initially was introduced in Kenya by local distributors of imported merchandise, who relied on their suppliers to provide substantial advertising and promotional support, particularly when introducing a new product or brand name.[7]

An example of a small country with an active advertising industry is the U.S.-dominated market of Liberia. Here, the role of the United States in the economy is the leading factor. While advertising, relatively speaking, is not as widely used in Liberia as in the United States, the industry is growing in pace with the expansion of the money economy. Most major advertising media are available in Liberia, and a multimedia approach generally is considered the most effective in gaining acceptance for new products. Advertising campaigns are desirable and are used extensively in introducing certain consumer goods to the market. Leading American and European news magazines are read widely by the expatriate community and by Liberians in government, business, and professional circles. The country's radio and television are dependent on advertising revenue. Because of widespread illiteracy in the country, the broadcasting media are an important means of reaching consumers, especially those outside Monrovia, the capital city.[8]

Although advertising is permitted in all the media, statistics show that in Nigeria and Kenya the greatest concentration of advertising expenditure is directed to the press, to the radio, to outdoor posters and billboards, and to ads appearing on modes of transportation. The generally low level of development in the public-utilities sectors explains why none of these countries devotes more than 10 percent of its total advertising expenditure to television. Exhibitions, displays, posters, point-of-sale reminders, and demonstrations are important in Kenya and Nigeria. A wide variety of newspapers are read and circulated among East African and West African consumers. Billboard advertising and neon signs are permitted in railway stations and are used extensively by local advertisers. Mobile cinemas take entertainment to the rural population. Interior and exterior advertisements on public buses also are popular. In addition, foreign agencies have noted the effectiveness of contests as an advertising medium in these countries. For example, Unilever offers scholarships as prizes in an advertising campaign, and when asked to increase the sales of Vaseline, the Nairobi office of Ogilvy & Mather mounted a contest featuring a cow as first price.[9]

The most comprehensive regulatory regimes exist in Anglophone countries, reflecting two factors: (1) the British legacy of legal and institutional infrastructures, which have facilitated the regulatory process, and (2) the greater concentration of advertising activity in these countries. Protecting the domestic economy and promoting growth objectives have been prime motivators for controlling foreign advertising activity. There are no significant consumer organizations or movements in any countries; nevertheless, public-health considerations are reflected in product-specific laws. Attention drawn to consumer issues in international forums also have been reflected in national legislation, such as legislation concerning the marketing of infant formulas in Nigeria, Kenya, and Zambia. The regulations adopted bear marks of British and U.S. systems. Although no country has adopted comprehensive advertising laws, many have specific legislation regarding many consumer products and the use of the media. Foreign investment laws also affect the extent of foreign activity.

The most extensive regulation is found in Nigeria, which has food and drug legislation, administrative controls, self-regulation, indirect measures to control foreign activities through foreign-investment laws, and local state laws. The main control on message and content of advertisements is in food and drug legislation. In 1974 the Food and Drug Decree was enacted, and in 1982 sixty-one detailed regulations were drawn up as the basis for enforcing the decree. Sections 23–25 of the regulations prohibit falsehoods, half-truths, and misleading information in advertising. Other legislation includes the Pharmacy Act of 1958 and the Price Control Decree of 1970. All pharmaceuticals must be registered before being advertised.

The Nigerian government has established the Foods and Drugs Administration and Laboratory Services (FDALS) as the body responsible for implementing advertising rules and regulations. Procedures include screening advertising materials and products, monitoring ads in all the public media, and removing unapproved or faulty advertisements from the media. The FDALS also hears complaints.[10]

The government also has established the Advertising Council of Nigeria. This council handles policies and issues related to the formulation of a government code of advertising practice.

Indirect controls exist in the form of investment law. Under the Enterprise

Promotion Act of 1977, a formalized and comprehensive effort was made to enhance the role of Nigerians in business activities. The act reserved advertising to Nigerian agencies.[11] Since 1989 this policy has been reversed as economic conditions again prompt Nigeria to seek foreign investment. Permission to invest must still be approved by the Ministry of Internal Affairs. Total foreign ownership of local firms is permitted and tax and non-tax incentives are offered.

An industrywide system of self-regulation was inaugurated in 1972 with the establishment of the Association of Advertising Practitioners of Nigeria (AAPN). The association has attempted to regulate its members in accordance with the Nigerian Code of Advertising Practice, which is modeled on the British Code of Advertising Practice and the ICC code.

Local state governments have added their own restrictions on advertising. In northern Nigerian states, where the majority of the population is Moslem, advertising of alcoholic beverages is prohibited, and the appearance of women in advertisements is heavily restricted.

Extensive product-specific regulations exist in other countries. In 1972 the government of Zambia adopted the Food and Drug Act to protect the public against health hazards and fraud in the "sale and use of food, drugs, cosmetics, and medical devices, and for matters incidental thereto or connected therewith."[12] The act provides that "anyone shall be guilty of an offense, who advertises any food, drug, or device in a manner that is false, misleading, or deceptive as regards the product's character, nature, value, substance, quality, composition, merit, or safety, or in contravention of any regulations made in the Act."[13] Likewise, Kenya and Zimbabwe have rules on food and drug advertising.[14]

Media controls also are in effect in these countries. In Kenya and Zimbabwe, advertisements must receive approval before they are broadcast. In Kenya the government must screen advertisements in advance. In Zimbabwe this screening is done by the media in question.[15]

Investment policies in Kenya and Ghana have had discouraging impact on the activities of multinational advertisers. In Kenya the policy of Africanization poses a challenge to advertisers. As a result, exporters are obliged to consider government programs designed to favor African over noncitizen traders. Legislation restricting noncitizen merchants to trading in specific commodities and only at certain commercial centers limits the ability of foreign advertising agencies to provide adequate product representation in this market.[16] Ghana controls foreign advertisers through foreign investment regulations. There is minimal foreign advertising observed in Ghana today. Likewise, in Ghana's Investment Code Act of 1981, advertising agencies and public-relations businesses are classified as enterprises that should be wholly reserved for its citizens as individuals or for the State.[17]

Liberia, with its liberal use of advertising in the American style, is moving in the direction of consumer protection. According to the Ministry of Commerce, although no basic guidelines on consumer protection have yet been established, a grievance committee was established in 1976 to handle complaints affecting consumers and/or suppliers. The committee was inactive for several years but reportedly has been recently activated.[18]

Middle-Income Francophone Countries

In contrast to the situation in Anglophone Africa, foreign advertising activities in Francophone Africa are dominated by French commercial interests. Non-European businesses have tended to shy away from French African markets for a number of reasons, including the relatively small market size, slow growth, high production costs, and the strong French hold on the economy.[19] A small number of American businesses import locally produced and distributed consumer products in Senegal, Cameroon, the Congo's Brazzaville, and Gabon, which are commercially dominated by the French.[20,21] Greater opportunities for foreigners, other than the French, exist when a Francophone country seeks to diversify its source of supply and effectively integrates with the two regional organizations of which it is a member (the West African Economic Community and the sixteen-country Economic Community of West African States).

Francophone Africa's socioeconomic and political characteristics are similar to those of low-income and middle-income Anglophone Africa (see table 16–2). Seven countries fall into this group: the Ivory Coast, Gabon, Senegal, Zaire, the People's Republic of the Congo, and Cameroon. These countries tend to cluster at the lower end of the middle-income range. Although its per capita income figures are substantially higher, Gabon also belongs in this group because it shares most socioeconomic characteristics. Only its relatively high revenue from oil exports sets it apart from the others. The principal differences between Anglophone and Francophone countries lie in strong cultural and commercial links with France and Belgium and in the nature of the regulatory machinery. Because France adhered to a policy of central control over its colonies, it did not establish as extensive an institutional infrastructure as the British did in preparing their colonies for self-rule. Local government is less experienced in parliamentary traditions, and local government bureaus have had to establish themselves on their own. Business customs reflect French influence, and commercial law is patterned on the French civil code.

With the exception of Dakar and Abidjan, advertising in French West Africa is in an earlier stage of development than in Anglophone Africa. Markets for foreign and domestic consumer goods are generally small, but are slowly expanding. Dominant foreign imports include food grains and tobacco. Local affiliates of several foreign multinationals, including Colgate-

Table 16–2
Regulatory Profile: Low-Income and Middle-Income Francophone Africa

Countries:	Cameroon, the Congo, Ivory Coast, Senegal, Zaire and others (see map 16–1)
Government:	Republics; presidential systems; single (nationalist) party rule; elitist democracies
Politico-economic ideology:	Constitutionalism; capitalism
Economic system:	Mixed public and free enterprise
Legal system:	French civil code; customary tribal law; supplemented by legislated national law
Investment policy:	Liberal; special relations with France; preferential agreements with Common Market countries*
Ad regulation:	Developing; mainly product specific; modeled on French laws
Ad expenditure:	Not available; a few multinational agencies report small income and billings in some countries
Consumer market:	Small; growing urban middle class
Social indicators:	
Population:	5–12 million (Zaire: 32 million)
Urbanization:	35–40%
Per capita income:	$350–$800
Language:	French; local languages
Class structure:	Majority low income
Life expectancy:	47–53 years
Literacy:	40–50%

*African, Caribbean, and Pacific countries (ACP) affiliated with the EEC under the Lomé Convention.

Palmolive Co., Biotherm, Seagram Overseas Sales Co., and Star Kist Foods, Inc., operate in Francophone Africa. Because foreign advertising follows trade, there is noticeable, albeit limited, advertising activity in each country.

Multinational advertising firms operating in French West Africa include the Paris-based Eurocom Group, Publicis International, and Roux Seguela Cayzac and Goudard and the New York-based Lintas Worldwide. Statistics on French agency activity in West Africa are not readily available. According to what is available, highest concentrations of foreign activity are reported in the Ivory Coast. In 1987 Lintas reported close to $1 million in gross earnings of its affiliate in Abidjan.[22] Foreign advertising activity is easily observed in Senegal and throughout the region on billboards and in journals.

Foreign advertising abounds in international journals and magazines. Several Europe-based magazines enjoy wide circulation in urban centers. Well-known examples are *Bingo, Paris Match, Le redoute,* and *La vie africaine,* as well as the European editions of *Time* and *Newsweek.*

The small size of the advertising industry is also a factor reflected in the dearth of legislated restrictions on advertising. For example, Cameroon, with a small advertising industry, has not had the luxury of developing consumer protection, product liability, and advertising law. Least developed of all legislation in Cameroon is that concerning misleading, untruthful, and defamatory statements in advertising or other publications.[23] The picture is somewhat similar in Gabon, where according to a local attorney, there are no specific commercial laws that apply to consumer protection, product liability, and advertising.[24] However, the absence of laws directed at advertising is not an open invitation to abuse or to irresponsible behavior, nor are flagrant violations tolerated. There is always an element in the criminal codes to cover obvious transgressions of acceptable business practices.

There are few restrictions on the use of the media. An unintended benefit of the relative dearth of foreign commercial activity in the consumer-goods market is freedom to advertise at low cost through any available medium—newspapers and magazines, billboards, short films in local movie houses, radio networks, local exhibitions and displays, and direct mail. However, this freedom is circumscribed by the reach and impact of the media. Daily newspapers are few in number and have only a limited readership. The most effective media for illiterate audiences, public radio and television, cannot penetrate far beyond the urban capitals.[25] The foreign market is reached through shortwave radio.

The minimal regulations common to all countries exercise firm control over the trade in pharmaceuticals. Again, these are strongly influenced by French law. The French system of government monopoly over the pharmaceutical industry has generally been adopted in Francophone Africa. In Cameroon law in respect to pharmaceuticals emulates provisions of the French code of pharmacy and contains provisions for regulating advertising and authorizing advertising only under certain conditions. Technical advertisement to professionals is unregulated. Advice to the public must mention only trade names, provide the composition of the product, and state the name and professional qualifications of the pharmacist selling the product.[26] In Senegal the regulation of pharmaceutical sales and advertising is the responsibility of the Division for Administrative Inspection of Medicaments.[27] The law also provides that all products licensed by the minister of health for production must be legally sold in the country of origin; if a similar product is on the market, the new product will not be permitted. A law similar to Senegal's exists in the Congo.[28]

Low-Income Countries

In most low-income African countries, commercial advertising is an altogether low-priority issue. Countries in this category include Angola, Burkina-Faso, Chad, Burundi, Ethiopia, Mali, Mauritania, Mozambique, Rwanda, and Tanzania (see map 16–1). Lack of income and lack of markets for con-

Table 16–3
Regulatory Profile: Other Low-Income Africa

Countries:	Burundi, Chad, Mali, Mozambique, Ethiopia, Tanzania, and others (see map 16–1)
Government:	Republics; presidential systems; single (nationalist) party or military rule
Politico-economic ideology:	Nascent capitalism/socialism; Islamism (Saharan countries); traditionalism
Economic system:	Predominantly agrarian subsistence
Legal system:	Predominantly French civil code; customary tribal law; supplemented by a few national laws
Investment policy:	Under consideration; members of the Common Market*
Ad regulation:	Developing; mainly product specific; modeled on European laws
Ad expenditure:	Not available; presumed negligible
Consumer market:	Small urban middle class
Social indicators:	
Population:	4 to 23 million (except Ethiopia 43 million)
Urbanization:	20%
Per capita income:	Under $350
Language:	French; Portuguese; local languages
Class structure:	Majority low income
Life expectancy:	40–45 years
Literacy:	25%

*African, Caribbean, and Pacific countries (ACP) affiliated with the EEC under the Lomé Convention.

sumer goods are the primary factors (see table 16–3). Sparsely populated states with few resources and token consumer markets offer little incentive to exporters of foreign investors. In some more heavily populated countries (such as Ethiopia and Tanzania), economic constraints are compounded with a socialist political ideology to discourage foreign investment or the establishment of consumer markets before initial development goals have been attained. In these countries problems of international advertising are subordinate to the all-consuming fight for survival. Nevertheless, some minimal regulations on the marketing of pharmaceuticals have been adopted.

Examples of low-income environments occur in Burundi, Chad, Mali, and Mozambique. Burundi, a very poor and isolated country, has to date attracted virtually no multinationals or foreign advertising. The current body of legislation does not address the problems of advertising or consumer protection and product liability. There is no consumer movement.[29] Mozambique likewise has no legislation dealing with advertising, product liability, or consumer protection. There is no advertising of food and drug products; indeed, at present, there is a severe shortage of food and drugs.[30] However, the importation of goods with fraudulent or misleading labels or marks is prohibited.[31]

The governments of Rwanda, Chad, Burkina-Faso, and Mali, like many other Francophone countries, exercise monopoly control over trade in pharmaceuticals, including marketing. Rwanda has a law governing the advertising of pharmaceuticals that dates back to its colonial period.[32] Legislation in Chad provides that all commercial advertising of medicaments must be licensed by the Ministry of Public Health and Social Affairs after consultation with the Pharmaceutical Advertising Board. The law prohibits advertisements that are dangerous or objectionable for public health.[33] Burkina-Faso and Mali have established marketing licenses for pharmaceutical products.[34]

Notes

1. Because of the current political situation and because of the advanced economic status of the country, South Africa is not included in this analysis.

2. John Spencer, former professor of African studies, Fletcher School of Law and Diplomacy, interview in Madison, Ct. on 14 February 1989.

3. Cited in David R. Francis, "Ray of Hope For Africa's Economy." *Christian Science Monitor,* March 13, 1989.

4. John H. Barton et al., *Law in Radically Different Cultures* (St. Paul, Minn.: West Publishing, 1983), 43–44; Hilda Kuper and Leo Kuper, eds., *African Law Adaptation and Development* (Berkeley: University of California Press, 1965), 216–40; Rene David and John E.C. Brierley, *Major Legal Systems in the World Today* (London: Stevens and Sons, 1978), 505–33.

5. *World Advertising Expenditure 1983,* 18th ed., Starch INRA Hooper, Inc., in cooperation with the International Advertising Association, 7; "Foreign Agency Income Report," *Advertising Age,* 23 April 1984.

6. *Advertising in Nigeria 55,* May–June 1984, p. 9.

7. United States, Department of Commerce, "Marketing in Kenya," *Overseas Business Reports,* OBR 82-09 (May 1982): 10, 14.

8. United States, Department of Commerce, "Marketing in Liberia," *Overseas Business Reports,* OBR 82-12 (August 1982).

9. David Ogilvy, *Ogilvy on Advertising* (London: Pan Books, 1983), 184.

10. *Advertising in Nigeria,* March/April 1987, 37–39.

11. Nigeria, *Enterprises Promotion Act (1977),* A/63 (Decree No. 3, 1977), in the UN Center for Transnational Corporations, *National Legislation and Regulations Relating to Transnational Corporations,* ST/CTC/26 (1983), 228.

12. Zambia, *Food and Drugs Act of 1972, Act No. 22 of 1972,* in *Republic of Zambia Government Gazette,* Acts Supp. (25 August 1972): 133–49.

13. Ibid., 135.

14. Kenya, *Pharmacy and Poisons (Registration of Drugs) Rules of 1981,* Legal Notice no. 147, 26 August 1981.

15. International Advertising Association, *Food Advertising Regulation and Self-Regulation,* prepared by J.J. Boddewyn (New York: IAA, 1982).

16. U.S. Department of Commerce, "Marketing in Kenya," 11.

17. UN Center for Transnational Corporations, *National Legislation and Regulations Relating to Transnational Corporations,* ST/CTC/35 (1983).

18. American Embassy, Monrovia, Liberia, letter to author, 31 May 1984.

19. American Embassy, Dakar, Senegal, "Economic Trends Report," Cerp 0004, memorandum to the U.S. Department of State, 11 August 1983.

20. American Embassy, Yaoundé, Cameroon, letter to author, 16 May 1984.

21. U.S. Department of Commerce, "Marketing in Congo," *Overseas Business Reports,* OBR 83-13 (1983) and "Marketing in Gabon," *Overseas Business Reports,* OBR 82-10 (1982).

22. "Foreign Agency Report," *Ad Age,* 9 May 1988.

23. American Embassy, Yaoundé, letter.

24. American Embassy, Libreville, Gabon, letter to author, 18 May 1984.

25. See, for example, U.S. Department of Commerce, "Marketing in Gabon," 15–16, and "Marketing in Congo," 13.

26. Cameroon, *Law No. 68-LF-8 of 11 June 1968* (concerning the practice of the professional pharmacist), in *Official Gazette of the Federal Republic of Cameroon,* no. 2, supp. (15 July 1968): 35–54.

27. Senegal, *Law No. 65-33 to Amend the Provisions of Public Health Code Concerning the Preparation, Sale and Advertising of Pharmaceutical Specialties,* in *Journal officel de la République du Sénégal,* no. 3747 (5 June 1965): 637.

28. American Embassy, Brazzaville, Congo, letter to author, 21 May 1984; Congo, *Control of Trade in Pharmaceutical Products, Establishing a National Office for Sale of Pharmaceutical Products, Law No. 42/65,* in *Journal officiel de la République du Congo,* no. 18 (15 September 1965): 570.

29. American Embassy, Bujumbura, Burundi, letter to author, 4 June 1984.

30. Chief of cabinet, Ministry of Justice, Mozambique, reply to inquiry by American Embassy, cited by Commercial Officer, American Embassy, Maputo, Mozambique, in letter to author, 3 July 1984.

31. Bureau of National Affairs, "Mozambique," *International Trade Reporter,* U.S. Government Printing Office, Washington, D.C. (1983).

32. Rwanda, *L'Ordonnance No. 72/6 du janvier 1958 sur la publicité pharmaceutique;* cited in Rwasine J. Baptiste, Office of Pharmaceuticals, Kigali, Rwanda, letter to author, 29 August 1984.

33. Chad, *Decree No. 87-66 P,* 18 April 1966, and *Decree No. 76-66,* 14 April 1966.

34. Burkina-Faso, *President's Law of 17 August 1963 to Promulgate Law No. 38-63-AN of 24 July 1963 to Establish the National Pharmacy of (Upper Volta),* in *Journal officiel de la Répulik de Haute Volta,* no. 35 (17 August 1963): 47–48; Mali, Ministry of Health, *Interministerial Order No. 2135, MSP-AS CAB,* 21 July 1977, and *Decree No. 48, PG RM,* 18 March 1977.

Part V
International Controls

17
Global Advertising and International Control

International debates on advertising problems are, in some measure, extensions of current debates in national forums. The outcomes, however, are quite different. On the national scene, binding laws, standards, ordinances, and regulations are normal and expected outcomes when solutions are deemed necessary. Not so in international forums. Here, the multiplicity of experience, interests, and diversity in socioeconomic and legal systems, as well as in human experience, creates enormous obstacles to agreements or solutions that are simultaneously acceptable and effective. The international solutions are nonbinding, normative guidelines or codes whose implementation depends on the moral and political suasion of international public opinion.

The impact of these initiatives defies measurement. International rules, regulations, and other forms of control gain legal strength only if they are ratified and incorporated into national law. In a strict sense, these controls constitute a body of soft law, law that is voluntary or recommendatory in nature.

Maximalists and minimalists presently contend the legal status and function of international regulations. The maximalist favors legally finding, international rules of conduct. For international business this means that once international standards are set the maximalist would expect countries to seek compliance or at least to refrain from obstructing them. The minimalist argues that a voluntary and not legally enforceable code is without legal effect, but that it may exert some moral influence.[1] Despite the fray, in the final analysis, codes and other instruments elaborated by the United Nations systems have no more than moral and political influence.

Nevertheless, this influence is far from insignificant. One indication of this is the attention being given by advertisers to initiatives taken by international organizations. There is enough concern over such initiatives in the regulatory field to prompt the International Advertising Association and the International Chamber of Commerce to keep their membership regularly apprised of any related developments. In addition to special studies on advertising regulation and policy issues, the IAA issues a bimonthly magazine, the *International Advertiser,* which covers latest developments in national regulation and self-regulation, as well as relevant activities of the UN and the UN-specialized agencies. The IAA and the ICC are nongovernmental international organizations in the UN system.

High levels of emotionalism have enveloped particular causes, precipitating international regulatory proposals. "The Baby Killer," "Death by Prescription," and "Commerciogenic Malnutrition" are provocative titles of articles protesting various practices, articles that have attracted international attention. Their substance has raised the hackles of corporations and businesses and has enraged public sentiment. Arguments and accusations between antagonists have indicated that such issues are indicative of deep-seated ideological conflicts between public and private sectors of the world economy; between the political left and right; and among partisans of the north, south, east, and west corners of the earth.

In respect to commercial advertising, aggressive postures have been taken by nongovernmental representatives of consumer organizations and humanitarian groups, by concerned individuals, and by representatives of health and economic ministries in many Third World countries. These various groups have charged that advertising by international firms has serious negative consequences and should be effectively regulated, controlled, and in some cases, prohibited by the international community, as well as by home and host countries.

In the debates in international forums, the positions taken by corporations, producers, and advertising agencies through diplomats of Western governments and representatives of commercial and producer associations generally have been defensive. They have stressed the lack of empirical data on negative impacts of advertising. They also have stressed their compliance with relevant rules and regulations established by home and host governments, as well as compliance with their own self-regulation schemes, in performing services for the world's benefit.

The development of international regulations is a complex procedure involving many of the same factors found in national regulatory processes but multiplied several times. In international advertising it may be that only general solutions in the form of simple recommendations are feasible because of the enormous complexity of the issues and the diversity of cultures, values, and levels of development of the interested parties. However, international measures, simple or otherwise, have succeeded only when there was a clear and powerful majority preference. In these cases international regulations have been respected by the enterprises with vested interests in international public opinion.

International codes and guidelines serve a number of purposes. They are mediums for the harmonization of national laws. They provide direction for policy makers in national governments. Some are initiatives for legislation on subjects inadequately or unprotected under any national laws.[2] Usually, international measures, like national laws, are of a limiting or restrictive nature. They aim at protecting consumers from the excesses of multinational advertisers. The UN Consumer Protection Guidelines and the initiatives of Codex Alimentarius Commission provide models for countries attempting to harmonize their national legislation, as well as for countries intending to elaborate standards for international advertising. WHO's unique code concerning infant formula has served as a pilot for national legislatures in a subject area previously free of national laws and regulations. Its creation stems from roots peculiar to international marketing, the creation of inappropriate products according to criteria existing in particular national markets.

In the final analysis, however, international rules and regulations offer no protection to consumers unless countries themselves are willing and able to enforce them. This position has been clearly stated by WHO, wherein there is general understanding of the organization's role as being international, and not supranational. This perception of WHO also is true for other organizations in the UN system. Each is an association of member states, and their policies are collectively determined. Each member carries out individually what has been decided collectively. Policies are defined in international organizations, but they cannot be imposed by them. Once governments have adopted certain policies, they are expected to implement them domestically and in their relationship with other countries. If they do not wish to do so, they are expected to adopt other policies collectively.

A number of initiatives in the United Nations and its specialized agencies aim directly or indirectly at advertising and related aspects of consumer protection. They are both general and product-specific, and they take several forms: studies on various facets of marketing problems and public policies, discussions on the issues, resolutions calling for further research and debate, and codes and guidelines on content and diffusion.

What are these initiatives? In the following chapter, separate analyses are made of the codes and guidelines concerning advertising debated or adopted by the UN system. Moving from general to specific regulations, the analyses seek to identify the characteristics, strengths, and weaknesses of the international approach to marketing and advertising issues. A separate chapter is an account of the most famous of these regulations, the International Code of Marketing of Breast-Milk Substitutes.

Notes

1. Hans W. Baade, "The Legal Effects of Codes of Conduct for Multinational Enterprises," *Legal Problems of Code of Conduct For Multinational Enterprises,* ed. Norbert Horn (Deventer, Neth: Kluwer Law and Taxation Publishers, 1980), 20.

2. Cynthia Day Wallace, *Legislative Controls of Multinational Enterprises* (The Hague, Neth: Martinis Nijhoff Publishers, 1982) 321–26.

18
International Guidelines and Standards

Attempts have been made within the UN system to elaborate general codes on advertising and on transnational corporations. Thus far, these overall efforts have not met with success, and by the end of the 1980s, the political atmosphere within the industrialized countries was not favorable to their revival. On the other hand, several guidelines and standards have been adopted or are being developed. Attempts, failures, and successes of the UN system are described in this chapter.

General Code on Advertising

The possibility of formulating a general code on advertising has been discussed in UNESCO. The aim of such a code would be the preservation of cultural identity and moral values. Preliminary work began in 1976 through a study on world communications and society. Four years later, the MacBride Report (so named after Sean MacBride, a Nobel laureate and Irish diplomat) was submitted. The UNESCO director general's comments on the report were adopted at UNESCO's general conference in October 1980. The main purpose of advertising, the report says, is "selling goods and services to promote lifestyles that extol acquisition and consumption at the expense of other values."[1]

Subsequently, a program of case studies was developed at the beginning of the 1980s to analyze the impact of advertising, the content of messages, and the management of national communications media. Studies were undertaken on the social, economic, and cultural effects of advertising in various countries and regions (notably in India, Latin America, and the Soviet Union) and on self-regulation. A paper summarized the findings of these studies.[2]

Perhaps because of the strong bias of the project, and certainly as a result of the political difficulties confronting UNESCO (including the withdrawal of the United States and the United Kingdom from the organization), the general code on advertising has been set aside. It would seem that its resurrection would demand political conditions very different from those currently prevailing.

Guidelines on Consumer Protection

A symbolic and painful step toward the development of international measures to control advertising practice was made by the United Nations. Its Guidelines on Consumer Protection were adopted by consensus in the General Assembly on April 9, 1985.[3]

The history of the development of these guidelines provides a case study of the obstacles confronting international efforts aimed at transferring some of the basic protections accorded to consumers in industrialized free-market countries to their Third World counterparts. The compromises necessary to achieve a consensus were such that the final document is vague, ambiguous, and of uncertain practical value.

The proposal that the UN's Economic and Social Council (ECOSOC) undertake the elaboration of consumer guidelines came in the late 1970s on a wave of controversy over so-called product dumping and over sales promotion of infant formula in developing countries.[4] Advertising and marketing practices in general, as well as in specific areas of foods and pharmaceuticals, were key issues. Negotiations spanned eight years.

At its sixty-third session in 1977, ECOSOC adopted Resolution 2111 (63) on Consumer Protection. This resolution was the fruition of efforts by the International Organization of Consumers Unions to persuade the UN to take up the consumer problem.[5] Following the preparation of a number of studies and the Regional Consultation on Consumer Protection, held by the Economic and Social Commission for Asia and the Pacific in 1981, a consultant was requested to draft a set of guidelines for national legislation, which was circulated to governments for comments in the fall of 1982.

More than one hundred developing countries expressing their common position as that of the Group of 77, or all the developing countries that are UN members, championed the guidelines in their original form.[6] The representative for the group was Pakistan. The chief protagonist for the Western world was the United States, whose support was considered a prerequisite to the successful implementation of the guidelines. Sweden played a mediating role. The major objective of the Eastern bloc was to exclude state enterprises from the scope of the resolution that should focus on transnational corporations.[7]

In the United States strong opposition came from the Association of National Advertisers, the American Association of Advertising Agencies, and the Grocery Manufacturers Association. Opinions favoring the guidelines, particularly those emanating from consumer-interest groups, were expressed by Esther Peterson, consumer affairs adviser to both Presidents Lyndon Johnson and President Jimmy Carter. Her defense focused on the duty of the United States, a strong defender of its own consumers, to share its protection with the rest of the world. She lamented the exclusion of the consumer voice in the determination of the U.S. position on the guidelines.[8] Her arguments stressed that the proposed guidelines would offer models to countries without these protections on how to protect themselves from hazardous or shoddy products being dumped on the world market. Such guidelines would help in establishing testing protocols for pharmaceuticals and minimal health standards for foods and in providing examples of ways to offer redress to consumers with complaints. She emphasized that all of these basic protections are embodied in U.S. federal law.[9]

The administration's arguments against the guidelines were frequently expressed by Murray L. Weidenbaum, chairman of President Ronald Reagan's Council of Economic Advisors, in testimony before congressional committes.[10] He expressed the official view that regulation of internal economic activities should be strictly a matter of national concern. Even at this national level, regulation was imperfect, costly, and at times counterproductive. In addition, the draft guidelines on consumer protection were inconsistent with the principles underlying a private-enterprise economy. They were designed to promote a larger government role in the private sector.

Indeed, the final guidelines are based on a number of principles relevant to the regulation of international advertising. Governments are called upon to develop, to strengthen, or to maintain strong consumer-protection policies while establishing their own priorities in light of their socioeconomic circumstances and in light of a cost-benefit analysis of the proposed measures. The legitimate need of consumers, supported in the guidelines, is access to adequate information to enable informed choices according to individual wishes and needs. The guidelines suggest that measures for consumer protection should be designed to benefit all population groups. All enterprises are called upon to obey the relevant laws and regulations of the countries in which they do business. They also should conform to the appropriate provisions of international standards for consumer protection to which the competent authorities of the country in question have agreed.

In promoting and protecting consumers' economic interests, the guidelines provide that consumer organizations be encouraged to monitor adverse practices, including false and misleading claims in marketing and service frauds, and that governments ensure that all involved in the provision of goods and services adhere to mandatory standards. Moreover, governments should encourage fair and effective competition in order for consumers to maximize their choices and minimize their costs. Three paragraphs of the guidelines, quoted below, deal with fair treatment of the consumer in the provision of commercial information and with the development of codes of marketing and other business practices. They appear to endorse the principle of self-regulation, which is so important from the perspective of the private business community:

> 20. Promotional marketing and sales practices should be guided by the principle of fair treatment of consumers and should meet legal requirements. This requires the provision of the information necessary to enable consumers to make informed and independent decisions, as well as measures to ensure that the information provided is accurate.
> 21. Governments should encourage all concerned to participate in the free flow of accurate information on all aspects of consumer products.
> 22. Governments should, within their own national context, encourage the formulation and implementation by business, in cooperation with consumer organizations, of codes of marketing and other business practices to ensure adequate consumer protection. Voluntary agreements may also be established jointly by business, consumer organizations and other interested parties. These codes should receive adequate publicity.[11]

Finally, business is invited to play a role in consumer information and education programs. The guidelines provide that governments should encourage consumers and other interested groups, including the media, to undertake such programs, in particular for the benefit of low-income consumer groups in rural and urban areas. Businesses should, when appropriate, undertake and participate in factual and relevant comparable programs.

The resolution was adopted by consensus, and there was a general feeling that the guidelines would assist countries in protecting their consumers. Nevertheless, a number of concerns remained, notably for the United States.

A critical U.S. concern was that the guidelines posed a potential obstacle to international trade. In an effort to overcome this problem, two clauses stress that when regulations for consumer protection are implemented, regard should be given to assure that the regulations do not become barriers to international trade and that they are consistent with international trade obligations. Thus, under the guidelines, it would not be consistent to ban trade of any product. However, to protect consumers from potential harm, the guidelines call on governments to develop or to strengthen information links regarding products banned, withdrawn, or seriously restricted in importing countries and to ensure that the quality of products and of relevant information does not vary significantly from country to country to the detriment of consumers.

The United States also regretted the failure of the guidelines to qualify risks and hazards by the term *unreasonable* and regretted as well the frequent references to specific product lines. The guidelines were found to be biased toward government interference in the marketplace, although self-regulation and free-market forces were the most effective protectors of consumer interests. Moreover, there remained the fear that the guidelines would justify protectionist measures and discrimination against foreign investment. Finally, the United States was dubious about the role of the UN in the regulatory area; according to the United States, there were better ways for the organization to spend its resources.

The representative for the Eastern bloc countries was not altogether satisfied with the resolution either. According to this group, the issue of consumer protection was an internal matter subject to national guidelines. It became a matter for international regulation only when it involved international trade. There was also regret over deletion of any reference to transnational corporations.

The government of Sweden, reflecting the country's strong commitment to international action in the area of consumer regulation, stated that the guidelines should be seen as a major accomplishment in the economic field. In addition, the guidelines would benefit consumers worldwide.

Code of Conduct for Transnational Corporations

Advertising falls under the rubric of consumer protection in the UN's Draft Code of Conduct for Transnational Corporations. The code, if adopted, will incorporate all the codes and guidelines adopted in the UN system pertaining to multinational enterprises. The negotiations on this code are particularly relevant in light of the political and legal issues impeding progress in its elaboration.

The UN Commission on Transnational Corporations was established by the sixth special session of the General Assembly in 1974 in Resolution 3202 S-V6, Sec. 5. This initiative was a direct follow-up of hearings of the Group of Eminent Persons on Multinational Corporations, convened in 1972 by ECOSOC. The report of this group constituted the first step in an overall program of study, negotiation, and practical action that was intended to result in a code of conduct for transnational corporations.

The justification for the code was based on the evolutionary nature of international norms. Its objectives were to minimize the negative impact of the operations of MNEs and to maximize their positive contribution to economic progress in an interdependent world. Work on this code began in 1976 and was to be completed by 1978.

Consumer protection has always been considered an objective of UN work on transnational corporations. The Group of Eminent Persons accepted the proposition that because products of multinationals are often geared to consumption patterns of advanced countries, the needs of the majority of the population in poor countries may not be fulfilled. It asserted the right of government to discourage or even ban socially undesirable products, as well as to control advertising that exploited the consumer.[12]

In its present state, the draft code consists of two sets of provisions; those that are provisionally agreed upon (concluded provisions) and those that are not yet concluded. The code addresses human rights and consumer protection in separate paragraphs; these are among the concluded provisions.

Consumer protection is one of the areas that pertains to economic, financial, and social matters. Provisionally agreed-upon paragraphs express the need for respect of host-government laws and regulations; regard for international standards; provision of all information to competent authorities on products that may prejudice health and safety of consumers, including relevant measures adopted in countries of origin; and disclosure to the public of all relevant information by means of proper labeling and informative and accurate advertising. Contents of products should not be misrepresented.

The draft code also calls for respect of human rights and fundamental freedoms by the MNEs in the countries where they operate. They are to conform to government policies designed to extend equality of opportunity and treatment. They are expected to refrain from interference in the internal affairs of countries. In this context they should refrain from activities that undermine national, political, and social systems. There are, however, fundamental disagreements on the formulation of the noninterference clause.

In 1988 the code was still in draft state. While two-thirds of its provisions had been provisionally accepted, there were several outstanding issues. The nonconcluded parts blocking the code's adoption are concerned with the different concepts of the international commercial world and international law held on one hand by the industrialized free-enterprise economies and on the other hand by a majority of the developing countries. These issues relate to the relevance of international law and obligations to the norms of the code, to the use of the principle of preferential treatment for developing countries, to the position of free choice of law and means of dispute settlement, and to the scope to be given to the concept of noninterference in internal affairs.[13]

On the first issue, there are at least two schools of thought. The first, subscribed to by the industrialized market-economy countries, holds that customary international legal principles should be applicable in the amplification and qualification of broad standards in the code. For example, customary law would hold states responsible for injuries to aliens and property and for maintaining a common international standard of fair and equitable treatment. The Third World subscribes to the second school of thought, which questions the existence of universally recognized principles of customary international law applicable to matters concerning MNEs or foreign investment. This position maintains that the subject falls wholly within the purview of national law, subject to norms, undertakings, and obligations expressly stipulated in contemporary negotiated international instruments to which states have freely subscribed.

The second unresolved issue concerns the provisions of exceptions from the principle of national treatment, exceptions justified by development policies. In other terms, it refers to recognition of the principle of preferential treatment in the code for developing countries.

The third issue turns on whether or not all contracts with private parties, as well as with governments and their agencies, are subject to the law of the host country. One school holds that in contracts between private parties, the parties may choose the law governing their contract. The opposition holds that all contracts are subject to the law of the host country.

The fourth issue is centered on the scope of the concept of noninterference. While all countries agree with the principle of noninterference by an MNE in the internal affairs of a state, disagreement centers on whether or not, and the extent to which, this term should be qualified. The underlying rationale for this principle is perceived in an unequal balance of economic bargaining power between the MNE and the poor developing country; a fundamental purpose of the code should be to strengthen the governments of these countries in their dealings with MNEs.

These issues are not unique to negotiations on the Code of Conduct for Transnational Corporations, but reappear in variations on these themes in many negotiations between the developed, market-economy countries and Third World countries. They will arise in any international initiatives to develop overall standards for marketing or advertising practice. The future of such an endeavor would seem to depend on progress in the resolution of these issues.

The Work of the Codex Alimentarius Commission

The purpose of the Joint Food and Agricultural Organization and World Health Organization Food Standards Program, which formally came into existence in 1963, is to protect the health of consumers, to ensure fair practices in the food trade, to promote coordination of all food standards work undertaken by international governmental and nongovernmental organizations, to determine priorities and initiate and guide the preparation of draft standards through and with the aid of appropriate organizations, and to finalize these standards. After acceptance by governments, such standards would be published either as regional or worldwide standards.[14]

The implementing body of the program is the Codex Alimentarius Commission (CAC), whose membership is open to all countries that are members or associate members of FAO and WHO. To date it has 129 members. The commission's main function has been the establishment of global standards applicable to a wide variety of foodstuffs in international trade. The Codex Alimentarius is the collection of these internationally adopted food standards. The standards, recommendations to countries that are commission members, become binding only when accepted by these countries. The CAC's procedural manual prescribes three degrees of acceptance by member states: (1) full acceptance, (2) target (intended) acceptance, and (3) acceptance with specified deviations. Full acceptance means that a complying domestic or imported product is allowed to circulate free of any legal impediment in the territory concerned, except for any consideration of health not specified in the relevant standard. Conversely, noncomplying products will not be allowed to circulate under the name and description in the standards. A country that does not comply with the standard must explain the ways its present or proposed requirements differ from the general standard and, if possible, the reasons for these differences.[15]

In 1984 the commission subjected its mandate for advertising to legal scrutiny. There was considerable discussion over whether it could promote standards on food advertising by electronic and mass media. It was agreed that although no such prima facie mandate existed (the term *advertising* is never used in the statutes), a mandate to deal with mass media advertising did stem from the legal premise that "any statutory body . . . also has powers which extend beyond those expressly given to it, if such powers are necessary and proper to fulfill the purposes for which the body was established, as well as if the powers are incidental or consequential to these purposes."[16] Viewing advertising as an essential marketing and trade activity and as having the power to mislead consumers and thus to endanger health, the councils of FAO and WHO concluded that the commission had implied powers to deal with advertising of food products in international trade. And, by definition, *advertising* embraces messages conveyed through any media, including mass media and electronic advertising.

The commission's work on advertising is carried out by its Committee on Food Labeling (CCFL). Established in 1965, this committee considered in 1972 the possibility of elaborating guidelines for food advertising. A draft code of practice for food advertising was prepared, but the CCFL decided to adopt only a general guideline applying to all food products, prepackaged or not. The general principles for labeling of prepackaged food proscribed presentations that were false, misleading, deceptive, or likely to create an erroneous impression regarding the product's character. Also prohibited was to present foods in a manner that would generate confusion with other products. The general guideline was supported by the ICC.

In 1983 the question of developing guidelines for food advertising was raised again in the CCFL. Having established that the terms of reference of the commission extended to mass-media advertising, the commission requested the CCFL to give further consideration to the subject of advertising.[17]

As background to drafting the new proposed code of practice, numerous national and international codes were reviewed. The background paper was prepared by the delegation from Canada.[18] On the basis of its review and an examination of the earliest working paper on advertising, the Canadian delegation concluded that the major concerns regarding food advertising had been addressed and that there was no need to formulate a code of practice for food advertising.[19]

A substantial number of delegations and observers felt that an adequate array of advertising codes already existed both nationally and internationally and that little value would be gained by adding another.[20] Notably, the ICC stated that the proposed code would be redundant in that several of the articles were already incorporated in the ICC's Code of Advertising and the CAC's Guidelines on Claims.[21]

Today, the code of practice is still promoted by Sweden and many other countries including Norway, India, Thailand, Poland, Iraq, and Australia.[22] It is opposed mainly by the United States, Canada, and the EC. The issue continues to be considered in the CCFL and the Commission.

General Guidelines on Claims

With obstacles confronting the development of a code on advertising, the Committee on Food Labeling has restricted itself to the elaboration of the Guidelines on Claims.[23] In 1979 the thirteenth session of the commission adopted the Guidelines on Claims that had been developed by the CAC Committee on Food labeling.[24] The Guidelines on Claims are, in essence, a listing of examples of claims for which the general principle, expressed in the general principles section of the General Standard for Labeling of Pre-Packaged Foods, applies.

The definition of *claim* in the text of the guidelines implies a link between *claim* and *advertising*. This definition states the following: "For the purpose of these guidelines, a claim is any representation which states, suggests or implies that a food has particular qualities relating to its origins, nutritional properties, nature, processing, composition, or any other quality."[25]

There is a lack of agreement, however, among countries and interested organizations as to whether the guidelines on claims extend to advertising. Those opposing a code of practice on advertising have implied that the guidelines on claims make the code a duplication. Thus, the existence of the Guidelines of Claims prompted the ICC representative at the 11–18 March 1985 meeting in Ottawa to propose that a draft code of practice was redundant.[26] Those favoring the code of practice take the opposite view. In proposing further work toward developing this code, the delegate from Sweden "pointed out that the Guidelines on Claims elaborated by the Commission applied to labels only and not to advertising."[27] There is no agreement yet on whether claims are the equivalent of advertising. Countries appear more comfortable with the ambiguity, being able or not to find a definitional overlap when it suits their policy. The issue remains to be resolved.

The guidelines distinguish between claims that should be prohibited, claims that might be misleading, and claims that should be controlled. In the former category are claims that any given food would provide an adequate source of all essential nutrients or that a balanced diet would not do that job; claims that cannot be substantiated; with certain exceptions, claims concerning the suitability of a food for medicinal purposes; and claims giving rise to doubts about the safety of a food or that arouse or exploit the fear in a consumer. In the second category are uses of comparatives and superlatives; use of terms concerning good hygienic practice, such as *wholesome, healthful,* and *sound;* and claims that the nature or origin of a food is organic or biological. In the third category are claims that additives have increased nutritional value; the use of the terms *natural, pure, fresh,* and *home made;* and statements related to religious or ritual preparation of food.

Advertising Related to Claims in Food Standards

Because codex standards contain requirements for food aimed at ensuring for the consumer a sound, wholesome food product free from adulteration, correctly labeled and presented, advertising, broadly interpreted, is implicitly concerned with the development of standards.[28] Claims considered in the product-specific commodity committees will determine advertising limits, for example, in respect to qualities and descriptions of specific products.[29]

Advertising and the Code of Ethics
for International Trade in Food

The CAC Committee on General Principles also has dealt with the question of advertising in connection with international trade in food. In response to the consideration that many member states, particularly developing countries, do not yet have adequate food control infrastructures to protect consumers against possible health hazards in food and against fraud, the committee drew up its Draft Code of Ethics for International Trade in Food. In December 1979 the commission adopted this draft as a recommended international code that would be circulated to members with a view to implementation.[30]

The Code of Ethics for International Trade in Food recommends "that all those engaged in international trade in food, commit themselves morally to the Code and undertake voluntarily to support its implementation."[31] With respect to advertising, one of its basic principles provides that "no food should be in international trade which . . . is labelled, or presented in a manner that is false, misleading or deceptive."[32]

The code also provides that when principles, as expanded in specific terms, are not covered by appropriate legal or administrative procedures in importing countries, food exporters should conform with the code provisions and other instruments adopted by the commission.

Pharmaceuticals

International attention on pharmaceuticals is intense. Many international organizations have received proposals to initiate work on a code of conduct for the pharmaceutical industry. Few phases of the activities of this industry, be they production, sales, research and development, advertising or direct sales, or exports or imports, have escaped public scrutiny and designs for control. Studies have been carried out by, among others, the UN, UNCTAD, UNIDO, OECD, and WHO. The OECD, CTC, UNCTAD, and UNIDO have focused on economic and social aspects of the international pharmaceutical problem. A primary objective of these organizations is to help Third World countries develop comprehensive policies identifying potential drug needs, production capacity, and national plans for imports and/or foreign direct investment in the local industry. Advertising and direct sales promotion by the MNEs in some circumstances have been considered detrimental to these ends.[33]

The organization that has dealt the most specifically with marketing and advertising of pharmaceuticals is WHO. Since its inception, this organization has been monitoring national regulations on the advertising and promotion of pharmaceuticals. Periodic reports on regulation of pharmaceutical advertising have been issued since the early 1960s in the WHO *International Digest of Health Legislation*.[34]

In 1968 the World Health Assembly adopted a resolution on pharmaceutical advertising. According to its preamble, pharmaceutical advertising in whatever form, *if not objective,* was detrimental to the health of the public.[35] The Assembly held that adherence to certain fundamental principles for advertising of pharmaceutical products was essential and urged member states to enforce the application of ethical and scientific criteria for pharmaceutial advertising. The criteria are reproduced as an appendix to this chapter.

Although there have been many suggestions that a marketing code for pharmaceuticals be adopted, this has not reached the stage of serious proposal. The following quotation from the *Biennial Report of the Director General* is indicative of the WHO Secretariat's position on this issue:

> There are no simple solutions to this issue. Wise drug procurement and efficient production are important, but to insure optimal benefits from them requires the definition and determined implementation of clear national policies that include the identification of therapeutic needs, the selection of corresponding drugs, their rational distribution and their proper use. The intricate web of relationships between governments, national drug industries, multinational drug companies, the medical and other health professions, and consumers, has not yet been disentangled. In this circumstance, it is not surprising that aggressive or defensive postures have been adopted by some of the involved. Nor is it surprising that consumer groups have become more

vociferous, in keeping with the enhanced role of people in shaping their own health destiny which is of the very stuff of the Strategy for Health For All. WHO has been highly active in fulfilling its international coordination role in the field of drugs, acting neither as the neutral pacifier among the parties concerned nor as the subjective supporter of any one of them, but as an objective pathfinder marking out for every one the best ways of complying with the policy on essential drugs adopted by the WHO Assembly in 1982. It has done so in the interest of people everywhere, and in particular of the underprivileged people in the developing countries.[36]

The World Health Organization, however, is expecting to continue its work in this area. Some of the other initiatives of WHO have a significant, albeit indirect, bearing on advertising and promotion of pharmaceuticals. Among those are the Essential Drug Program, the Drug Certification Scheme, and the Drug Information Bulletins.

The objective of the Essential Drug Program is to persuade governments to formulate national drug policies to meet the needs of the great majority of their populations with products of proven efficacy and safety. Work on this program was initiated in 1975 by the World Health Assembly, which requested the WHO director general to implement the proposals for possible new drug policies for developing countries and, in particular, to advise governments on the selection and procurement, at reasonable cost, of essential drugs of established quality, corresponding to their national health needs.[37] The WHO Technical Committee spelled out the guidelines for establishing national lists and provided a model list of two hundred essential drugs that were to be understood as a tentative identification of a "common core" of basic needs which has universal relevance and applicability.[38] It has been stressed by WHO that lists of essential drugs should be drawn up at the national level in order to reflect the health needs of the national environment.

The WHO list has encouraged governments to be more selective in importing pharmaceuticals and in purchasing drugs for national health programs. For example, in July 1982 the government of Bangladesh promulgated a new drug policy and used the Essential Drug List as the basis for dramatic cuts in drug imports. This action caused considerable consternation in some pharmaceutical enterprises.[39] However, the International Federation of Pharmaceutical Manufacturers Associations has pledged to provide, at low cost, essential drugs to developing countries with the expectation that this action would blunt the impetus for a code of conduct for pharmaceutical corporations.[40]

Since 1976, WHO has been issuing bimonthly Drug Information Bulletins to member governments and interested parties. These bulletins contain up-to-date information provided by member governments on general policy topics, reports on individual drugs, lists of pharmaceutical products approved annually, and regulatory decisions by member governments on individual drugs.[41]

They are devoted to international transfer of information on current drug problems. The documents do not constitute formal publications.

The Certification Scheme on the Quality of Pharmaceutical Products Moving in International Commerce was set in operation in 1976. The scheme provides a mechanism whereby importing countries can obtain assurance that a given product has been authorized for sale in an exporting country. If this is not the case, the importing country can obtain information on the reasons for products not having been placed on the market of the exporting country. It also assures importing countries a means of ascertaining quality standards. Certificates for specific products are issued only by the competent authority of the exporting country upon request of the importing authority. Although seventy-four countries subscribe to the scheme, many developing countries fail to avail themselves of its benefit.[42]

Tobacco

The World Health Organization has focused considerable attention on the promotion of tobacco to consumers. The multinational tobacco industry has also been a subject of interest in UNCTAD and the FAO, whose main concerns center on the economic importance and potential of the industry. Some analysts are weighing the economic benefits of tobacco as an important cash crop in developing economies against the cost of smoking as a health threat.

The WHO campaign to combat the smoking epidemic and its socioeconomic costs began in 1970. The objective was to promote action by governments to control and discourage smoking. To this end, a series of resolutions were adopted during the 1970s.[43]

In laying the basis for the development of its antismoking policies, WHO convened two expert committees. The first one, The Expert Committee on Smoking and Its Effects on Health, convened in 1974 and proposed legislative action by member governments to combat smoking. In particular, this committee recommended that "legislative action should be considered for the following purposes: (a) to restrict or prohibit all forms of advertising and sales promotion of tobacco."[44] This was followed in 1978 by the Expert Committee on Smoking Control, whose recommendations endorsed and strengthened the recommendations adopted in 1974.[45]

In 1980 another resolution was adopted, and it generated WHO's program on Smoking and Health.[46] This resolution encouraged the adoption of certain measures, such as increased taxation on tobacco, restrictions on advertising, and protection of nonsmokers by national governments. The first paragraph of the resolution addressed the advertising problem. The resolution

> urges Member States to strengthen and to initiate where lacking, the smoking control strategies outlined in [previous resolutions of the WHO Executive

Board and the Assembly] laying special emphasis on educational approaches, particularly with respect to youth, and on measures to ban, restrict or limit advertising of tobacco products.[47]

In 1985 the director general issued a report on the WHO tobacco program.[48] The report examined the tobacco situation, including the extent of the public-health problems, trends in tobacco use, and the positive and negative effects of tobacco production and consumption. It also reviewed WHO actions since 1970 and attempted to define prevention strategies on the basis of an evaluation of the effectiveness of smoking-control measures at the national level.

Upon consideration of this report, the executive board of WHO adopted a resolution in January 1986.[49] The resolution noted the encouragement of the board by the existence of total bans, restrictions, or limitations on tobacco advertising in several countries. It deplored all direct and indirect practices promoting the use of tobacco, as this product is addictive and dangerous even when used as promoted. The resolution urged those member states that had not yet done so to implement smoking-control strategies. The strategies would include measures leading to the progressive elimination of incentives that maintain and promote the use of tobacco and would promote viable economic alternatives to tobacco production, trade, and taxation.

Alcohol

Since its inception, WHO has assumed a role in the prevention of a wide range of health problems associated with alcohol. More recently, this organization has been giving increasing attention to alcohol-related problems. This attention reflects the concern of many countries where alcoholism has been linked with major social problems and where advertising is viewed as an enticement to this end. A study was published in 1985 on the implications of production, trade, and consumption of alcoholic beverages.[50] WHO also is planning to undertake a review of national regulations on alcohol advertising.

Spurred on by the initiatives of WHO, the alcoholic beverage industry and the International Chamber of Commerce have initiated marketing self-regulation. This action reflects growing national and international concern over alcohol-related social problems.

Appendix: Ethical and Scientific Criteria for Pharmaceutical Advertising

All advertising on a drug should be truthful and reliable. It must not contain incorrect statements, half-truths or unverifiable assertions about the contents, effects (therapeutic as well as toxic) or indications of the drug or pharmaceutical specialty concerned.

Advertising to the Medical and Related Professions

In describing the properties of a drug and its use, stress should be laid on rendering facts and data, whereas general statements should be avoided. Statements should be supported by adequate and acceptable scientific evidence. Ambiguity must be avoided. Promotional material should not be exaggerated or misleading.

A full description, based on current scientific knowledge, should include information on the producer and sponsor of the product advertised; full designation (using generic or non-proprietary names) of the nature and content of active ingredient(s) per dose; action and uses; dosage, form of administration, and mode of application; side-effects and adverse reactions; precautions and contra-indications; treatment in case of poisoning; and reference to the scientific or professional literature.

A fair balance should be maintained in presenting information on effectiveness on the one hand and adverse reactions and contra-indications on the other.

Advertising to the Public

Advertisements to the public should not be permitted for prescription drugs, for the treatment of certain diseases and conditions which can be treated only by a doctor and of which certain countries have established lists, or in a form which brings about fear or distress, or which declares specific remedies to be infallible, or suggests that they are recommended by members of the medical profession.[51]

Notes

1. UN, UNESCO, *Rapport de la Commission Internationale de l'Étude des Problèmes de la Communication, Voix Multiples Un Seul Monde* (Paris: La Documentation Française; Les Nouvelles Editions Africaines, 1980).

2. UN, UNESCO, *Mass Communications and the Advertising Industry,* Reports and papers on mass communications, no. 97, Paris 1985. The following were commissioned by UNESCO: Noreen Janus, *Advertising and the Communications Media in Latin America: History, Regulation, and Social Effects,* Instituto Latinoamericano de Estudios Transnationales, Mexico City, 1982; N.N. Pillai, *A Study of Advertising in India,* Indian Institute of Mass Communication, New Delhi, 1982; V. Shestakov, *Nature, Scope, and Impact of Advertising in the Communication Media in the USSR,* Institute of USA and Canada, Moscow, 1982; and P.P. de Win, *Self-Regulation in the Field of Advertising,* Brussels, 1983.

3. UN, General Assembly, *Resolution 39/248 on Consumer Protection,* A/INF/39/7 (9 April 1985), 67–73.

4. Product dumping is the export of products banned in the country of origin. The infant formula case is discussed in chapter 19.

5. UN, ECOSOC, *Transnational Corporations, Proposal for Consumer Protection under United Nations Auspices: Statement Submitted by the International Organization of Consumers Unions,* E/NGO/52 (19 July 1976).

6. The Group of 77 includes all the developing countries, now around 120, that are members of the United Nations.

7. The views of each of these groups of countries are contained in UN, General Assembly, *Comments of Governments on the Draft Guidelines for Consumer Protection: Report of the Economic and Social Commission,* A/C.2/39/L.2 (24 September 1984).

8. U.S. Congress, House Committee on Foreign Affairs, *Testimony by Esther Peterson to Subcommittee on Human Rights and International Organizations, and to Subcommittee on International Economic Policy and Trade,* 98th Cong., 2d sess., 28 June 1984, (typescript).

9. Esther Peterson, "Trade Imbalance in Exporting Democracy," typescript, 16 July 1984.

10. Murray L. Weidenbaum, "The UN May Become Global Nanny," Testimony before the Senate Foreign Relations Committee, Washington, D.C., 19 May 1983, (typescript); idem, "The UN's Bid to Play Consumer Cop," *New York Times,* 26 June 1983; idem, "UN's Regulatory Riptide Poses Threat to International Trade," *Christian Science Monitor,* 5 January 1984, 10. Weidenbaum was the first chairman of President Ronald Reagan's Council of Economic Advisers.

11. UN, General Assembly, *Resolution 39/248 on Consumer Protection,* A/INF/39/7 (9 April 1985), par. 20–22.

12. Peter Goldman, *Multinationals and the Consumer Interest* (The Hague: International Organization of Consumer Unions, 1974).

13. UN, ECOSOC, *Work on the Formulation of the United Nations Code of Conduct on Transnational Corporations: Outstanding Issues in the Draft Code,* E/C.10/1985/S/2 (22 May 1985).

14. UN, Joint FAO/WHO Food Standards Program, *Codex Alimentarius Commission: Procedural Manual* (1981), 1. (hereinafter cited as *Codex Procedural Manual*).

15. UN, *Codex Procedural Manual,* 22–28, par. 4A, 5A.

16. UN, Joint FAO/WHO Food Standards Program, Codex Committee on Food Labeling, 18th sess., *"Advertising" in the Mandate of the Codex Alimentarius Commission and Its Subsidiary Bodies: Note Prepared by the Legal Counsels of FAO and WHO,* CX/FL 85-7, appendix 1 (March 1984).

17. UN, Joint FAO/WHO Food Standards Program, Codex Alimentarius Commission, *Report of the Fifteenth Session,* 4–15 July 1983, ALINORM 83/43, par. 122.

18. UN, Joint FAO/WHO Food Standards Program, Codex Committee on Food Labeling, 18th sess., *Working Paper on Advertising, Prepared by the Canadian delegation,* CX/FL 85/7 (March 1985). See also *Proposed Draft Code of Practice for Food Advertising for Consideration by the Codex Committee on Food Labeling at its*

Eighteenth Session, annexed to *Working Paper on Advertising,* CX/FL 85/7, appendix 2.

19 UN, *Proposed Draft Code,* par. 7; UN, Joint FAO/WHO Food Standards Program, Codex Committee on Food Labeling, *Draft Report of the Eighteenth Session,* 11-18 March 1985, ALINORM 85/22A, par. 171.

20. UN, *Draft Report of the Eighteenth Session,* par. 172.

21. ICC, *Statement Submitted to the Codex Committee on Food Labeling,* Ottawa, 11-18 March 1985, Doc. no. 250-24/115.

22. UN, Joint FAO/WHO Food Standards Program, Codex Alimentarius Commission, *Report of the Sixteenth Session,* Geneva, 1-12 July 1985, ALINORM 85/47, par. 204-05. The delegation of Sweden stated that it was in favor of establishing ethical standards in food advertising for the benefit of consumer protection as well as fair trade practices. The delegation pointed out that food advertising and especially transnational advertising was increasing and that ethical standards should be elaborated within the CAC framework. The legal opinions of FAO and WHO had confirmed that such work was within the terms of reference of CCFL. It was of the opinion that work on ethical standards in food advertising should continue and care should be taken not to duplicate the code established by the International Chamber of Commerce. Sweden proposed that a study should be prepared by a consultant setting out the problems and how to resolve them for submission to the labeling committee. See also report of the 17th session of CAC, July 1987.

23. UN, Working Paper on Advertising, par. 6.

24. UN, Joint FAO/WHO Food Standards Program, Codex Alimentarius Commission, *Report of the Thirteenth Session,* Rome, 3-14 December 1979, ALINORM 79/38, par. 137-42.

25. UN, Joint FAO/WHO Food Standards Program, CAC Committee on Food Labeling, Report of the Thirteenth Session, Ottawa, 16-20 July 1979, ALINORM 72/22, par. 4-7, and appendix 2, par. 1.2.

26. ICC, *Statement on FAO/WHO Codex Alimentarius Proposal for Code on Advertising Practice,* par. 3, Ottawa, Canada, 11-18 March 1985.

27. UN, Joint FAO/WHO Food Standards Program, Codex Alimentarius Commission, *Report of the Sixteenth Session,* par. 205.

28. UN, Joint FAO/WHO Food Standards Program, *Codex Alimentarius Commission: Procedural Manual.* Geneva, 1981. 1, 52-53.

29. For a discussion of this subject, see Sami Shubber, "Codex Alimentarius Commission under International Law," *International and Comparative Law Quarterly* 21 (October 1972): 652-53.

30. UN, Joint FAO/WHO Food Standards Program, Codex Alimentarius Commission, *Report of the Thirteenth Session,* par. 122; UN, Joint FAO/WHO Food Standards Program, Codex Alimentarius Commission, *Code of Ethics for International Trade in Food,* CAC/RCP 20 (1979). The code was originally drafted by a consultant, then the President of IOCU. C. Feldberg, "World Wide Regulatory Overview," *Food, Drug, Cosmetic Law Journal,* September 1979.

31. UN, *Code of Ethics,* Preamble, 1.

32. Ibid., Article 4.2.

33. See UN, CTC, *Transnational Corporations in the Pharmaceutical Industry of Developing Countries,* ST/CTC/49 (1984); UN, Conference on Trade and Devel-

opment, *Technology Policies and Planning for the Pharmaceutical Sector in the Developing Countries,* TD/B/C.6/56 (1980) with a series of individual country profiles prepared as addenda to this report; UN, Industrial Development Organization, *Global Study of the Pharmaceutical Industry,* ID/WG.331/6 and add. 1 (22 October 1980); Organization for Economic Cooperation and Development, *Multinational Enterprises, Governments and Technology: Pharmaceutical Industry,* Report by M.L. Burstall, J.H. Dunning, and A. Lake (Paris: OECD), 1981.

34. UN, WHO, *International Digest of Health Legislation (IDHL)* 12 (1961); *IDHL* 19 (1968); *IDHL* 31 (1980).

35. UN, WHO, Assembly, *Resolution WHA 21.41,* 21st sess. (1968); UN, WHO, *WHO Handbook of Resolutions and Decisions of the World Health Assembly and the Executive Board, 1948-1972,* vol. 1 (1973), 144. (hereinafter cited as *WHO Handbook* 1).

36. UN, WHO, "Introduction by the Director-General," *The Work of WHO 1982-1983; Biennial Report of the Director General* (1984), xiii.

37. UN, WHO, Assembly, *Resolution WHA 28.66,* 28th sess. (1975); UN, WHO, *WHO Handbook of Resolutions and Decisions of the World Health Assembly and the Executive Board, 1973-1984,* vol. 2 (1985), 134. (hereinafter cited as *WHO Handbook* 2).

38. UN, WHO, *The Selection of Essential Drugs: First Report of the WHO Expert Committee,* WHO Technical Report Series 615 (1977); Ibid., *The Selection of Essential Drugs: Second Report of the WHO Committee* (WHO Technical Report Series 641 (1979); Ibid., *The Use of Essential Drugs: Report of the WHO Expert Committee,* WHO Technical Report Series 685 (1983).

39. UN, WHO, The Danish International Development Association (DANIDA), and the Swedish International Development Association (SIDA), *Essential Drugs for Primary Health Care in Bangladesh—Report of a Project Preparation Mission,* Report in collaboration with Hoff and Overgaard A/S Health Planning Division (January 1984); "U.S. Asks Bangladesh to Delay Ban on Many Drugs Rated as Ineffective," *International Herald Tribune,* 20 August 1982.

40. IAA, *Intelligence Survey,* no. 26 (February/March 1982).

41. Series denoted as UN, WHO, *Drug Information Bulletins.*

42. UN, WHO, Assembly, *Resolution WHA 28.65,* 28th sess. (1975); UN, WHO, *WHO Handbook* 2, 129; UN, WHO, *Certification Scheme on the Quality of Pharmaceutical Products Moving in International Commerce,* WHO Official Records, No. 226, 1975, 88.

43. UN, WHO, Assembly, *Resolution WHA 23.32,* 23rd sess. (1970) on health hazards of smoking, and Ibid., *Resolution WHA 24.48* (1971), see *WHO Handbook* 1, 110-11; Ibid., *Resolution 29.55,* 29th sess. (1976), and Ibid., *Resolution 31.56,* 31st sess. (1978) on Control of smoking, *WHO Handbook* 2, 173-75.

44. UN, WHO, "Recommendations of the 1974 WHO Expert Committee on Smoking and Its Effect on Health," par. 5, in *WHO Expert Committee on Smoking and Its Effects on Health,* WHO Technical Report Series 568 (1975).

45. UN, WHO, *Controlling the Smoking Epidemic: Report of Expert Committee on Smoking Control,* WHO Technical Report Series 636 (1979).

46. UN, WHO, Assembly, *Resolution WHA 33.35,* 33d sess. (1980) on WHO Action Program against Tobacco Use, *WHO Handbook* 2, 175.

47. Ibid., par. 1.

48. UN, WHO, Executive Board, *WHO Program on Tobacco or Health: Report by the Director General,* 77th sess., EB77/22, add. 1 (15 November 1985).

49. UN, WHO, Executive Board, *Resolution on Tobacco and Health,* 77th sess., EB77.R5 (16 January 1986).

50. UN, WHO, *Public Health Implications of Alcohol Production and Trade,* prepared by Brendan Walsh and Marcus Grant, WHO Offset Pub. 880 (1985).

51. UN, WHO, Assembly, *Resolution WHA 21.41,* 21st sess. (1968) on pharmaceutical advertising, *WHO Handbook* 1, 144.

19
The International Code of Marketing of Breast-Milk Substitutes

The International Code of Marketing of Breast-Milk Substitutes was adopted in the World Health Organization on May 21, 1981, with a vote of 118 in favor, 3 abstentions, and 1 against. Argentina, Japan, and the Republic of Korea abstained. The United States voted against adopting the code.[1]

This is the first marketing code adopted by an intergovernmental organization. It aims at the provision of safe and adequate nutrition for infants by the protection and promotion of breast-feeding and by the regulation of marketing practices. It calls for a ban on commercial advertising and other forms of promotion of breast-milk substitutes, including infant formula; other milk products, foods and beverages, including bottle-fed complementary foods, when marketed or otherwise represented to be suitable for use as a partial or total replacement of breast milk; and feeding bottles or teats.[2]

The code is based on the general assumption that advertising is the principal controlling factor causing mothers to turn from breast milk to substitutes. According to the explanation for this assumption, these products are glamorized through pictures of healthy-looking infants and through statements suggesting that the products are as beneficial to the baby as breast milk. Mothers thus increasingly resort to artificial feeding and are faced with all the dangers that such practice seemingly entails, particularly in poor countries and among certain social groups.

The Crusade against the "Baby Killer"

The events leading to the adoption of the code began in the 1960s with the concern of health workers and some pediatricians, notably Dr. Derrick Jelliffe, over the steady decline in the incidence of breast-feeding, particularly in the urban areas of developing countries.[3] In some reports a correlation was made between declining breast-feeding and increased malnutrition in children due to the absence of immunological protection gained from breast milk and to greater bacteriological infection from the complements of bottle-feeding.

Meetings were organized by the international health community, notably in Bogota in 1970 and in Paris in 1972, with the participation of the infant-formula industry, to address the concerns over the alleged increasing infant malnutrition. The thrust of these discussions was that, indeed, breast milk was the best food for infants and would, if present in adequate quantities, satisfy the needs of a child up until four to six months of age. However, in situations when breast-feeding was insufficient or impossible, the use of nutritional substitutes should be encouraged.

Public attention was dramatically drawn to the controversy in 1973 and 1974. A journalist wrote a booklet entitled *The Baby Killer* condemning the promotional activities of infant formula manufacturers Unigate and Nestlé for discouraging breast-feeding.[4] This thirty-two page booklet was translated into German by the Swiss Third World Action Group (TWAG) Arbeitsgruppe Dritte Welt Bern and was retitled *Nestlé Kills Babies*.[5] It was stated that Nestlé was responsible for death or permanent damage to thousands of children and was using unethical and immoral methods in the Third World, especially with respect to advertising.

Nestlé was incensed by this accusation, and on behalf of Nestlé, Dr. A. Furer stated emphatically, "No one has the right to accuse us of killing babies. No one has the right to assert that we are pursuing unethical and immoral sales practices . . . this is why we have brought libel actions against [TWAG]."[6] He went on to accuse TWAG of using infant malnutrition as a way "to attack one of those capitalist multinational creations in the hope of convincing a sufficient number of dupes" by means of "lies, distortions, and false allegations."[7]

Nestlé sued for libel all those involved with the booklet and with other publications on the same subject. In February 1975 the canton (state) of Bern was given jurisdiction over all the cases. The authors of the questioned materials were tried for slander, and the press was tried for overstepping its rights by printing the brochure. On trial were the methods of the consumer-activist groups to gain public support for their cause against advertising by multinationals in the Third World. Also on trial were the advertising practices of Nestlé.

As a witness for the defense, Jelliffe linked the increased rate of infant mortality in developing countries to the activities of the companies manufacturing baby food. Basing his testimony on experience in the Caribbean, he stated that the milk nurses employed by Nestlé influenced mothers in such a way that the mothers backed away from nursing.[8] Believing that advertising messages had to be adjusted for different audiences, Jelliffe stated, "I am of the opinion that the means of advertising should be adjusted to the given reality, the naivete of the audience, their strife to adjust to modern life as a status symbol, and to the given sanitary circumstances."[9]

According to Jelliffe, ads in the press were damaging, as they appealed to the desire to reach a pseudo–status symbol, and they were false in their picturing of overfed babies next to the product. Recognizing that Nestlé's advertising attempted to promote breast-feeding, Jelliffe said that such information was not understood by those who could not read and who were, to the contrary, influenced by the pretty-looking baby on the can or jar.

The court appreciated the predicament of the accused. In the view of the court, the defendants were people who, in general, had attained a high level of education; who ethically valued their work, research, and information; and who, therefore, expected to be taken seriously. They also were perceived as having great difficulty attracting public attention. Because they were a small group, they had to strive to reach the forefront. With the exaggerated title of their translation, they gained the public attention they would not have had otherwise. Their concerns were considered honest. They recognized a problem and tried to solve it. The method they chose was unfortunate, but it did not change their reasons for doing what they did.

However, a question of honor had been raised, and the plea for acquittal was not successful. The court determined that the translation, in its legal sense, implied that Nestlé kills infants, premeditatedly or carelessly, and that the public would interpret the title in its more limited sense of premeditated murder. The title went beyond accusations of moral responsibility, and blamed Nestlé of punishable doings and of extreme immoral behavior. It was held by the court that a person who "accuses of killing should know that this, if untrue, is an insult of honor."[10] The accused were guilty of exercising "too little carefulness."[11]

The sentence required the defendants to publish notification of their guilt in their publications for benefit of their readers. Payment of one-thirteenth of the trial costs were to be borne by each of the thirteen people found guilty. However, the court admonished Nestlé to rethink its advertising of infant formula in developing countries because its advertising practices could change a life-saving product into a dangerous, deadly one. If, in the future, Nestlé wished to avoid accusations of immoral and unethical behavior, it must change its methods of advertising.

The accusations against Nestlé were well covered by the print press and by television in Europe. This publicity brought the infant-formula issue to international attention.

In November 1975, following the trial, a number of large infant-formula companies, led by Nestlé, formed the International Council of Infant Food Industries (ICIFI) and adopted a self-regulatory code of ethics for formula promotion.[12] The code provided that all advertising should emphasize that human milk is best for infants and that professional advice should be sought when a supplement or alternative is required. Two of the largest U.S. manufacturers of infant formula, Abbott Laboratories and Bristol-Myers, refused to join the coalition and adopted their own self-regulation codes appropriate to the marketing practices of pharmaceutical companies not engaged in mass-media advertising.

Meanwhile, a drama was evolving on the American stage, where the actors were American formula producers as well as Nestlé. In 1974 the Consumer's Union published a book by Robert J. Ledogar entitled *Hungry for Profit*. It contained the results of a study providing further evidence on the dangers of breast-milk substitutes, evidence cited in a report entitled *Formula for Malnutrition*. This report focused on the promotional practices of the leading American formula manufacturers. By the end of the year, member groups of the Interfaith Center on Corporate Responsibility (ICCR) had filed shareholder resolutions with Abbott Laboratories, American Home Products, and Bristol-Myers Co., requesting information on sales and promotional practices and requesting that these companies desist from the offending market practices.[13] These resolutions were withdrawn in the case of Abbott/Ross and American Home Products after a number of meetings and the companies' agreement to desist from the offending practices.

In 1976 the Sisters of the Precious Blood, Inc., an order of catholic nuns, filed suit against Bristol-Myers Co. for alleged violation of section 14(a) of the Securities Exchange Act of 1934 and rule 14 a-9 and item 22 of schedule 14A adopted pursuant to the act.[14] Plaintiff shareholders accused the corporate defendant of having responded to a shareholder's request for infant-formula marketing information with false and misleading statements that were repeated in proxy material. They sought an injunction ordering the company to submit the proposal, with full explanation, at an official stockholders' meeting. The company denied the allegation, the case was dismissed in court, and the Sisters of the Precious Blood filed an appeal. Eventually, each party independently concluded that all parties involved shared common goals and that further court proceedings would be counterproductive to their mutual interests.[15]

On July 4 1977, the Infant Formula Coalition Action (INFACT) organized a worldwide boycott against Nestlé products.[16] This boycott would not end until January 26, 1984, when both INFACT/ICCR and Nestlé agreed to accept UNICEF's recommendations on the interpretation of four controversial points in the WHO Code: educational materials, health hazards on labels, gifts to health professionals and free supplies to hospitals.

Supported by Dr. Benjamin Spock, Ralph Nader, Cesar Chavez, and other national figures, the boycott aimed at the cessation of all promotion of Nestlé infant formula, including mass-media advertising, the distribution of free samples, the use of milk nurses, and promotion by medical professionals. In July 1978 over 9 million Americans were estimated to have watched a nationwide CBS television broadcast of a half-hour documentary film, "Into the Mouths of Babes," on the health problems related to infant formula being given to babies in the Dominican Republic. Moderated by television journalist

Bill Moyers, the program also revealed a kickback scheme involving companies paying a percentage of formula sales revenues to the Dominican Medical Association.

Also in 1976 a joint resolution was introduced in the U.S. Congress calling on the Agency for International Development (AID) to cooperate with developing countries to elaborate and implement a strategy to promote breast-feeding. On May 23, 1978, the Senate Subcommittee on Health and Scientific Research, chaired by Senator Edward Kennedy, a leading proponent of a global code on advertising, held a seminar on the issues raised by the promotion of infant formula. Thus, by the end of the 1970s, citizens in the United States and throughout the world were aware of the controversy. The time was ripe for the WHO initiative.

Characteristics of the WHO Code

Because breast-feeding is better for the infant, its practice should be encouraged, substitutes should be used only when necessary, and commercial advertising should be prohibited. This is the position of the International Code of Marketing of Breast-Milk Substitutes.

The scope of the code extends to the marketing of all substitutes. Not only infant formula is involved, but also other milk products, foods, and beverages when these are marketed or otherwise represented to be suitable for replacing breast milk. For consumer activists, such as the International Baby Food Action Network (IBFAN), such wording has allowed products used as breast-milk substitutes but not marketed as such to fall outside the code, including powdered milks, cereal infant foods, teas, and vegetable gruels. On the other hand, the producers, notably Nestlé, question whether or not so-called weaning foods are included, as by nature they are substitutes. Because the authority to interpret the code is left to member countries and to the WHO Assembly, the WHO Secretariat could not address directly such criticism. However, the Secretariat provided statements and notes on subjects that are addressed in the code. These notes confirm that the code's references to products used as partial or total replacements for breast milk apply to complementary foods only when these foods are marketed as suitable for partial or total replacement of breast milk.

The code does not set any age limit in the scope of its application, It is, however, stated in the annex to the code that during the first four to six months of life, breast milk is generally adequate to meet the normal infant's nutritional requirements. After this initial period, foods such as cow's milk, cereals, and vegetables are no longer bona fide substitutes, but should be seen as complementary foods.[17]

Article 4 of the code outlines the type of information that should be provided to mothers with infants. Governments should ensure that objective and consistent information is given on feedings for infants and young children. All informational and educational materials should specify the health hazards resulting from unnecessary or improper use of substitutes and should not contain any promotional element that could be used for advertising, directly or indirectly, of products covered by the code, including use of pictures or texts that idealize use of substitutes.

The most significant aspect of the code is the ban on commercial advertising. It is formulated in the following terms:

> There should be no advertising or other form of promotion to the general public of products within the scope of this code. . . . There should be no point-of-sale advertising . . . or any other promotion device to induce sales directly to the consumer at the retail level, such as special displays, discount coupons, premiums, special sales, loss-leaders and tie-in sales, for products within the scope of this code.[18]

The motivation behind this suggested ban on advertising is to protect mothers and pregnant women from the temptation, through advertisements and promotion, to use breast-milk substitutes for feeding their infants. Therefore, the code recommends prohibiting any advertisement or promotion of any kind relating to the products covered in the code and addressed to the general public, be this promotion through television, radio, newspapers, magazines, posters, or in any other form.

The code, however, does not clearly define such terms as *information, promotion, education,* and *advertising*. Regarding the latter, it appears from WHO sources that in the absence of an explicit definition, the term should be given its ordinary meaning, in accordance with article 31 of the Vienna Convention on the Law of Treaties, 1969, and that such meaning, taken from the Concise Oxford Dictionary, is the following: " 'advertise' (means) . . . to describe (goods) publicly with view to increasing sales."[19] Nevertheless, the failure to provide definitions of terms that, according to common usage, have somewhat blurred meanings has certainly complicated the task of translating the code into operational instructions at the national and industrial levels.

Another controversial aspect of the code relates to article 5.5, which states that "marketing personnel, in their business capacity, should not seek direct or indirect contact of any kind with pregnant women or with mothers of infants and growing children."[20] According to Nestlé's interpretation, this article should not (and therefore did not) prevent appropriately qualified personnel from responding to complaints or unsolicited requests for information on product use. The company felt it would be negligent and in violation of consumers' rights if it did not reply to an unsolicited request for information on the proper use of the product. This interpretation is confirmed by the annex to the code, in which it is noted that any information given by manufacturers and distributors to health professionals regarding products covered by the code should be limited to scientific and factual matters and should not imply or create a belief that bottle-feeding is equivalent or superior to breast-feeding.

In the view of consumer activist groups, article 5.5 offers a critical loophole through which companies could continue to enlarge their markets in the Third World through promotions to medical professionals. Samples and information to these individuals can be seen as forms of disguised advertising. This is a significant criticism, as promotion to the medical and health professionals has always been the channel used by pharmaceutical manufacturers who did not participate in mass-media campaigns. Indeed, it was through the hospitals that many of the Third World mothers were said to have become introduced to bottle-feeding.

The Legal Nature of the Code

According to the WHO constitution, the Assembly had the choice between three legal forms for the code: treaty, regulation, or recommendation.[21] The authority to adopt a treaty on any matter within its competence by a two-thirds majority is granted under article 19. This article has never been invoked and was not considered for the code.

Under article 21 of the same constitution, WHO has authority to adopt regulations concerning, among other things, "advertising and labeling of biological, pharmaceutical and similar products moving in international commerce."[22] After adoption by a simple majority vote, regulations become legally binding following due notice by the Assembly, unless a member notifies the WHO director general of rejection or reservation within the set period of time. They are quasi-legislative in that they do not bind member states without their consent. In light of its substance and according to the theory of implied powers as defined by the International Court of Justice, the code would have qualified for regulation status.

According to the theory of implied power, it has been argued that because WHO, according to article 1 of its constitution, has the objective of "attainment by all peoples of the highest possible level of health," it has functions embracing the promoting of maternal and child health and welfare; the developing, establishing, and promoting of international standards with respect to food; and generally the taking of all action necessary to attain its objective.[23] Such action would include authority to develop a regulation on breast-milk substitutes. This alternative, however, was not chosen, and there appear to be no plans to revise the code's status from a recommendation to a regulation.

The third alternative was elected. The code is a recommendation and falls under article 23 of the WHO constitution, which stipulates that the Health

Assembly shall have authority to make recommendations to members on any matters within its competence and thus to lay down general principles, provide advice, and call on member states to take certain stands on public-health issues. Not legally binding, the code carries only a moral and political authority, derived from the collective judgment of the membership of WHO. Its legal effect is derived by incorporation of the code into national laws. In light of this necessity, in 1982 the WHO Assembly unanimously adopted a further recommendation urging member states to give renewed attention to the need to adopt national legislation, regulations, or other measures to enable the code and the director general to provide the necessary support and guidance.

The Impact of the Code

The director general of WHO reports biannually to the Assembly on the status of implementation of the code. Details on national measures are reported in the quarterly journal *International Digest of Health Legislation.*

About twenty-five developing countries have formally adopted legislation encompassing at least some of the provisions of the code. At least nine of them, Nicaragua, Papua, New Guinea, India, Sri Lanka, Tunisia, Egypt, Lebanon, and the United Arab Emirates, have adopted legislation banning advertising of breast-milk substitutes and complementary products to the general public. For example, Tunisia's law provides that

> There may be no advertising of any nature whatsoever that promotes the use as breast-milk substitutes of the products referred to in Section 1 of this law, nor any distribution of samples thereof. The same shall apply to utensils and articles of such a nature as to promote the above mentioned products or bottle feeding.[24]

The Indian law reflects the WHO code almost verbatim, inserting however, the mandatory *shall* instead of *should* with respect to the ban on advertising. In Nicaragua infant formula is declared to be a medication and thus is under the strict supervision of the Ministry of Health.

The governments of Ghana, Libya, and Iran exercise monopoly control over the formula industry and have banned advertising. This does not mean that these countries adhere wholeheartedly to the spirit of the code. For example, cans of infant milk food sold by the state monopoly in Iran are adorned with images of fat, healthy babies. The government of Ghana has authorized the development of a reasonably priced, nutritionally satisfactory local product for infants who have to be fed substitutes.

A number of other countries, including Kenya, Nigeria, Malaysia, and Singapore, all middle-income Commonwealth countries with significant multinational advertising presence, have adopted comprehensive legislation on infant and child feeding but depart from the code's strict ban on advertising of infant formula and other breast-milk substitutes. The Nigerian code, prepared in consultation with the infant-formula industry, provides that media communications on infant-feeding practices should not carry a brand name and should be approved by the Federal Ministry of Health. A similar situation prevails in a number of Latin American countries. Advertising of infant formula is not banned but is regulated in Brazil, Chile, Colombia, Ecuador, Guatemala, Peru, and Venezuela. In Thailand modified milks for infants have been declared controlled foods, subject to quality standards and regulated advertising.

In addition to the countries banning or regulating the advertising of infant formulas through formal legislation, more than twenty other developing countries in Africa and the Middle East have prohibited advertising of breast-milk substitutes to the general public through regulation of the media. Advertising of breast-milk substitutes via mass media has ceased through voluntary arrangements with the infant-formula industry in Denmark, Norway, Sweden, Ireland, Canada, the United Kingdom, and the United States.

It is not clear what action the countries of Eastern Europe have taken. Images of fat, healthy babies and/or baby bottles appear on boxes of powdered milks sold in Hungary and Poland. In Western Europe, the Nordic countries, France, and the United Kingdom, as well as in Canada and the United States, measures have been adopted to promote breast-feeding and/or infant nutrition.

Finally, many other countries throughout the world have draft legislation pending, are studying the problem, or are initiating programs to encourage breast-feeding. Moreover, overall national advertising rules and regulations generally apply to the advertising of infant foods as well as other products.

Apart from its enactment in national law, the code suggests that its provisions and principles be honored by manufacturers and distributors, even in the absence of national legislation. Concerning the code's suggestions, three stages can be defined in terms of the marketing behavior of producers of infant formula and other substitutes.

The first stage was from 1974 until the adoption of the code in 1981. During this period, the infant-formula business slowly changed its policies from open and free sales promotion to more restrained marketing campaigns, more heavily concentrated on the health sector. All the major producers adopted or participated in self-regulatory schemes calling for more careful marketing procedures and more emphasis on natural breast-feeding as the preferred source of infant nutrition. The ICIFI code of ethics stipulated, in particular, that product claims would reflect scientific integrity without implying that any product was inferior to breast milk.

The second period dated from the adoption of the code in 1981 until the end of the Nestlé boycott in September 1984. Members of the industry, notably Nestlé, revised their self-regulatory schemes to conform to the spirit of the code and began to monitor violations of their own codes or policies.

The third period is the present postboycott period, during which certain members of the industry are seen as beginning to relax their restraints. It seems that marketing campaigns are targeted to health professionals in both industrialized and developing countries. This activity is not a violation of the code, but illustrates one of the loopholes regretted by some consumer activists. The code permits the industry to give educational materials to health professionals and their clients. Prizes and awards also are permitted, as long as no promise to endorse specific positions or products is required of the recipients.

Nevertheless, the code and its follow-up seems to have quieted all but the most intense opponents of bottle-feeding. The public apparently has recognized that the code coincided with many overt changes in marketing practices of the infant-formula companies. Milk nurses, mass-media advertising, and exaggerations of the benefits of formula feeding are no longer making headlines in the Western world. The boycott has ended. Formula sales are reported to be as high as ever.

The Future of Similar Codes

Three questions need to be addressed. First, was the uproar over infant formula necessary and useful? Second, has the code changed practices and attitudes? Third, will and should other comparable regulations be adopted?

Regarding the first question, it should be noted that in the 1940s infant formula was the food of choice recommended by pediatricians in industrialized countries. It "liberated" the women, did not appear to harm the child, and contributed indirectly to the war effort in Western countries by enabling women to leave home to work. Infant formula was a product viewed by the public as having net social benefits.

These attitudes changed over time, and the controversy over Nestlé and infant formula was the result of the conjunction of at least three forces. First, a back to nature movement, away from the excesses and sophistication of the industrialized societies, erupted in the 1960s. Second, a related dislike for large companies and large profits in general appeared in consumer and other groups. Third, the controversy over infant formula centered on marketing in Third World countries. Some consumer groups and individuals from wealthy countries suddenly became outraged by the attraction that a woman from an African or Asian village could feel for a nicely presented bottle of breast-milk substitute. Implicitly, the rich were saying to the poor to avoid the path and attitudes that led to what is commonly perceived as social and economic progress, if not affluence. Poor people and poor countries do want progress, and an attractive path to that progress has yet to be found.

Practices and attitudes of consumers in both industrialized and developing countries do not appear to have changed. As noted earlier, the companies selling the products covered by the code are prosperous. Yet advertising is banned, at least in its most visible practice. This suggests that the demand for infant formula was and remains real, that advertising was perhaps not the problem, and that the controversy and the ensuing code were artificial and unnecessary. Clearly, no empirical study has ever proven that there was a correlation between milk-substitute use and infant mortality. On the other hand, it would be unfair and incorrect not to recognize that corporate responsibility and corporate ethics have been enhanced by the controversy.

The code and the controversy that led to its adoption did play a role in the emergence of this new responsible culture. Also, the excesses of the consumer activists were unquestionably instrumental in bringing about more self-regulation within these movements themselves. A more sober, more scientific, and less ideological attitude appears currently to be prevalent.

Will similar codes be discussed and adopted for other products, such as tobacco, alcohol, or pharmaceuticals? The methods used to achieve the code and a ban on promotion of infant formula included dramatization of the facts to evoke global sympathy and support combined with economic and legal pressure. This approach was facilitated by the universal appeal of the cause. The general public and politicians found difficulties in opposing the code for the sake of business profits.

Surely the infant formula crisis is unique in that there were strong emotional elements on the side of the proponents of the code. Few could argue against a proposal whose stated aim was the protection of the lives of innocent babies. Even questioning the legitimacy of the argument of the code's proponents was difficult, despite the redeeming qualities of the product as a nutritional food for babies. If other possible codes are discussed, it is likely that self-regulation and a few more steps in the emergence of corporate ethics will be the outcome. Business was fighting a losing battle from the beginning, and most U.S. companies were quick to recognize this. By adopting self-regulating codes stronger than the ICIFI code subscribed to by Nestlé and the majority of non–U.S. formula producers and by reforming their promotion campaigns even before the code was adopted, most of the U.S. formula manufacturers provided indications of the efficacy of the measures employed by the protagonists of the code. Whether the same measures would reap success in the pursuit of international advertising codes on other products, such as alcohol, tobacco, or pharmaceuticals, is a matter for debate.

Notes

1. UN, WHO, Assembly, *Resolution WHA 34.22,* 34th sess., 4–22 May 1981, WHA 34/1981/REC/1, 21, and annex 3; idem, *Records of Plenary Meetings—Reports of Committees,* WHA34/1981/REC/2, 266.

2. UN, WHO, *International Code of Marketing of Breast-Milk Substitutes* (1981). Adopted by the 34th session of the World Health Assembly, 4–22 May 1981.

3. Throughout the period, Dr. Derrick Jelliffe, director of the Caribbean Food and Nutrition Institute in Jamaica, was a key figure in identifying problems of infant formula feeding in developing countries and in bringing this issue to international attention. His findings were cited by international organizations and used by various consumer activist groups, in particular War on Want, ICCR, and INFACT in their campaign to stop the market promotion of breast-milk substitutes to the public. In one article Jelliffe is quoted as estimating that there occur some 10 million cases per year of infectious disease and infant malnutrition directly attributable to improper bottle feeding. Jim Post and Ed Baer, "International Code of Marketing for Breast-Milk Substitutes: Consensus, Compromise, and Conflict in the Infant Formula Controversy," *The Review: International Commission of Jurists,* December 1980.

4. Mike Muller, *The Baby Killer: A War on Want Investigation into the Promotion and Sale of Powdered Baby Milks in the Third World* (London: War on Want, 1974). War on Want was founded in the early 1950s as a campaign to make world poverty an urgent social and political issue. Today it is one of the major Third World aid agencies in the United Kingdom.

5. TWAG is an activist group in Switzerland and is made up of teachers, clergy, and students. The group disseminates information to schools on national foreign-aid programs.

6. A. Furer, "Nestlé and Baby Food in the Third World," Nestlé press release (1975), 3.

7. Ibid.

8. *Nestlé Alimentana SA/Arbeitsgruppe Dritte Welt Bern Criminal Procedure,* Strafrerfahren Nr. 627/74, Richterampt 8, Bern, 2 July 1976. The original text has been translated into English by Monika Whipple, German scholar, teaching in the Groton School, Groton, Mass. Subsequent excerpts in English are derived from her translation. The case was procured from the Bern Cantonal Court. (typescript)

9. Idem, *Audienz des Gerichtsprasidenten,* VIII von Bern, 26 February 1976, 4.

10. Idem, *Erwagungen,* 995.

11. Ibid., 1023.

12. International Council of Infant Food Industries, *Code of Ethics and Professional Standards for Advertising, Product Information, and Advisory Services for Breast-Milk Substitutes,* Zurich, 20 November 1975, amended 14 September 1976. Companies adopting the code included Nestlé (Switzerland); Wyeth, Intl. (United States); Unigate (United Kingdom); Dumex (Denmark); and Mieji Milk, Morinaga Milk, Snow Brand Milk, and Wakado (Japan).

13. ICCR is an ecumenical agency, related to the National Council of Churches, made up of more than 12 Protestant denominations and at least 150 Roman Catholic orders. These groups, as stockholders in U.S. corporations, analyze the social performance of these corporations and raise social and corporate responsibility issues they believe arise from the activities of the corporations in which they invest.

14. *Sisters of the Precious Blood, Inc., v. Bristol Myers,* No. 76 Civ. 1734(MP), 431 F. Supp. 385, (S.D.N.Y. 1977), *appeal docketed,* No. 77-7299 (2d Cir. June 8, 1977) (settled Dec. 22, 1977, settlement agreement revised Jan. 6, 1978). Rule 14 a-9 provides that no solicitation shall be made by means of any proxy statement that, in

given circumstances, was false and misleading in regard to statements of material facts, or through omissions of material facts was rendered false and misleading. Item 22 concerns statement of vote required for approvals of nonprocedural matters submitted to a vote of security holders. Id. at 385, 386, nn. 1, 2.

15. In 1977 the ICCR also had filed a shareholder's suit with Borden. In response Borden agreed to modify certain advertising and labeling of infant formulas, Klim, to oversee its marketing, to minimize conditions for misuse, and to withdraw New Biolac from Asian markets where advertising was no longer socially acceptable.

16. INFACT was established in late 1976. The group was based in Minneapolis, Minnesota. Its membership included a number of individuals and church and welfare organizations joined with a study group at the Third World Institute of the Newman Center. The purpose of the group was to halt the unethical and dangerous promotion of infant milk formula in Third World countries.

17. For members of IBFAN, the silence of the code on the age limit is a weakness. They believe that breast-feeding is always a valuable source of nutrition and must be utilized throughout infancy.

18. WHO, *Code on Marketing Breast-Milk Substitutes,* article 5.

19. *Vienna Convention on the Law of Treaties,* p. 885, fn. 62, par. 1 of art. 31 provides that "a treaty shall be interpreted in good faith in accordance with the ordinary meaning to be given to the terms of the treaty in their context and in the light of its object and purpose." For text of the convention see the United Nations, *Official Records of the United Nations Conference on the Laws of Treaties,* Documents of the Conference, A/Conf.39/23 (1969). Also, the *Concise Oxford Dictionary,* 7th ed., S.V. "advertise."

20. UN, WHO, *Code on Marketing Breast-Milk Substitutes,* article 5.5.

21. UN, WHO, *World Health Organization Constitution,* adopted by the International Health Conference, New York, 19 June–22 July 1946, and signed on 22 July 1946 by the representatives of sixty-one states. Amendments adopted by the twelfth World Health Assembly (*Resolution WHO 12.43*) came into force on 25 October 1960.

22. Ibid., Article 21.

23. Ibid., Article 1 as interpreted by Sami Shubber, "The International Code of Marketing of Breast-Milk Substitutes," *International Digest of Health Legislation* 36, (No. 4, 1985): 883–84.

24. Government of Tunisia, Law No. 83–24 on the Quality Control, Marketing and Information Concerning Use of Breast-Milk Substitutes, 4 March 1983, *Journal officiel de la République Tunisienne,* No. 18, 8 March 1983), 632–33, par. 5.

20
Concluding Observations

The regulatory systems identified in this guide radiate from three different levels. These are the national level, the intergovernmental-international level, and, in-between, the domain of self-regulation. Within these three systems, however, there are a number of variations, and, of course each type of regulation overlaps with the others, influences them, and evolves as an element of a living organism. A simplified summary of the contours of this complex universe might therefore be useful.

National Systems

Four national regulatory systems can be identified. These are: (1) the broad-spectrum legislative and administrative control system, (2) the state-enterprise monopoly system, (3) the national-development system, and (4) the skeletal customary-law system.

Broad-spectrum legislative and administrative control systems prevail in the industrialized market-economy countries. About 80 percent of global expenditure on advertising and 15 percent of the world's population fall under this type of regulatory system. These systems can be interpreted as an outgrowth of a constitutional/legalist ideology, according to which the purpose of government is to maintain order, to preserve fundamental liberties, and to protect the well-being of society. The regulation of advertising is primarily geared to these ends.

These regimes boast an effective array of government legislation, case law, and administrative rules and regulations. General rules prescribe basic ethical standards founded on the principles of truth in advertising, decency, and fairness. A host of detailed laws and standards pertain to advertising of specific products with potential health and safety risks and govern advertisers' use of the media and influence in advertising to vulnerable target audiences. In addition, in some countries consumers have access to courts to recover losses from damages or harm attributed to reliance on defective advertising.

The *state-enterprise monopoly system* exists in the centrally planned socialist countries. Advertising regulation consistent with socialist ideology has been used to advance socialist objectives. In the absence of private ownership of the media, government control is almost complete. The government and the governed being one, the state is both regulator and regulated. Thus, all advertising is under the control of the state advertising enterprise, which determines what products will be advertised and how they will be advertised. Socialist regulation stresses the information function of advertising.

Commercial advertising by multinational advertisers until recently has been relatively inconspicuous in most centrally planned countries (excluding China). Foreign industrial advertising, which has almost always been permitted, generally is channeled through government agencies with a monopoly over advertising activity and is issued in technical journals. These agencies control foreign advertising messages for image and information content. This rigid system has slowly begun to dissolve in the 1980s, first in China under its modernization program and now in the Soviet Union as a result of *glasnost* and *perestroika*. New regulatory regimes combining elements of the old system and broad-spectrum controls, allowing for more free-enterprise operations in the advertising industry, are evolving. The system in China can be considered a preliminary prototype.

National-development systems define regulation in many middle-income and large low-income Third World countries. In general, these countries have sizeable upper and middle classes, rural as well as urban, that are literate, traveled, and educated, and a much larger mass of poor urban wage earners, often illeterate. In most places the rural poor are outside the market for consumer goods. These countries include upper–middle-income Latin America and middle-income densely populated countries in Africa, Latin America, and Asia.

In contrast to the centrally planned states, these countries have open economies, and potentially profitable free-enterprise markets have been or are being established. In contrast to the industrialized free-market economies, the regulatory systems of these countries are not fully developed, nor are the countervailing social forces oranized so that capitalism can be counterbalanced by consumerism in the legislative process whereby consumer regulations are developed.

Developmentalism, nationalism, and *dependencia* theories are prevalent in economic policy making. Many advertising regulations are by-products of policies aimed at development objectives, such as legislation to encourage local industry, promote national pride, and discourage imports. Foreign-investment laws, tax laws, exchange restrictions, and copyright laws often have a restrictive impact on foreign advertising. Consumer-protection laws exist as well, but in many countries they are not fully developed. Where general consumer-protection laws do not exist, product-specific health laws are issued by the health ministries and are basically incorporated in overall food and drug laws. Often these regulations are modeled on U.S. or Western European prototypes.

Skeletal customary-law systems are characteristic in the least developed countries of Africa. In these countries advertising is generally insignificant. Rule of law is not well established, and what regulations do exist are found in customary laws and laws on the books since they were written by colonial governments.

In general, consumerism does not exist in these countries, and legislation is spotty. There is little incentive to consider consumers' welfare as a priority business objective. In most, however, there is a minimum of product-specific legislation. Government regulations are limited to prohibiting deceptive practices in the advertising of foods and drugs. Advertising of tobacco products is increasingly restricted.

Self-Regulation

Self-regulatory systems are both national and international. In national systems, industries have established voluntary codes that operate either in parallel with government controls, as is generally the case, or as an integral part of an overall government regulatory system. Self-regulation in some form exists in all the developed market-economy countries and some of the larger, more advanced Third World countries. Self-regulatory systems are found in Brazil, Venezuela, India, the Philippines, Malaysia, and Singapore. Self-regulation in the absence of consumer movements and the threat of tough government regulation is not widespread.

Internationally, self-regulation is promoted by cross-industry associations, such as the International Chamber of Commerce and the International Advertising Association. Having established an international advertising code, the work of these organizations is to promote the establishment of international standards on a country by country basis.

International Rules and Regulations

On the international plane, governments have discussed the elaboration of codes and guidelines that should be observed by industry and promoted by national governments. A few have been adopted, notably those with strong health objectives, such as the WHO International Code of Marketing of Breast-Milk Substitutes and the WHO Ethical and Scientific Criteria for Pharmaceutical Advertising.

A Word on the Future

It was beyond the scope and objective of this guide to speculate about the future of advertising and its regulation. A few observations, prompted by features of the current situation and of the historical trends that have led to it, are, however, in order. First, the complex array of national, regional and international regulations on advertising may be moving towards increasing unity. There is a growing convergence of interest and concepts of regulation as a result of debates in regional and international forums. The focus no longer is to limit as much as possible the damage that profit-oriented advertising was supposed to inflict on society, as was the case not so long ago in a number of countries, rich and poor alike. It is rather to channel this creative force in the mainstream of the dominant culture of the times. And this culture is evolving common characteristics that bind the three worlds: East with West, as well as the North with the South. Advertising is, at the end of this century, a respected and essential aspect of a set of universal values. The direction of the regulatory process is toward more cooperation between private and public spheres of society. Increasingly the legislators and the advertisers recognize common goals. Advertising is gaining increasing respect as a legitimate element of the international socio-economic fabric. What has been obvious for the American consumer over many decades is now also conceived by the Russian, the Chinese, the Brazilian, and the French citizens.

A second and related observation pertains to the changing relationships between advertising and the ethical realm of our culture. During the 1950s and 1960s, a reasonably informed intellectual of the Western hemisphere would have perceived advertising, in its various forms, as, at best, a morally neutral and economically useful endeavor. Morally neutral, for it was reflecting the aspirations of individuals and groups anxious to benefit from the fruits of the philosophy of progress developed during the eighteenth and nineteenth centuries. Economically useful, for it was contributing to the creation of demand that was fueling the productive system. The same intellectual would have noted that in non-liberal or totalitarian countries and societies, advertising was ethically wrong because it aimed at mobilizing people for a cause, or worse, a particular leader. Advertising there was propaganda. Today, such a discourse would no longer be typical. Partly because of the pressure of consumers, partly because of shifts in politico-economic ideology, and partly through regulations of all types (including self-regulation), advertising today expresses and even promotes aspects of the ethics of contemporary societies. On one hand, the philosophical and moral objections to "consumerism" have abated and, on the other hand, societies that use to limit advertising to propaganda are now allowing it as part of a project of modernization and liberalization. And, above all, the notion of social responsibility of the advertisers themselves has and will continue to increase. It seems quite probable that the political and social debate will, in most societies, shift slowly from traditional economic issues of production and distribution to ethical questions on the distribution of power, the values that sustain or destroy a community and the dialogue between philosophy and science. In such a perspective, advertising and its regulatory process will take a new dimension. For all the actors concerned, including private and public international organizations, the challenges ahead are indeed interesting.

Index

Abbott Laboratories, 329, 330
Action for Children's Television, 30
Acuerdo de Cartagena, 228
Addison, Joseph, 7
Administrative/aedilian law, 12
Advertisement Regulation Act of, 119
Advertisers as targets of regulation, 17
Advertising: benefits of, 39–40; development of regulation, 11–14; early history of, 6–7; perceptions of, 40–41; spread of multinational, 10–11; theory and definitions, 5. *See also* Commercial advertising
Advertising Age, 11, 18, 75, 154, 193
Advertising agencies: comparison of gross billings of top multinational, 18, 19; conglomerates, 20, 23; expenditure by country, 24–27; geographic distribution of, 24, 25–26; structure of, 20, 24; as targets of regulation, 17, 18–20, 24, 26–27; top fifty, 20–21; world wide operations of, 22
Advertising Agencies Association of India, 258
Advertising Control Law, 158
Advertising Council of Nigeria, 293
Advertising Standards Authority (ASA), 123–124, 258
Advertising Standards Council of India (ASCI), 258
Africa: advertising expenditure in, 32, 34, 281; advertising in low- and middle-income Anglophone countries, 289–295; advertising in low-income countries, 297–299; advertising in middle-income Francophone countries, 295–297; advertising tools used in, 286–287; breast-milk substitutes in, 335; development of commercial advertising in, 9, 10; effects of economic development on advertising, 281–285; legal systems in, 287–288; problems with multiple tribal customs and languages, 286; regulations in, 14, 288–289; regulatory profile of northern, 214; types of goods advertised in, 285. *See also under specific country*
Agency for International Development (AID), 331
Agfa Films, 10
Agpol, 182, 254
Alcoholic beverages, regulation of, 61; in Africa, 294; in Asia, 257, 259; in Latin America, 237, 244; WHO and, 320
Algeria, 212, 220–221
Alien Business Law, 269
All Soviet Conference, 9, 167
American Advertising Federation (AAF), 35, 88
American Association of Advertising Agencies (AAAA), 35, 88
American Association of Retired Persons (AARP), 30
American Brands, Inc., 27
American Home Products Corp., 27, 99, 330
American Law Institute, 89, 97
American Marketing Association, 5
American Tobacco Co. (British), 10
Andean Common Market (ANCOM), 37, 228

Andean Foreign Investment Code, 229
Angola, 287
Argentina: advertising expenditure in, 230, 232; foreign activity in, 206; minority-share affiliations in, 24; multinational agencies in, 26, 240; regulations in, 235, 240; self-regulation, 240
Asia: advertising expenditure in, 32, 34; advertising in high-middle-income, 272–277; advertising in low-income, 250; advertising in middle-income, 260–262; development of commercial advertising in, 9–10; differences between countries in, 249–250; minority-share affiliations in, 24; ownership requirements in, 58; regulations in, 14, 249. *See also under specific country*
Associated Advertising Clubs of America (AACA), 35
Associated Advertising Clubs of America and the World, 13
Association of Advertising Practitioners in Nigeria (AAPN), 291, 294
Association of National Advertisers (ANA), 35, 88, 89, 308
Australia: advertising expenditure in, 34; expansion of agencies in, 19; regulations in, 126, 127, 130–131
Austria, 58, 72

Baby Killer, The, 328
Bacardi Corp., 27
Backer Spielvogel Bates WW, 75
Bahrain, 212, 216, 217, 219–220
Bangladesh, 250, 259, 318
Barbados, 242
B.A.T. Industries PLC, 27
Baxter v. Ford, 96
Bayer AG, 10, 27
BBDO Worldwide, 289
Beijing Advertising Corp., 193
Benelux countries, 72
Berkbile v. Brantly Helicopter, 94
Bersch v. Drexel Firestone, 98
Bhopal, India, 99, 258
Biennial Report of the Director General, 317–318
Biotherm, 296
Bolivia, 229, 244

Borden, Neil, 46–47
Botswana, 287
Branch v. Federal Trade Commission, 97
Brazil: advertising expenditure in, 230, 232, 238; breast-milk substitutes in, 335; consumer groups in, 207, 229, 239–240; development of commercial advertising in, 10, 238; expansion of agencies in, 19, 238; foreign activity in, 206; multinational agencies in, 26; print media advertising in, 238–239; regulations in, 233–236, 239–240; self-regulation, 239; television advertising in, 238
Breast-milk substitutes, 17; WHO Code of Marketing of, 60, 88, 327–337
Bristol-Myers, 27, 329, 330
British Code of Advertising Practice (BCAP), 123
Broadcasting Act of 1981, 122
Bulgaria, 182
Burkina-Faso, 208, 297, 299
Burma, 198–199
Burundi, 297, 298
Business Contact, 175

Cadbury Schweppes PLC, 27
Cahier, 136
Calvo Doctrine, 230
Cameroon, 295, 296–297
Canada, 126, 127–130, 335
Caribbean countries: advertising expenditure in, 24; description of population and culture of, 225–227; legal system in, 227; regulations in, 242–244
Carlill v. Carbolic Smoke Ball Co., 118
Carmichael v. Reitz, 94
Caveat emptor, 12
CBS, 193
Central American Common Market, 228
Central American countries, advertising expenditure in, 24, 242. *See also under specific country*
Central Hudson Gas v. Public Service Commission, 87
Chad, 297, 298, 299

Chavez, Cesar, 330
Chiat/Day, 19
Chile, 26, 335
China: advertising agencies in, 191-192; advertising expenditure by media in, 188-191; advertising expenditure in, 32, 34, 188; advertising in early, 6; concept of *li* and *fa*, 193-194; development of commercial advertising in, 8, 9, 10, 185-192; foreign advertising activity, 192-193; future of advertising in, 197-198; joint ventures in, 24, 192, 195; laws on misleading and unfair advertising in, 57; legal system in, 165-166, 193-197; regulation of foreign advertising, 193-197; regulatory profile of, 186; self-regulation, 197; types of products advertised in, 187-188
China International Advertising Corp., 192
China National Advertising Association for Foreign Economic Relations and Trade, 193
China National Foreign Trade Advertising Association, 192
China National United Advertising Corp., 192
China Popular Science Press, 193
Ciba-Geigy AG, 27
Civil law, 52, 53, 70, 71
Clayton Act, 81
Coca-Cola Co., 27, 176, 258, 266
Code of Conduct for Transnational Corporations, Draft, 60, 230, 311-313
Code of Ethics for Advertising Professionals, 239
Code of Ethics for International Trade in Food, 316
Code of the International Federation of the Pharmaceutical Manufacturers, 62
Code on Foreign Investment, 228
Codex Alimentarius Commission, 36, 60, 208, 305, 313-316
Colgate-Palmolive Co., 27, 295-296
Colombia, 206, 208, 229, 244, 335
Combustion Engineering, 176
COMECON countries, 174, 175

Comisión Inter-Societaria de Autoregulación Publicitaria (CIAP), 240
Commercial advertising: definition of, 5; disadvantages of, 40; international development of, 7-10; in socialist countries, 167-168
Commercial Code of Bolivia, 244
Committee of Advertising Practice, 123
Common law, 52, 53, 70
Conference of Advertising Workers in Socialist Countries, 9, 167
Confucian law, 53, 55
Consumer Complaints Council (CCC), 258
Consumer Federation of America, 30
Consumer Guidance Society, 258
Consumer interest groups: in Asia, 207, 257, 258; in Latin America, 229, 239-240; regulation and, 17-18, 27-31; in Third World countries, 207
Consumer Product Safety Act, 14
Consumer Product Safety Commission, 14
Consumer Protection Act of 1975 (Singapore), 276-277
Consumer Protection Act of 1979 (Thailand), 270
Consumer Protection Act of 1987 (United Kingdom), 120, 126
Consumer protection and rights, 29; UN guidelines on, 52, 60, 305, 308-311
Consumer Protection Fundamental Act of 1968, 159
Consumerism, definition of, 17, 27
Consumer's Union, 330
corpus juris, 12
Cosmetics, Devices, and Drugs Act, 260
Cosmetics, regulations for, 85, 260
Council for Fair Business Practices, 258
Council for Mutual Economic Assistance (CMEA), 175
Council of Better Business Bureaus (CBBB), 35, 88
Crist v. Art Metal Works, 91
Cyprus, 219
Czechoslovakia, 181

Danish Broadcasting Act, 111, 142
Deception, definition of, 83–84
Demand, impact of advertising on, 42–43
Demonstration effect, 43–44
Denmark, 139–142, 335
Dentsu, Inc., 153, 154, 193
Directorate of Audio-Visual Publicity (DAVP), 257
Discover Magazine, 193
Djibouti, 221
Dr. Williams' Medicines, 10
Dominican Republic, 330–331
Drug Certification Scheme, 318
Drug Information Bulletins, 318–319
Drugs. *See* Pharmaceuticals
Drugs Act of 1972 (Pakistan), 259
Drugs Act of 1979 (Thailand), 270
Drugs and Magic Remedies Acts and Rules of 1954, 257
Dubai, 216
Ducote v. Chevron Chemical, 92
Dunhill, 27
Dunlop, 10

Eastern Europe: advertising expenditure in, 32, 169; affects of Gorbachev on advertising in, 169; development of commercial advertising in, 8, 9; legal system in, 165; media restrictions in, 58; ownership requirements in, 58
Eastman Kodak Co., 10
Economic goods, definition of, 5
Ecuador, 229, 244, 335
Egypt, 212; advertising expenditure in, 216; breast-milk substitutes in, 334; consumerism in, 29, 207; foreign activity in, 206; radio advertising in, 219; regulations in, 220; television advertising in, 217, 219
Emblem and Names of Act, 257
England, 6–7, 71
Enterprise Promotion Act, 293–294
Erie v. Tompkins, 80
Essential Drug Program, 318
Esso, 46
Ethiopia, 287, 297, 298
Eurocom, 153, 296
Europe: advertising expenditure in, 11, 32, 34, 67, 105; development of commercial advertising in, 7, 8;
expansion of agencies in, 19; majority-owned subsidiaries in, 24. *See also* Eastern Europe
European Community (EC)/Common Market, regulations in, 14; Directive on Misleading Advertising, 37, 73, 111–115; Directive on Product Liability, 115–116; regulatory profile of, 110–111; Single European Act and, 105–109
European Economic Community (EEC), 47, 57, 73, 105

Fair Trading Act of 1973, 120, 122
False advertising, definition of, 83
Federal Cigarette Labeling and Advertising Act, 86
Federal Communication Commission (FCC), 82
Federal Consumer Protection Law, 236
Federal Food, Drug, and Cosmetic Act, 85, 97
Federal Republic of Germany: advertising expenditure in, 24; legal system in, 72; media restrictions in, 58; multinational agencies in, 24
Federal Trade Commission (FTC), 13, 35, 43; powers of, 82–83, 85, 86; truthful comparative advertising and, 72–73
Federal Trade Commission Act, 13, 82, 97
Federation Internationale des Vins et Spiritueux (FIVES), 36
Fei, Han, 6
Finnav, 176
Food Act of 1966 (Nepal), 259, 260
Food Act of 1979 (Thailand), 270
Food Act of 1983 (Malaysia), 259, 260
Food and Agricultural Organization (FAO): regulation of advertising and, 36, 60; /Who Codex Alimentarius Commission, 36, 60, 208, 305, 313–316; /Who Joint Food Standards Program Guidelines on Claims and Code of Ethics for International Trade in Food, 60, 313
Food and Drug Act: U.S., 13, 85, 97; Zambia, 294

Food and Drug Administration (FDA), 82, 85–86
Food and Drug Decree (Nigeria), 293
Foods and Drugs Administration and Laboratory Services (FDALS) (Nigeria), 293
Ford Motor Co., 10
Foreign Capital Inducement Law, 273
Foreign Exchange and Foreign Trade Control Law, 150–151
Foreign Investment Law (India), 258
Foreign Investment Law (Japan), 150
Foreign trade organizations (FTOs), 169, 181, 182
Formula for Malnutrition, 330
Forum non conveniens, 99
Four Modernizations Program, 186
France: advertising expenditure in, 24; advertising in early, 6; expansion of agencies in, 19; influence of nationalism, 58; legal system in, 70–71, 73, 132–139; multinational agencies in, 24
France, regulations in: liability cases, 138–139; misrepresentation in, 111, 134–137; profile of, 132–133; self-regulation, 137–138; unfair competition, 133–134; use of French language, 137
Furer, A., 328

Gabon, 295, 296, 297
Galbraith, John Kenneth, 31, 41, 43, 45
General Agreement on Tariffs and Trade (GATT), 37
General Foods, 136–137
Ghana: breast-milk substitutes in, 334; government of, 287; ownership requirements in, 58; regulations in, 208, 294
Gillette, 27
Girardin, Emile de, 6
Global American Television, Inc., 176, 179
Goldman, Marshall, 8, 170
Gorbachev, Mikhail, 169
Gostel-radio, 176, 179
Grand Metropolitan P/C, 27
Grant Advertising, 240
Greyser, Stephen, 30, 40

Grocery Manufacturers Association, 308
Group Against Smoking and Pollution, 30
Guatemala, 244, 335
Guidelines on Consumer Protection, 52, 60, 305, 308–311
Gulf Oil v. Gilbert, 99

Harvard Business School, 44
HDM World-wide, 153–154, 193
Health, issues of, 41–42, 59–61
Henkel, KGaA, 27
Hidden Persuaders, The, (Packard), 81
Hodson, L.J., 119
Hoffman-La Roche, 10
Home Trade Law of 1978, 181
Hong Kong: advertising expenditure in, 24, 272; multinational agencies in, 24; regulatory profile of, 273
Hungary, 169, 180–181, 335
Hungexpo, 180
Hungry for Profit (Ledogar), 330

IBM, 258
Imperial Chemical Corp., 10
Indecent Advertisements Act, 119
Independent Broadcasting Authority Act of 1973, 122, 123
India: advertising expenditure in, 252; Bhopal, 99, 258; breast-milk substitutes in, 334; consumer groups in, 207, 257, 258; consumerism in, 29; development of commercial advertising in, 10, 252; expansion of agencies in, 252–254; foreign activity in, 206, 207, 255–256, 257; government in, 249; language barriers in, 256; majority-owned subsidiaries in, 24; multinational agencies in, 26, 253–254; print media advertising in, 256; profile of, 250–252; regulations in, 208, 257–258; regulatory profile of, 252; self-regulation, 258; television advertising in, 256
Indian Society of Advertisers, 258
Indonesia: attitudes toward foreign activity, 260; consumer groups in, 207; development of commercial advertising in, 10, 264–266; foreign

Indonesia (*continued*)
    activity in, 206, 207; government in, 250; legal system in, 266–267; multinational agencies in, 262; nonequity contractual arrangements in, 24; regulations in, 208, 263–267
Infant Formula Coalition Action, 330
Infant formulas. *See* Breast-milk substitutes
Inoreklama, 175
Institutional advertising, 5
Intelligence Summary, 304
Interads Advertising, 254
Interfaith Center on Corporate Responsibility (ICCR), 330
International Advertising Association (IAA), 28, 35, 88, 125, 193, 207, 303–304, 308
International Association of Infant Food Manufacturers (IFM), 36
International Baby Food Action Network (IBFAN), 331
International Chamber of Commerce (ICC), 13, 303; Code of Marketing Practices, 14; Code of Standards of Advertising Practice, 13, 35, 58, 62, 69, 239; purpose of, 13, 35
International Code of Marketing of Breast-Milk Substitutes, 17, 60, 88, 327–337
International Convention for Settlement of Investment Disputes, 230
International Council of Infant Food Industries (ICIFI), 329
International Digest of Health Legislation, 317, 334
International Federation of Pharmaceutical Manufacturers Association (IFPMA), 36, 318
International Organization of Consumers Unions (IOCU), 30, 308
International regulation, 59–61, 343
Interpress, 180
Interpublic Jardine China, 193
Inter Vista Advertising, 265
Investment Code Act of 1981 (Ghana), 294
Iran, 334
Iraq, 212
Ireland, 72, 335

Islamic law, 53, 54, 212–213, 214–215
Israel, 67
Italy, 72
Ivory Coast, 295, 296
Iwaarden, Theo Van, 43
Izvestia, 176

Jacobs, Everett M., 9
Jamaica, 242, 243
Japan: advertising expenditure by media in, 154–155; advertising expenditure in, 32, 34, 67, 149; environmental influences on advertising, 156–158; expansion of agencies in, 19, 153; legal system in, 67, 69, 72, 158; political makeup of, 149; regulatory profile of, 150–153, 158–160; self-regulation, 159
Japan Advertising Review Organization (JARO), 160
Japanese Advertising Statute, 159
Jelliffe, Derrick, 327, 328–329
Jevons, W.S., 5
Johnson & Johnson, 27
Joint Venture Law, 195
Joint ventures: in China, 24, 192, 195; in the Soviet Union, 24, 178–180
Jordan, 212, 216, 217, 219, 220
Jungle, The, (Sinclair), 80
jus civile, 11–12
J. Walter Thompson Co., 75, 176, 238, 240, 241–242

Kampuchea, 198
Kellogg Co., 27
Kennedy, Edward, 331
Kennedy, John F., 28–29
Kenya, 208, 286, 289, 292, 294, 334–335
Kindleberger, Charles, 44
Klages v. General Ordinance Equipment, 96
Komplexreklama, 175
Korea Broadcast Advertising Corp. (KOBACO), 273–274
Korea Broadcasting Ethics Committee (KOBEC), 274–275
Kuwait, 212, 216, 220

La Gazette, 6
Langridge v. Levy, 125

Laos, 198
Latin America: advertising expenditure in, 32, 34, 227; attitudes toward foreign investors, 227–229; consumerism in, 29; consumer protection in, 229; description of population and culture of, 225–227; development of commercial advertising in, 9, 10; legal system in, 227; majority-owned subsidiaries in, 24; minority-share affiliations in, 24; ownership restrictions in, 229; regulations in, 14, 230; regulations in high-income, 231–242; regulations in middle-income, 242–244. *See also under specific country*
Latin America Free Trade Area, 228
Lawson, R.G., 121
Lebanon, 212, 216, 217, 220, 334
Ledogar, Robert J., 330
Legal systems: actors, structures, and processes and, 4; civil law, 52, 53, 70, 71; common law, 52, 53, 70; comparison of criminal, private and administrative law, 72; Confucian law, 53, 55; culture and, 4; extension of, 3–4; in industrialized countries, 67, 69–74; Islamic law, 53, 54; penetration of, 4; in socialist countries, 165–166; socialist law, 52, 53–54; traditional/customary law, 53, 55. *See also under specific country*
Lenin, Vladimir Ilyich, 8, 170
Leo Barnett, 242
Liability: European Community Directive on Product, 115–116; laws in France, 138–139; laws in the United Kingdom, 125–126
Liability laws in the United States, 59, 69; comparison under contract and tort law, 90; international application of, 96–100; negligence and, 90–91; misrepresentation, 94, 96; strict liability per se, 93–94; uniform codes for, 89–90, warranty and, 91–93
Libel and Defamation Act of 1959, 259
Liberia, 292, 294–295

Libya, 212, 220, 334
Lintas Worldwide, 10, 253, 258, 289, 290, 296
Love v. Wolfe, 91, 94

MacBride Report, 307
McCann Erickson, 176, 180, 238, 240, 289
McDonald's, 27
Madhya Pradesh (Bhopal) Consumer Protection Act of 1984, 258
Mahir, 180
Majority-owned subsidiaries, 24
Malaysia: advertising expenditure in, 24, 268; attitudes toward foreign activity, 260; breast-milk substitutes in, 334–335; consumer groups in, 207; consumerism in, 29; government in, 249; influence of nationalism, 58; multinational agencies in, 26, 262; regulations in, 208, 267–269
Mali, 297, 298, 299
Manipulative model, 40–41
Mansour, Mohammed, 204
Mars Inc., 27
Marx, Karl, 8, 167
Maslow, Abraham H., 45
Maynes, E. Scott, 31
Media as targets of regulation, 17, 58, 70, 111, 140
Menger, Carl, 5
Merchandise Marks Act of 1887, 120
Merrell Dow Pharmaceuticals, Inc., 99
Merryman, John, 3
Mexico: advertising expenditure in, 230; consumer groups in, 207, 229; foreign activity in, 206, influence of nationalism, 58; laws on misleading and unfair advertising in, 57, 236–237; multinational agencies in, 26; ownership restrictions in, 229; regulations in, 208, 236–238; self-regulation, 236
Middle East: advertising expenditure in the, 24, 32, 34, 211, 216; breast-milk substitutes in the, 335; characteristics of advertising in the, 216–219; development of commercial advertising in the, 10; differences between countries in the, 211–215; legal systems in the, 215;

Middle East (continued)
   media restrictions in the, 58;
   nonequity contractual arrangements in the, 24; ownership requirements in the, 58; pan-Arab print media in the, 216; position of women in the, 215, 221–222; radio advertising in the, 219, 220; regulations in the, 219–222; regulatory profile of the, 213; television advertising in the, 217, 219, 220. See also under specific country
Ministry of Foreign Economic Relations and Trade (MOFERT) (CHINA), 192, 195
Minority-share affiliations, 24
Misrepresentation Act of 1967, 120, 121–122, 126
Misrepresentation advertising: European Community Directive on, 37, 73, 111–115. See also under specific country
Model Uniform Product Liability Act, 89–90, 93
Mojo, 19
Mongolia, 198
Monopolies and Restrictive Trade Practices Act of 1969, 257
Montaigne, Michel de, 6
Morocco, 212, 216, 221
Moyers, Bill, 331
Mozambique, 287, 297, 298

Nader, Ralph, 330
Nasser, Gamal Abdul, 211
National Advertising Review Board (NARB), 35, 88–89
National Advertising Review Council, Inc. (NARC), 88
National Commission for Advertising Self-Regulation (CONAR), 239
National Council of Consumer Protection, 239
National regulations: broad-spectrum legislative and administrative control systems, 341; general laws on misleading and unfair advertising, 57; important characteristics of legal systems, 52–55; indirect controls, 58–59; influence of nationalism, 56, 58; national-development system, 342–343; OECD on, 51–52; skeletal customary-law systems, 343; state-enterprise monopoly system, 342; type of products that are targets for, 57–58; UN General Assembly on, 52
National Vigilance Committee, 35
Nedelia, 176
Needham Harper and Steers, 193
Negligence, 90–91
Nepal, 249, 259
Nestlé, 10, 27, 36, 60, 328–330
Nestlé Kills Babies, 328
Netherlands, 24
New Guinea, 334
New Zealand, 26, 126, 127
Nicaragua, 244, 334
Nigeria: advertising agencies in, 290–291; advertising expenditure in, 289, 292; breast-milk substitutes in, 334; consumer groups in, 207; consumerism in, 29, 207; development of commercial advertising in, 10, 290–292; foreign activity in, 206; government of, 287; ownership requirements in, 58, 294; regulations in, 293–294; self-regulation, 294
Noncommercial advertising, 5
Nonequity contractual arrangements, 24
North Korea, 198
Norway, 139–142, 335
Nurkse, R., 44
N.W. Azur and Son, 238

Obligation, civil-law concept of, 71
Occidental Petroleum, 176
Ogilvy & Mather, 176, 180, 193, 253, 258, 289, 293
Oman, 212, 216, 220
Ombudsman, 71, 111, 140–141
100,000,000 Guinea Pigs (Kallet and Schlink), 80
Organization for Economic Cooperation and Development (OECD), 37; Declaration on International Investments and Multinational Enterprises, 51–52; pharmaceuticals and, 60–61, 317

Packard, Vance, 81
Pakistan: advertising expenditure in, 24, 259; foreign activity in, 206,

207; government in, 250; regulations in, 208, 259
Papua, 334
Paraguay, 244
Parke-Davis and Co., 91
Pechiney, 176
People's Republic of the Congo, 295, 296
PepsiCo Inc., 27, 176
Peru: breast-milk substitutes in, 335; influence of nationalism, 58; ownership restrictions in, 229; regulations in, 208, 242, 244
Peter Stuyvesant, 27
Peterson, Esther, 309
Pfizer, Inc., 27
Pharmaceutical Act of 1978 (Nepal), 259
Pharmaceuticals, regulations of: in Africa, 293, 294, 297, 299; in Asia, 257, 259, 270; international organizations and, 60–61, 62, 317, 320–321; in Latin America, 237, 241; in the Middle East, 219–220; OECD and, 60–61, 317; in Third World countries, 208–209; in the U.S., 85–86, 97, 99; World Health Assembly and, 317, 318, 320–321; WHO and, 61, 317–319
Pharmacy Act of 1958 (Nigeria), 293
Philip Morris Inc., 27, 193
Philippine Board of Advertising, 271–272
Philippines: advertising expenditure in, 24, 271; attitudes toward foreign activity, 260; consumer groups in, 207; foreign activity in, 206, 207; government in, 250; influence of nationalism, 58; multinational agencies in, 262; regulations in, 208, 271–272; self-regulation, 271–272
Piper Aircraft v. Reyno, 99–100
Poland, 181–182, 335
Police Regulations of 1908, 158
Portugal, 24
Powers of Criminal Courts Act, 126
Prevention of Food Adulteration Act of 1954, 257
Price Competitions Act of 1955, 257
Price Control Decree of 1970, 293
Primary demand, definition of, 5
Procter & Gamble, 10, 27

Product-specific issues, 41–42
Prohibition on Advertisements Relating to Smoking Act of 1970, 277
Prosser, William L., 12
Publicis International, 296
Publick Advertiser, 6
Puffing, 46, 92, 118

Qatar, 212, 216, 217, 220

Regulations: critics of, 17, 27–31; development of early, 11–14; general laws on misleading and unfair advertising, 57; international, 59–61, 343; media as targets of regulation, 17, 58; national, 51–59, 341–343; self-, 61–62, 343; targets of, 17. *See also under specific country*
Regulations for Advertising Management, 195–197
Regulations of the People's Republic of China on the Registration of Joint Ventures Using Chinese and Foreign Investment, 195, 198
Regulators, who are the, 18; host and home countries, 31–33; intergovernmental, 36–37; self-regulators, 33–36
Renaudot, Theophraste, 6
Restatement (second) of Foreign Relations Law, 97
Restatement (Second) of Torts, 89–90, 93, 94, 96
RJR Nabisco, Inc., 27, 176
Rogers v. Toni Home Permanent, 92
Rolex, 193
Romano-Germanic civil law, 52, 53
Rostorgreklama, 174
Rothmans International, 27
Roux Seguela Cayzac and Goudard, 296
Royal Typewriter Co., 10
Royer Act of 1973, 135–136
Russian Soviet Federative Socialist Republic (RSFSR), 177
Rwanda, 297, 299

Saatchi & Saatchi Advertising Worldwide, 75, 77, 176, 179, 253, 289
Sale of Food Act of 1973, 277
Sale of Goods Act of 1893, 12

Saudi Arabia, 212; advertising expenditure in, 216; regulations in, 208, 219, 220, 221; television advertising in, 217
Scandinavia: legal system in, 71, 72, 139–142; media restrictions in, 58, 70, 140; misrepresentation in, 111; regulations in, 139–142
Seagrams, Joseph E., & Sons, 27, 296
Searle Laboratories, Inc., 99
Securities and Exchange Commission, 82
Selective demand, definition of, 5
Self-regulation: codes regarding, 62; history of, 33–36, 61–62; national and international, 343. *See also under specific country*
Senegal, 295, 296, 297
Service model, view of advertising, 41
Shanghai, 10
Sherman Anti-Trust Act of 1890, 13, 81
Sinclair, Upton, 80
Singapore: advertising expenditure in, 24, 67, 272; breast-milk substitutes in, 334–335; consumerism in, 29; government in, 249; regulations in, 208, 276–277; regulatory profile of, 273
Singer Sewing Machine Co., 10
Single European Act, 105–109
Sisters of the Precious Blood, Inc., 330
Smith, Adam, 41
Socialist law, 52, 53–54
Societal issues: impact of advertising on demand, 42–43; impact of advertising on society, 43–45; truthfulness in advertising, 45–46
South Africa: advertising expenditure in, 67; multinational agencies in, 26; regulations in, 126, 127, 131–132
South Korea: advertising expenditure in, 272; consumer groups in, 207; foreign activity in, 206, 207; government in, 250; nonequity contractual arrangements in, 24; regulations in, 273–275
South Magazine, 193
Sovero, 175

Soviet Export, 175
Soviet Union: advertisements of multinational enterprises in the, 175–176; advertising expenditure in the, 32, 172; advertising expenditure by foreigners in the, 172; development of commercial advertising in the, 8–9, 170–172; domestic advertising, 174; foreign advertising, 175–176; future of advertising in the, 178–180; joint ventures in the, 24, 178–180; regulatory profile of the, 171–174, 176–178
Soyuztorgreklama, 174, 179–180
Spain, 24
Spencer, John, 284
Spock, Benjamin, 330
Sri Lanka, 208, 249, 259, 260, 334
Stalin, Joseph, 8, 170–171
Star Kist Foods, Inc., 296
State Administration for Industry and Commerce, 187, 192, 195, 196, 197
Stolichnya Vodka, 176
Sudan, 208, 212
Sunday Entertainment Act, 119
Sunday Observance Act, 119
Sweden, 139–142, 335
Switzerland, 19, 24
Syndicat du Commerce des vins de Champagne c. Ackerman-Laurance, 134
Syntex Laboratories, Inc., 99
Syria, 212

Taiwan, 250; advertising expenditure in, 272; regulations in, 277; regulatory profile of, 273
Tanzania, 297, 298
Tatler, The, 7
Technical Trends, 175
Thailand: advertising expenditure in, 270; attitudes toward foreign activity, 260; breast-milk substitutes in, 335; consumerism in, 29; foreign activity in, 206, 207; government in, 249–250; influence of nationalism, 58; multinational agencies in, 26, 262; regulations in, 208, 269–270; -U.S. Treaty of Amity and Economic Relations, 269

Third World Action Group (TWAG), 328
Third World Advertising Congress, 193
Third World countries: advertising issues in, 47–48; consumer groups in, 207; consumers and the UN, 29; definition of, 203; growth of advertising in, 204; regulations in, 208–209; types of consumers in, 204–206. *See also under specific country*
Thomson, Peter, 118, 119
Time, Inc., 193
Tisza, 180
Tobacco products, regulation of: in Asia, 257, 277; international organizations and, 61; in Latin America, 237, 244; in the Middle East, 220; in the U.S., 85, 86; WHO and, 319–320
Tobago, 243
Trade Descriptions Act of 1968, 120, 121
Trade Marks Act of 1938, 120
Traditional/customary law, 53, 55
Transactional model, 41
Transnational Corporations, Draft Code of Conduct for, 60, 230, 311–313
Treaty of Rome (1957), 105, 106
Trinidad, 242, 243
Tripartito Comisión Inter-Societaria, 240
Trud, 176
Truthfulness in advertising, 45–46
Truth in Advertising slogan, 13
Tunisia, 212, 334
Turkey, 206

Uganda, 287
Ukrtorgreklama, 174
Unfair competition in France, 133–134
Unfair practices, definitions of, 13, 84
Uniform Commercial Code (UCC), 89
Uniform Compliance Act of 1923, 181
Uniform Sales Act of 1906, 89
Unigate, 328
Unilever, 10, 27, 265, 293
United Arab Emirates (UAE), 212, 216, 217, 234
United Kingdom: breast-milk substitutes in the, 335; expansion of agencies in the, 19; legal system in the, 71, 72, 116–122; multinational agencies in the, 24
United Kingdom, regulations in the: common law and the, 118–119; liability cases in the, 125–126; misrepresentation in the, 111–112, 118, 120–122; profile of the, 116–118; self-regulation, 122–125; statutory law and the, 119–122
United Nations: Charter of Economic Rights and Duties of States, 230; Code of Conduct for the Transfer of Technology, 230; Consumer Protection Guidelines, 305, 308–311; Draft Code of Conduct for Transnational Corporations, 60, 230, 311–313; International Organization of Consumers Unions and the, 30; pharmaceuticals and the, 317; regulation of advertising and the, 36–37, 59–60; Third World consumers and the, 29; Universal Declaration of Human Rights, 87, 98
UN Center for Transnational Corporations (CTC), 36, 60–61
UN Commission on Transnational Corporations, 311
UN Conference on Trade and Development (UNCTAD), 37, 60, 61, 317, 319
UN Economic and Social Council (ECOSOC), 36, 308
UN Educational Scientific and Cultural Organization (UNESCO), 36–37, 59, 307–308
UN Food and Agricultural Organization. *See* Food and Agricultural Organization
UN General Assembly, 36, 52, 59–60
UN Industrial Development Organization (UNIDO), 60, 61, 317
United Nations Report for Advertising and Marketing, 304
UN World Health Organization. *See* World Health Organization
United States: advertising expenditure by media in the, 78; advertising expenditure in the, 10–11, 32, 34,

United States (continued) 67, 75–76; breast-milk substitutes in the, 335; Department of Commerce, 89; development of commercial advertising in the, 7, 8; expansion of agencies in the, 18–19; House Committee on Energy and Commerce, 82; legal system in the, 71, 72, 73, 79–81; majority-owned subsidiaries in the, 24; multinational agencies in the, 24, 75, 76–77; Senate Committee on Commerce, Science, and Transportation, 82; UN Guidelines on Consumer Protection and the, 308–309, 310–311

United States, regulations in the, 13, 14; administrative bodies responsible for, 81–82; deception and, 83–84; false advertising and, 83; free speech and, 86–88; liability cases and, 89–96; pharmaceuticals and, 85–86, 97, 99; profile of, 79–81; role of the Federal Trade Commission, 82–83, 85, 86; self-regulation, 81, 88–89; tobacco products and, 85, 86; unfairness and, 84

U.S. Postal Service (USPS), 82
Uruguay Round, 37
Utility, definition of, 5

Valentine v. Chrestensen, 87
Value of goods, definition of, 5
Venezuela: advertising expenditure in, 230; breast-milk substitutes in, 335; consumer groups in, 207, 229; foreign activity in, 206; multinational agencies in, 26, 241–242; ownership restrictions in, 229; regulations in, 233–236, 241–242; self-regulation, 241
Vietnam, 198
Virginia State Board of Pharmacy v.

Virginia Citizens Consumer Council, 87
Vneshtorgreklama, 175, 179, 254

Wang, N.T., 9
Warner-Lambert Co., 27
Warranty and advertising, 91–93
Weidenbaum, Murray L., 309
Weights and Measures Acts, 257
West Africa Publicity (WAP), 290
West Germany. *See* Federal Republic of Germany
Wheeler-Lea Act, 13, 82, 85
Wiley, Harvey, 80
World Bank, 230, 281, 286
World Health Assembly, 317, 318, 320–321
World Health Organization (WHO): alcohol and, 320; Code of Marketing of Breast-Milk Substitutes, 17, 60, 88, 327–337; *Digest of Health Legislation*, 61; /FAO Codex Alimentarius Commission, 36, 60, 208, 305, 313–316; *International Digest of Health Legislation*, 317, 334; pharmaceuticals and, 61, 317–319; regulation of advertising and, 36, 60, 61, 259; tobacco products and, 319–320
World Intellectual Property Organization, 230
Wyeth Laboratories, Inc., 99

Yemen, Federal Republic of, 212
Yemen, People's Republic of, 212
Yemen Arab Republic, 216
Young & Rubicam, 153, 176, 179, 241, 289
Yukawa Hideki, 157

Zabranreklama, 254
Zaire, 295, 296
Zambia, 208, 289, 294
Zimbabwe, 208, 287, 289–290, 294

About the Author

Barbara Baudot has a wide background in international political/economic and legal relations. She served the United Nations for several years in New York and Geneva, where, as an economic affairs officer, she participated in north/south negotiations in UNCTAD, prepared numerous studies on problems of foreign investment, and participated in meetings of planners from Eastern Bloc and Western Bloc countries. She was Fulbright Scholar in Norway and an International Relations Fellow with the Rockefeller Foundation. She received her doctorate degree from the Fletcher School of Law and Diplomacy. Over the years she has traveled widely and lectured on international business, international law, politics, and economics at several colleges and universities. Currently she is an assistant professor in the Politics Department of St. Anselm College. She is also associated with ConsultAmerica Inc., a firm advising U.S. business on overseas markets and regulatory regimes.

DATE DUE

JAN 0 4 2010	

GAYLORD — PRINTED IN U.S.A.